D1383365

Visual Basic® Design Patterns

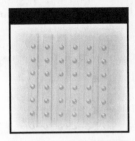

Visual Basic®
Design Patterns

Mark Grand
Brad Merrill

Wiley Publishing, Inc.

Visual Basic® Design Patterns

Published by
Wiley Publishing, Inc.
10475 Crosspoint Boulevard
Indianapolis, IN 46256
www.wiley.com

Copyright © 2005 by Wiley Publishing, Inc., Indianapolis, Indiana

Published simultaneously in Canada

ISBN-13: 978-0-471-26860-4
ISBN-10: 0-471-26860-7

Manufactured in the United States of America

10 9 8 7 6 5 4 3 2 1

1B/SZ/QW/QV/IN

No part of this publication may be reproduced, stored in a retrieval system or transmitted in any form or by any means, electronic, mechanical, photocopying, recording, scanning or otherwise, except as permitted under Sections 107 or 108 of the 1976 United States Copyright Act, without either the prior written permission of the Publisher, or authorization through payment of the appropriate per-copy fee to the Copyright Clearance Center, 222 Rosewood Drive, Danvers, MA 01923, (978) 750-8400, fax (978) 646-8600. Requests to the Publisher for permission should be addressed to the Legal Department, Wiley Publishing, Inc., 10475 Crosspoint Blvd., Indianapolis, IN 46256, (317) 572-3447, fax (317) 572-4355, or online at http://www.wiley.com/go/permissions.

Limit of Liability/Disclaimer of Warranty: The publisher and the author make no representations or warranties with respect to the accuracy or completeness of the contents of this work and specifically disclaim all warranties, including without limitation warranties of fitness for a particular purpose. No warranty may be created or extended by sales or promotional materials. The advice and strategies contained herein may not be suitable for every situation. This work is sold with the understanding that the publisher is not engaged in rendering legal, accounting, or other professional services. If professional assistance is required, the services of a competent professional person should be sought. Neither the publisher nor the author shall be liable for damages arising herefrom. The fact that an organization or Website is referred to in this work as a citation and/or a potential source of further information does not mean that the author or the publisher endorses the information the organization or Website may provide or recommendations it may make. Further, readers should be aware that Internet Websites listed in this work may have changed or disappeared between when this work was written and when it is read.

For general information on our other products and services or to obtain technical support, please contact our Customer Care Department within the U.S. at (800) 762-2974, outside the U.S. at (317) 572-3993 or fax (317) 572-4002.

Wiley also publishes its books in a variety of electronic formats. Some content that appears in print may not be available in electronic books.

Library of Congress Cataloging-in-Publication Data:
Grand, Mark.
 Visual Basic design patterns / Mark Grand, Brad Merrill.
    p. cm.
 Includes bibliographical references and index.
 ISBN-13: 978-0-471-26860-4 (paper/website)
 ISBN-10: 0-471-26860-7 (paper/website)
1. Microsoft Visual BASIC. 2. BASIC (Computer program language) 3. Software patterns.
I. Merrill, Brad. II. Title.
 QA76.73.B3G683 2005
 005.2'768--dc22

                          2005007862

Trademarks: Wiley and the Wiley logo are trademarks or registered trademarks of John Wiley & Sons, Inc. and/or its affiliates, in the United States and other countries, and may not be used without written permission. Visual Basic is a registered trademark of Microsoft Corporation in the United States and/or other countries. All other trademarks are the property of their respective owners. Wiley Publishing, Inc., is not associated with any product or vendor mentioned in this book.

About the Authors

Mark Grand is an Atlanta-based consultant specializing in Distributed Systems Object Oriented Design and Java. He was the architect of the first commercial B2B e-commerce product for the Internet. Prior to his involvement with Java, Mark spent over 11 years as a designer and implementer of 4GLs. His most recent role in that vein was as the architect and project manager for an electronic data interchange product. Mark has worked with a number of MIS organizations in capacities such as Software Architect, Database Architect and Network Designer.

Mark has been involved with object-oriented programming and design since 1982 and is now most widely known for his best-selling patterns books. Mark has taught for U.C. Berkeley, Sun and other organizations. You can find more information about Mark Grand at http://www.markgrand.com/.

Brad Merrill currently works as a software engineer on the ASP.NET team at Microsoft. He's previously worked as a .NET technology evangelist at Microsoft, and as a software engineer at Sybase and Digital Equipment Corporation. His areas of expertise are in distributed systems, transaction processing, operating systems, and compiler technology. Brad lives in Redmond, Washington, and is an avid tournament chess player and bridge player. He can be reached at zbrad@cybercom.net or http://www.cybercom.net/~zbrad.

Credits

Executive Editor
Robert M. Elliott

Development Editors
Emilie Herman
Eileen Bien Calabro
Ami Frank Sullivan

Technical Editors
Brad Abrams
Geoffrey Mroz
Rod Stephens

Production Editor
Angela Smith

Copy Editor
Foxxe Editorial Services

Editorial Manager
Mary Beth Wakefield

Vice President & Executive Group Publisher
Richard Swadley

Vice President and Publisher
Joseph B. Wikert

Project Coordinator
Erin Smith

Graphics and Production Specialists
April Farling
Carrie A. Foster
Denny Hager
Stephanie D. Jumper

Quality Control Technicians
Leeann Harney
Jessica Kramer
Joe Niesen
Brian H. Walls

Proofreading and Indexing
Johnna Van Hoose
TECHBOOKS Production Services

Contents

About the Authors   **v**

Credits   **vii**

Introduction   **xxiii**
    A Brief History of Patterns   xxiv
    Organization of this Book   xxiv
    Description of Patterns   xxv
      Pattern Name   xxvi
      Synopsis   xxvi
      Context   xxvi
      Forces   xxvi
      Solution   xxvi
      Implementation   xxvi
      Consequences   xxvii
      .NET Usage   xxvii
      Code Example   xxvii
      Related Patterns   xxvii
    Who Should Read this Book   xxvii
    What's on the Companion Web Site   xxviii

Chapter 1   **Overview of UML**   **1**
    Class Diagram   2
    Collaboration Diagram   14
    Statechart Diagram   22

Chapter 2   **The Software Life Cycle**   **25**
    Case Study   28
      Business Case   28
      Define Requirements Specification   29

	Develop High-Level Essential Use Cases	30
	Object-Oriented Analysis	32
	Object-Oriented Design	34
Chapter 3	**Fundamental Design Patterns**	**45**
	Delegation (When Not to Use Inheritance)	47
	Synopsis	47
	Context	47
	Forces	50
	Solution	51
	Implementation	51
	Consequences	52
	.NET Usage	52
	Code Example	52
	Related Patterns	54
	Interface	55
	Synopsis	55
	Context	55
	Forces	56
	Solution	56
	Implementation	56
	Delegates	57
	Constructors	57
	Consequences	58
	.NET Usage	58
	Code Example	58
	Related Patterns	59
	Abstract Base Class	61
	Synopsis	61
	Context	61
	Forces	62
	Solution	63
	AbstractBaseclass	63
	ConcreteClass1, ConcreteClass2, . . .	64
	Implementation	64
	Consequences	64
	.NET API Usage	64
	Code Example	64
	Related Patterns	67
	Interface and Abstract Class	69
	Synopsis	69
	Context	69
	Forces	69
	Solution	69
	Consequences	70
	.NET API Usage	70
	Code Example	71
	Related Patterns	72

Immutable   75
  Synopsis   75
  Context   75
  Forces   76
  Solution   76
  Implementation   77
  Consequences   79
  .NET API Usage   79
  Code Example   79
  Related Patterns   80
Proxy   81
  Synopsis   81
  Context   81
  Forces   82
  Solution   82
  Implementation   83
  Consequences   83
  Code Example   83
  Related Patterns   91

Chapter 4   Creational Patterns   93
Factory Method   95
  Synopsis   95
  Context   95
  Forces   97
  Solution   97
  Implementation   99
    Class Determination by Configuration   99
    Data-Driven Class Determination   100
  Consequences   101
  .NET API Usage   101
  Code Example   102
  Related Patterns   107
Abstract Factory   109
  Synopsis   109
  Context   109
  Forces   110
  Solution   111
  Implementation   113
  Consequences   113
  Code Example   114
  Related Patterns   119
Builder   121
  Synopsis   121
  Context   121
  Forces   124
  Solution   124

Implementation   126
   The Build Process   126
Consequences   127
.NET API Usage   128
Code Example   128
Related Patterns   129
Prototype   131
  Synopsis   131
  Context   131
  Forces   132
  Solution   132
  Implementation   133
  Consequences   134
  .NET API Usage   135
  Code Example   135
  Related Patterns   139
Singleton   141
  Synopsis   141
  Context   141
  Forces   142
  Solution   142
  Implementation   143
    Concurrent GetInstance Calls   144
  Consequences   145
  .NET API Usage   145
  Code Example   146
  Related Patterns   147
Object Pool   149
  Synopsis   149
  Context   149
  Forces   151
  Solution   152
    Reusable   153
    Client   153
    ReusablePool   154
  Implementation   154
    Hiding the Object Pool   154
    Delegating Object Creation   155
    Ensuring a Maximum Number of Instances   155
    Data Structure   155
    Limiting the Size of the Pool   155
    Managing Stateful Objects   156
  Consequences   156
  Code Example   156
  Related Patterns   161

Chapter 5   Partitioning Patterns   **163**
          Filter   165
               Synopsis   165
               Context   165
               Forces   166
               Solution   166
               Implementation   169
               Consequences   170
               .NET API Usage   170
               Code Example   170
               Related Patterns   174
          Composite   175
               Synopsis   175
               Context   175
               Forces   177
               Solution   177
               Implementation   179
               Consequences   179
               .NET Usage   180
               Code Example   180
               Related Patterns   185
          Read-Only Interface   187
               Synopsis   187
               Context   187
               Forces   189
               Solution   189
               Implementation   190
               Consequences   191
               Code Example   191
               Related Patterns   192

Chapter 6   Structural Patterns   **193**
          Adapter   195
               Synopsis   195
               Context   195
               Forces   196
               Implementation   198
               Consequences   199
               Code Example   199
               Related Patterns   204
          Iterator   205
               Synopsis   205
               Context   205
               Forces   206
               Solution   206

Implementation   207
    Generics   207
    Additional Functions   208
    Multiple Orderings   208
    Null Iterator   208
    Modification to the Underlying Collection   208
Consequences   209
.NET API Usage   209
Code Example   209
Related Patterns   211
Bridge   213
    Synopsis   213
    Context   213
    Forces   216
    Solution   216
    Implementation   218
    Consequences   218
    .NET API Usage   218
    Example   218
    Related Patterns   223
Façade   225
    Synopsis   225
    Context   225
    Forces   226
    Solution   226
    Implementation   227
    Consequences   228
    .NET API Usage   228
    Example   228
    Related Patterns   231
Flyweight   233
    Synopsis   233
    Context   233
    Forces   236
    Solution   236
    Implementation   238
    Consequences   239
    .NET API Usage   239
    Example   239
    Related Patterns   244
Dynamic Linkage   245
    Synopsis   245
    Context   245
    Forces   247
    Solution   247
    Implementation   248
        Incompatible Classes   248
        Security Risk   249

Consequences   249
.NET API Usage   250
Code Example   250
Related Patterns   253
Virtual Proxy   255
　Synopsis   255
　Context   255
　Forces   256
　Solution   257
　　Service   257
　　Client   257
　　ServiceProxy   258
　　IService   259
　Implementation   259
　　Shared Service Objects   259
　　Deferred Class Loading   259
　Consequences   260
　Code Example   261
　Related Patterns   263
Decorator   265
　Synopsis   265
　Context   265
　Forces   267
　Solution   267
　Implementation   269
　Consequences   269
　Code Example   270
　Related Patterns   272
Cache Management   273
　Synopsis   273
　Context   273
　Forces   274
　Solution   275
　Implementation   275
　　Structural Considerations   275
　　Implementation of the Cache   276
　　Performance-Tuning a Cache   277
　　GetHashCode( )   281
　Consequences   281
　Code Example   282
　Related Patterns   292

Chapter 7　**Behavioral Patterns**   **293**
Chain of Responsibility   295
　Synopsis   295
　Context   295
　Forces   296
　Solution   297

Implementation   297
Consequences   299
.NET API Usage   299
Code Example   299
Related Patterns   304
Command   305
Synopsis   305
Context   305
Forces   305
Solution   305
Implementation   307
Undo/Redo   307
Avoid User Interface Dependencies   308
Consequences   309
.NET API Usage   310
Code Example   310
Related Patterns   315
Little Language   317
Synopsis   317
Context   317
Forces   328
Solution   328
Implementation   329
Consequences   330
.NET API Usage   331
Code Example   331
Related Patterns   342
Mediator   343
Synopsis   343
Context   343
Forces   345
Solution   345
Colleague1, Colleague2 . . .   345
EventHandler1, EventHandler . . .   346
Mediator   346
Implementation   347
Recursive Events   348
Consequences   348
Code Example   349
Related Patterns   354
Snapshot   355
Synopsis   355
Context   355
Forces   359
Solution   359
Implementation   363
Consequences   370

Code Example   370
Related Patterns   372
Observer   373
Synopsis   373
Context   373
Forces   374
Solution   374
Implementation   376
Observing the Observable   376
Eliminating the Multicaster   377
Batching Notifications   378
Veto   378
Consequences   378
.NET API Usage   379
Code Example   379
Related Patterns   382
State   383
Synopsis   383
Context   383
Forces   386
Solution   386
Implementation   388
Consequences   388
Code Example   389
Related Patterns   394
Strategy   395
Synopsis   395
Context   395
Forces   396
Solution   396
Implementation   397
Consequences   397
.NET API Usage   397
Code Example   398
Related Patterns   400
Null Object   401
Synopsis   401
Context   401
Forces   402
Solution   402
Implementation   403
Consequences   403
Code Example   404
Related Patterns   405
Template Method   407
Synopsis   407
Context   407
Forces   408

Solution   408
Implementation   410
Consequences   410
Code Example   410
Related Patterns   413
Visitor   415
Synopsis   415
Context   415
Forces   417
Solution   417
Implementation   421
Consequences   421
Code Example   422
Related Patterns   425
Hashed Adapter Objects   427
Synopsis   427
Context   427
Forces   430
Solution   431
Implementation   432
The Hash Table Data Structure   432
Alternate Data Structures   433
Consequences   433
Code Example   433
Related Patterns   435

Chapter 8   **Concurrency Patterns**   **437**
Single Threaded Execution   439
Synopsis   439
Context   439
Forces   442
Solution   442
Implementation   442
Consequences   443
Code Example   444
Related Patterns   446
Static Locking Order   447
Synopsis   447
Context   447
Forces   447
Solution   448
Consequences   448
Implementation   449
Known Uses   449
Code Example   450
Related Patterns   451

Lock Object   453
  Synopsis   453
  Context   453
  Forces   454
  Solution   454
  Implementation   455
  Consequences   456
  Code Example   457
  Related Patterns   458
Guarded Suspension   459
  Synopsis   459
  Context   459
  Forces   460
  Solution   460
  Implementation   461
  Consequences   463
  .NET API Usage   464
  Code Example   464
  Related Patterns   465
Balking   467
  Synopsis   467
  Context   467
  Forces   468
  Solution   468
  Implementation   469
  Consequences   469
  Code Example   469
  Related Patterns   470
Scheduler   471
  Synopsis   471
  Context   471
  Forces   473
  Solution   473
  Implementation   476
  Consequences   476
  Code Example   476
  Related Patterns   481
Read/Write Lock   483
  Synopsis   483
  Context   483
  Forces   484
  Solution   485
  Implementation   486
  Consequences   486
  .NET API Usage   487
  Code Example   487
  Related Patterns   492

Producer-Consumer   493
  Synopsis   493
  Context   493
  Forces   494
  Solution   494
  Implementation   496
  Consequences   496
  .NET API Usage   496
  Code Example   496
  Related Patterns   498
Double Buffering   499
  Synopsis   499
  Context   499
  Forces   500
  Solution   501
  Implementation   502
    Multiple Buffers   502
    Threads   502
    Exception Handling   503
  Consequences   503
  .NET API Usage   504
  Code Example   504
  Related Patterns   518
Asynchronous Processing   519
  Synopsis   519
  Context   519
  Forces   521
  Solution   521
  Implementation   522
    Request Management and Thread Allocation   522
    Outcome Management   524
  Consequences   524
  .NET API Usage   525
  Code Example   525
  Related Patterns   527
Future   529
  Synopsis   529
  Context   529
  Forces   530
  Solution   531
  Implementation   532
    Polling   532
    Proxy   533
    Launching a Synchronous Computation   533
    Rendezvous   534
    Exceptions   534

Consequences   534
.NET API Usage   534
Code Example   536
Related Patterns   540

Bibliography   **541**
Index   **543**

Introduction

Experience gives programmers a variety of wisdom. As programmers gain experience, they may recognize new problems as being similar to problems they have solved before. With even more experience, they recognize that solutions for similar problems follow recurring patterns. By being aware of these patterns, experienced programmers recognize situations that patterns apply to and immediately use the solution without having to stop, analyze the problem, and pose possible strategies.

Software patterns are reusable solutions to recurring problems you encounter during software development. When a programmer discovers a pattern, it is just an insight. In most cases, to go from an unverbalized insight to a well thought out idea that the programmer can clearly articulate is surprisingly difficult. It is also an extremely valuable step. When we understand a pattern well enough to put it into words, we are able to intelligently combine it with other patterns. More importantly, once put into words, a pattern can be used in discussions among programmers who know the pattern. That allows programmers to more effectively collaborate and combine their wisdom. It can also help avoid the situation of programmers arguing over different solutions to a problem, only to find that they were really thinking of the same solution but expressing it in different ways.

Putting a pattern into words has an additional benefit for less experienced programmers who have not yet discovered the pattern. Once a pattern has been put into words, more experienced programmers can teach it to programmers who do not know the pattern.

The value of this book is that it gives experienced programmers a common vocabulary to discuss patterns. It also allows programmers who have not yet discovered a pattern to learn about the pattern.

Though this book includes a substantial breadth of patterns, there are additional patterns the author knows but did not have time to put in the book. You, dear reader, may discover some patterns yourself. Some patterns you discover may be highly specialized and only of interest to a small number of people. Other patterns may be of very broad interest and worthy of inclusion in a future volume of this book. If you wish to communicate such a pattern to this book's author, you may send e-mail to mgrand@mindspring.com.

The patterns cataloged in this book convey constructive ways of organizing parts of the software development cycle. There are other patterns that recur in programs that are not constructive. These are called *anti-patterns*, because anti-patterns can cancel out the benefits of patterns. This book does not attempt to catalog anti-patterns, as the subject is well covered in other books. Readers who are interested in anti-patterns may enjoy reading [BMMM98].

Note

Because this book is all about software patterns, they are simply referred to as patterns in the rest of this book.

A Brief History of Patterns

The idea of software patterns originally came from the field of building architecture. An architect named Christopher Alexander wrote some books describing patterns in building architecture and urban planning. Some of those books are *A Pattern Language: Towns, Buildings, Construction* (Oxford University Press) and *The Timeless Way of Building* (Oxford University Press).

The ideas presented in those books are applicable to a number of fields outside of architecture, including software.

In 1987, Ward Cunningham and Kent Beck used some of Alexander's ideas to develop five patterns to guide the design of user interfaces. They published a paper on them at OOPSLA-87. The paper was titled, "Using Pattern Languages for Object-Oriented Programs".

In the early 1990s, four authors began work in a very influential book called *Design Patterns* by Erich Gamma, Richard Helm, John Vlissides, and Ralph Johnson (Addison-Wesley). It popularized the idea of patterns and was the largest single influence on this book. The Design Patterns book is often called the "gang of four book" or GoF. This book used C++ and Smalltalk for its examples, as UML did not exist when it was written. UML is now widely accepted as the preferred notation for object-oriented design, so UML is the notation used in this book. *Visual Basic .NET Design Patterns* uses VB.NET for its examples. The pattern descriptions are presented from a VB.NET point of view.

Organization of this Book

This book focuses on design patterns that are used at the micro-architectural level. The first two chapters contain material to help you understand the patterns presented in the chapters that follow.

- Chapter 1 begins with a description of the subset of UML used in this book.

- Chapter 2 contains an overview of the software life cycle, to provide a context in which the patterns are used. This chapter also provides a case study that will show you where applications of design patterns can be applied.

The remaining chapters describe different sorts of patterns:

- Chapter 3 contains patterns that are fundamental in their nature. These patterns can be applied to a wide variety of situations. They are used by other patterns.

- Chapter 4 contains patterns that describe how to organize the creation of objects in various situations.

- Chapter 5 contains patterns that use a divide-and-conquer approach to solving a problem.

- Chapter 6 contains patterns that describe ways to combine objects into different sorts of structures.

- Chapter 7 contains patterns that describe different ways of organizing behavior.

- Chapter 8 contains patterns for managing concurrency.

Description of Patterns

The patterns in this book are described using a format that includes the following information:

- A name that is commonly used for the pattern. Alternative names are given in cases where the pattern is known by more than one name.

- A description of the problem that includes a concrete example and a solution specific to the concrete problem.

- A summary of the considerations or forces that lead to the formulation of a general solution or the avoidance of the solution.

- A general solution.

- The consequences, good and bad, of using the given solution to solve a problem.

- A list of related patterns.

Pattern books differ in how they present this information. The patterns in this book are all related to the design phase. The descriptions of design phase related patterns in this book are organized into sections with the following headings:

Pattern Name

The heading of this section consists of the name of the pattern. Under the heading may be a bibliography reference indicating where the pattern came from. Most patterns do not have any additional text under this heading. For those that do, this section contains alternate names for the pattern or information about the derivation or general nature of the pattern.

Synopsis

This section contains a brief description of the pattern. The synopsis conveys the essence of the solution provided by the pattern. The synopsis is primarily directed at experienced programmers who may recognize the pattern as one they already knew, but may not have known a name for.

   If you do not recognize a pattern from its name and synopsis, don't be discouraged. You should read through the rest of the pattern description carefully to understand it.

Context

This section describes the problem that the pattern addresses. For most patterns, the problem is presented in terms of a concrete example. After presenting a concrete problem, the context section presents a design solution to the concrete problem.

Forces

The Forces section summarizes the considerations that lead to the general solution presented in the following section. It may also present reasons to not use the solution. The reasons to use or not use the solution are presented as a bulleted list:

   ☺ Reasons to use the solution are bulleted with a happy face.

   ☹ Reasons not to use the solution are bulleted with a sad face.

Solution

The Solution section is the core of the pattern. It describes a general-purpose solution to the problem that the pattern addresses.

Implementation

The implementation section describes important considerations to be aware of when implementing the solution. It may also describe some common variations or simplifications of the solution.

Consequences

The consequences section explains the implications, good and bad, of using the solution. Most consequences are organized into bullet points like this:

- ☺ Good consequences are bulleted with a happy face.
- Neutral consequences are bulleted with a dot. (Bullets are also used in standard bullet lists.)
- ☹ Bad consequences are bulleted with a sad face.

.NET Usage

Where there is a suitable example of the pattern in the .NET Framework, it is pointed out in this section. Patterns that are not used in the .NET Framework do not have this section in their description.

Code Example

This section contains a code example that shows a sample implementation of a design that uses the pattern. Usually, the design implemented in this section is the design described previously in the "Context" section.

Related Patterns

This section contains a list of patterns that are related to the pattern being described.

Who Should Read this Book

This book should be of value to programmers of all levels who are working in a .NET environment. Programmers at different levels of experience will get different things from this book. The less experienced programmers will focus on the problem that each pattern solves and its solution.

More experienced programmers who are already familiar with the problem and solution described in a pattern will benefit from the discussion of the reasons to use or not use a solution and its consequences.

Programmers at all levels will benefit from having a name for the solutions described. Those who are already familiar with UML or the software life cycle may skip those chapters.

The pattern chapters may be read in sequence. Some people will prefer to skim and just read those patterns that appear to have immediate relevance to their current assignment. People who have co-workers also reading this book may find it helpful to organize a discussion group to share each other's insights gained from studying these patterns. Also there are pattern discussion groups that have been organized in many places. There is a listing of them at http://c2.com/cgi/wiki?PatternsGroups.

What's on the Companion Web Site

There will be a web site related to this book at http://www.wiley.com/go/vbdesign patterns. It contains a synopsis of the patterns that appear in this book, as well as the code examples in this volume.

Overview of UML

The Unified Modeling Language (UML) is a notation you can use for object-oriented analysis and design. This chapter contains a brief overview of UML to introduce you to the subset of UML and extensions to UML used in this book. For a complete description of UML, see www.omg.org/technology/documents/formal/uml.htm.

Books on UML call the pieces of information stored in instances of a class *attributes*; they call a class's encapsulations of behavior *operations*. Those terms, like UML, are not specific to any implementation language. However, this book is not language neutral. It assumes that you are using VB.NET as your implementation language. This book also uses VB-specific terms in most places, rather than terms that are language neutral but less familiar to VB.NET programmers. For example, it uses the words *operation*, *function*, and *subroutine* interchangeably, preferring the VB.NET-specific terms *function* and *subroutine*.

UML defines a number of different kinds of diagrams. The rest of this chapter is organized into sections that describe different kinds of UML diagrams and the elements that appear in them.

If you are experienced with object-oriented design, you will find most of the concepts that underlie the UML notation to be familiar. If you find that many concepts in this chapter are unfamiliar, read only as much of this chapter as you feel comfortable with. In later chapters, if a UML diagram contains something that you want explained, return to Chapter 2 and find a diagram that contains that UML element.

Class Diagram

A *class diagram* is a diagram that shows classes, interfaces, and their relationships. The most basic element of a class diagram is a class. Figure 1.1 shows many of the features that a class can have in a class diagram.

Classes are drawn as rectangles. The rectangles can be divided into two or three compartments. The class rectangle shown in Figure 1.1 has three compartments. The top compartment contains the name of the class. The middle compartment lists the class's variables. The bottom compartment lists the class's functions and subroutines.

The symbols that precede each variable, function, and subroutine are *visibility indicators*. The possible visibility indicators and their meanings are:

+	Public	Unrestricted access
#	Protected	Access only by containing class or derived types (children)
-	Private	Access restricted to containing class

UML does not have any simple way of indicating `Friend` variables or functions. The variables in the middle compartment are shown as:

```
visibilityIndicator name : type
```

Therefore, the two variables shown in the class in Figure 1.1 are private variables. The name of the first variable is `instance` and its type is `KeyManager`. The name of the second variable is `prevKey`, and its type is `Key`.

Though not shown in Figure 1.1, an initial value can be indicated for a variable by following the variable's type with an equals sign and the value like this:

```
shutDown:Boolean = false
```

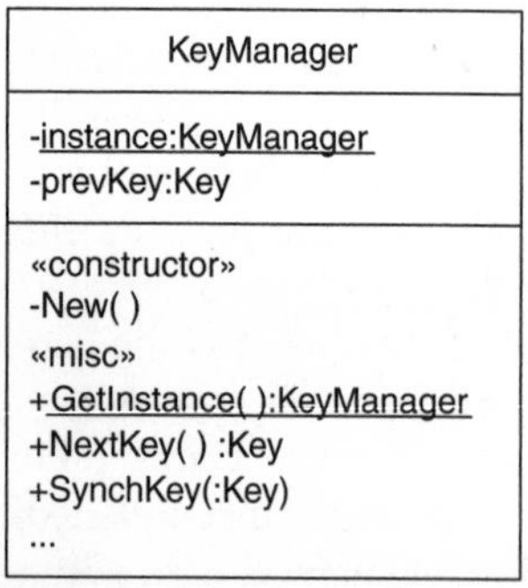

```
KeyManager
────────────────────────
-instance:KeyManager
-prevKey:Key
────────────────────────
«constructor»
-New( )
«misc»
+GetInstance( ):KeyManager
+NextKey( ) :Key
+SynchKey(:Key)
...
```

Figure 1.1 Basic Class

Notice that the first variable shown in the class is underlined. If a variable is underlined, it means that the variable is a shared variable. This applies to functions and subroutines too. Underlined functions and subroutines are shared.

The functions and subroutines in the bottom compartment are shown as:

```
visibilityIndicator name  ( formalParameters ) : returnType
```

The `GetInstance` function shown in Figure 1.1 returns a `KeyManager` object.

The UML indicates a subroutine by leaving out the `: returnType` to indicate that it does not return anything. An example of this is the `synchKey` subroutine shown in the class in Figure 1.1. A formal parameter of a function or subroutine consists of a name and a type, like this:

```
AddToken(token:String)
```

If a function or subroutine has multiple parameters, commas separate them:

```
DisplayTokenList (tokenList:ArrayList, separator:String)
```

Formal parameters may each be preceded by one of the words `in`, `out`, or `inout`, like this:

```
GetInfo(inout status:StatusCode, out msg:string):Boolean
```

A UML formal parameter that is preceded by `in` or nothing is equivalent to a `ByVal` parameter in VB.NET. A UML formal parameter that is preceded by `inout` is similar to a VB.NET parameter that is preceded by `ByRef`. A UML formal parameter that is preceded by `out` is used only to pass a value out of the function or subroutine.

A function and subroutine shown in the class in Figure 1.1 are preceded by a word in guillemets, like this:

```
«constructor»
```

In a UML drawing, a word in guillemets is called a *stereotype*. A stereotype is used like an adjective to modify what comes after it. The «`constructor`» stereotype indicates that the subroutines following it are constructors. The «`misc`» stereotype indicates that the functions and subroutines following it are regular functions and subroutines. Additional uses for stereotypes are described later in this chapter.

One last element that appears in Figure 1.1 is an ellipsis (...). If an ellipsis appears in the bottom compartment of a class, the class has additional functions and subroutines that the diagram does not show. If an ellipsis appears in the middle compartment of a class, it means that the class has additional variables that the diagram does not show.

Often, it is not necessary or helpful to show as many details of a class as were shown in the preceding class. As is shown in Figure 1.2, a class may be drawn with only two compartments.

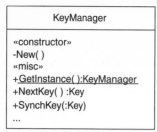

Figure 1.2   Two-Compartment Class

It is common in UML diagrams not to include all possible details. The usual reason for leaving a detail out of a diagram is either that the detail is not relevant or that the detail has not yet been decided. UML syntax allows most details of a class, other than its name, to be omitted.

When a class is drawn with only two compartments, as shown in Figure 1.2, its top compartment contains the class's name; its bottom compartment shows the class's functions and subroutines. Leaving out the compartment that contains the variables just means that the class's variables are not shown. It does not mean that the class has no variables.

The visibility indicators may be omitted from functions, subroutines, and variables. When a function, subroutine, or variable is shown without a visibility indicator, it means that there is no indication of the function's, subroutine's, or variable's visibility. It does not imply that they are public, protected, or private.

A function's parameters may be omitted if its return values are also omitted. Omitting a function's or subroutine's parameters is common in a high-level design that just identifies functions and subroutines. For example, the return values and parameters are omitted from the class shown in Figure 1.3.

The simplest form of a class has just one compartment that contains the class name, as shown in Figure 1.4.

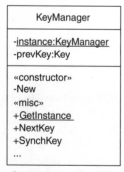

Figure 1.3   Simplified Class

A one-compartment representation of a class merely identifies the class. It provides no indication about what variables, functions, or subroutines the class has.

Interfaces are drawn in a manner similar to classes. The difference is that the name in the top compartment is preceded by an «interface» stereotype. Figure 1.5 is an example of an interface.

A .NET delegate can be similarly indicated by using a «delegate» stereotype and showing exactly one function or subroutine.

Generic classes and interfaces are indicated by an additional box with a dashed border in the upper-right corner of the class or interface. The dashed box contains the names of the type parameters that can be specified for the class or interface. Figure 1.6 shows an example of this.

The generic interface shown in Figure 1.6 has a method that returns whatever type of value is specified as a parameter of the interface. If a generic class or interface has more than one parameter, they are separated by commas in the dashed box.

What is shown in Figure 1.6 is actually a family of interfaces that work with different types that are specified through a parameter. Classes or interfaces that belong to such a generic family and work with specific types are named by specifying the generic class or interface followed by its parameters specified in angle brackets like this:

```
IEnumerator<Product>
```

```
┌─────────────────┐
│  KeyManager     │
└─────────────────┘
```

Figure 1.4 One-Compartment Class

```
┌─────────────────────┐
│    «interface»      │
│    IMetaBean        │
├─────────────────────┤
│ Clear( )            │
│ Contains( ) : Boolean│
│ ...                 │
└─────────────────────┘
```

Figure 1.5 Interface

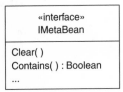

```
┌─────────────────────┐
│    «interface»      │
│    IEnumerator      │
├─────────────────────┤
│ MoveNext() : Boolean │
│ GetCurrent() : T    │
└─────────────────────┘
```

Figure 1.6 Generic Interface

Classes and interfaces are important elements of class diagrams. Other elements of a class diagram show relationships between classes and interfaces. Figure 1.7 is a typical class diagram.

The lines in Figure 1.7 indicate the relationships between the classes and an interface. A solid line with a closed hollow head such as the one in Figure 1.8 indicates the relationship of a subclass that inherits from a base class.

The class diagram in Figure 1.7 shows the abstract (MustInherit) class `Product` as the base class of the `ConcreteProduct` class. You can tell that it is abstract because its name is italicized. You can tell that its functions and subroutines are abstract because they are also italicized.

A similar sort of line is used to indicate that a class implements an interface. It is a dotted or dashed line with a closed head, like the one in Figure 1.9.

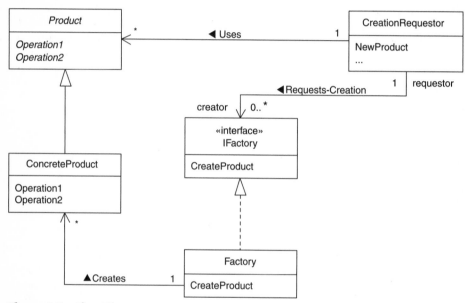

Figure 1.7   Class Diagram

Figure 1.8   Inherits from Base Class

Figure 1.9 Implements an Interface

The class diagram in Figure 1.7 shows that the Factory class implements the IFactory interface.

The other lines show other types of relationships between the classes and interface. UML calls these other types of relationships *associations*. A number of things can appear with associations that provide information about the nature of an association. The following items are optional, but this book uses them wherever it makes sense.

Association name: Somewhere around the middle of an association there may be an *association name*. The name of an association is always capitalized. There may be a triangle at one end of the association name. The triangle indicates the direction in which you should read the association. Looking at Figure 1.7, you will see that the association between the Factory and ConcreteProduct classes has the name Creates.

Navigation arrows: Arrowheads that may appear at the ends of an association are called *navigation arrows*. Navigation arrows indicate the direction in which you may navigate an association.

Looking at the association named Creates in Figure 1.7, you will see a navigation arrow pointing from the Factory class to the ConcreteProduct class. Because of the nature of creation, it seems clear that means the Factory class is responsible for creating instances of the ConcreteProduct class.

The nature of some associations is less obvious. To make the nature of such associations clear, it may be necessary to supply additional information about the association. One common way to clarify the nature of an association is to name the role that each class plays in the association.

Role name: To clarify the nature of an association, the name of the role each class plays in the association can appear at each end of an association, next to the corresponding class. *Role names* are always lowercase. This makes them easier to distinguish from association names, which are always capitalized.

In Figure 1.7, the CreationRequestor class and the IFactory interface participate in an association named Requests-Creation. The Creation Requestor class participates in that association in a role called requestor. The IFactory interface participates in that association in a role called creator.

Multiplicity Indicator: Another helpful detail of an association is how many instances of each class participate in an occurrence of the association. A multiplicity indicator may appear at each end of an association to provide this information. A multiplicity indicator can be a simple number like 0 or 1. It can be a range of numbers indicated like this:

```
0..2
```

An asterisk as the high value of a range means an unlimited number of occurrences. The multiplicity indicator 1..* means at least one instance; 0..* means any number of instances. A simple * is equivalent to 0..*.

Looking at the multiplicity indicators in Figure 1.7, you will see that each one of the associations in the drawing is a one-to-many relationship.

Figure 1.10 is a class diagram that shows a class with multiple subclasses.

Though the drawing in Figure 1.10 is perfectly valid, the UML allows a more aesthetically pleasing way to draw a class with multiple subclasses. You can combine the arrowheads, as shown in Figure 1.11. The diagram in Figure 1.11 is identical in meaning to the diagram in Figure 1.10.

Sometimes there is a need to convey more structure than is implied by a simple one-to-many relationship. The type of one-to-many relationship where one object contains a collection of other objects is called an *aggregation*. If the many objects will be managed as a collection, then the relationship should be drawn as an aggregation.

A hollow diamond at the end of the association indicates aggregation. A hollow diamond appears at the end of the association attached to the class that contains instances of the other class. The class diagram in Figure 1.12 shows an aggregation.

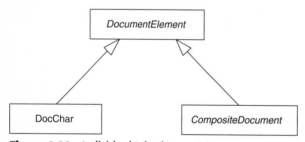

Figure 1.10 Individual Inheritance Arrows

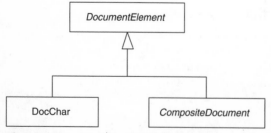

Figure 1.11 Combined Inheritance Arrow

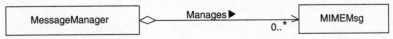

Figure 1.12 Aggregation

The class diagram In Figure 1.12 shows a class named `MessageManager`. Each of its instances contains zero or more instances of a class named `MIMEMsg`.

UML has another notation to indicate an even more structured relationship than aggregation. This relationship is called *composite aggregation*. For an aggregation to be composite, two conditions must be satisfied:

- Aggregated instances must belong to only one composite at a time.

- Some operations must propagate from the composite to its aggregated instances. For example, when a composite object is cloned, its `Clone` function will typically clone the aggregated instances so that the cloned composite will own clones of the original aggregated instances.

Figure 1.13 is a class diagram that contains a composite aggregation. The class diagram shows a `Document` class. `Document` objects can contain `Paragraph` objects. `Paragraph` objects can contain `DocChar` objects. Because of the composite aggregation, you know that `Paragraph` objects do not share `DocChar` objects, and `Document` objects do not share `Paragraph` objects. Because the classes involved in a composite aggregation propagate operations to each other, they generally implement a common interface or extend a common superclass.

Some associations are indirect. Instead of classes being directly associated with each other, they are associated indirectly through a third class. Consider the class diagram in Figure 1.14. The association in Figure 1.14 shows that instances of the `Cache` class refer to instances of the `Object` class through an instance of the `ObjectID` class.

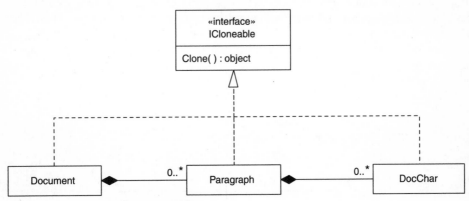

Figure 1.13 Composite Aggregation

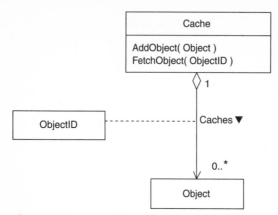

Figure 1.14 Association Class

There is another use for ellipsis in a class diagram. Some class diagrams need to show a class that has a large or open-ended set of subclasses, while only showing a few subclasses as examples of the sort of subclasses the class has. The class diagram in Figure 1.15 shows how ellipsis can be used to show this.The class diagram in Figure 1.15 shows a class named DataQuery. The DataQuery class has subclasses named OdbcQuery, OracleQuery, and Db2Query and an indefinite number of other classes indicated by the ellipsis.

An association between classes or interfaces implies a dependency that involves an object reference connecting two objects. Other types of dependencies are possible. A dashed line with an open arrowhead is used to indicate a dependency in the more general sense. Figure 1.16 shows an example of such a dependency.

The classes in a class diagram can be organized into packages. Packages are drawn as a large rectangle with a small rectangle above the large rectangle. The small rectangle contains the name of the package. The small and large rectangles are arranged to have an overall shape similar to a manila folder. The class diagram in Figure 1.17 contains a package named ServicePackage. A visibility indicator can precede the name of classes and interfaces that appear within a package. Public classes are accessible to classes outside of the package; private classes are not.

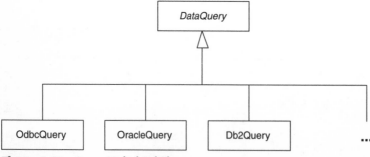

Figure 1.15 Open-Ended Subclasses

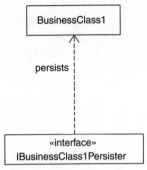

Figure 1.16 Dependency

UML packages can be used to model namespaces and assemblies. The visibility indicators of a package are not relevant to namespaces. They can be used when modeling assemblies to distinguish between public and friend[1] classes.

Some classes and interfaces are declared inside of a class. The UML terminology for such classes is nested class. Nested classes are considered to be members of the class they are declared in. Figure 1.18 shows how the nested class relationship is indicated in UML.

Figure 1.18 shows the class GameItem, which is a private member of the Game Model class. The circle with a cross in it on the end of a line indicates the nested class relationship. However, it does not indicate the visibility of the nested class. Figure 1.18 uses a comment to indicate that the visibility of the nested class is private.

Comments in UML are drawn as a rectangle with its upper-right corner turned down. Comments are attached to the diagram element they relate to by a dashed line. The class diagram in Figure 1.18 contains a comment attached to the GameModel class.

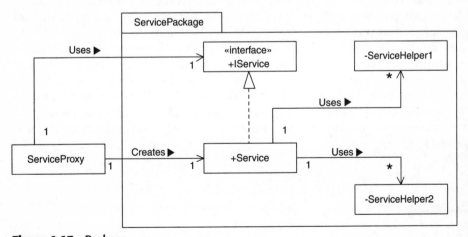

Figure 1.17 Package

[1]Friend is an accessibility modifier that indicates that a class will be accessible only to other classes in the same assembly. Public classes are available to all classes in all assemblies.

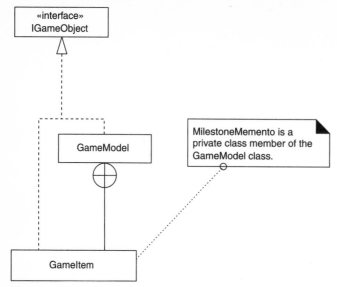

Figure 1.18   Private Classes

Class diagrams can include objects. Most objects in the diagrams in this book are drawn as shown in Figure 1.19. The object shown in this figure is an instance of a class named `Area`. The underline tells you that it is an object.[2] A name may appear to the left of the colon (:). The only significance of the name is that it you can use it to identify the individual object.

Some diagrams indicate an object as just an empty rectangle with nothing inside of the rectangle. Obviously, blank objects cannot be used to identify any particular kind of object. However, they can be used in a diagram that shows a runtime structure in which objects of unspecified types are connected. The class diagram in Figure 1.20 shows such a structure.

The lines that connect two objects are not associations. The lines that connect objects are called links. Links are connections between objects, whereas associations are relationships between classes. A link is an occurrence of an association, just as an object is an instance of a class. Links can have association names, navigation arrows, and most of the other embellishments that associations can have. However, since a link is a connection between two objects, links may not have multiplicity indicators or aggregation diamonds.

Figure 1.19   Object

---

[2]It is sometimes confusing to people that an underline is used to indicate two different things. In the middle or bottom compartment, it indicates shared functions, subroutines, and variables. In the top or only compartment, an underline indicates an object.

Some diagrams consist of just objects and links. Such diagrams are considered a kind of class diagram. However, there is a special name for this kind of diagram. A diagram that consists of just objects and links is called an object diagram. Figure 1.21 is an example of an object diagram.

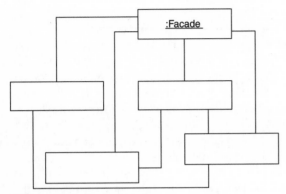

Figure 1.20   Blank Objects

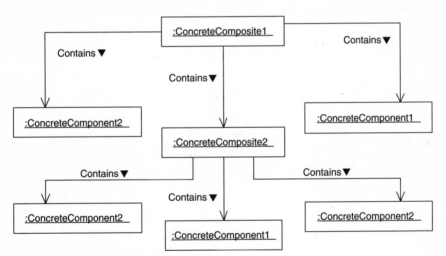

Figure 1.21   Object Diagram

Collaboration Diagram

Class and object diagrams show relationships between classes and objects. They also provide information about interactions between classes. They do not show the sequence in which the interactions occur or any concurrency that they may have.

Collaboration diagrams show objects, the links that connect them, and the interactions that occur over each link. They also show the sequence and concurrency requirements of each interaction. Figure 1.22 is a simple example of a collaboration diagram

Any number of interactions can be associated with a link. Each interaction involves a function or subroutine call. Next to each interaction or group of interactions is an arrow that points to the object whose function or subroutine is called by the interaction. The entire set of objects and interactions shown in a collaboration diagram is collectively called a *collaboration*.

Each interaction shown in Figure 1.22 begins with a sequence number and a colon. Sequence numbers indicate the order in which function or subroutine calls occur. An interaction with the number 1 must come before an interaction with the number 2 and so on. The function or subroutine name that sits on the link belongs to the object at the end of the link. In Step 1 of Figure 1.22, the `MessageManager` object's `Receive()` function is called, which in turn calls the `MIMEParser` object's `Parse` function.

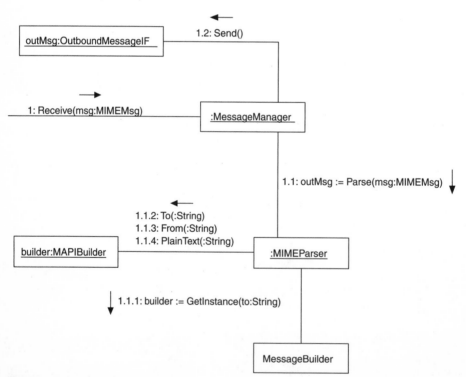

Figure 1.22   Collaboration Diagram

Multilevel sequence numbers consist of two or more numbers separated by a period. Notice that most of the sequence numbers in Figure 1.22 are multilevel sequence numbers. Multilevel sequence numbers correspond to multiple levels of calls. The portion of multilevel sequence number to the left of its rightmost period is called its prefix. For example, the prefix of 1.3.4 is 1.3.

Interactions numbered with a multilevel sequence number occur during another interaction's function or subroutine call. The other call is determined by the interaction's prefix. The function or subroutine calls of the interactions numbered 1.1 and 1.2 are made during the call of interaction 1. Similarly, interactions numbered 1.1.1, 1.1.2, 1.1.3. . . occur during the function or subroutine call of interaction 1.1.

Among interactions numbered with the same prefix, their functions or subroutines are called in the order determined by the last number in their sequence numbers. Therefore, the interactions numbered 1.1.1, 1.1.2, 1.1.3. . . are called in that order.

UML does not have any standard way to show delegates in a collaboration diagram. Figure 1.23 shows how calls using delegates are shown in this book. The delegate object is shown with the stereotype «delegate». The call to the delegate is shown with its sequence number and parameters, but without any name.

As mentioned earlier, links represent a connection between two objects. For this reason, links may not have any multiplicity indicators. That works well for links that represent an occurrence of an association between a definite number of objects. Associations that have a star multiplicity indicator on either end involve an indefinite number of objects. There is no way to draw an indefinite number of links to an indefinite number of objects. UML provides a symbol that allows us to draw links that connect an indefinite number of objects. That symbol is called a *multiobject*. It represents an indefinite number of objects. It looks like a rectangle behind a rectangle. The collaboration diagram in Figure 1.23 contains a multiobject.

The collaboration diagram in Figure 1.23 shows a WidgetModel object calling a delegate object's subroutine. The delegate object happens to be a Multicast Delegate that may call the subroutines of multiple objects when its subroutine is called. To signify that this particular delegate may call the Notify subroutine of multiple objects, the target of the Notify call is a multiobject.

Objects created as the result of a collaboration may be marked with the property {new}. Temporary objects that exist only during a collaboration may be marked with the property {transient}. The collaboration diagram in Figure 1.24 shows a collaboration that creates an object.

Figure 1.23 Multiobject

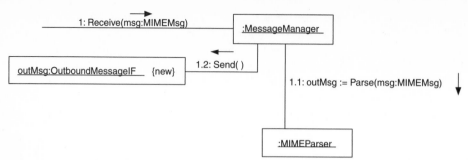

Figure 1.24   New Object

Some interactions happen concurrently, rather than sequentially. A letter at the end of a sequence number indicates concurrent interactions. For example, in Figure 1.25 the methods of interactions numbered 1.2a and 1.2b would be called concurrently with each call running in a separate thread. The top-level interaction is the one numbered 1. During that interaction, first interaction 1.1 is invoked. Then interactions 1.2a and 1.2b are invoked at the same time. After that, interactions 1.3 and 1.4 are invoked, in that order.

The collaboration in Figure 1.26 begins by calling the `TollBooth` object's `Start` subroutine. The `Start` subroutine repeatedly calls the object's `CollectNextToll` function. The `CollectNextToll` function calls the `TollBasket` object's `Collect Toll` function and the `TollGate` object's `RaiseGate` subroutine.

One other thing to notice about the collaboration diagram in Figure 1.26 is the «`self`» stereotype that appears next to the link for interaction 1.1. It serves to clarify the fact that the link is a self-reference.

An asterisk after a sequence number indicates a repeated interaction. Consider the collaboration diagram in Figure 1.26.

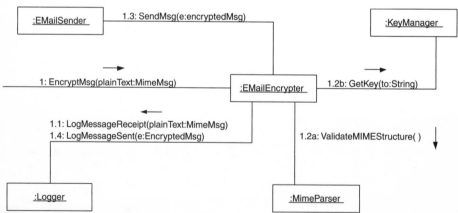

Figure 1.25   E-Mail Encrypter

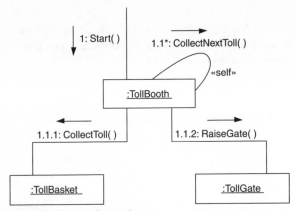

Figure 1.26   Toll Booth

Unlike the example in Figure 1.26, most repetitive interactions occur conditionally. UML allows a condition to be associated with an interaction by putting it inside of square brackets before the colon. The collaboration diagram in Figure 1.27 shows an example of a conditional repetitive interaction.

Figure 1.27 shows an `IEnumerator` object being passed to a `DialogMediator` object's `Refresh` subroutine. Its `Refresh` subroutine, in turn, calls a `Widget` object's `Reset` subroutine and then repeatedly calls its `AddData` subroutine while the `IEnumerator` object's `MoveNext` function returns true.

It is important to note that the definition of UML does not define the meaning of conditions associated with repetitive interactions very precisely. In particular, the definition of UML says that what appears between the square brackets can "be expressed in pseudocode or an actual programming language." This book consistently uses VB.NET for that purpose.

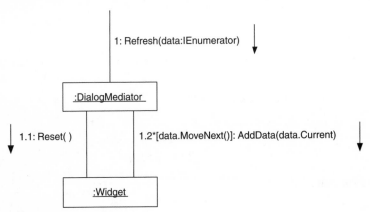

Figure 1.27   Refresh

When dealing with multiple threads, something that often needs to be specified about functions and subroutines is what happens when two threads try to call the same function or subroutine at the same time. UML allows this to be specified by placing one of the following constructs after a function or subroutine:

```
{concurrency = sequential}
```

This means that only one thread at a time should call a function or subroutine. No guarantee is made about the correctness of its behavior if the function or subroutine is called by multiple threads at a time.

```
{concurrency = concurrent}
```

This means that if multiple threads call a function or subroutine at the same time, they will all execute it concurrently and correctly.

```
{concurrency = guarded}
```

This means that if multiple threads call a function or subroutine at the same time, only one thread at a time will be allowed to execute the function or subroutine. While one thread is executing the function or subroutine, other threads will be forced to wait for their turn. This is usually implemented with a SyncLock statement that uses Me as the object to use for locking.

The collaboration diagram in Figure 1.28 shows an example of a guarded subroutine.

There are refinements to thread locking used in this book for which there is no standard representation in UML. This book uses some extensions to the {concurrency=guarded} construct to represent those refinements.

Sometimes the object that threads need a lock on is not the same object whose function or subroutine is called by an interaction. Consider the collaboration diagram in Figure 1.29.

Figure 1.28 Guarded Subroutine Call

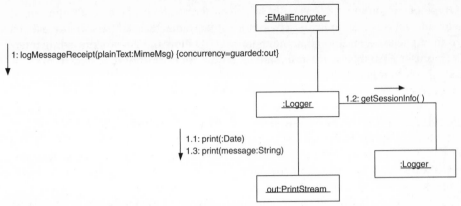

Figure 1.29 Synchronization Using a Third Object

In Figure 1.29, `{concurrency=guarded:lockObject}` refers to the object labeled `lockObject`. Before the subroutine call can actually take place, the thread that controls the call must own the lock associated with the object labeled `lockObject`. This is identical to VB.NET's semantics for a `SyncLock` statement.

Sometimes there are preconditions beyond acquiring ownership of a lock that must be met before a thread may proceed with a function or subroutine call. Such preconditions are indicated by vertical bar followed by the precondition. The collaboration diagram in Figure 1.30 shows such preconditions following `guarded` and a vertical bar.

The collaboration diagram in Figure 1.30 shows two asynchronous interactions. One interaction calls a `PrintQueue` object's `AddPrintJob` subroutine to add a print job to the `PrintQueue` object. In the other interaction, a `PrintDriver` object calls the `PrintQueue` object's `GetPrintJob` function to get a print job from the `PrintQueue` object. Both interactions have synchronization preconditions. If the print queue is full, then the interaction that calls the `addPrintJob` subroutine will wait until the print queue is not full before proceeding to make the call to the `AddPrintJob` subroutine. If the print queue is empty, then the interaction that calls the `getPrintJob` function will wait until the print queue is not empty before proceeding to make the call to the `GetPrintJob` function.

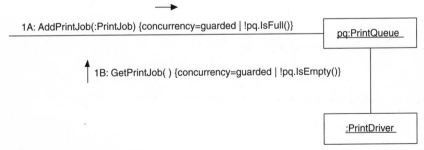

Figure 1.30 Print Queue

A type of precondition not usually indicated with an expression is a requirement that an interaction not start until two or more other interactions finish. All interactions have an implicit precondition that they cannot start before the directly preceding interactions finishes. An interaction numbered 1.2.4 cannot start until the interaction numbered 1.2.3 is completed.

Some interactions are required to wait for additional interactions to complete before they can start. Such additional predecessor interactions are indicated by listing them at the left side of the interaction followed by a slash (/) and the rest of the interaction. The collaboration diagram in Figure 1.31 contains an example.

In Figure 1.31, the interaction labeled 2.1a.1 cannot start until interaction 1.1.2 finishes. If an interaction must wait for more than one additional interaction to finish before it starts, they all appear before the slash, separated by commas.

The mechanisms discussed so far determine when the functions or subroutines of a collaboration are called. They do not say anything about when the calls return. The arrows that point at the objects whose functions or subroutines are called provide information about when the calls may return.

Most of the arrows in Figure 1.31 have a closed head. This indicates that the calls are synchronous. The calls do not return until they have completed doing whatever they do.

An open arrowhead indicates an asynchronous call. An asynchronous function or subroutine call returns to its caller immediately, while the function or subroutine does its work asynchronously in a separate thread. The collaboration diagram in Figure 1.32 shows an asynchronous call.

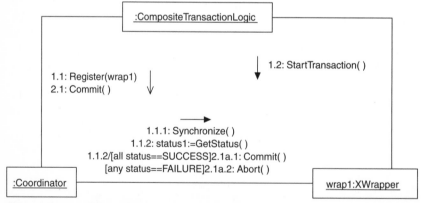

Figure 1.31   Additional Predecessor Interactions

Figure 1.32   Asynchronous Subroutine Call

The UML only defines arrowheads for synchronous and asynchronous calls. UML allows other types of arrows to indicate different types of function or subroutine calls as extensions to UML. To indicate a balking call, this book uses a bent back arrow, as shown in Figure 1.33.

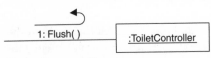

Figure 1.33 Balk

When a balking call is made to a function or subroutine, if there is nothing preventing the call from proceeding immediately, then it does proceed to do whatever it does and then returns. However, when a balking call is made and there is a reason that the function or subroutine cannot execute immediately, then it returns immediately without doing anything.

You may have noticed that the object making the top-level call that initiates a collaboration is not shown in all of the preceding collaboration diagrams. This means the object that initiates the collaboration is not considered to be a part of the collaboration.

The objects you have seen how to model in UML, up to this point, are passive in nature. They do nothing until one of their functions or subroutines is called.

Some objects are active. They have a thread that allows them to initiate operations asynchronously and independently of whatever else is going on in a program. Active objects are indicated as an object with a thick border. Figure 1.34 contains an example of an active object.

Figure 1.34 shows an active Sensor object that calls a SensorObserver object's subroutine without another object first calling one of its functions or subroutines.

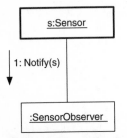

Figure 1.34 Active Sensor

Statechart Diagram

Statechart diagrams are used to model a class's behavior as a state machine. If you don't know what a state machine is, then you can skip the rest of this chapter and come back to it when you read about the State pattern in Chapter 7.

Figure 1.35 is an example of a simple state diagram.

A statechart diagram shows each state as a rounded rectangle. All the states in the preceding diagram are divided into two compartments. The upper compartment contains the name of the state. The lower compartment contains a list of events that the object responds to while in that state, without changing state. Each event in the list is followed by a slash and the action it performs in response to the event. UML predefines two such events:

- The `enter` event occurs when an object enters a state.
- The `exit` event occurs when an object leaves a state.

If there are no events that a state responds to without changing state, then its rectangle is not divided into two compartments. Such a state is drawn as a simple rounded rectangle that just contains the state's name.

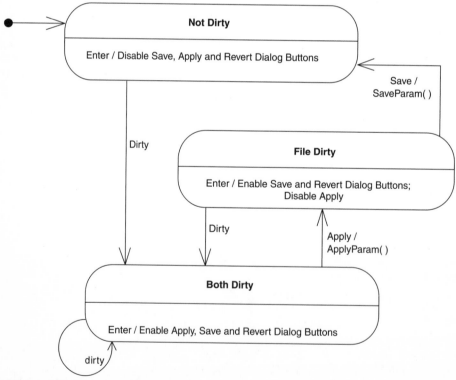

Figure 1.35   Statechart Diagram

Every state machine has an initial state that is the state an object is in before the first transition occurs. The initial state is drawn as a small solid filled-in circle.

Transitions between states are shown in statechart diagrams as lines between states. Normally, transition lines are required to have a label that indicates the event that triggers the transition. The event may be followed by a slash and the action that occurs when the transition takes place.

If a statechart includes a final state, the final state is drawn as a small solid circle inside of a larger circle.

CHAPTER 2

The Software Life Cycle

The purpose of this chapter is to help you understand how design patterns are used by explaining the context in which they are used.

A recurring theme in most activities related to software development is *getting organized*. There are many different ways to get organized. They all involve making decisions. The software development activity that involves the most decisions is design, which involves determining the software's internal organization from some sort of problem analysis.

Patterns give us guidance in making decisions. Because design involves many decisions, patterns related to design have been of greatest interest to programmers.

This book is devoted to patterns used during design. This chapter describes how patterns are used by putting them into the context of a software development process. There are many different kinds of development processes that have different merits. Without intending to promote any particular development process, this chapter first describes the life cycle of a software development process. It uses this software development as a context for the use of patterns, then it presents the object-oriented design portion of a case study.

A variety of activities take place during the lifetime of a piece of software. Figure 2.1 shows some of the activities that lead up to the deployment of a piece of business software.

Figure 2.1 is not intended to show all the activities that occur during a software project. It merely shows some common activities for the purpose of understanding the context for the patterns discussed in this book. This book describes recurring patterns that occur during the portion of the software life cycle labeled in Figure 2.1 as "Build."

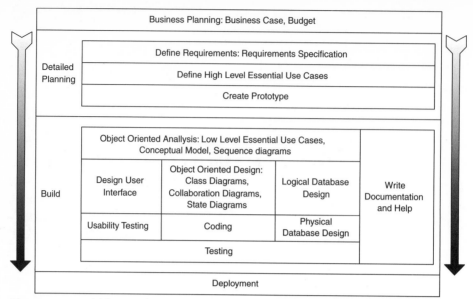

Figure 2.1   Activities Leading to Software Deployment

The diagram in Figure 2.1 shows very clear boundaries between each activity. In practice, the boundaries are not always so clear. Sometimes it is difficult to say if a particular activity belongs in one box or another. The precise boundaries are not important. What is important is to understand the relationships between these activities.

Earlier activities, such as defining requirements and object-oriented analysis, determine the course of activities that follow them, such as defining essential use cases or object-oriented design. However, in the course of those later activities, deficiencies in the products of earlier activities emerge. For example, in the course of defining a use case, it may become apparent that there is an ambiguous or conflicting requirement. Making the necessary changes to the requirements will generally result in the need to modify existing use cases or write new ones. You should expect such iterations. So long as the trend is for later iterations to produce fewer changes than earlier iterations, consider the iterations to be part of the normal development process.

The following are brief descriptions of some of the activities shown in Figure 2.1. These short descriptions only provide enough information about these activities to understand how the patterns discussed in this work apply to a relevant activity. The case study that follows the descriptions provides deeper insights into these activities.

> **Business Planning:** This typically starts with a proposal to build or modify a piece of software. The proposal evolves into a *business case*. A business case is a document that describes the pros and cons of the software project and also includes estimates of the resources that will be required to complete the project. If a decision is made to proceed with the project, then a preliminary schedule and budget are prepared.
>
> **Define Requirements:** The purpose of this activity it to produce a requirements specification that says what the software produced by the project will and won't do. This typically begins with goals and high-level requirement from the

business case. Additional requirements are obtained from appropriate sources to produce an initial requirements specification.

As the requirements specification is used in subsequent activities, necessary refinements to the requirements are discovered. The refinements are incorporated into the requirements specification. The products of subsequent activities are then modified to reflect the changes to the requirements specification.

Define Essential Use Cases: A use case describes the sequence of events that occurs in a specific circumstance between a system and other entities. The other entities are called actors. Developing use cases improves our understanding of the requirements, analysis, or design that the use case is based on. As we develop better understanding of requirements, analysis, and design, we are able to refine them.

Essential use cases describe events in terms of the problem domain. Use cases that describe events in terms of the internal organization of software are called real use cases.

The type of use case most appropriate for refining requirements are high-level essential use cases. Such use cases are high level in the sense that they explore the implications of what they are based on, but do not try to add additional details.

Create Prototype: Create a prototype of the proposed software. A prototype can be used to get reactions to a proposed project. Reactions to a prototype can be used to refine requirements and essential use cases.

Define High-Level System Architecture: Determine the major components of the system that are obvious from the original proposal. Also determine their relationships.

Object-Oriented Analysis: The purpose of this activity is to understand what the software produced by the project will do and how it will interact with other entities in its environment. The goal of analysis is to create a model of what the software is going to do, but not how to do it. The products of object-oriented analysis model the situation in which the software will operate, from the perspective of an outside observer. The analysis does not concern itself with what goes on inside the software.

Object-Oriented Design: The purpose of this activity is to determine the internal organization of software. The products of the design effort identify the classes that will comprise the internal logic of the software. They also determine the internal structure of the classes and their interrelationships.

More decisions are made during object-oriented design than during any other activity. For that reason, this work includes more patterns that apply to object-oriented design than any other activity.

Coding: The purpose of this activity is to write the code that will make the software work.

Testing: The purpose of this phase is to ensure that the software works as expected.

Case Study

What follows is a case study that involves the design and development of an employee timekeeping system for a fictitious business called Henry's Food Market. To keep the size of this reasonable, the artifacts of the development process are simplified and abbreviated. Details of deriving those artifacts are also abbreviated. The point of this case study is to set the stage for a situation where applications of design patterns can be demonstrated.

Business Case

What follows is an abbreviated business case that sets out the motivation and schedule for building an employee timekeeping system.

Henry's Food Market operates five retail stores. To support those stores, it also operates a warehouse and a commercial bakery that produces the baked goods that the stores sell. Most of its employees are paid by the hour. The hours of employees are tracked by a time-clock system. When each employee begins work, goes on break, returns from a break, or leaves work the employee is supposed to slide his or her employee badge through a timekeeping clock that records the hours worked.

Henry's Food Market wants to expand, increasing the number of its stores from 5 to 21 over the next two years at a rate of two stores every three months. One challenge facing the company is that if it continues to use the existing timekeeping system, it will have to hire more people to handle the system's administrative functions. Currently, each location requires a person working half-time at each location as a timekeeper to administer its timekeeping system. Following are the activities that the timekeeper is required to perform:

- The timekeeper prints reports for supervisors, showing the number of hours that each employee worked the previous day, so that supervisors can verify that their subordinates worked the stated number of hours. Here are some common errors that supervisors uncover by reviewing these reports:

  - Employees not clocking out when they go on break or leave work.
  - Coworkers clocking in employees who are late to work.
  - Employees clocking in before the beginning of their shift, hoping to be paid for the extra time.

- The timekeeper enters corrections into the timekeeping system.

- The timekeeper prepares weekly reports showing the number of hours every employee in a location worked and sends those reports to the payroll department.

Because the timekeeping system provides employee hours in the form of a printed report only, there is currently one person working full-time to enter employee hours into the payroll system and review the entered hours. That person costs the company $28,000 a year. If the company continues to use the same system, it will have to hire another person to enter employee hours at an additional cost of $28,000 a year.

The cost of having a person working half-time as a timekeeper in each location is $12,000 per person per year. The current cost of paying people to be timekeepers is $60,000/year.

The total current cost of labor for timekeeping is $88,000/year. In two years, when the company's expansion is complete, that labor cost for timekeeping will have increased to $308,000.

The proposed project is to build a replacement timekeeping system that will keep the labor cost of timekeeping at current or lower levels after the expansion. The timekeeping system will be expected to pay for itself in 18 months. It is expected to be deployed within 6 months of the beginning of the project.

Define Requirements Specification

Minimally, a requirements specification should specify the required functions and attributes of what is produced by a project. Required functions are things that the system must do, such as record the time when an employee begins work. Required attributes are characteristics of the system that are not functions, such as requiring that users of the timekeeping terminals not need more than an eighth grade education. Some of the other things that will normally be in a requirements document that are not in the following example are:

- **Assumptions:** This is a list of things that will be assumed to be true, such as the minimum educational level of employees or that the company will not become unionized.

- **Risks:** This is a list of things that may go wrong, leading to delay or failure of the project. That may include technical uncertainties, such as the availability of devices that are suitable for use as timekeeping terminals. It may include nontechnical concerns, such as anticipated changes to labor laws.

- **Dependencies:** This is a list of resources the project may depend on, such as the existence of a wide area network.

It is helpful to number the requirements in a requirements specification. That allows decisions based on a requirement to be easily noted in use cases, design documents, and even code. If inconsistencies are found later on, it is then easy to trace them back to the relevant requirements. It is also common to number requirements hierarchically by functions. The following are some of the required functions for the timekeeping system:

R1. The system must collect the times that employees start work, go on break, return from break, and leave work.

    R1.1 In order to work with the timekeeping terminal, employees will be required to identify themselves by sliding their employee badge through a badge reader on the timekeeping terminal.

    R1.2 After an employee is identified to a timekeeping terminal, the employee will be able to press a button to indicate if he or she is starting a work shift, going on break, returning from break, or ending a work shift. The timekeeping system will keep a permanent record of each such event in a form that it is later able to incorporate into a report of the employee's hours.

R2. Supervisors must be able to review the hours of subordinates at a timekeeping terminal without any need to get hard copy.

    R2.1 Timekeeping terminals will present options to supervisors to allow them to review and modify an employee's recorded hours.

        R2.1.1. All revisions made to an employee's timekeeping record will leave an audit trail that will retain the original records and identify the person who made each revision.

    R2.2 To ensure the simplest possible user interface for nonsupervisors, non-supervisors will not see any options related to supervisory functions when they use a timekeeping terminal.

    R2.3 Supervisors will only be able to modify the timekeeping records of their own subordinates.

R3. At the end of each pay period, the timekeeping system must automatically transmit employee hours to the payroll system.

As we develop some use cases, you can expect to discover additional required functions.

Develop High-Level Essential Use Cases

When developing use cases, it is usually best to first focus on the most common cases and then develop uses cases for less common cases. Use cases for common situations are called primary use cases. Use cases for less common situations are called secondary use cases. Here is a use case for the most common use of the timekeeping system:

Use Case:	Employee Uses Timekeeping Terminal, version 1
Actors:	Employee
Purpose:	Inform timekeeping system of an employee's comings and goings.
Synopsis:	An employee is about to begin a work shift, go on break, return from break, or end a work shift. The employee identifies him/herself to the timekeeping system and lets it know which of those four things he/she is about to do.
Type:	Primary and essential
Cross-References:	Requirements R1, R1.1, R1.2, R1.3, and R2.2

Course of Events

Employee	System
1 Employee slides his/her badge through a timekeeping terminal's badge reader.	2 The timekeeping terminal reads the employee ID from the badge and verifies that it is a legitimate employee ID. The timekeeping terminal then prompts the employee to tell it if he/she is starting a work shift, going on break, returning from break, or ending a work shift.
3 The employee indicates to the timekeeping terminal whether he/she is starting a work shift, going on break, returning from break, or ending a work shift.	4 The timekeeping terminal makes a permanent record of the employee's indication. It then acknowledges the employee by displaying the current time, indicating that it is ready for use by the next employee.

Now we will consider a larger use case that is less detailed.

Use Case:	Employee Uses Multiple Timekeeping Terminals to Track Hours, version 1
Actors:	Employee
Purpose:	Inform timekeeping system of an employee's comings and goings during an entire shift.
Synopsis:	An employee who is not restricted to the use of a single timekeeping terminal notifies the timekeeping system when he/she starts a shift, goes on break, returns from break, and ends a shift.
Type:	Primary and essential
Cross-References:	Requirements R1 and R1.2

Course of Events

Employee	System
1 An employee uses a timekeeping terminal to notify the timekeeping system that he/she is beginning a shift.	2 The system makes a record of the time that the employee began the shift.

(continued)

Course of Events *(continued)*	
Employee	System
3 An employee uses a timekeeping terminal to notify the timekeeping system that he/she is going on break.	4 The system makes a record of the time that the employee went on break.
5 An employee uses a timekeeping terminal to notify the timekeeping system that he/she has returned from break.	6 The system makes a record of the time that the employee returned from break.
7 An employee uses a timekeeping terminal to notify the timekeeping system that he/she is ending a shift.	8 The system makes a record of the time that the employee ended the shift.

Analyzing the preceding use case, we find a potential problem: There is no requirement that the timekeeping terminals all keep the correct time. Employees are likely to notice if the time on different timekeeping terminals is not the same. They will want to start their shift on the terminal that shows the earlier time and end their shift on the terminal that shows the later time. To prevent employees from cheating the company in this way, we will add another requirement to the early timekeeping scenario:

R1.3   The times displayed and recorded by different timekeeping terminals must be within five seconds of each other.

As we develop additional essential use cases, additional refinements to the requirements will be found. However, that is all that we will present in this case study.

Object-Oriented Analysis

Object-oriented analysis is concerned with building a model of the problem to be solved. It answers the question of what the software will do without being concerned with how it will do it.

The primary product of object-oriented analysis is a conceptual model of the problem that shows the proposed system and the real-world entities that the system will interact with. The conceptual model also includes the relationships and interactions between the entities and between the entities and the system.

Conceptual models are usually constructed in two phases:

1.   Identify the entities that are involved in the problem. It is very important to identify all of the entities involved. When in doubt, it is best to include an entity in the model. On one hand, if the entity is unnecessary for subsequent design activities, then it will become apparent as the design develops. On the other hand, if an entity is missing from the analysis, the missing entity may not be detected later on.

2. Build a conceptual model consisting of identifying relationships between the entities.

UML uses the same symbols to represent the entities and relationships of a conceptual model as it uses to represent classes and associations in a class model. Figure 2.2 is a diagram that shows just the entities that are apparent from the requirements and the use cases.

The entities in Figure 2.2 are in no particular order. The diagram in Figure 2.3 adds some of the more obvious relationships.

Looking at the diagram in Figure 2.3, you will notice two entities that are not involved in any of the indicated relationships: `TimekeepingSystem` and `Employee ID`.

Figure 2.3 is supposed to be a conceptual model of the problem to be solved. Because the `TimekeepingSystem` entity does not seem to have a relationship to anything else in the problem, we conclude that it is really part of the solution rather than the problem. For that reason, we will drop it from the model.

The `EmployeeID` entity is very closely related to the `Employee` entity. It is so closely related to the `Employee` entity that it seems more appropriate to represent it as an attribute. The diagram in Figure 2.4 shows the conceptual model with attributes added.

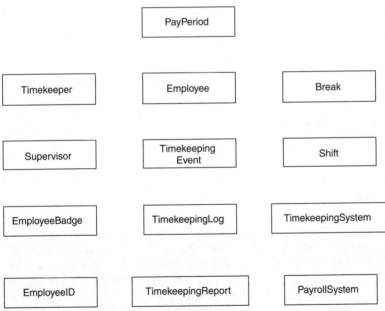

Figure 2.2 Conceptual Model (Entities Only)

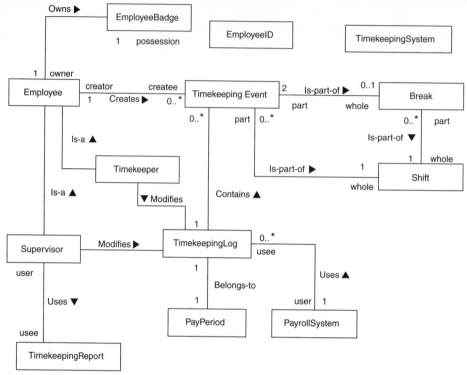

Figure 2.3   Conceptual Model (with Associations)

The diagram in Figure 2.4 is as far as we will take the analysis of this problem.

Object-Oriented Design

Object-oriented design is concerned with designing the internal logic of a program. In this case, we are concerned with the internal logic of the timekeeping system. It is not concerned with how the user interface presents that logic. It is not concerned with how data is stored in a database. The ultimate goal of object-oriented design is to provide a detailed design of the classes that will provide that internal logic.

There are various strategies for using the results of analysis to produce a design. The strategy we use here is to create a class diagram that models the structural relationships in the conceptual model. We then develop collaboration diagrams to model the behavioral relationships in the conceptual model. We then refine the class diagrams with what we learned from the collaboration diagrams. We then refine the collaboration and class diagrams with requirements not covered by the conceptual model.

Throughout this process, we will use design patterns to guide us in our decision making. In the following paragraphs, we will work through this process. At points in the process, we will find the opportunity to use patterns and explain how the patterns help.

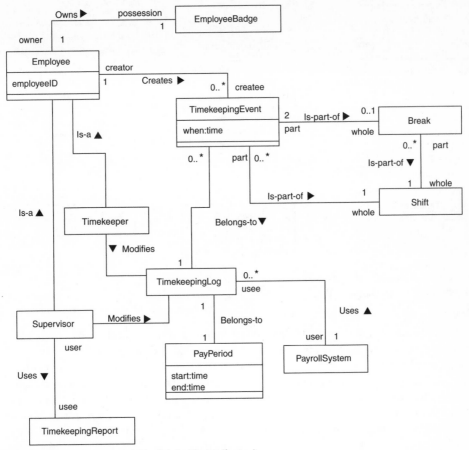

Figure 2.4   Conceptual Model (with Attributes)

We construct our first class diagram by assuming that there will be a class to represent each entity in the conceptual model. This is shown in Figure 2.5.

Rather than assume the representation of the entity attributes in the conceptual model, the class diagram in Figure 2.5 indicates *accessor methods* for the attributes.

Next we consider the "Is-a" relationships in the conceptual model.[1] Though an obvious way to represent an "Is-a" relationship in a class diagram is through inheritance, the Delegation pattern (described in Chapter 3) tells us that it is not always the best way to represent "Is-a" relationships. In particular, it tells us to use delegation instead of inheritance to represent "Is-a" relationships to represent roles that instances of a class may play, if instances of the class play different roles at different times. Since non-supervisor employees may be promoted to supervisors, be transferred from another job to the timekeeper job or become timekeeping supervisors, we will use delegation to represent those roles. Figure 2.6 is a version of the class diagram that adds the role relationships.

[1]Relationships labeled "Is-a" are commonly used in conceptual models to indicate that a kind of entity is a kind of another entity.

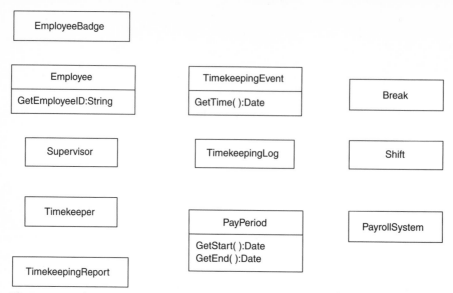

Figure 2.5 Class Diagram Version 1

The "Is-part-of" relationships in the conceptual diagram are another structural relationship that we might consider designing into the class diagram at this point.[2] We notice that there is some redundancy between two sets of "Is-part-of" relationships: The "Is-part-of" relationship between Shift and TimekeepingEvent appears to have some redundancy with the set of "Is-part-of" relationships between Shift and Break and between Break and TimekeepingEvent. For that reason, we postpone including those relationships in the design until we have clarified the relationships through the construction of collaboration diagrams.

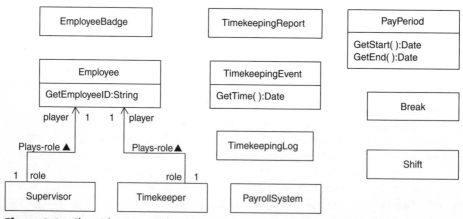

Figure 2.6 Class Diagram version 2

[2]Relationships labeled "Is-part-of" are commonly used in conceptual models to indicate that one kind of entity is a part of another kind of entity.

We will guide the construction of collaboration diagrams with use cases, so we construct the following real use case to describe a day's usage of the timekeeping system for a typical employee.

Use Case:	Employee Uses Timekeeping Terminal to Track Hours, version 1
Actors:	Employee
Purpose:	Inform timekeeping system of an employee's comings and goings.
Synopsis:	An employee is about to begin a work shift, go on break, return from break, or end a work shift. The employee identifies him/herself to the timekeeping system and lets it know which of those four things he/she is about to do.
Type:	Primary and real
Cross References:	Requirements R1, R1.1, R1.2, R1.3, and R2.2 Essential use case "Employee Uses Timekeeping Terminal"

Course of Events

Employee	System
1 Employee slides his or her badge through a timekeeping terminal's badge reader.	2 The timekeeping display replaces its display of the current time indicating it is available for use with a display indicating that it is looking up the employee id that the badge reader read. After the timekeeping terminal has looked up the employee's information, it first checks if the employee is allowed to use this particular timekeeping terminal. The timekeeping terminal then prompts the employee to tell it if he/she is starting a work shift, going on break, returning from break or ending a work shift.
3 The employee indicates to the timekeeping terminal whether he/she is starting a work shift, going on break, returning from break or ending a work shift.	4 The timekeeping terminal makes a permanent record of the employee's indication. It acknowledges the completion of the timekeeping transaction by displaying the current time, indicating that it is ready for use by the next employee.

Looking that the preceding use case, we can see that it involves classes that are not in the previous class diagram. The use case talks about a timekeeping terminal interacting with a user, so we include a user interface class in our design. We may later refine that into additional classes if it seems necessary.

The use case also mentions creating a permanent record of timekeeping events. To manage that and the employee information the timekeeping terminal looks up, we infer the existence of a database object. Again, we leave open the possibility of later additional refinement.

We want to minimize the number of dependencies between the user interface and the classes that implement the timekeeping terminal's internal logic. Maintaining loose coupling between the user interface and the internal logic will make the software more maintainable. To achieve this, we use the Façade pattern. The Façade pattern tells us that we can maintain low coupling between a functionally related set of classes and their client classes by interposing an additional façade class between the set of classes and their clients. Most or all of the client's access to the set of classes is through the façade class. The façade class also encapsulates the common logic that is needed to use also the set of classes.

The façade class that we add to the design is called `TimekeepingController`. It will be responsible for controlling the sequence of events that occurs when a time-keeping terminal interacts with a user.

Based on the preceding use case, we construct the collaboration diagram shown in Figure 2.7.

Here is a description of the interactions shown in the collaboration diagram in Figure 2.7.

1   The `UserInterface` object begins the collaboration by passing an employee ID to the `TimekeepingController` object's `DoTransaction` subroutine.

   1.1   The `TimekeepingController` object gets information about the employee associated with the employee ID by passing the employee ID to the `Database` object's `LookupEmployee` function. The `LookupEmployee` function returns an `Employee` object that encapsulates information about the employee.

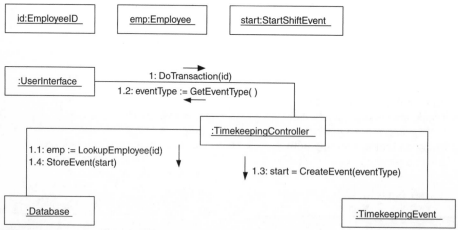

Figure 2.7   Start Shift Collaboration

1.2 The `TimekeepingController` object calls the `UserInterface` object's `GetEventType` function, which causes the user interface to prompt the employee for the type of event that should be recorded. The function returns a value that indicates the type of event to record.

1.3 The `TimekeepingController` object passes the event type it got from the user interface to the `TimekeepingEvent` class' `CreateEvent` function. The `CreateEvent` function returns an object that encapsulates the event.

1.4 The `TimekeepingController` object passes the event object to the Database object's `StoreEvent` subroutine so that it can be stored in the database.

What follows is some of the rationale behind the construction of the collaboration diagram in Figure 2.7.

- The `Database` class's `LookupEmployee` operation creates an object to encapsulate the employee information it finds. The Creator pattern, described in [Grand98], says that if an object contains, aggregates, records instances of, or provides initializing data for instances of a class, then that object is a good choice of creator for instances of that class. Therefore, the objects that the `Database` class' `LookupEmployee` operation creates will be instances of the `Employee` class. [Grand98]

- Since a start of shift event is a kind of timekeeping event, objects that represent a start of shift event will be an instance of a subclass of `TimekeepingEvent`. There will be other subclasses of `TimekeepingEvent` to represent other kinds of timekeeping events. We don't want the user interface to know about the subclasses of the `TimekeepingEvent` class because we want to minimize the dependencies between the user interface and the internal logic. To achieve that we will use the Factory Method pattern (described in Chapter 4).

  The Factory Method pattern puts one class in charge of creating instances of other classes that have a common superclass or implement a common interface. Following that pattern, we put the `TimekeepingEvent` class in charge of creating instances of its subclasses.

Figure 2.8 is another version of the class diagram we have been working on that includes refinements from what we have learned from the collaboration diagram in Figure 2.6. The `EmployeeBadge` class has been removed from the design, since the mechanism for capturing an employee's employee ID is part of the user interface and not part of the internal logic.

For the next refinement to the design, we will take a closer look at the `Database` class. The intent of the `TimekeepingLog` entity in the conceptual model was to maintain a log of all timekeeping events. We created a class that corresponds to it in our initial design. Now we notice that the `Database` class has been given that responsibility. That means that we don't need the `TimekeepingLog` class in the design, so we will remove it.

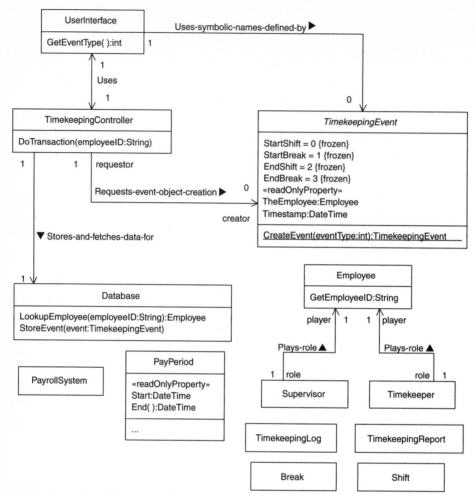

Figure 2.8   Class Diagram version 3

An area of the design that we have not yet addressed is the generation of timekeeping reports. Supervisors will use timekeeping reports to review the hours that their subordinates have worked. Specially formatted timekeeping reports will be fed to the payroll system.

Timekeeping reports organize timekeeping events into shifts. A shift is a range of time during which an employee is at work. During a shift, an employee is supposed to be working, except for periods within a shift called breaks. Breaks are periods when an employee stops working for such reasons as eating lunch or going to the bathroom.

For the purposes of computing an employee's pay, the time during a shift is broken down into three categories:

- *Regular time* is time that an employee is paid at his/her usual hourly rate.

- *Overtime* is time beyond the time that an employee is normally expected to work. An employee is paid for overtime at a multiple of his/her regular time rate.

■ *Unpaid time* is time that an employee is not paid for. Some or all of an employee's break time may be unpaid time.

Timekeeping reports must break down the time an employee has worked into these three categories and indicate the amount of money an employee has earned before taxes and other deductions.

The rules for classifying time as regular time, overtime, and unpaid time vary from state to state. The rules for computing the multiple of the regular rate that is paid for overtime also vary from state to state. The company currently operates in only one state. However, there are plans to expand into other states. Therefore, the design must account for different rules being used to classify an employee's hours and compute the employee's pay.

To allow different sets of rules to be selected for timekeeping computations, we will need to devise a way to organize a set of rules as a set of objects. We can represent a set of rules as finite state machines that take timekeeping events as input and respond to the input by performing timekeeping computations. The statechart diagram in Figure 2.9 shows a sample state machine that, omitting states and transitions for error handling, models timekeeping rules for the state of Georgia.

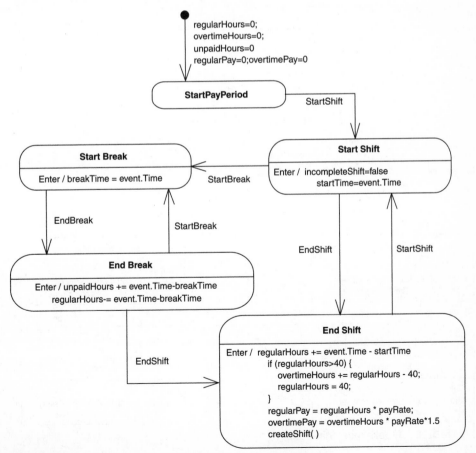

Figure 2.9 Sample State-Based Timekeeping Computation

To implement the state machine shown in Figure 3.9, we can use the State pattern (described in Chapter 7). The State pattern tells us to implement the states of a state class as classes that implement a common interface. The class diagram in Figure 2.10 shows how the State pattern can be used to implement the state machine in the Figure 2.9.

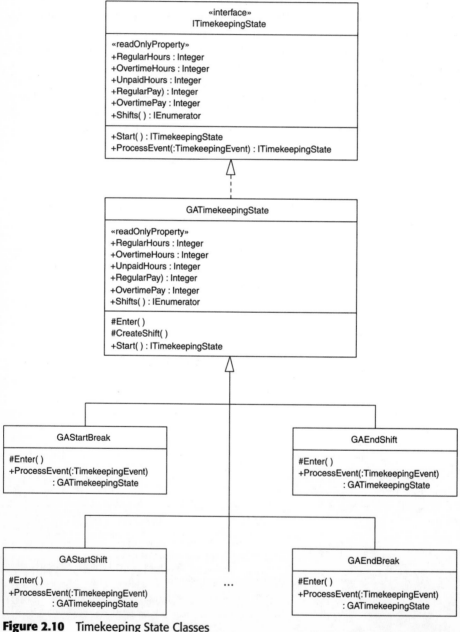

Figure 2.10 Timekeeping State Classes

Here is how the classes in Figure 2.10 are used. A program that will get an employee's timekeeping events from the database creates a GATimekeepingState object. It uses an instance of each of its subclasses to represent each of the state machine's states. The GATimekeepingState object's Start function returns the state machine's initial state and makes that state the current state.

After a program creates an instance of GATimekeepingState, it calls its Start function to get the initial state. Then the program begins fetching an employee's time-keeping events from the database. It passes each fetched timekeeping event to the ProcessEvent function of the current state object. The ProcessEvent function causes the state machine to transition to another state based on the type of timekeeping event that is passed to it. The ProcessEvent function returns the new current state. When the ProcessEvent function causes the state machine to enter a state, it calls that state object's enter function.

As the state machine shifts from state to state, it computes the employee's hours and gross pay. It also organizes the timekeeping events into shifts. When the program is finished passing an employee's timekeeping events to the state machine, it can call appropriate functions of the GATimekeepingState object to get the employee's hours, gross pay, or an Enumeration of the shifts that the employee worked.

This is as far as we will take this case study. Hopefully, it has provided you with some insight about how to use design patterns.

If you are interested in a more in-depth treatment of object-oriented design and analysis with patterns, you might want to read [Larman01].

CHAPTER 3

Fundamental
Design Patterns

Delegation (47)

Interface (55)

Abstract Base Class (61)

Interface and Abstract Class (69)

Immutable (75)

Proxy (81)

The patterns in this chapter are the most fundamental and most important design patterns to know. You will find these patterns used extensively in other design patterns.

The Delegation, Interface, Abstract Base Class, and Interface and Abstract Class patterns provide guidance on how to organize relationships between classes. Most other patterns use at least one of these patterns. They are so ubiquitous that they are not mentioned in the "Related Patterns" section of most other patterns.

The Immutable pattern describes a way to avoid bugs and delays when multiple objects want to access the same object. Though the Immutable pattern is not explicitly part of most other patterns, it can be used to advantage with most other patterns.

The Proxy pattern is the basis for a number of patterns that share the common concept of an object managing access to another object in a relatively transparent way.

Delegation (When Not to Use Inheritance)

SYNOPSIS

In some situations, using inheritance to extend a class leads to a bad design. Though less convenient, delegation is a more general-purpose way to extend classes. Delegation works well in many situations where inheritance does not work well.

CONTEXT

Inheritance is a common way of extending and reusing the functionality of a class. Delegation is a more general way to extend a class's behavior. Delegation extends a class by using another class's functions, subroutines, and properties rather than inheriting them. Inheritance is inappropriate for many situations in which delegation works well.

For example, inheritance is useful for capturing "is-a-kind-of" relationships because of their very static nature. However, "is-a-role-played-by" relationships are awkward to model by inheritance. Instances of a class can play multiple roles. Consider the example of an airline reservation system.

An airline reservation system will include such roles as passenger, ticket-selling agent, and flight crew. It is possible to represent this as a class called `Person` that has subclasses corresponding to these roles, as shown in Figure 3.1.

The problem with the model in Figure 3.1 is that the same person can fill more than one of these roles. A person who is normally part of a flight crew can also be a passenger. Some airlines float flight crew to the ticket counter. This means the same person can fill any combination of these roles. To model this situation, you would need seven subclasses for `Person`, as shown in Figure 3.2. The number of subclasses this sort of model needs increases exponentially with the number of roles. To model all the combinations of 6 roles would require 63 subclasses.

A more serious problem is that the same person can play different combinations of roles at different times. Inheritance relationships are static. They do not change over time. To model different combinations of roles over time using inheritance relationships, it is necessary to use different objects at different times to represent the same person in order to capture changes in role. This gets complicated.

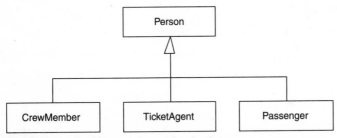

Figure 3.1 Modeling Roles with Inheritance

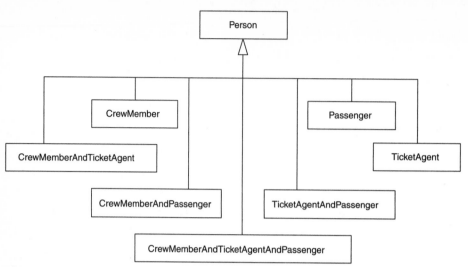

Figure 3.2 Modeling Multiple Roles with Inheritance

On the other hand, it is possible to represent persons in different roles using delegation without having any of these problems. Figure 3.3 shows how the model could be reorganized using delegation.

Using the organization shown in Figure 3.3, a `Person` object delegates the responsibility of filling a particular role to an object that is specific to that role. You need only as many objects as there are roles to fill. Different combinations do not require additional objects. Because delegation objects can be dynamic, role objects can be added or removed as a person fills different roles.

In the case of the airline reservation software, a predetermined set of role objects may become associated with different `Person` objects over time. For example, when a flight is scheduled, it will be determined that a certain number of flight-crew members must be on board. When the flight is staffed, specific persons will be associated with the crew member roles. As schedules change, a person may be shifted from one crew member role to another. Let's consider an example.

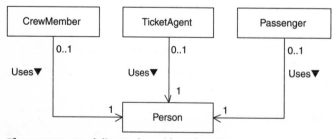

Figure 3.3 Modeling Roles with Delegation

Let's consider an example. Figure 3.4 shows four roles scheduled to be filled by three people today:

- Joe fills the role of attendant #1 on flight A.
- Sue is ticket agent #1 at the ticket counter and attendant #2 on flight A.
- Jill is agent #2 at the ticket counter.

Suppose that Sue has a personal emergency that requires her to fly out of town today instead of working. The airline needs to shift people around to fill roles, as shown in Figure 3.5.

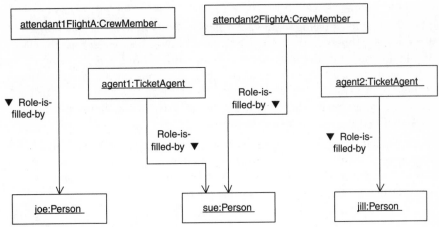

Figure 3.4 Today's Initial Role Assignments

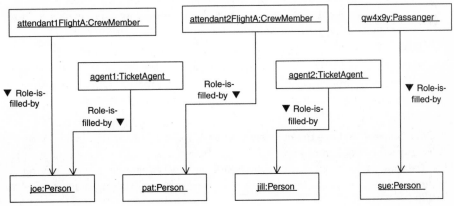

Figure 3.5 Revised Role Assignments

In the revised assignment of roles, Sue is now a passenger, not a ticket agent or a flight crew member. Joe fills the role of ticket agent #1 in Sue's place. Another person named Pat fills the attendant #2 role. There is no reasonable way to achieve this sort of flexibility using inheritance.

FORCES

☺ Inheritance is a static relationship; it does not change over time. If you find that an object needs to be a different subclass of a class at different times, then it should not be a subclass of that class in the first place. If an object is created as an instance of a class, it will always be an instance of that class. However, an object can delegate behavior to different objects at different times.

☺ If you find yourself trying to prevent a class's clients from using functions, subroutines, properties, or variables it inherits from a base class, then the class should not inherit from the base class. There is no effective way to prevent client classes from attempting to access public or internal functions, subroutines, properties, or variables inherited from a base class. You may take measures to cause such attempts to fail, but such measures leave the possibility that client classes will erroneously attempt the access.

A simpler solution is for an object to use another object's functions, subroutines, properties, and variables, while ensuring that it is the only object has that access to the other object. This accomplishes the same thing as inheritance, but uses dynamic relationships that can be changed over time.

☺ If a class is related to a program's problem domain, then it should not be a subclass of a utility class. There are two reasons for this:

First, if you declare a class to be a subclass of a class like `ArrayList` or `Hashtable`, you run the risk that classes not under your control will change in an incompatible way. Though the risk is low, there is usually no corresponding benefit to offset it when subclassing a utility class.

Second, a problem-domain-specific class as a subclass of a utility class is written, usually the intention is to use the functionality of the utility class to implement problem domain functionality. The problem with using inheritance this way is that it weakens the encapsulation of the problem domain class's implementation.

Client classes that use the problem domain class may be written in a way that assumes the problem domain class is a subclass of the utility class. If the implementation of the problem domain changes in a way that results in its having a different base class, client classes that rely on its having its original base class will break.

An even more serious problem is that client classes can use the public methods of the utility base class, which defeats its encapsulation.

☹ Delegation imposes less structure on classes than inheritance. In designs where it is important to constrain the structure of classes, the structure and inflexibility of inheritance may be a virtue. This is often the case in frameworks. See the Template Method pattern for more on this issue.

☹ Delegation can be less convenient than inheritance because it requires more code to implement.

Some inappropriate uses of inheritance are so common that they are classified as anti-patterns. In particular, subclassing utility classes and using inheritance to model roles are common design flaws.

☺ Much or even most reuse and extension of a class is not appropriately done through inheritance.

☺ The behavior a class inherits from its base class cannot easily be changed over time. Inheritance is not useful when the behavior a class should build on is not determined until run time.

SOLUTION

Use delegation to reuse and extend the behavior of a class. You do this by writing a new class (the delegator) that incorporates the functionality of the original class by using an instance of the original class (the delegatee) and calling its methods. Figure 3.6 shows a class that is in a `Delegator` role uses a class in the `Delegatee` role.

Delegation is more general purpose than inheritance. Any extension to a class that can be accomplished by inheritance can also be accomplished by delegation.

IMPLEMENTATION

The implementation of delegation is very straightforward. It simply involves acquiring a reference to an object you want to delegate to and calling its methods. For example, the following `ToString` method delegates part of its object's string representation to other objects it refers to as `leftArg` and `rightArg`.

```
Public Overrides Function ToString() As String
    Return leftArg.ToString() & "+" & rightArg.ToString()
End Function
```

The best way to ensure that a delegation is easy to maintain is to make its structure and purpose explicit. One way to do this is to make the delegation through an interface or .NET delegate using the Interface pattern.

Figure 3.6 Delegation

CONSEQUENCES

Delegation can be used without the problems that accompany inheritance. Another advantage of delegation is that it is easy to compose behavior at run time.

The main disadvantage of delegation is that it is less structured than inheritance. Relationships between classes built using delegation are less obvious than those built using inheritance. Here are some strategies for improving the clarity of delegation-based relationships:

- Use consistent naming schemes to refer to objects in a particular role. For example, if multiple classes delegate the creation of widget objects, the role of the delegatee object becomes more obvious if all the classes that delegate that operation refer to delegatee objects through a variable called `widgetFactory`.

- Clarify the purpose of a delegation by writing comments.

- In extreme cases, these indirect delegations can make an intermediate class less coherent by adding functions, subroutines, or properties unrelated to the class's purpose. In such cases, refactor the unrelated functions, subroutines, or properties into a separate class, using the Pure Fabrication pattern (also described in [Grand98]).

- Use well-known design and coding patterns. A person reading code that uses delegation will be more likely to understand the role that the objects play if the roles are part of a well-known pattern or a pattern that recurs frequently in your program.

Note that it is possible and advantageous to use all three of these strategies at the same time when you can.

.NET USAGE

The .NET Framework is full of examples of delegation. It is the basis for .NET's event model, in which event sender objects send events to event receiver objects. Event sender objects do not generally decide what to do with an event. Instead, they delegate the responsibility of handling the event to receiver objects (also called handlers).

Another example is that some of the `StringWriter` class's functions and subroutines are implemented by delegating to the `StringBuilder` class.

CODE EXAMPLE

For an example of delegation, we look at another part of an airline reservation system. Suppose that the reservation system is responsible for tracking checked pieces of luggage. We can expect this part of the system to include classes to represent a flight segment[1], a luggage compartment, and pieces of luggage, as shown in Figure 3.7.

---

[1]A flight segment is a portion of a trip that you take on an airline without changing planes.

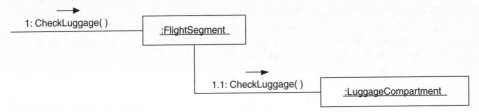

Figure 3.7 Check Luggage

In Figure 3.7, the `FlightSegment` class has a subroutine called `CheckLuggage`. It checks a piece of luggage onto a flight. The flight class delegates the operation to an instance of the `LuggageCompartment` class.

Another common use for delegation is to implement a collection. Consider the diagram in Figure 3.8.

The `LuggageCompartment` class maintains a collection of other objects. Such classes normally delegate the responsibility for the collection to another object, such as an instance of `ArrayList`. Because implementing a collection by delegation is so common, the separate collection class is usually omitted from design drawings.

Here are code fragments that implement the preceding design:

```
' The FlightSegment class delegates the CheckLuggage
' operation to the LuggageCompartment class.
Public Class FlightSegment
    ' The luggage compartment that contains luggage for
    ' this flight segment.
    Private myLuggageCompartment As LuggageCompartment

    ' constructor for a new FlightSegment
    Public Sub New()
        myLuggageCompartment = New LuggageCompartment()
    End Sub 'New

    ' Check a pieceof luggage onto this flight segment.
    Public Sub CheckLuggage(ByVal piece As Luggage)
        myLuggageCompartment.CheckLuggage(piece)
    End Sub 'CheckLuggage
End Class 'FlightSegment

' Here is the LuggageCompartment class that delegates the
' collection of pieces of luggage to the ArrayList class
Public Class LuggageCompartment
    ' The luggage checked into this luggage compartment
    Private pieces As New ArrayList()

    ' my running weight total
    Private myWeight As Single

    ' Check a piece of luggage into this luggage compartment.
```

```
Public Sub CheckLuggage(ByVal thePiece As Luggage)
    Dim newWeight As Single = thePiece.Weight + myWeight
    SyncLock pieces
        pieces.Add(thePiece)
    End SyncLock
    myWeight = newWeight
End Sub 'CheckLuggage
End Class 'LuggageCompartment
```

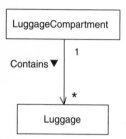

Figure 3.8 Luggage Compartment

RELATED PATTERNS

Most other patterns use delegation. Some of the patterns that rely most heavily on delegation are the Decorator pattern and the Proxy pattern. In addition, the Interface pattern can be useful in making the structure and motivation for a delegation explicit and easier for maintainers to understand.

Interface

SYNOPSIS

Instances of a class provide data and services to instances of other classes. You want to keep client classes sufficiently independent of specific data-and-service-providing classes, so you can substitute another data-and-service-providing class in its place with minimal impact on its client classes. You accomplish this by having other classes access the data and services through an interface.

CONTEXT

Suppose that you are designing some reusable classes to perform a variety of business functions. You are also designing an environment to allow people to browse business object instantiated from these classes for the purpose of understanding how they have been configured. One of the things that you will want the environment to display about a business object is a description of the object.

You want the implementation of the environment to be simple and reusable, so it should display the object descriptions without having to be aware of the specific class of the object. With that in mind, you design the environment to work with business objects through an interface instead of their class. This organization is shown in Figure 3.9.

Using the organization shown in Figure 3.9, a browser object is able to display the description of any object whose class implements the `IDescription` interface.

For the sake of simplicity, the interface used in this example has only one property. It is common to use this pattern with interfaces that have multiple functions, subroutines, or properties.

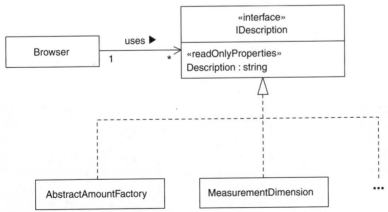

Figure 3.9   Indirection through Reference Interface

FORCES

☺ An object depends on another object for data or services. If the dependent object must assume that the other object belongs to a particular class, then the reusability of the dependent object's class is limited.

☺ You want to vary the kind of object another object uses for a particular purpose without making the object dependent on any class other than its own.

☹ A class's constructors cannot be accessed through an interface, since VB.NET interfaces cannot have constructors.

SOLUTION

To avoid classes having to depend on other classes because of a uses/used-by relationship, make the usage indirect through an interface. Figure 3.10 shows this relationship. Here are the roles that these classes and interface play:

Client: The `Client` class uses classes that implement the `IIndirection` interface.

IIndirection: The `IIndirection` interface provides indirection that keeps the `Client` class independent of the class that is playing the `Service` role.

Service: Classes in this role provide a service to classes in the `Client` role.

IMPLEMENTATION

Implementation of the Interface pattern is straightforward. Define an interface to provide a service, write client classes to access the service through the interface, and write service-providing classes that implement the interface.

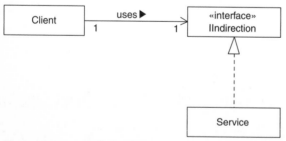

Figure 3.10 Interface Pattern

Delegates

.NET delegates serve a purpose similar to that of interfaces. Delegates provide a sort of indirection similar to the indirection you get with an interface. In some places where your design has an interface that declares a single function or subroutine, the interface can be implemented by using a delegate instead of an interface. From this point of view, you can think of a delegate as an interface that contains a single function or subroutine and creates its own implementation when you instantiate it.

Sometimes you have a class that expects to use a function, subroutine, or property of a class that implements an interface, and you want it to use a function, subroutine, or property of a class that does not implement the interface. You can make this happen by constructing an adapter class (see the Adapter pattern) that implements the interface with functions, subroutines, and properties that delegate their work to another class that does not implement the interface. Delegates accomplish this without anyone having to write the additional code for another class. However, you are generally better off using an interface if you can. Indirection through interfaces is generally less bug prone than indirection through delegates. If the signature of the method called by a delegate changes, you may not find out about it until run time. If the nature of the service or data changes in a way that client classes need to call more than one function or subroutine to use the service or data, then you will want to go to the trouble of changing all of the uses of the delegate to an interface. However, there is one situation in which you should use a delegate instead of an interface.

You may find yourself designing VB.NET classes to use data or a service provided by objects that do not implement an interface. This may be because you have no control over the design of the classes that provide the data or service in question.

If there is no way to arrange for the data or service-providing classes to implement an appropriate common interface, then there are two alternative implementation strategies:

- If the interface in the design only involves one method, you are certain that there will never be additional methods, and you are sure that all of the method implementation will take exactly the same parameters, then use a delegate. However, you are rarely sure of that much, so using a delegate in this situation is unusual.

- When you cannot use a delegate, use an adapter object, as discussed in the description of the Adapter pattern. This is always the safest choice.

Constructors

Interfaces cannot have constructors. For this reason, interfaces are not helpful in keeping a class responsible for creating objects independent of the class of the objects that it creates. The .NET Framework includes a class called System.Reflection. ConstructorInfo that can be used to construct objects without knowing what class they will be an instance of. First an instance of ConstructorInfo is created by an object that does know the class to be instantiated. The other objects use the

ConstructorInfo object to construct objects without knowing what class is being instantiated.

Note that it may take significantly longer to construct objects through a ConstructorInfo object than by using the new operator.

CONSEQUENCES

☺ The Interface pattern allows objects to use a service from another object without being coupled to any specific class.

☹ Like any other indirection, the Interface pattern can make a program more difficult to understand.

.NET USAGE

A window or dialog implemented by the System.Windows.Forms.Form class can have buttons associated with it as OK or Cancel buttons. These button controls are not required to be an instance of any particular class. However, they are required to implement the System.Windows.Forms.IButtonControl interface.

CODE EXAMPLE

Here is a listing of code implementing the design shown under the "Context" heading. The first listing is of the IDescription interface shown in Figure 3.9:

```
' Any class that implements the IDescription interface has a
' read-only property named Description whose value is a
' description of the instance it belongs to. A reference to an
' object that implements the IDescription interface can get the
' object's description. The class using the reference does not
' need to know the actual class of the referenced object.
'
Public Interface IDescription

    ' A description of this object.
    ReadOnly Property Description() As String
End Interface 'IDescription
```

Figure 3.9 shows a class named Browser using the IDescription interface. A browser is actually a complex object that is composed from instances of a number of classes. The particular class that is responsible for handling the reference to the IDescription interface is named DescriptionModel. Here is a listing of the DescriptionModel class.

```
' This class is the data model for displaying the
' description of a framework object.
Public Class DescriptionModel
```

```
' This object is used by the browser as the data
' model for the description of an object.  The object
' that this object provides a description for is the
' object referred to by the myObject variable.
'
' The myObject variable is set by this
' object's constructor.  If the object passed to the
' constructor does not implement the IDescription
' interface, then myObject will be Nothing.
Private myObject As IDescription


' Constructor
'
' theObject - The object that this object will provide a
' description for.
Public Sub New(ByVal theObject As IDescription)
    myObject = theObject
End Sub 'New


' The description of the object being browsed.
Public ReadOnly Property Description() As String
    Get
        If myObject Is Nothing Then
            Return "No Description available"
        End If
        Return myObject.Description
    End Get
End Property
End Class 'DescriptionModel
```

The `DescriptionModel` class does not care about the class of the object it describes; it just cares whether or not it implements the `IDescription` interface.

RELATED PATTERNS

Delegation: The Delegation and Interface patterns are often used together.

Adapter: The Adapter pattern allows classes that use a particular interface to work with classes that don't implement the interface.

Strategy: The Strategy pattern uses the Interface pattern.

Abstract Base Class

This pattern is also known as Abstract Superclass. It was originally described in [Rhiel00].

SYNOPSIS

Ensure consistent behavior of conceptually related classes by giving them a common abstract base class.

CONTEXT

You want to write classes to provide sequential and read-only access to some data structures. You decide that these classes will implement the interface IEnumerator interface.

The documentation for the IEnumerator interface specifies some behavior that implementations of this interface should share. You want to your classes that implement the IEnumerator interface to implement the common behavior in a consistent way.

The common behavior in question involves throwing an exception in certain situations. IEnumerator objects have a read-only property named Current. When an IEnumerator object is first created, or immediately after its reset subroutine is called, the IEnumerator object is considered to be positioned before the first member of the data structure. When the object is in this state, you want attempts to get the value of its Current property to throw an exception.

Calls to an IEnumerator object's MoveNext function advance it to the next member of the data structure. While the position of IEnumerator object in the data structure corresponds to a member of the data structure, the value of its Current property is the member of the data structure. After some number of calls to the MoveNext function, the IEnumerator object will be positioned after the last member of the data structure. When the object is in this state, you want attempts to get the value of its Current property to throw an exception.

There is one other situation in which you want your IEnumerator objects to throw an exception. If the data structure associated with an IEnumerator object is modified, then any calls to the IEnumerator object's MoveNext or Reset methods should throw an exception.

To ensure that your IEnumerator classes implement the common behaviors in the same way, you create an abstract base class for all of your Iterator classes to inherit from. This organization is shown in Figure 3.11.

The abstract class AbstractEnumerator implements the IEnumerator interface. It implements the methods of the IEnumerator interface with skeletal logic that tests for situations where an exception should be thrown. All logic specific to navigating a data structure is delegated to the abstract function NextElement and the abstract subroutine ResetImpl. Concrete subclasses of the AbstractEnumerator class must override these to provide logic for the data structure they are supposed to work with.

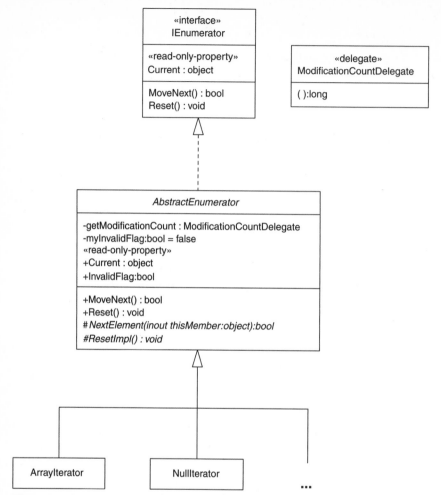

Figure 3.11   Enumerators with Abstract Base Class

Because all your concrete `IEnumerator` classes inherit their exception-throwing logic from the `AbstractEnumerator` class, you are confident that they will have the same exception-throwing behavior.

FORCES

☺ You want to ensure that logic common to related classes is implemented in a consistent way.

☺ You want to avoid the runtime and maintenance overhead of redundant code.

☺ You want to make it easy to write related classes.

☹ In many situations, inheritance is not an appropriate way to organize common behavior. The Delegation pattern describes this in detail.

SOLUTION

Organize the common behavior of related classes into an abstract base class.

To the extent possible, organize variant behavior into functions and subroutines with common signatures[2] and common properties. Declare the abstract base class to have abstract functions and subroutines with these common signatures. Figure 3.12 shows this organization.

Here are the roles that classes play in the Abstract Base Class pattern.

AbstractBaseclass

A class in this role is an abstract base class that encapsulates common logic for related classes. The related classes extend this class, so they inherit its functions, subroutines, and properties. Functions and subroutines whose signature and logic are common to the related classes are put in the base class so that their logic is shared. Common properties are also put into the base class. Functions and methods with different logic but the same signature are declared in the abstract class as abstract. This ensures that each concrete subclass has functions and subroutines with those signatures. Similarly, common properties with different underlying logic are declared in the abstract class as abstract properties.

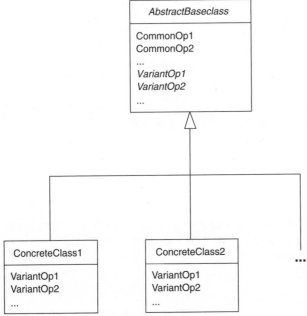

Figure 3.12 Abstract Base Class Pattern

[2]A method's signature is the combination of its name and formal parameters.

ConcreteClass1, ConcreteClass2, . . .

A class in this role is a concrete class whose logic and purpose are related to other concrete classes. Functions and subroutines common to these related classes are refactored into the abstract base class.

Common logic that is not encapsulated in common functions or subroutines is refactored into common functions or subroutines.

IMPLEMENTATION

If the common function and subroutine signatures are public, then, if possible, they should be organized into an interface that the abstract class implements. The reasons for this are described in the Interface and Abstract class pattern.

Implement the abstract class in VB.NET as a `MustInherit` class. Common function and subroutine signatures that are not public should be declared in the `MustInherit` class as `MustOverride`.

CONSEQUENCES

☺ Fewer test cases may be needed to completely test your classes because there are fewer pieces of code to test.

☹ Using the Abstract Base Class pattern creates dependencies between the base class and its subclasses. Changes to the base class may have unintended effects on some subclasses, thus making the program harder to maintain.

.NET API USAGE

The .NET Framework includes the `System.Attribute` class. It is an abstract base class for classes that can be used as attributes. The .NET Framework also includes the `System.IO.Stream` class, which is an abstract class for classes that can read or write streams of data from and to various data sources and destinations.

CODE EXAMPLE

Implementations of the classes discussed under the "Context" heading are the code example for this pattern. These classes are part of the framework that appears in Appendix A on this book's Web site.

Here is a listing of the `AbstractEnumerator` class:

```
Imports System.Collections

' delegate for counting modifications
Public Delegate Function ModificationCountDelegate() As Long

' common abstract base class for Iterator classes
```

```vbnet
Public MustInherit Class AbstractEnumerator
Implements IEnumerator

' Delegate that this object will use to get the
' modification count of the data structure it is
' responsible for navigating. Every time the data
' structure is modified, this count is supposed to
' be incremented.
Private getModificationCount As ModificationCountDelegate

' The modification count of the underlying data
' structure at the time this object was created.
Private originalCount As Long

' The current member of the data structure being
' navigated
Private myCurrent As Object = Nothing

' If this is true, the current property is not mapped to
' any member of the underlying data structure.
Private currentIsMapped As Boolean = False

' Constructor
Public Sub New(ByVal theDelegate As ModificationCountDelegate)
    getModificationCount = theDelegate
    originalCount = getModificationCount()
End Sub

' The current member of the underlying data structure
'
' Throws System.InvalidOperationException
' if the current position in the data
' structure does not correspond to any element. This
' is true when this object is first created, after
' its MoveNext function returns false and after
' its Reset subroutine is called.
Public ReadOnly Property Current() As Object _
                        Implements IEnumerator.Current

    Get
        If Not currentIsMapped Then
            Dim msg As String
            msg = "No current data structure member."
            Throw New System.InvalidOperationException(msg)
        End If
        Return myCurrent
    End Get
End Property

' True if the underlying data structure is modified.
Public ReadOnly Property InvalidFlag() As Boolean
```

```vbnet
    Get
        Return getModificationCount() <> originalCount
    End Get
End Property


' Throw an exception if the underlying
' data structure has been modified.
Private Sub CheckModified()
    If InvalidFlag Then
        Dim msg As String
        msg = "Underlying data structure modified"
        Throw New System.InvalidOperationException(msg)
    End If
End Sub 'CheckModified


' This function is responsible for navigating to the
' next member of the underlying data structure.
' obj - The variable to update with the new current data
' returns: true if navigation to the next data structure
' member was successful or false if we are past the last
' member of the data structure.
Protected _
MustOverride Function NextElement(ByRef obj As Object) _
                    As Boolean


' Move this enumerator to the next member of the
' underlying data structure.
'
' returns: true if this enumerator advanced to the next
' data structure element or false if this
' enumerator is past the last member of the data
' structure.
' Throws System.InvalidOperationException if the
' underlying data structure has been modified.
Public Function MoveNext() As Boolean _
                Implements IEnumerator.MoveNext
    CheckModified()
    currentIsMapped = NextElement(myCurrent)
    Return currentIsMapped
End Function 'MoveNext


' Navigate to before the first member of the
' underlying data structure.
Protected MustOverride Sub ResetImpl()


' Navigate to before the first member of the
' underlying data structure.
' Throws System.InvalidOperationException
' if the underlying data structure has been modified.
Public Sub Reset() Implements IEnumerator.Reset
```

```
        CheckModified()
        ResetImpl()
    End Sub 'Reset
End Class 'AbstractEnumerator
```

RELATED PATTERNS

Interface and Abstract Class: The Interface and Abstract Class pattern uses the Abstract Base Class pattern.

Template Method: The Template Method pattern uses the Abstract Base Class pattern.

Interface and Abstract Class

SYNOPSIS

You need to keep client classes independent of classes that implement a behavior and ensure consistency of behavior between the behavior-implementing classes. Don't choose between using an interface and an abstract class. Have the classes implement an interface *and* extend an abstract class.

CONTEXT

You are designing a framework. You want client classes that use services provided by the framework not to rely on the specific classes that provide the services. You know you can do this by having client classes access service-providing classes through an interface. To promote consistency and convenience of implementation, you want the classes to extend a common abstract class. You are not sure how to decide between basing the classes on an interface or an abstract class.

FORCES

☺ Using the interface pattern, VB.Net interfaces can be used to hide the specific class that implements a behavior from the clients of the class.

☺ Organizing classes that provide related behaviors with a common base class helps to ensure consistency of implementation. Through reuse, it may also reduce the effort required for implementation.

☹ There is a common tendency, when people are presented with two different ways to improve the organization of classes, to choose either one or the other rather than use both improvements.

SOLUTION

If you need to hide the class of an object that provides a service from its clients, then use the Interface pattern. Have client objects access the service-providing object indirectly through an interface. The indirection allows the clients to access the service-providing object without having to know what kind of objects they are.

If you need to design a set of related classes that provide similar functionality, then organize the common portions of their implementation into an abstract base class.

If you are presented with both of these needs in the same object design, then use both an interface and an abstract class, as shown in Figure 3.13.

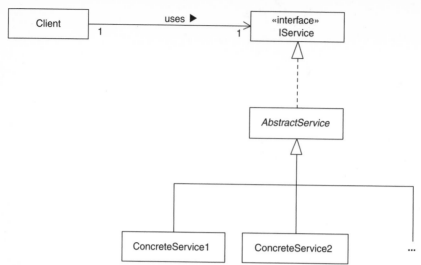

Figure 3.13 Interface and Abstract Class

The ConcreteService classes inherit common logic from the AbstractService class. Helper classes that are involved in the common portion of the implementation of ConcreteService classes access them through the AbstractService class. All client classes access ConcreteService classes through the IService interface.

CONSEQUENCES

☺ Using the Interface and Abstract Class pattern allows an object design to benefit from the benefits of both an interface and an abstract class. Clients of concrete classes that implement the interface can access the concrete classes through the interface without having any dependencies on their implementation. The concrete classes can share common implementation details with the abstract class without exposing these implementation details to their clients.

.NET API USAGE

ASP.NET allows you to attach validation controls to an input control to test whether the contents of a control is valid. ASP.NET provides a class named System.Web.UI. WebControls.BaseValidator that is the base class for most validation control objects. However, ASP.NET does not require that validation controls be instances of System.Web.UI.WebControls.BaseValidator. Instead, it requires the class of validation controls to implement the System.Web.UI.IValidator interface. These relationships are shown in Figure 3.14.

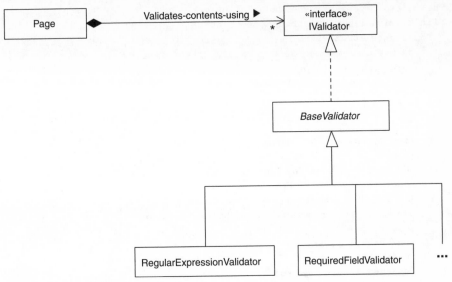

Figure 3.14 Validator Organization

CODE EXAMPLE

The code example for the Interface and Abstract Class pattern consists of an interface and classes for managing a data structure called a doubly linked list. There is a class called `DoubleLinkedList`, which performs insert and delete operations on the elements of a doubly linked list. The `DoubleLinkedList` class does not require the objects in the doubly linked list to be instances of any particular class. It does require all the objects in the list to implement an interface called `IDoubleLink`. There is an abstract class called `AbstractDoubleLink` that implements the `IDoubleLink` interface. Extending the `AbstractDoubleLink` class is a convenient way to write concrete classes that can be manipulated in a doubly linked list. These classes are part of the framework that appears in Appendix A on this book's Web site.

Here is a listing of the `IDoubleLink` interface:

```
' defines the properties to be implemented for an IDoubleLink
Public Interface IDoubleLink
    ' The previous member of the Doubly linked list this
    ' object belongs to or Nothing.
    Property Previous() As IDoubleLink
    ' The next member of the Doubly linked list this
    ' object belongs to or Nothing.
    Property NextElement() As IDoubleLink
End Interface 'IDoubleLink
```

Here is a listing of the abstract class `AbstractDoubleLink` that implements the `IDoubleLink` interface:

```
' This class implements the IDoubleLink interface
Public MustInherit Class AbstractDoubleLink
    Implements IDoubleLink
    ' The previous member of the Doubly linked list this
    ' object belongs to or Nothing.
    Private myPrevious As IDoubleLink

    ' The next member of the Doubly linked list this
    ' object belongs to or Nothing.
    Private myNext As IDoubleLink

    ' The previous member of the Doubly linked list this
    ' object belongs to or Nothing.
    Public Property Previous() As IDoubleLink _
                    Implements IDoubleLink.Previous
        Get
            Return myPrevious
        End Get
        Set(ByVal value As IDoubleLink)
            myPrevious = value
        End Set
    End Property

    ' The next member of the Doubly linked list this
    ' object belongs to or Nothing
    Public Property NextElement() As IDoubleLink _
     Implements IDoubleLink.NextElement
      Get
            Return myNext
        End Get
        Set(ByVal value As IDoubleLink)
            myNext = value
        End Set
    End Property
End Class 'AbstractDoubleLink
```

Classes that extend the `AbstractDoubleLink` class generally add additional information of their own.

RELATED PATTERNS

Interface: The Interface and Abstract Class pattern uses the Interface pattern.

Abstract Class: The Interface and Abstract Class pattern uses the Abstract Base Class pattern.

DOUBLY LINKED LIST

A doubly linked list is a data structure organized into a sequence so that each element contains a reference to its successor and predecessor. Figure 3.15 shows an example of this structure.

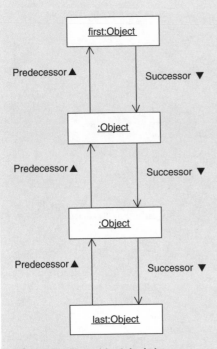

Figure 3.15 Doubly Linked List

The advantage of a doubly linked list over an array is the amount of work it takes to insert and delete objects. When you insert or delete objects in an array, you must shift everything in the array after the insertion or deletion point. The larger the array, the longer the average insertion and deletion will take. Inserting or deleting objects in a doubly linked list involves adjusting predecessor and successor references.

Inserting or deleting an element in a doubly linked list always takes the same amount of time, no matter how many elements there are. The drawback is that finding the nth element of a doubly linked list requires a search through the first n elements in the list. The larger n is, the longer this takes.

Immutable

The Immutable pattern is fundamental in a different sense than other patterns in this chapter. It is fundamental because the more appropriate places you use it, the more robust and maintainable your programs will be.

SYNOPSIS

Increase the robustness of objects that share references to the same object and reduce the overhead of concurrent access to an object. Accomplish this by not allowing the shared object's contents to change after the object is constructed. This also avoids the need to synchronize multiple threads of execution that share an object.

CONTEXT

The primary purpose of a value object is to encapsulate values, rather than to provide behavior. For example, the class `System.Drawing.Rectangle` encapsulates the position and dimensions of a rectangle.

In situations where multiple objects share access to the same value object, a problem can arise if changes to the shared object are not properly coordinated between the objects that share it. This requires careful programming that is easy to get wrong. If the changes to and fetches of the shared objects' state are done asynchronously, then in addition to the greater likelihood of bugs, correctly functioning code will have the overhead of synchronizing the accesses to the shared objects' state.

The Immutable pattern avoids these problems by organizing a class so that the state information of its instances never changes after they are constructed.

Suppose that you are writing a game program that involves the placement and occasional movement of objects on a playing field. Pieces can be moved by only one player at a time. All players are aware of the position of all pieces at all times.

In the course of designing classes for the program, you decide to use immutable objects to represent the position of objects on the playing field. An organization of a class for modeling position is shown in Figure 3.16.

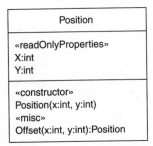

Figure 3.16 Immutable Position

Figure 3.16 shows a class named `Position` that has an x and y value associated with its instances. The class has a constructor that specifies the x and y value. It also has read-only properties named X and Y. Lastly, it has a function that creates a new `Position` object at a given x and y offset from an existing position. It does not have any functions, subroutines or writable properties to modify its x or y value. If an object's position changes, then it is made to refer to a new position object.

FORCES

☺ Your program uses instances of a class that is passive in nature. The instances do not ever need to change their own state. Instances of the class are used by multiple objects.

☺ Coordinating changes to the contents of a value object used by multiple objects can be a source of bugs. When the contents of a value object change, all the objects that use it may need to be informed. When multiple objects use an object, they may attempt to change its state in inconsistent ways.

☺ If multiple threads modify the contents of a value object, then the modification operations must be synchronized to ensure the consistency of the contents. The overhead of synchronizing the threads may add an unacceptable overhead to accessing the value object's contents.

☺ An alternative to modifying the contents of a value object is replacing the entire object with another object that has different contents. This eliminates any need for synchronization among threads that only fetch the contents of the value object.

☹ If there are multiple threads that update the contents of an object, then replacing the object instead of updating its contents does not eliminate the need for synchronizing the threads that do the updating.

☹ Replacing a value object with a new value object that contains an updated version of the values in the old object involves copying unchanged values from the old object to the new. If the changes to an object are frequent or an object has a large amount of state information associated with it, then the cost of replacing value objects may be prohibitive.

SOLUTION

To avoid having to manage the synchronization of changes to value objects used by multiple other objects, make the shared objects immutable. Prevent any changes to their instance variables after they are constructed. You can accomplish this by not including any properties or functions or subroutines, other than constructors, in their class that modify state information. The class shown in Figure 3.17 has a constructor that sets its instance variables. It has read-only properties to query the values of its instance variables. It has functions that perform various computations without modifying any of the class's instance variables. Because there is nothing in the class to change the value of its instance variables after their value is set by the constructor, we are sure that after an instance has been created the values of its instance variables will never change.

The class shown in Figure 3.17 has a constructor that sets its instance variables. It has read-only properties to query the values of its instance variables. It has functions that perform various computations without modifying any of the class's instance variables.

The class does not have any way to change the values of one of its instance variables after the instance has been constructed.

IMPLEMENTATION

There are two concerns you should have when implementing the Immutable pattern:

- Only constructors should modify the values of a class's instance variables. The class should have no writable properties. None of its functions or methods should modify the values of a class's instance variables.

- Any method that computes new state information must store the information in a new object, rather than modifying the existing object's state.

The instance variables of a class designed using the Immutable pattern will generally be declared `Private ReadOnly`. The properties of a class designed using the immutable pattern will generally be declared `ReadOnly`.

Figure 3.17 Immutable Pattern

CONSEQUENCES

☺ Since the state of immutable objects never changes, there is no need to write code to manage such changes.

☺ An immutable object is often used as the value of another object's attribute. If the value of an object's attribute is an immutable object, then it may not be necessary for access to the value's attribute to be synchronized. This is because VB.NET guarantees that assigning an object reference to a variable is always done as an atomic operation. If the value of a variable is an object reference, and one thread updates its value and another thread fetches its value, then the other thread will either fetch the new object reference or the old object reference.

☹ Operations that would otherwise change the state of an object must create a new object. This is overhead that mutable objects do not incur.

.NET API USAGE

Instances of the String class are immutable. The sequence of characters that a String object represents is determined when it is constructed. The String class does not provide any functions, subroutines, or writable properties to change the sequence of characters that a String object represents. Methods of the String class that compute a new sequence of characters, such as ToLower and Substring, return the new character sequence in a new String object.

CODE EXAMPLE

Here is what the code for the Position class described under the "Context" heading might look like:

```
' a class for modeling an immutable position
Public Class Position
    Private myX As Integer
    Private myY As Integer

    ' Constructor
    '
    ' x - This object's X coordinate
    ' y - This object's Y coordinate
    Public Sub New(ByVal x As Integer, ByVal y As Integer)
        myX = x
        myY = y
    End Sub 'New
```

```
' This object's X coordinate.
Public ReadOnly Property X() As Integer
    Get
        Return myX
    End Get
End Property

' This object's Y coordinate
Public ReadOnly Property Y() As Integer
    Get
        Return myY
    End Get
End Property

' Calculates and returns a new Position that is at the given
' X and Y offset from this Position
'
' xOffset - The X offset
' yOffset - The Y offset
' Returns: new Position
Public Function Offset(ByVal xOffset As Integer, ByVal yOffset As
Integer) As Position
    Return New Position(myX + xOffset, myY + yOffset)
    End Function 'Offset
End Class 'Position
```

RELATED PATTERNS

Single Threaded Execution: The Single Threaded Execution pattern is the pattern
most frequently used to coordinate access by multiple threads to a shared object.
The Immutable object pattern can be used to avoid the need for the Single
Threaded Execution pattern or any other kind of access coordination.

Read-Only Interface: The Read-Only interface pattern is an alternative to the
Immutable object pattern. It allows some objects to modify a value object, while
other objects can only fetch its values.

Proxy

Proxy is a very general pattern that occurs in many other patterns. The proxy pattern was described previously in [GoF95].

SYNOPSIS

Force client objects to use an object's functions, subroutines, and properties indirectly through a proxy object that acts as a surrogate for the object, delegating method calls to the object. Classes for proxy objects are declared in a way that usually eliminates client objects' need to know they are dealing with a proxy.

CONTEXT

A proxy object is an object that receives function, subroutine, and property calls on behalf of another object. Client objects call the proxy object's functions, subroutines, and properties, which do not directly provide the services that its clients request. Instead, the proxy object uses the functions, subroutines, and properties of the object that provides the actual service. Figure 3.18 shows this structure.

A client requests services through a proxy object rather than directly because the proxy object provides some management of the services. Proxy objects share a common interface with the service-providing object. Whether client objects directly access a service-providing object or a proxy, they access it through the common interface rather than as an instance of a particular class. This allows client objects to be unaware they are using the functions, subroutines, and properties of a proxy object rather than of the actual service-providing object. Transparent management of another object's services is the essential reason for using a proxy.

A proxy can be used to provide many different types of service management. Some of the more important ones are documented elsewhere in this work as patterns in their own right. Here are some of the more common uses for proxies:

- Make a function that can take a long time to complete appear to return immediately.

- Create the illusion that an object that exists on a different machine is an ordinary local object. This kind of proxy is called a remote proxy or a stub. It is used by Web services, .NET Remoting, and other ORBs (object request brokers). Stub classes are described as part of the discussion of the Object Request Broker pattern in [Grand01].

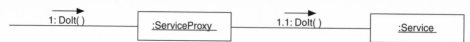

Figure 3.18 Function Calls through a Proxy

- Control access to a service-providing object based on a security policy. This use of proxy is described as the Protection proxy pattern in [Grand01].

- Create the illusion that a service object exists before it actually does. This can be useful if a service object is expensive to create and its services may not be needed. This use of proxies is documented in this book as the Virtual Proxy pattern.

FORCES

☺ It is not possible for a service-providing object to provide a service at a time or place that is convenient.

☺ Gaining visibility to an object is nontrivial, and you want to hide the complexity.

☺ Access to a service-providing object must be controlled without adding complexity to the service-providing object or coupling the service to the access control policy.

☺ The management of a service should be provided in a way that is transparent to the clients of that service.

☺ The clients of a service-providing object do not care about the identity of the object's class or which instance of its class they are working with.

SOLUTION

Transparent management of a service-providing object can be accomplished by forcing all access to the service-providing object to be accomplished through a proxy object. In order for the management to be transparent, the proxy object and the service-providing-object should implement a common interface:

Figure 3.19 shows the organization of the Proxy pattern. Though not shown in the diagram, `ServiceProxy` objects have a way to access a corresponding `Service` object. This can be because of a direct association between the `ServiceProxy` and `Service` classes, an indirect association between the `ServiceProxy` and `Service` classes, or a more complex mechanism.

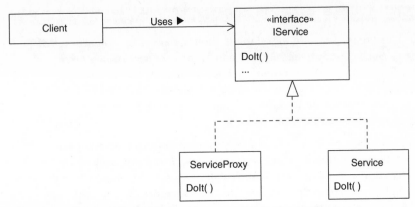

Figure 3.19 Proxy Class Diagram

Figure 3.19 does not show details for implementing any particular access management policy. However, the Proxy pattern is not very useful unless it implements some particular access management policy. The Proxy pattern is so commonly used with some access management policies that these combinations are described elsewhere as patterns in their own right.

IMPLEMENTATION

Without any specific management policy, the implementation of the Proxy pattern simply involves creating a class that shares a common interface with a service-providing class and delegates operations to instances of the service-providing class.

CONSEQUENCES

☺ The service provided by a service-providing object is managed in a manner transparent to the object and its clients.

☺ Unless the use of proxies introduces new failure modes, there is normally no need for the code of client classes to reflect the use of proxies.

CODE EXAMPLE

The Proxy pattern is not useful in its pure form. It must be combined with a service-management behavior to accomplish anything useful. This example of the Proxy pattern uses proxies to defer an expensive operation until it is actually needed. If the operation is not needed, the operation is never performed.

ICLONEABLE

Some classes are responsible for enabling their instances to make copies of themselves. Such classes generally implement the System.ICloneable interface. The ICloneable interface declares a function named Clone. When you call the Clone function of an object whose class implements ICloneable, it is expected to return an object that is an instance of the same class and contains the same values.

When implementing the Clone function, you need to decide whether you want the copying operation to be deep or shallow. A *shallow copy* of an object refers to the same objects as the original object. The objects that the original object refers to are not copied, just the references to the other objects. A *deep copy* of an object refers to copies of the objects that the original object refers to. A deep copy does *not* refer to the same objects as the original object. Figure 3.20 illustrates this.

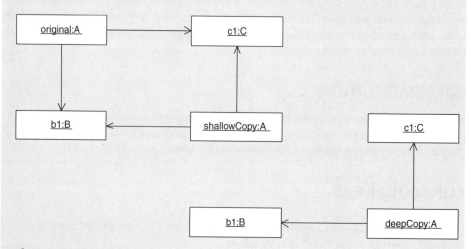

Figure 3.20 Deep and Shallow Copies

All classes inherit the MemberwiseClone function from the System.Object class. An object's MemberwiseClone function returns a shallow copy of the object. The object that MemberwiseClone returns is an instance of the same class as the original object. Its fields all have the same values as in the original object. The fields of the copy refer to the same objects as the original object.

The MemberwiseClone function is protected. Its primary use is implementing the ICloneable.Clone function. A typical implementation of the clone function begins with a call to the MemberwiseClone function. If the Clone implementation is supposed to copy any of the objects the cloned object refers to, it then calls their Clone function.

The example is a proxy for instances of classes like `System.Collections.`
`Hashtable` that implement both the `System.Collections.IDictionary` interface and the `System.IClonable` interface. The purpose of the proxy is to delay
cloning the underlying `IDictionary` object until it is known that this expensive operation will actually be needed.

One reason for cloning an `IDictionary` object is to avoid holding a lock on the
object for a long time when all that is desired is to fetch multiple key-value pairs. In a
multithreaded program, to ensure that an `IDictionary` object is in a consistent state
while fetching key-value pairs from it, use a mechanism such as a lock statement to
obtain exclusive access to the `IDictionary` object. While a thread has exclusive
access to the `IDictionary` object, other threads will wait to gain access to the same
`IDictionary` object. Such waiting may be unacceptable.

If the concern is for guaranteeing the integrity of the data rather than sharing
data, then cloning is an alternative to locking. If each thread has its own copy of an
`IDictionary` object, then no thread will interfere with another thread's operations on
the `IDictionary` object.

Not every class that implements the `IDictionary` interface also implements
the `ICloneable` interface. However, some `IDictionary` classes, such as `System.`
`Collections.Hashtable` and `System.Collections.SortedList`, do implement the `ICloneable` interface.

Cloning an `IDictionary` object prior to fetching values out of it is a defensive
measure. Cloning the `IDictionary` object avoids the need to obtain a synchronization lock on a `Hashtable` beyond the time it takes for the clone operation to complete.
When you have a freshly cloned copy of an `IDictionary` object, you can be sure that
no other thread has access to the copy. Since no other thread has access to the copy, you
will be able to fetch key-value pairs from the copy without any interference from other
threads.

If, after you clone an `IDictionary` object, there is no subsequent modification to
the original `IDictionary` object, then the time and memory spent in creating the
clone was wasted. The point of this example is to avoid that waste. It does that by
delaying the cloning of an `IDictionary` object until a modification to it actually does
occur.

The name of the proxy class is `LazyCloneDictionary`. Instances of `LazyClone`
`Dictionary` are a copy-on-write proxy for an `IDictionary` object. When a proxy's
clone function is called, it returns a copy of the proxy but does not copy the underlying
`IDictionary` object. At this point, both the original and copy of the proxy refer to the
same underlying `IDictionary` object. When one of the proxies is asked to modify the
underlying `IDictionary` object, the proxy recognizes that it is using a shared underlying `IDictionary` object. It clones the underlying `IDictionary` object before it
makes the modification. The organization of the `LazyCloneDictionary` class is
shown in Figure 3.21.

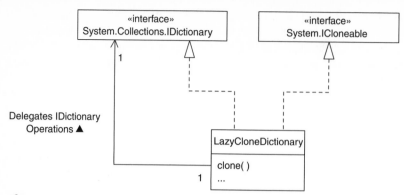

Figure 3.21 LazyCloneDictionary

Let's look at a listing of the LazyCloneDictionary class:

```
Imports System
Imports System.Collections

' This is a sample implementation of a proxy pattern.
' We are wrapping System.Collections.IDictionary objects and
' System.ICloneable objects with a single class. The wrapped
' object must implement ICloneable.  This class
' provides a "cloning on write" behavior to allow
' multithreaded use of seperate dictionaries.
Public Class LazyCloneDictionary
    Implements IDictionary
    Implements ICloneable

    ' The Dictionary object that this object is a proxy for.
    Private dict As IDictionary
```

Proxy classes have a way for a proxy object to refer to the object it is a proxy for. This proxy class has an instance variable dict that refers to the underlying IDictionary object. LazyCloneDictionary objects know if they are sharing their underlying IDictionary object with other LazyCloneDictionary objects by keeping a count of how many refer to the underlying IDictionary object. It keeps this count in an instance of a class name MutableInteger. The MutableInteger object is shared or not by the same LazyCloneDictionary objects that share the underlying IDictionary object. The listing for MutableInteger appears later.

```
    ' This is the number of proxy objects that share the same
    ' underlying dictionary.
    Private refCount As MutableInteger
```

The constructor clones the wrapped `IDictionary` object to be sure that no other object has a reference to the wrapped object. `IDictionary` objects. Since the `LazyCloneDictionary` class is useful only for wrapping objects that implement both the `IDictionary` and the `ICloneable` interfaces, the constructor assumes that the `IDictionary` object passed into it also implements the `ICloneable` interface.

```
' Constructor
' d - IDictionary object this object should be a proxy for.
Public Sub New(ByVal d As IDictionary)
    ' Clone wrapped dictionary if
    dict = CType(CType(d, ICloneable).Clone(), IDictionary)
    refCount = New MutableInteger(1)
End Sub 'New
```

This class's `clone` method does not copy the underlying `IDictionary` object. It does increment the reference count that is also shared by the original `LazyClone Dictionary` object and the copy. Incrementing the value allows `LazyClone Dictionary` objects to know that they share their underlying `IDictionary` object.

```
' Creates a copy of the dictionary
Public Function Clone() As Object _
              Implements ICloneable.Clone
    Dim theClone As LazyCloneDictionary = _
      CType(MemberwiseClone(), LazyCloneDictionary)
    SyncLock refCount
        refCount.Value = refCount.Value + 1
    End SyncLock
    Return theClone
End Function 'Clone
```

The following private method is called by public methods of the `Lazy CloneDictionary` class, such as `put` and `clear`, that modify the underlying `IDictionary` object. They call this method before modifying the underlying `IDictionary` object to ensure that they are not sharing the underlying `IDictionary` object:

```
Private Sub ensureUnderlyingDictionaryNotShared()
    SyncLock refCount
        If refCount.Value > 1 Then
            ' this will copy the entries
            dict = CType(CType(dict, ICloneable).Clone(), _
                         IDictionary)
            ' update shared refCount
            refCount.Value = refCount.Value - 1
            ' create new local refCount
            refCount = New MutableInteger(1)
        End If
    End SyncLock
End Sub 'ensureUnderlyingDictionaryNotShared
```

The ensureUnderlyingDictionaryNotShared method begins by determining if the value of the reference count is greater than one. A reference count greater than one means this LazyCloneDictionary object shares its underlying IDictionary object with other LazyCloneDictionary objects. The ensureUnderlying DictionaryNotShared method clones the underlying IDictionary object, so this LazyCloneDictionary object will have its own copy of the underlying IDictionary object that it does not share with any other LazyCloneDictionary object. It decrements the reference count so that the other LazyCloneDictionary objects this object was sharing an underlying IDictionary object with will know they are no longer sharing the underlying Map object with this object. Finally, it creates a new object to contain the reference count of 1 that indicates this LazyClone Dictionary object does not share its underlying Map object.

The rest of the members of the LazyCloneDictionary class delegate their work to the corresponding method of the underlying IDictionary object. The next portion of the listing shows members that implement the members of the ICollection interface:

```
' number of key-value pairs.
Public ReadOnly Property Count() As Integer _
                            Implements ICollection.Count
    Get
        Return dict.Count
    End Get
End Property


' indicates if dictionary access is thread-safe
Public ReadOnly Property IsSynchronized() As Boolean _
                        Implements IDictionary.IsSynchronized
    Get
        Return dict.IsSynchronized
    End Get
End Property


' object used for synchronization
Public ReadOnly Property SyncRoot() As Object _
                            Implements IDictionary.SyncRoot
    Get
        Return dict.SyncRoot
    End Get
End Property


' Copies the dictionary to a 1-dimensional System.Array,
' starting at the speficied index
Public Sub CopyTo(ByVal a As Array, ByVal i As Integer) _
        Implements ICollection.CopyTo
    dict.CopyTo(a, i)
End Sub 'CopyTo
```

The following function implements the only member of the `IEnumerator` interface:

```
Function IEnumGetEnumerator() As IEnumerator _
        Implements IEnumerable.GetEnumerator
    Return dict.GetEnumerator()
End Function 'IEnumerable.GetEnumerator
```

The following class members implement the members of the `IDictionary` interface:

```
' indicates if fixed size
Public ReadOnly Property IsFixedSize() As Boolean _
                            Implements IDictionary.IsFixedSize
    Get
        Return dict.IsFixedSize
    End Get
End Property


' indicates if read-only
Public ReadOnly Property IsReadOnly() As Boolean _
                            Implements IDictionary.IsReadOnly
    Get
        Return dict.IsReadOnly
    End Get
End Property


' keys in dictionary
Public ReadOnly Property Keys() As ICollection _
                            Implements IDictionary.Keys
    Get
        Return dict.Keys
    End Get
End Property


' values in dictionary
Public ReadOnly Property Values() As ICollection _
                            Implements IDictionary.Values
    Get
        Return dict.Values
    End Get
End Property

' Determines whether the dictionary contains a specific key
Public Function Contains(ByVal key As Object) As Boolean _
            Implements IDictionary.Contains
    Return dict.Contains(key)
End Function 'Contains
```

```
Function GetEnumerator() As IDictionaryEnumerator _
        Implements IDictionary.GetEnumerator
    Return dict.GetEnumerator()
End Function 'IDictionary.GetEnumerator
```

Because the next property and three methods modify the underlying IDictionary object, they call the ensureUnderlyingDictionaryNotShared method before they delegate their work to the underlying IDictionary object:

```
' gets or sets value associated with key
Default Public Property Item(ByVal index As Object) As Object _
            Implements IDictionary.Item
    Get
        Return dict(index)
    End Get
    Set(ByVal value As Object)
        ensureUnderlyingDictionaryNotShared()
        dict(index) = value
    End Set
End Property


' Add to dictionary
Public Sub Add(ByVal key As Object, ByVal value As Object) _
            Implements IDictionary.Add
    ensureUnderlyingDictionaryNotShared()
    dict.Add(key, value)
End Sub 'Add


' Clear dictionary
Public Sub Clear() Implements IDictionary.Clear
    ensureUnderlyingDictionaryNotShared()
    dict.Clear()
End Sub 'Clear


' Removes the element with the specified key from the dictionary
Public Sub Remove(ByVal key As Object) _
        Implements IDictionary.Remove
    ensureUnderlyingDictionaryNotShared()
    dict.Remove(key)
End Sub 'Remove


' Determines whether two Object instances are equal
Public Overloads Overrides Function Equals(ByVal o As Object) _
                        As Boolean
    Return CType(dict, Object).Equals(o)
End Function 'Equals


' Hash function for current type
Public Overrides Function GetHashCode() As Integer
    Return CType(dict, Object).GetHashCode()
End Function 'GetHashCode
End Class 'LazyCloneDictionary
```

Here is a listing of the `MutableInteger` class that the `LazyCloneDictionary` class uses:

```
' Reference counting class
Public Class MutableInteger
    Private val As Integer

    ' reference tracking integer
    Public Sub New(ByVal value As Integer)
        val = value
    End Sub 'New

    ' gets or sets the reference count
    Public Property Value() As Integer
        Get
            Return val
        End Get
        Set(ByVal value As Integer)
            val = value
        End Set
    End Property
End Class 'MutableInteger
```

RELATED PATTERNS

Protection Proxy: The Protection Proxy pattern (described in [Grand01]) uses a proxy to enforce a security policy on access to a service-providing object.

Façade: The Façade pattern uses a single object as a front end to a set of inter-related objects, rather than as a front end to a single object.

Object Request Broker: The Object Request Broker pattern (described in [Grand01]) uses a proxy to hide the fact that a service object is located on a different machine than the client objects that want to use it.

Virtual Proxy: This pattern uses a proxy to create the illusion that a service-providing object exists before it has actually been created. It is useful if the object is expensive to create and its services may not be needed. The copy-on-write proxy discussed under the "Code Example" heading for the Proxy pattern is a kind of virtual proxy.

Decorator: The Decorator pattern is structurally similar to the Proxy pattern in that it forces access to a service-providing object to be done indirectly through another object. The difference is a matter of intent. Instead of trying to manage the service, the indirection object in some way enhances the service.

Creational Patterns

Factory Method (95)
Abstract Factory (109)
Builder (121)
Prototype (131)
Singleton (141)
Object Pool (149)

Creational patterns provide guidance for organizing the creation of objects when their creation involves making decisions. These decisions typically involve dynamically deciding which class to instantiate or which objects a new object will delegate responsibility to. Creational patterns tell us how to structure and encapsulate these decisions.

You may wonder why there are specialized patterns that focus on just the creation of objects. Creating an object from a class presents some challenges that are unique to object creation. Here are two of the more obvious problems.

- Object creation is normally done using the new operation. The name of the class to be instantiated directly follows the word new. Because it is the actual name of the class rather than a variable, no indirection is possible. If the actual class to be instantiated will vary or be decided at run time, then other arrangements must be made.

- When an object is being constructed, it can only access Shared data and what is passed to its constructor's parameters. Access to other information must be arranged through these mechanisms.

Often, there is more than one creational pattern you can apply to a situation. Sometimes you can combine multiple patterns advantageously. In other cases, you must choose between competing patterns. For these reasons, it is important to be acquainted will all the patterns described in this chapter.

If you have just time to learn one pattern in this chapter, the most commonly used one is Factory Method. The Factory Method pattern is a way for an object to initiate the creation of another object without having to know the class of the object being created.

The Abstract Factory pattern is a way for objects to initiate the creation of different kinds of objects without knowing the classes of the objects being created, but ensuring that the classes are a correct combination.

The Builder pattern is a way to determine the class of an object to be created from its contents or context.

The Prototype pattern allows a class to initiate the creation of an object without knowing the class of the object or the details of how to create the object. It accomplishes this by copying an existing object.

The Singleton pattern is a way for multiple objects to share a common object without having to know if it already exists.

The Object Pool pattern is a way to reuse existing objects rather than create new ones.

Factory Method

This pattern was previously described in [GoF95].

SYNOPSIS

You need to create an object to represent external data or process an external event. The type of object to create depends on the contents of the external data or type of event. You do not want the data source, the event source or the object's clients to be aware of the actual type of object created or any special initialization it requires. You encapsulate the decision of what class of object to create in a different class.

CONTEXT

Consider the problem of writing a framework for applications organized around documents or files. Their operation usually begins with a command to create or edit a word processing document, spreadsheet, time line, or other type of document the application is intended to work with.

A framework to support this type of application will include high-level support for common operations such as creating, opening or saving documents. Such support will include a consistent set of methods to call when the user issues a command. For the purpose of this discussion, we will call the class providing the `DocumentManager` class.

Because the logic to implement most commands varies with the type of document, the `DocumentManager` class delegates most commands to some sort of document object. The logic in document objects for implementing commands varies with the type of document. However, some operations, such as displaying the title of a document, will be common to all document objects. This suggests an organization that includes:

- An application-independent document interface
- An abstract class that provides application-independent logic for concrete document classes
- Concrete application-specific classes that implement the interface for specific types of documents

Figure 4.1 shows this organization.

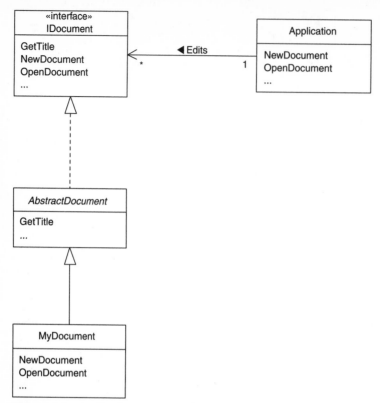

Figure 4.1   Application Framework

Neither Figure 4.1 nor the preceding discussion show how a DocumentManager object creates instances of application-specific document classes without itself being application-specific.

One way to accomplish this is for programmers using the framework to provide a class that encapsulates logic for selecting and instantiating application-specific classes. To enable the DocumentManager class to call the programmer-provided class without having any dependencies on it, the framework should provide an interface that the programmer provided class must implement. Such an interface would declare a function that the programmer-provided class would implement to select and instantiate a class. The DocumentManager class works through the framework-provided interface and not with the programmer-provided class. Figure 4.2 shows this organization.

Using the organization shown in Figure 4.2, a DocumentManager object calls the createDocument function of an object that implements the IDocumentFactory interface. It passes a string to the CreateDocument function. The CreateDocument function uses the string to infer which of the classes to instantiate that implement the IDocumentFactory interface. The DocumentManager class does not need to know the actual class of the object whose function it calls or which subclass of the Document class it instantiated.

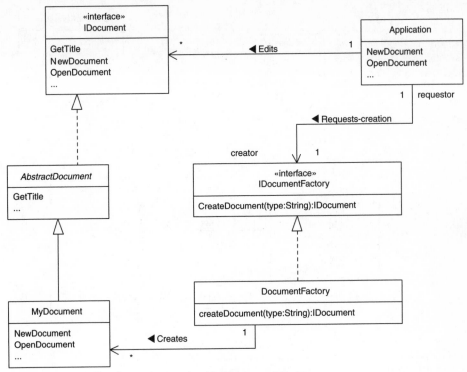

Figure 4.2 Application Framework with Document Factory

FORCES

☺ A class must be able to initiate the creation of objects without having any dependencies on the class of the created objects.

☺ The set of classes a class may be expected to instantiate may be dynamic and change as new classes become available.

SOLUTION

Provide application-independent objects with an application-specific object to which they delegate the creation of other application-specific objects. Require the application-independent objects that initiate the creation of application-specific objects to assume that the objects implement a common interface.

Figure 4.3 shows the interfaces and classes that typically make up the Factory Method pattern.

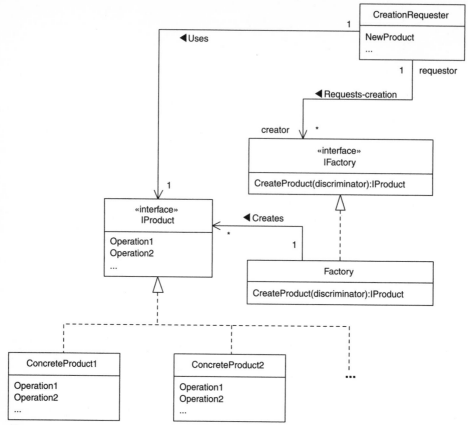

Figure 4.3   Factory Method Pattern

The class diagram in Figure 4.3 shows the roles classes and interfaces play in the Factory Method pattern:

IProduct: The objects created using this pattern must implement an interface in this role.

ConcreteProduct1, ConcreteProduct2, . . .: Classes in this role are instantiated by a `Factory` object. Classes in this role must implement the `IProduct` interface.

CreationRequester: A class in this role is an application-independent class that needs to create application-specific classes. It does so indirectly through an instance of a class that implements the `IFactory` interface.

IFactory: This is an application-independent interface. Objects that create `IProduct` objects on behalf of `CreationRequester` objects must implement this interface. Interfaces of this sort declare a function that a `Creation Requester` object calls to create concrete product objects. This function's arguments are discussed under the "Implementation" section for this pattern.

Interfaces filling this role will typically have a name that includes the word "Factory," such as IDocumentFactory or IImageFactory.

Factory: This is an application-specific class that implements the appropriate IFactory interface and has a function to create ConcreteProduct objects. Classes that fill this role typically have a name like DocumentFactory or ImageFactory that contains the word "Factory".

IMPLEMENTATION

In many implementations of the Factory Method pattern, the ConcreteProduct classes do not directly implement the IProduct interface. Instead, they extend an abstract class that implements the interface. See the Interface and Abstract Class pattern in Chapter 3 for a discussion of the reasons for this.

Class Determination by Configuration

There are two main variations on the Factory Method pattern. The general case is where the class of the object to create is determined when object creation is initiated. There is also the less common case where the class of objects that will be created is always the same and is determined before any object's creation is initiated.

A program may use a factory object that always creates an instance of the same class if the class is determined by some configuration information. For example, suppose that a company sells a point-of-sale system that is responsible for communicating with a remote computer to process credit card payments. Its classes expect to send messages to the remote computer and receive responses by using objects that implement a particular interface. The exact format of the messages to send will depend on the company that processes the credit card transactions. For each credit card–processing company, there is corresponding class that implements the required interface and knows how to send the messages that company expects. There is also a corresponding factory class. This organization is shown in Figure 4.4.

Here is an explanation of the design shown in Figure 4.4. When the point-of-sale system starts, it reads its configuration information. The configuration information tells the point of sale that it is to pass credit card transactions either to BancOne or Wells Fargo for processing. Based on this information, it creates either a BancOneCC Factory or WellsCCFactory object. It accesses the object through the ICredit CardProcessorFactory interface. When it needs an object to process a credit card transaction, it calls the CreateProcessor function of its ICreditCard ProcessorFactory, which creates an object that uses the configured credit card–processing company.

Note that the factory class's create function does need any arguments because it always returns the same type of object.

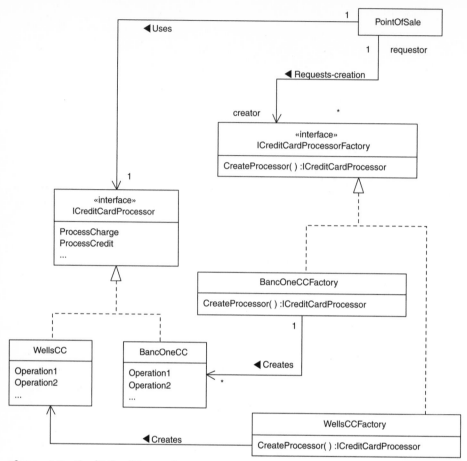

Figure 4.4 Credit Card Processing

Data-Driven Class Determination

Very often, the class of an object created by a factory object is determined by the data it is intended to encapsulate. The class is determined by the factory object's `CreateProduct` function. The determination is usually based on information passed into the function as a parameter. Such `CreateProduct` functions generally look something like this:

```
Public Function createDrawing(ByVal theFile As FileInfo) As Drawing
    Select Case theFile.Extension
        Case "gfx1"
            Return New Gfx1Drawing(theFile)
        Case "mxfi"
            Return New MfxiDrawing(theFile)
        ...
    End Select
End Function
```

A select statement works well for createProduct functions that have a fixed set of product classes to instantiate. To write a createProduct function that handles a variable or large number of product classes, you can use the Hashed Adapter Objects pattern (described in [Grand98]). Alternatively, you can use the objects that indicate which class to instantiate as keys in a hash table with System.Reflection. Emit.ConstructorBuilder objects for values. Using this technique, you look up an argument value in the hash table and then use the ConstructorBuilder object found in the hash table to instantiate the desired object.

Another point the preceding example illustrates is that factory methods are a reasonable place to find select statements or chains of if statements. In many situations, the presence of select statements or chains of if statements in code indicates that a method should have been implemented as a polymorphic method. Factory methods cannot be implemented using polymorphism, because polymorphism is useful only after an object has been created.

For many implementations of the Factory Method pattern, the valid arguments to the factory object's createProduct function are a set of predetermined values. It is often convenient for the factory class to define symbolic names for each of the predetermined values. Classes that ask the factory class to create objects can use the constants that define the symbolic names to specify the type of object to create. If the values are all integers, it is better to define the symbolic names using a single Enum statement than to define them as individual constants.

Sometimes, there is more that one layer of data-driven class determination. For example, there may be a top-level factory object responsible for creating the factory object that will create the actual product object. For this reason, the data-driven form of the Factory Method pattern is sometimes called *layered initialization*.

CONSEQUENCES

The primary consequences of using the Factory Method pattern are:

- ☺ The creation requester class is independent of the class of concrete product objects actually created.

- ☺ The set of product classes that can be instantiated may be changed dynamically.

- ☹ The indirection between the initiation of object creation and the determination of which class to instantiate can make a program more difficult for maintenance programmers to understand.

.NET API USAGE

The .NET Framework's security architecture includes a permission mechanism. At a high level, the way it works is that System.Security.IPermission objects become associated with a method's context. When a method is called that wants to know if its caller has permission to do what is being requested, the called method checks if its caller's context includes a particular permission.

It uses `System.Security.IPermission` objects to determine if the caller of a method has the right to request whatever it is requesting of a method. Some kinds of `IPermission` objects directly convey the right of a caller to request a particular service. For example, a `System.Drawing.Printing.PrintingPermission` object conveys the right to print something. The meaning of some other kinds of `IPermission` objects is less direct.

Some `IPermission` objects just imply an identity. It is up to the method checking permissions what inference it makes from identity. For example, `System.Security.Permissions.PublisherIdentityPermission` objects encapsulate the identity of a software publisher. There are similar `IPermission` classes that encapsulate such things as the URL an assembly came from or the name of an assembly.

Classes that represent identity information do not generally implement the `IPermission` interface. It is therefore necessary for classes that need `IPermission` objects that assert an identity to create them from identity objects. The .NET Framework uses the Factory Method pattern to avoid burdening classes that use identity-based `IPermission` objects with having to know about different kinds of identity objects.

All of the identity classes that the .NET Framework provides implement the `System.Security.Policy.IIdentityPermissionFactory` interface. The `IIdentityPermissionFactory` interface declares the function `CreateIdentityPermission`. The `CreateIdentityPermission` function takes an argument that is a collection of the identities to be asserted by an `IPermission` object and returns an `IPermission` object that asserts the identities.

CODE EXAMPLE

For our example, suppose that you are developing an application to process records in a journal file created by a point-of-sale system.[1] Every line that appears on every register tape has a corresponding record in the journal file. Your application will read all the records in a journal file and generate transaction-level summaries of them.

Your application will be required to work with point-of-sale systems from multiple manufacturers. Since the journal file produced by each manufacturer's point-of-sale system has a different format, it is especially important to keep the classes responsible for generating the summaries independent of the journal file format.

You notice that all the journal file formats consist of a sequence of records. The types of records in the journal files are similar. You decide to make the summary generating classes independent of the journal file formats by representing the journal files internally as a sequence of objects that correspond to the records in the journal file. With this in mind, you design a set of classes that correspond to different types of records that occur in the journal files.

The focus of this example is how your application will create objects that represent the records in the journal files. This example uses both forms of the Factory Method pattern.

---

[1]A point-of-sale system is a high-tech cash register.

- As the application reads records from a journal file, it uses a factory object to create the objects that correspond to each record in the journal file. Each time the factory object is asked to create an object, it selects the class to instantiate based on information in the record. This is an example of a factory that performs runtime class determination.

- The class of the factory object that creates objects to represent records depends on the type of journal file that the application will be reading. Because the class of this factory object depends on configuration information, it is created by another factory object when the application reads its configuration information.

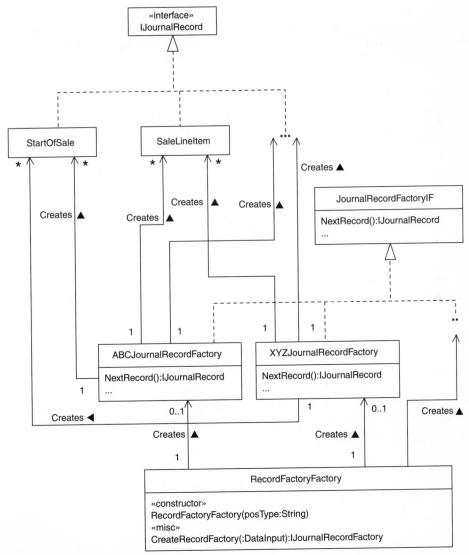

Figure 4.5 Journal-File-Related Factory Classes

Figure 4.5 shows the class organization this code example is based on. Here are descriptions of the classes and interfaces shown in Figure 4.5.

IJournalRecord: An Object that encapsulates the contents of a journal record is an instance of a class that implements this interface. Only two such classes are shown in Figure 4.5. However, in the complete application there would be many more.

StartOfSale: Instances of this class represent a journal record that indicates the beginning of the sale transaction.

SaleLineItem: Instance of this class represent a journal record that contains the details of a sale item on a register receipt.

IJournalRecordFactory: This interface is implemented by classes responsible for taking the information in journal file records and encapsulating them in objects that implement the `IJournalRecord` interface. Instances of classes that implement this interface create objects that implement the `IJournalRecord` interface, such as `StartOfSale` objects and `SaleLineItems` objects.

ABCJournalRecordFactory: Instances of this class are responsible for understanding the format of journal files produced by ABC point-of-sale systems. They read the next journal record from a `System.IO.BinaryReader` object and encapsulate its contents in an instance of a class that implements the `IJournalRecord` interface.

XYZJournalRecordFactory: Instances of this class are responsible for understanding the format of journal files produced by XYZ point-of-sale systems. They read the next journal record from a `System.IO.BinaryReader` object and encapsulate its contents in an instance of a class that implements the `IJournalRecord` interface.

RecordFactoryFactory: The name of a type of point-of-sale system is passed to this class's constructor. The constructed object is then used to create instances of the appropriate class that implements the `IJournalRecordFactory` interface for the specified type of point-of-sale system.

You may notice some structural similarity between this example that uses both forms of the Factory Method pattern and the next pattern in this book, the Abstract Factory pattern. One of the distinguishing characteristics of the Abstract Factory pattern is that the client objects are concerned with the interface implemented by the objects to be created rather than with their content.

Now let's look at code that implements this design. We will begin with a listing of the `RecordFactoryFactory` class.

```
Imports System
Imports System.IO
Imports System.Reflection
```

```vbnet
'When an instance of this class is created,
'its constructor is passed a string indicating the
'type of point of sale system that the object will be a
'factory for. It gets a ConstructorInfo object
'that it will use to construct objects and make the Constructor
'object the value of the factoryConstructor instance variable.
Public Class RecordFactoryFactory
    Private factoryConstructor As ConstructorInfo


    ' POS Types
    Public Enum PosTypes
        ABC
    End Enum


    'constructor
    '
    'posType - The type of point of sale system that this object
    'will be creating IJournalRecordFactory object for.
    Public Sub New(ByVal posType As PosTypes)
        Dim args() As Type = {GetType(StreamReader)}
        Dim factoryClass As Type
        If posType = PosTypes.ABC Then
            factoryClass = GetType(ABCJournalRecordFactory)
        Else
            Dim msg As String = "Unknown POS type: " & posType.ToString
            Throw New ApplicationException(msg)
        End If
        Try
            factoryConstructor = factoryClass.GetConstructor(args)
        Catch e As Exception
            Dim msg As String = "Error while constructing factory"
            Throw New ApplicationException(msg, e)
        End Try
    End Sub


    'This method creates IJournalRecordFactory objects
    Public Function CreateFactory(ByVal input As StreamReader) _
                As IJournalRecordFactory
        Dim args() As Object = {input}
        Dim factory As Object
        Try
            factory = factoryConstructor.Invoke(args)
        Catch e As Exception
            Dim msg As String = "Error creating factory"
            Throw New ApplicationException(msg, e)
        End Try
        Return CType(factory, IJournalRecordFactory)
    End Function
End Class 'RecordFactoryFactory
```

```
' Objects that encapsulate the contents of a journal record
' implement this interface.
Public Interface IJournalRecord
End Interface
```

Here is the IJournalRecordFactory interface:

```
' This interface is implemented by classes that are
' responsible for creating objects that encapsulate the
' contents of a point of sale journal file record.
Public Interface IJournalRecordFactory
    'Return an object that encapsulates the next record in a
    'journal file.
    Function NextRecord() As IJournalRecord
End Interface
```

Here is the class ABCJournalRecordFactory that implements the IJournal RecordFactory interface for a type of point-of-sale system named "ABC."

```
' This class implements the IJournalRecordFactory
' interface for a type of point of sale system named "ABC".
Public Class ABCJournalRecordFactory
    Implements IJournalRecordFactory

    ' Record Types
    Private Shared SALE_LINE_ITEM As String = "17"
    Private Shared START_OF_SALE As String = "4"

    Private input As StreamReader

    ' Counter for sequence number.
    Private sequenceNumber As Integer = 0

    Sub New(ByVal i As StreamReader)
        input = i
    End Sub

    ' Return an object that encapsulates the next record in a
    ' journal file.
    Public Function NextRecord() As IJournalRecord _
      Implements IJournalRecordFactory.NextRecord
        Dim record As String = input.ReadLine()
        Dim tokens As String() = record.Split(New Char() {","c})
        sequenceNumber += 1

        If tokens(0) = START_OF_SALE Then
            Return CType(constructStartOfSale(tokens), _
                        IJournalRecord)
        ElseIf tokens(0) = SALE_LINE_ITEM Then
            Return CType(constructSaleLineItem(tokens), _
```

```
                      IJournalRecord)
        End If
        Throw New IOException("Unknown record type")
    End Function 'NextRecord


    Private _
    Function constructStartOfSale(ByVal tok() As String) _
            As StartOfSale
        Dim index As Integer = 1
        Dim transactionID As String = tok(index)
        index += 1 ' Move past ID
        index += 1 ' Skip mode indicator.
        Dim timestamp As DateTime = DateTime.Parse(tok(index))
        index += 1 ' Move past DateTime
        Dim terminalID As String = tok(index)
        Return New StartOfSale(terminalID, sequenceNumber, _
                               timestamp, transactionID)
    End Function 'constructStartOfSale


    Private _
    Function constructSaleLineItem(ByVal tok() As String) _
            As SaleLineItem
        Dim index As Integer = 1
        Dim transactionID As String = tok(index)
        index += 1 ' Move past ID
        index += 1 ' Skip mode indicator.
        Dim timestamp As DateTime = DateTime.Parse(tok(index))
        index += 1 ' Move past DateTime
        Dim terminalID As String = tok(index)
        Return New SaleLineItem(terminalID, sequenceNumber, _
                                timestamp, transactionID)
    End Function 'constructSaleLineItem
End Class 'ABCJournalRecordFactory
```

RELATED PATTERNS

Hashed Adapter Objects: The Hashed Adapter Objects pattern can be used in the implementation of the Factory Method pattern. It is useful if the set of classes that a factory object instantiates may change during the running of a program.

Abstract Factory: The Factory Method pattern is useful for constructing individual objects for a specific purpose without the construction requestor knowing the specific classes being instantiated. If you need to create a matched set of such objects, then the Abstract Factory pattern is a more appropriate pattern to use.

Template Method: When The Factory Method pattern is implemented to determine the type of what will be created using configuration information, the implementation often uses the Template Method pattern.

Prototype: The Prototype pattern provides an alternate way for an object to work with other objects without knowing the details of their construction.

Strategy: If you are considering using the Factory Method pattern to vary behavior, the Strategy pattern may be a better alternative.

Abstract Factory

Abstract Factory is also known as Kit orToolkit. This pattern was previously described in [GoF95].

SYNOPSIS

Given a set of related interfaces, provide a way to create objects that implement those interfaces from a matched set of concrete classes. The Abstract Factory pattern can be very useful for allowing a program to work with a variety of complex external entities such as different windowing systems with similar functionality.

CONTEXT

Suppose that you have the task of building a user interface framework that works on top of multiple windowing systems, such as Windows, Motif, or MacOS. It must work on each platform with the platform's native look and feel. You organize it by creating an abstract class for each type of widget (text field, push button, list box . . .) and then writing a concrete subclass of each abstract class for each supported platform. To make this robust, you need to ensure that the widget objects created are all for the desired platform. That is where the abstract factory comes into play.

An abstract factory class defines functions to create an instance of each abstract class that represents a user interface widget. Concrete factories are concrete subclasses of an abstract factory that implements its functions to create instances of concrete widget classes for the same platform.

In a more general context, an abstract factory class and its concrete subclasses organize sets of concrete classes that work with different but related products. For a broader perspective, consider another situation.

Suppose that you are writing a program that performs remote diagnostics on computers made by a manufacturer called Stellar Microsystems. Over time, Stellar has produced computer models having substantially different architectures. Their oldest computers used CPU chips manufactured by Enginola that had a traditional complex instruction set. Since then, they have released multiple generations of computers based on their own RISC architectures called ember, super-ember, and ultra-ember. The core components used in these models perform similar functions, but involve different sets of components.

In order for your program to know which tests to run and how to interpret the results, it will need to instantiate objects that correspond to each core component in the computer being diagnosed. The class of each object will correspond to the type of component being tested. This means that you will have a set of classes for each computer architecture. There will be a class in each set that corresponds to the same type of computer component.

Figure 4.6 is a class diagram that shows the organization of classes that encapsulate diagnostics for different kinds of computer components. It shows just two kinds of components. The organization for any additional kind of component would be the same. There is an interface for each type of component. For each supported computer architecture, there is a class that implements each interface.

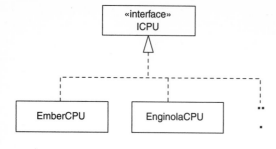

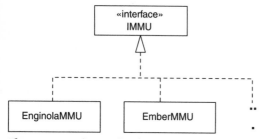

Figure 4.6   Diagnostic Classes

This organization shown in Figure 4.6 leads us to the problem that the Abstract Factory pattern solves. You need a way to organize the creation of diagnostic objects. You want classes that use the diagnostic classes to be independent of the specific diagnostic classes being used. You could use the Factory Method pattern to create diagnostic objects, but there is a problem that the Factory Method pattern does not solve.

You want to ensure that objects you use to diagnose a computer are all for that computer's architecture. If you simply use the Factory Method pattern, the classes that use the diagnostic classes will have the burden of telling each factory which computer architecture the diagnostic objects are for. You want to find a cohesive way of ensuring that all of the diagnostic objects used for a computer are for the correct architecture without adding dependencies to the classes that use the objects.

FORCES

☺   A system that works with multiple products should function in a way that is independent of the specific product it is working with.

☺   It should be possible to configure a system to work with one or multiple members of a family of products.

☺   Instances of classes intended to interface with a particular product should be used together and only with the product they are intended to work with. This constraint must be enforced.

☺ The rest of a system should work with a product without being aware of the specific classes used to interface with the product.

☺ A system should be extensible so that it can work with additional products by adding additional sets of classes and changing at most only a few lines of code.

☹ The interface that a class implements is not sufficient to distinguish it from other classes that may be instantiated to create an object.

SOLUTION

Figure 4.7 is a class diagram that shows the roles classes play in the Abstract Factory pattern.

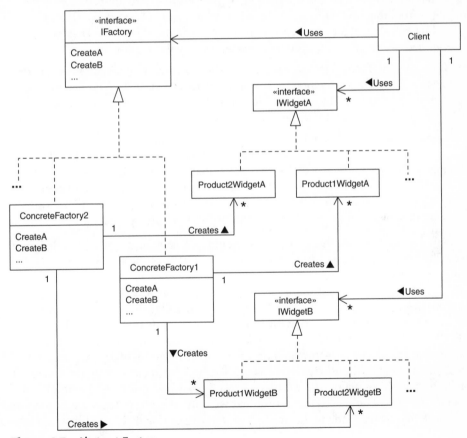

Figure 4.7   Abstract Factory

Here are descriptions of the roles that the classes and interfaces shown in Figure 4.7 play in the Abstract Factory pattern.

IWidgetA, IWidgetB, . . .: Interfaces in this role correspond to a service or feature of a product. Classes that implement one of these interfaces work with the service or feature to which the interface corresponds.

Only two of these interfaces are shown due to limited space. Most applications of the Abstract Factory pattern have more than two of these interfaces. There will be as many of these interfaces as there are distinct features or services of the products that are being used.

Product1WidgetA, Product2WidgetA . . .: Classes in this role correspond to a specific feature of a specific product. You can generically refer to classes in this role as concrete widgets.

Client: Classes in this role use concrete widget classes to request or receive services from the product that the client is working with. Client classes interact with concrete widget classes through an `IWidget` interface only. They are independent of the actual concrete widget classes they work with.

IFactory: Interfaces in this role declare methods for creating instances of concrete widget classes. Each method returns an instance of a class that implements a different `IWidget` interface. Classes responsible for creating concrete widget objects implement an interface in this role.

ConcreteFactory1, ConcreteFactory2 . . .: Classes in this role implement an `IFactory` interface to create instances of concrete widget classes. Each class in this role corresponds to a different product that a `Client` class may work with. Each function of a `ConcreteFactory` class creates a different kind of concrete widget. However, all the concrete widgets its functions create are for working with the product that the `ConcreteFactory` class corresponds to.

Client classes that call these functions should not have any direct knowledge of these concrete factory classes, but instead access instances of these classes through the `IFactory` interface.

If it is not clear to you what all this accomplishes, another way of looking at what the solution does is shown in Table 4.1. Table 4.1 is a matrix that shows different products that a program will need to work with and the common features of the products.

Each column of Table 4.1 corresponds to a different product. Each row of Table 4.1 corresponds to a different feature of a product. For each feature of a product, an interface is defined for working with the product. The body of Table 4.1 contains names of classes that implement a particular interface for a particular product. The point of the Abstract Factory pattern is to make sure that we only use classes from the column of the matrix that corresponds to the product we are working with.

Table 4.1 Product/Feature Matrix

	PRODUCT1	PRODUCT2	PRODUCT3
WidgetA	Product1WidgetA	Product2WidgetA	Product3WidgetA ...
WidgetB	Product1WidgetB	Product2WidgetB	Product3WidgetB ...
WidgetC	Product1WidgetC	Product2WidgetC	Product3WidgetC ...
...	...	...	... ...

We ensure that we only use classes from the correct column of the matrix by creating objects with a ConcreateFactory object that corresponds to the product that the program is working with. Each ConcreateFactory class has methods to create objects that implement the various widget interfaces for only one product.

IMPLEMENTATION

The main implementation issue for the Abstract Factory pattern is the mechanism that the client classes use to create and access IFactory objects. The simplest situation is when client objects only need to work with one product during the run of a program. In that case, some class will typically have a static variable set to the Concrete Factory class that is used during the program run. The variable may be public or its value accessed though a public static property.

If the abstract factory object uses information provided by the requesting client to select among multiple concrete factory objects, you can use the Factory Method pattern to select a concrete factory object.

CONSEQUENCES

☺ Client classes are independent of the concrete widget classes that they use.

☺ Adding (as opposed to writing) classes to work with additional products is simple. The class of a concrete factory object usually needs to be referenced in only one place. It is also easy to change the concrete factory used to work with a particular product.

☺ By forcing client classes to go through an IFactory interface to create concrete widget objects, the Abstract Factory pattern ensures that client objects use a consistent set of objects to work with a product.

☹ The main drawback of the Abstract Factory pattern is that it can be a lot of work to write a new set of classes to interface with a product. It can also take a lot of work to extend the set of features that the existing set of classes is able to exercise in the products that they work with.

Adding support for a new product involves writing a complete set of concrete widget classes to support the new product. You must write a concrete widget class for each IWidget interface. The more IWidget interfaces there are, the more work it will be to support an additional product.

Adding access to an additional feature of the products interfaced to can also take a lot of work if there are many supported products. It involves writing a new IWidget interface corresponding to the new feature and a new concrete widget class corresponding to each product.

⊗ Client objects may have a need to organize widget classes into a hierarchy that serves the needs of client objects. The basic Abstract Factory pattern does not lend itself to this because it requires concrete widget classes to be organized into a class hierarchy that is independent of client objects. This difficulty can be overcome by mixing the Bridge pattern with the Abstract Factory pattern.

Create a hierarchy of product-independent widget classes that suits the needs of the client classes. Have each product-independent widget class delegate product-specific logic to a product-specific class that implements a WidgetIF interface.

CODE EXAMPLE

For this pattern's code example, we will return to the problem discussed under the "Context" section. Figure 4.8 shows an expanded class diagram that incorporates the Abstract Factory pattern.

An instance of the Client class manages the remote diagnostic process. When it determines the architecture of the machine it has to diagnose, it passes the architecture type to the createToolkit function of a ToolkitFactory object. The function returns an instance of a class such as EmberToolkit or EnginolaToolkit that implements the IArchitectureToolkit interface for the specified computer architecture. The Client object can then use the IArchitectureToolkit object to create objects that model CPUs, MMUs (memory management units), and other components of the required architecture.

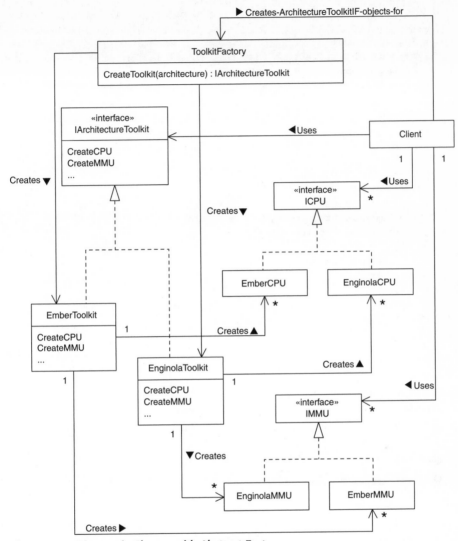

Figure 4.8 Diagnostic Classes with Abstract Factory

Here is some of the code that implements the design for remote computer diagnostics shown in Figure 4.8.

```
' Classes for testing all kinds of CPUs must implement this
' interface.
Public Interface ICpu
    ' The type of architecture that this object is for
    ReadOnly Property Type() As String


    ...
End Interface
```

```vbnet
' Classes for testing all kinds of memory management units must
' implement this interface.
Public Interface IMmu
    ' The type of architecture that this object is for
    ReadOnly Property Type() As String


    ...
End Interface


' Class for testing the CPU of a machine that uses the Ember
' architecture.
Public Class EmberCpu
    Implements ICpu

    Public ReadOnly Property Type() As String _
        Implements ICpu.Type
        Get
            Return "Ember"
        End Get
    End Property


    ...
End Class


' Class for testing the MMU of a machine that uses the Ember
' architecture.
Public Class EmberMmu
    Implements IMmu

    Public ReadOnly Property Type() As String _
        Implements IMmu.Type
        Get
            Return "Ember"
        End Get


        ...
    End Property
End Class


' Class for testing computers that use the Ember architecture.
Public Class EmberToolkit
    Implements IArchitectureToolkit

    ' Return an object for testing the CPU of a computer that
    ' uses the Ember architecure
    Public Function CreateCpu() As ICpu _
        Implements IArchitectureToolkit.CreateCpu
        Return New EmberCpu()
    End Function
```

```
        ' Return an object for testing the CPU of a computer that
        ' uses the Ember architecure
        Public Function CreateMmu() As IMmu _
            Implements IArchitectureToolkit.CreateMmu
            Return New EmberMmu()
        End Function
        ...
End Class

' Class for testing computers that use the Enginola
' architecture.
Public Class EnginolaCpu
    Implements ICpu

    Public ReadOnly Property Type() As String _
        Implements ICpu.Type
        Get
            Return "Enginola"
        End Get
    End Property
End Class

' Class for testing the MMU of a machine that uses the Enginola
' architecture.
Public Class EnginolaMmu
    Implements IMmu

    Public ReadOnly Property Type() As String _
        Implements IMmu.Type
        Get
            Return "Enginola"
        End Get
    End Property

    ...
End Class

' Class for testing computers that use the Enginola
' architecture.
Public Class EnginolaToolkit
    Implements IArchitectureToolkit

    ' Return an object for testing the CPU of a computer that
    ' uses the Enginola architecure
    Public Function CreateCpu() As ICpu _
        Implements IArchitectureToolkit.CreateCpu
        Return New EnginolaCpu()
    End Function
```

```vb
' Return an object for testing the MMU of a computer that
' uses the Enginola architecure
Public Function CreateMmu() As IMmu _
    Implements IArchitectureToolkit.CreateMmu
    Return New EnginolaMmu()
End Function

...

End Class


' Abstract toolkit classes that create objects for testing
' different components of the same architecture implement this
' interface.
Public Interface IArchitectureToolkit
    Function CreateCpu() As ICpu
    Function CreateMmu() As IMmu
    ...
End Interface


' This class is responsible for crating an instance of a class
' that implements the IArchitectureToolkit interface for a
' specified architecture.
'
' This class is a singleton.
Public Class ToolkitFactory
    ' The single instance of this class.
    Private Shared myInstance As New ToolkitFactory()

    ' Symbolic names to identify computer architectures
    Public Enum ComputerArchitecture
        ENGINOLA = 900
        EMBER = 901
    End Enum


    ' Return this class's single instance.
    Public Shared ReadOnly Property Instance() As ToolkitFactory
        Get
            Return myInstance
        End Get
    End Property

    '
    ' Return a newly created object that implements the
    ' ArchitectureToolkitIF interface for the given computer
    ' architecture.
    '
    Public Function CreateToolkit(ByVal architecture As ComputerArchitecture) _
        As IArchitectureToolkit
        Select Case architecture
            Case ComputerArchitecture.ENGINOLA
                Return New EnginolaToolkit()
```

```
              Case ComputerArchitecture.EMBER
                    Return New EmberToolkit()
          End Select
          Throw New System.ArgumentException("ArchId=" & architecture.ToString)
      End Function
End Class

' Very simple client class
Public Class Client
    Public Shared Sub Main()
        Dim myFactory As ToolkitFactory
        myFactory = ToolkitFactory.Instance
        Dim af As IArchitectureToolkit
        af = myFactory.CreateToolkit(ToolkitFactory.ComputerArchitecture.EMBER)
        Dim cpu As ICpu = af.CreateCpu()
        System.Console.WriteLine("Created Toolkit for cpu " & cpu.Type)
    End Sub
End Class
```

RELATED PATTERNS

Factory Method: In the preceding example, the abstract factory class uses the Factory Method pattern to decide which concrete factory object to give to a client class.

Singleton: Concrete factory classes are usually implemented as `Singleton` classes.

Builder

This pattern was previously described in [GoF95].

SYNOPSIS

The Builder pattern allows a client object to construct a complex object by specifying only its type and content. The client is shielded from the details of the object's construction.

CONTEXT

The context example for this pattern is a tool for automatically generating the source for a kind of class called a *wrapper class*.

The implementation of some of the design patterns discussed in this book, such as the Proxy pattern and the Façade pattern, involve the use of a wrapper class. A wrapper class is a class that implements an interface by delegating all of the functions, subroutines, and property implementations to another object with the same interface.

Typically, a wrapper class has a constructor with an argument refers to an object that implements the same interface as the wrapper class. The constructor sets an instance variable to refer to the given object. The functions and subroutines of the constructed wrapper instance pass their parameters to the corresponding functions and subroutines of the reference object. Each function returns the result returned by its call to the referenced object's function. We call these pass-through functions and subroutines because parameters and results just pass through them.

A wrapper object is used by interposing it between a client and the object that actually provides the services or data that the client uses as is shown in Figure 4.9. A client object uses an object that implements the `IFoo` interface. That object may be a `WrapperFoo` object that delegates all of its calls to a `FooImpl` object.

All by itself, a wrapper class is not very useful. An instance of a wrapper class provides just the behavior of the object it refers to. It does not add any value. However, a wrapper class is useful in implementing the Decorator pattern.

The Decorator pattern involves creating a class that implements the same interface as another class in order to modify *some* of its behavior. Implementing the Decorator pattern may involve creating a class that is like a wrapper in that it most of its functions and subroutines are pass-through functions and subroutines, but some do something else. Much of the work of implementing such a class may consist or writing pass-through functions and subroutines, unless the decorator class is implemented as a subclass of a wrapper class.

If a decorator class is implemented as a subclass of a wrapper class, then the decorator class inherits all the pass-through functions and subroutines it needs from the wrapper class. The person implementing the decorator class does not need to spend time writing any of the pass-through methods.

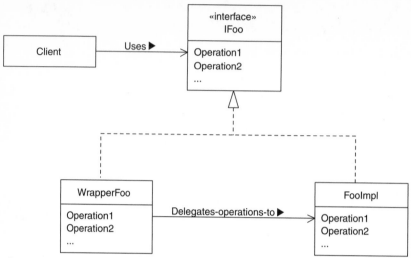

Figure 4.9   Wrapper

Implementing a decorator class by extending a wrapper class is not a real time savings if a programmer also has to write the wrapper class. Fortunately, it is possible to write a tool that automatically generates a wrapper class from a `System.Type` object that describes an interface.

Here is a partial listing of a class that is a wrapper for objects that implement the `System.IAppDomainSetup` interface:

```
Imports System
Namespace Wrappers

    Public Class WrapperIAppDomainSetup
        Implements System.IAppDomainSetup

        'Reference to wrapped object
        Private myWrappedObject As IAppDomainSetup

        Private _
        Sub New(ByVal myIAppDomainSetup As IAppDomainSetup)
            MyBase.New()
            myWrappedObject = myIAppDomainSetup
        End Sub

        ReadOnly Property WrappedObject() As IAppDomainSetup
            Get
                Return myWrappedObject
            End Get
        End Property

        Property ApplicationBase() As String _
                Implements IAppDomainSetup.ApplicationBase
            Get
```

```
                  Return myWrappedObject.ApplicationBase
            End Get
            Set(ByVal Value As String)
                  myWrappedObject.ApplicationBase = Value
            End Set
      End Property


      Property ApplicationName() As String _
                  Implements IAppDomainSetup.ApplicationName
            Get
                  Return myWrappedObject.ApplicationName
            End Get
            Set(ByVal Value As String)
                  myWrappedObject.ApplicationName = Value
            End Set
      End Property


      ...
      End Class
End Namespace
```

Suppose that you are designing a tool to create the source for a wrapper class from a `Type` object. You want to design the tool so that it can generate the source in VB.NET, C#, or other languages to be determined later. This is where the Builder pattern comes in.

You organize the tool so that it first determines what the members of the wrapper class will be. It then uses a code generator object to generate the source for the wrapper class. The rest of the tool accesses the code generator class through an interface. This allows the tool to use code generator objects without having to care what source code language it generates. The .NET Framework provides most of the classes that you will use to build your tool. Figure 4.10 shows the design.

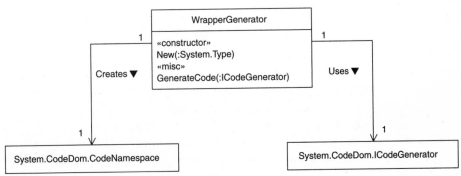

Figure 4.10 Builder Example Collaboration

Figure 4.10 shows a class named `WrapperGenerator`. The `Type` object that describes an interface is passed to the `WrapperGenerator` constructor. In the process of constructing a `WrapperGenerator` object, the constructor creates a `CodeName space` object that describes a wrapper class and its members. After the `Wrapper Generator` object is constructed, you can pass an `ICodeGenerator` object to the `WrapperGenerator` object's `GenerateCode` method. The `GenerateCode` method uses the `ICodeGenerator` object to generate source code without having to know what the language of the source is.

You can get an `ICodeGenerator` object that generates C# code by calling a `CSharpCodeProvider` object's `CreateGenerator` function. You can get an `ICodeGenerator` object that generates VB code by calling a `VBCodeProvider` object's `CreateGenerator` function.

FORCES

☺ A program must to be able to produce multiple external representations of the same data.

☺ The classes responsible for providing content should be independent of any external data representation and the classes that build them. If content-providing classes have no dependencies on external data representations, then changes to external data representation classes will not require any maintenance to content-providing classes.

☺ The classes responsible for building external data representations are independent of the classes that provide the content. Their instances can work with any content-providing object without knowing anything about the content-providing object.

SOLUTION

Figure 4.11 is a class diagram showing the participants in the Builder pattern.
Here are the roles that these classes and interface play in the Builder pattern:

Product: A class in this role defines a type of data representation. All `Product` classes should implement the `IProduct` interface so that other classes can refer to `Product` objects through the interface without having to know their class.

Iproduct: The Builder pattern is used to build a variety of different kinds of `Product` objects for use by `Client` objects. To avoid the need for `Client` objects to know the actual class of `Product` objects built for them, all `Product` classes implement the `IProduct` interface. `Client` objects refer to `Product` objects built for them through the `IProduct` interface, so they don't need to know the actual class of the objects built for them.

Client: An instance of a client class initiates the actions of the Builder pattern. It calls the `BuilderFactory` class's `CreateBuilder` function. It passes information to `getInstance` that tells it what sort of product it wants. The `CreateBuilder` function determines the `ConcreteBuilder` class to instantiate and returns it to the `Client` object. The `Client` object then passes the `ConcreteBuilder` object to a `Director` object's `Build` function, which builds the desired object.

Concrete Builder: A class in this role is a concrete subclass of the `Abstract Builder` class and implements the `IBuilder` interface. It is used to build a specific kind of data representation for a `Director` object.

AbstractBuilder: A class in this role is the abstract base class of `Concrete Builder` classes. An `AbstractBuilder` class provides common logic that is useful for implementing `ConcreteBuilder` classes in a consistent way.

IBuilder: Client objects access concrete builder objects through an interface in this role. Interfaces in this role define the functions and properties that `Client` and `Director` objects use to interact with `ConcreteBuilder` objects.

Director: A `Director` object calls the functions and subroutines of a `concrete builder` object to provide the concrete builder with content for the product object that it builds.

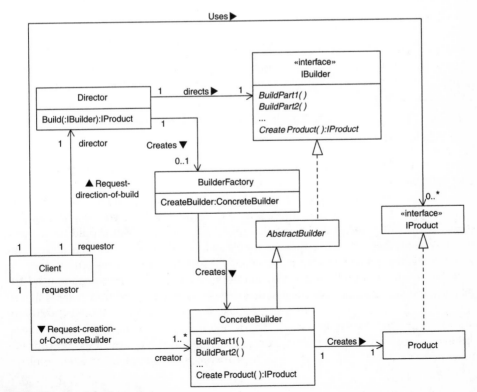

Figure 4.11 Builder Pattern

Figure 4.12 is a collaboration diagram showing how these classes work together.

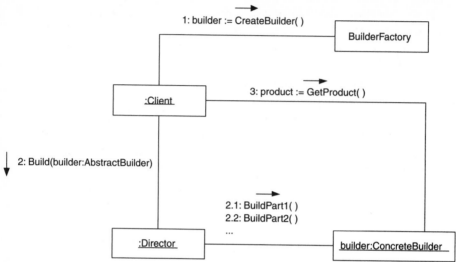

Figure 4.12   Builder Collaboration

IMPLEMENTATION

Some implementations of the Builder pattern do not build objects. Instead, as in the example under the "Context" heading, they generate a file of some sort. In such applications of the Builder pattern, there is no IProduct interface and there are no Product classes.

The Build Process

There are two fundamentally different ways to organize the process of building the product. One way is first build objects that describe everything about the final product, except those things that are specific to the kind of product to build. For example, if the goal is to create some kind of file containing formatted text, you might create a sequence of strings and other objects that describe how the strings should be formatted. You could then pass the sequence of objects to an appropriate builder object that would generate rich text, PostScript, or whatever sort of text file is desired.

If the product to build is relatively simple, first creating an intermediate product that is independent of the ultimate product to be produced may be more trouble that it is worth. Instead, it may be simpler just to describe the product to be built directly to the ConcreteBuilder object. If you decide on this approach, the biggest implementation issue for the Builder pattern becomes designing the set of functions and subroutines that the IBuilder interface defines to provide content to concrete builder objects. These functions and subroutines can be a major concern because there may be an excessive number of them. They should be general enough to allow all reasonable data representations to be constructed. On the other hand, an excessively general set of methods can be more difficult to implement and to use. The consideration of generality versus difficulty of implementation raises these issues in the implementation phase:

- Each content-describing function declared by the `IBuilder` interface may be provided with a default do-nothing implementation by the `Abstract Builder` class. However, not providing implementation in the `Abstract Builder` class allows concrete builder classes to inherit functions and subroutines as `MustOverride`, which causes the compiler to force programmers to supply an implementation. Forcing concrete builder classes to provide implementations for functions and subroutines is good in those cases where they provide essential information about content. It prevents implementers of those classes from forgetting to implement those functions and subroutines.

- However, functions and subroutines that provide optional content or supplementary information about the structure of the content may be unnecessary or even inappropriate for some data representations. Providing a default do-nothing implementation for such functions and subroutines saves effort in the implementation of concrete builder classes that do not need such functions and subroutines. See the Null Object pattern for more information about this technique.

- Organizing concrete builder classes so that calls to content-providing functions and subroutines simply add data to the product object is often good enough. In some cases, there is no simple way to tell the builder where in the finished product a particular piece of the product will go. In those situations, it may be simplest to have the content-providing function return an object to the director that encapsulates such a piece of the product. The director object can then pass the object to another content-providing function in a way that implies the position of the piece of the product within the whole product.

CONSEQUENCES

- ☺ Content determination and the construction of a specific data representation are independent of each other. The data representation of the product can change without any impact on the objects that provide the content. Builder objects can work with different content-providing objects without any changes.

- The Builder pattern provides finer control over construction than other patterns such as Factory Method by giving the director object step-by-step control over creation of the product object. Other patterns simply create the entire object in one step.

.NET API USAGE

As you can see from the example in the "Context" section, the .NET Framework provides support for the Builder pattern. The Visual Studio .NET development environment uses that support.

The `VBCodeProvider` class and `CSharpCodeProvider` class fill the `Builder Factory` role. They each have a function that creates an object that implements the `ICodeGenerator` interface. The `ICodeGenerator` interface fills the `IBuilder` role. The `ICodeGenerator` interface declares functions for generating source code. Classes that implement the `ICodeGenerator` interface fill the `ConcreteBuilder` role.

The implementation of the Builder pattern supported through these classes and interface does not include any interface to fill the `IProduct` role or classes to fill the `Product` role. `ICodeGenerator` objects do not create objects to encapsulate source code. Instead, they write the source code using a `TextWriter` object, which generally sends the output to a file. Similarly, no class fills the `Director` role. No `Director` class is needed because the name, attributes, members, members' statements, and so on are fully described by the already created objects that are passed to the methods of `ICodeGenerator` objects.

CODE EXAMPLE

Let us look at some sample code that implements the design from the context section in Figure 4.10. Here is part of the `WrapperGenerator` class:

```
' This class is responsible for generating source code for
' classes that wrap interfaces or other classes in a way that
' is suitble for coding a proxy or decorator class.
Public Class WrapperGenerator
    ' A model of the code to be generated.
    Private codeModel As CodeNamespace

    ' The name of the generated class's private instance variable
    Private Const VAR_NAME As String = "myWrappedObject"

    ' The name of the generated class's protected readonly property for
    ' accessing the wrapped object
    Private Const PROP_NAME As String = "WrappedObject"

    ' The argument for this constructor is the Type of the
    ' class or interface that this object will generate a
    ' wrapper for.
    Public Sub New(ByVal base As Type)
        codeModel = GenerateCodeModel(base)
    End Sub
```

The `WrapperGenerator` class's constructor calls a function named `Generate CodeModel`, which creates objects that describe a wrapper class for the interface described by its argument. It sets the instance variable `codeModel` to refer to these objects.

After a `WrapperGenerator` object is constructed, other objects can pass an `ICodeGenerator` object to the `WrapperGenerator` object's `GenerateCode` subroutine. The `GenerateCode` subroutine passes the description of the wrapper class to the `ICodeGenerator` object. The `ICodeGenerator` object takes the description of the wrapper class and generates source code for the wrapper class. The language of the source code depends entirely on the class of the `ICodeGenerator` object, which is something that the `WrapperGenerator` object does not know or care about.

```
Public Sub GenerateCode(ByVal generator As CodeDomProvider)
    Dim options As New CodeGeneratorOptions()
    generator.GenerateCodeFromNamespace(codeModel, _
                                        Console.Out, _
                                        options)

End Sub
...
End Class
```

Here is very simple client code that uses the `WrapperGenerator` class:

```
Sub Main()
    Dim w As WrapperGenerator = New
WrapperGenerator(GetType(System.IAppDomainSetup))
    w.GenerateCode(CodeDomProvider.CreateProvider("VisualBasic"))
    w.GenerateCode(CodeDomProvider.CreateProvider("CSharp"))
End Sub
```

RELATED PATTERNS

Interface: The Builder pattern uses the Interface pattern to hide the class of an `IProduct` object.

Composite: Typically, the `Product` object built using the Builder pattern is a composite or the object that describes the product to a `ConcreteBuilder` object is a composite.

Factory Method: The Builder pattern uses the Factory Method pattern to decide which concrete builder class to instantiate.

Template Method: The Abstract Builder class is often implemented using the Template Method pattern.

Null Object: Implementations of the Builder pattern must use the Null Object pattern to provide do-nothing implementations of methods.

Visitor: The Visitor pattern may be used to implement the Builder pattern. The Visitor pattern may also be used as an alternative to the Builder pattern.

Strategy: The Builder pattern is a specialized form of the Strategy pattern.

Prototype

This pattern was previously described in [GoF95].

SYNOPSIS

The Prototype pattern allows an object to create customized objects without knowing their exact class or the details of how to create them. It works by giving prototypical objects to an object that initiates the creation of objects. The creation-initiating object then creates objects by asking the prototypical objects to copy themselves.

CONTEXT

Suppose that you are designing a CAD program that allows users to draw diagrams from a palette of symbols. The program will have a core set of built-in symbols. However, people with different and specialized interests will use the program. The core set of symbols will not be adequate for people with a specialized interest. These people will want additional symbols that are specific to their interests. Most users of this program will have a specialized interest. It must be possible to provide additional sets of symbols for users to add to the program.

This gives you the problem of how to provide these palettes of additional symbols. You can easily organize things so that all symbols, both core and additional, are all descended from a common ancestor class. This will give the rest of your diagram-drawing program a consistent way to manipulate symbol objects. It does leave open the question of how the program will create these objects. Creating objects such as these is often more complicated than simply instantiating a class. It may also involve setting property values or combining objects to form a composite object.

A solution is to provide the drawing program with previously created objects to use as prototypes for creating similar objects. The most important requirement for objects to be used as prototypes is that their class implements the `ICloneable` interface. The `ICloneable` interface declares a function called `Clone` that is supposed to return a new object that is a copy of the original object. Figure 4.13 shows how this is organized.

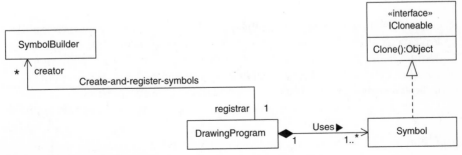

Figure 4.13   Symbol Prototype

The drawing program maintains a collection of prototypical Symbol objects. It uses the Symbol objects by cloning them. SymbolBuilder objects create Symbol objects and register them with the drawing program.

FORCES

☺ A system must be able to create objects without knowing their exact class, how they are created, or what data they represent.

☺ The system does not know which classes to be instantiated until run time, when they are acquired on the fly by techniques like dynamic linkage.

☺ The following approaches to allowing the creation of a large variety of objects are undesirable:

■ The classes that initiate the creation of objects directly create the objects. This makes them aware of and dependent on a large number of other classes.

■ The classes that initiate the creation of objects create the objects indirectly through a factory method class. A factory method that is able to create a large variety of objects may be very large and difficult to maintain.

■ The classes that initiate the creation of objects create the objects indirectly through an abstract factory class. In order for an abstract factory to be able to create a large variety of objects, it must have a large variety of concrete factory classes in a hierarchy that parallels the classes to be instantiated.

☺ The different objects that a system must create may be instances of the same class that contain different state information or data content.

SOLUTION

Enable a class to create objects that implement a known interface by giving it a prototypical instance of each kind of object it will create. It is then able to create new objects by cloning a prototypical instance.

Figure 4.14 shows the organization of the Prototype pattern. Here are descriptions of the roles these classes and interfaces play in the Prototype pattern:

Client: The client class represents the rest of the program for the purposes of the Prototype pattern. The client class needs to create objects that it knows little about. Client classes will have a method that can be called to add a prototypical object to a client object's collection. In the preceding diagram, this method is indicated with the name RegisterPrototype. However, a name that reflects the sort of object being prototyped, such as RegisterSymbol, is more appropriate in an actual implementation.

Prototype: Classes in this role implement the IPrototype interface and are instantiated for the purpose of being cloned by the client. Classes in this role are commonly abstract classes with a number of concrete subclasses.

Iprotype: All prototype objects must implement the interface that is in this role. The client class interacts with prototype objects through this interface. Interfaces in this role should extend the `Cloneable` interface so that all objects that implement the interface can be cloned.

PrototypeBuilder: This corresponds to any class instantiated to supply prototypical objects to the client object. Such classes should have a name that denotes the type of prototypical object that they build, such as `SymbolBuilder`.

A `PrototypeBuilder` object creates `Prototype` objects. It passes each newly created `Prototype` object to a `Client` object's `RegisterPrototype` function.

IMPLEMENTATION

An essential implementation issue is how the `PrototypeBuilder` objects add objects to a client object's palette of prototypical objects. The simplest strategy is for the client class to provide a function for that purpose for `PrototypeBuilder` objects to call. A possible drawback is that the `PrototypeBuilder` objects will need to know the class of the client object. If this is a problem, the `PrototypeBuilder` objects can be shielded from knowing the exact class of the client objects by providing an interface or abstract class for the client class to implement or inherit.

How to implement the clone operation for the prototypical objects is another important implementation issue. There are two basic strategies for implementing the clone operation:

- Shallow copying means that the variables of the cloned object contain the same values as the variables of the original object and that all object references are to the same objects. In other words, shallow copying copies only the object being cloned, not objects that it refers to. Both the original and a shallow copy refer to the same objects.

- Deep copying means that the variables of the cloned object contain the same values as the variables of the original object, except that variables that refer to objects refer to copies of the objects referred to by the original object. In other words, deep copying copies the object being cloned and the objects that it refers to. A deep copy refers to copies of the objects that the original refers to.

  Implementing deep copying can be tricky. You will need to decide if you want to make deep or shallow copies of the indirectly copied objects. You will also need to be careful about handling any circular references.

Shallow copying is easier to implement because all classes inherit a protected `MemberwiseClone` function from the `Object` class that returns a shallow copy of an object. You can implement the `ICloneable` interface's `Clone` function simply by having it call the implementing class's `MemberwiseClone` function.

Some kinds of objects, such as threads and sockets, cannot be simply copied or shared. Whichever copying strategy is used, if it involves references to such objects then equivalent objects must be constructed for the use of the copied objects.

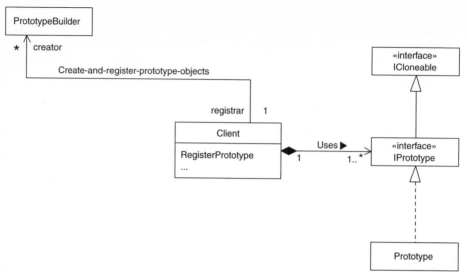

Figure 4.14   Prototype Pattern

Unless the Client object's palette of prototypical objects consists of a fixed number of objects having fixed purposes, it is inconvenient to use individual variables to refer to each prototypical object. It is easier to use a collection object that can contain a dynamically growing or shrinking palette of prototypical objects. A collection object that plays this role in the Prototype pattern is called a *prototype manager*. Prototype managers can be fancier than just a simple collection. They may allow objects to be retrieved by their attribute values or other keys.

If your program will have multiple client objects, then you have another issue to consider. Will the client objects have their own palette of prototypical objects or will they all share the same palette? The answer will depend of the needs of your application.

CONSEQUENCES

☺ A program can dynamically add and remove prototypical objects at run time. This is a distinct advantage offered by none of the other Creational patterns in this book.

☺ A PrototypeBuilder object can simply supply a fixed set of prototypical objects.

☺ A PrototypeBuilder object may provide the additional flexibility of allowing new prototypical objects to be created by object composition and changes to the values of object properties.

☺ The client object may also be able to create new kinds of prototypical objects. In the drawing program example that we looked at previously, the client object could very reasonably allow the user to identify a subdrawing and then turn the subdrawing into a new symbol.

☺ The client class is independent of the exact class of the prototypical objects that it uses. The client class does not need to know the details of how to build the prototypical objects.

☺ The `PrototypeBuilder` objects encapsulate the details of constructing prototypical objects.

☺ By insisting that prototypical objects implement an interface such as `IPrototype`, the Prototype pattern ensures that the prototypical objects provide a consistent set of functions and subroutines for the client object to use.

■ There is no need to organize prototypical objects into any sort of class hierarchy.

☹ A drawback of the Prototype pattern is the additional time spent writing `PrototypeBuilder` classes.

☹ Programs that use the Prototype pattern rely on dynamic linkage or similar mechanisms. Installation of programs that rely on dynamic linkage or similar mechanisms can be more complicated. They may require information about their environment that would otherwise not be needed.

.NET API USAGE

One way that .NET supports the Prototype pattern is through the combination of components and serialization.[2] You can have an application that configures and composes components and then serializes the components to a file. Once the components are in a file, they can be used by other applications without those applications knowing anything about how the components were originally created.

CODE EXAMPLE

Suppose that you are writing an interactive role-playing game. That is, a game that allows the user to interact with simulated characters. One of the expectations for this game is that people who play it will grow tired of interacting with the same characters and want to interact with new characters. For this reason, you are also developing an add-on to the game that consists of a few pregenerated characters and a program to generate additional characters.

The characters in the game are instances of a relatively small number of classes such as Hero, Fool, Villain, and Monster. What makes instances of the same class different from each other is the different attribute values that are set for them, such as the images that are used to represent them, height, weight, intelligence, and dexterity.

Figure 4.15 shows some of the classes involved in the game.

---

[2]Serialization is a facility that allows objects to be written as a stream of bytes from which a copy of the objects can be created.

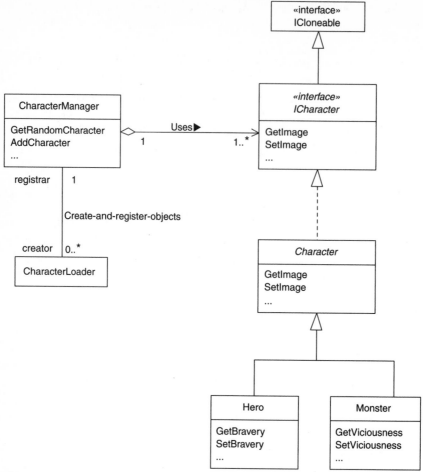

Figure 4.15 Prototype Example

Here is the code:

```
Imports System
Imports System.Drawing
Imports System.Collections
Imports System.IO
Imports System.Runtime.Serialization.Formatters.Binary


' All classes whose instances can participate as characters in
' the game must implement this interface
Public Interface ICharacter
    Inherits ICloneable
    Property Name() As String
    Property Image() As Image
    Property Strength() As Integer
    ...
End Interface 'ICharacter
```

```vbnet
' An abstract class for implementing game characters
Public MustInherit Class Character
    Implements ICharacter
    Private myName As String
    Private myImage As Image
    Private myStrength As Integer

    ' The character's name
    Public Property Name() As String Implements ICharacter.Name
        Get
            Return myName
        End Get
        Set(ByVal Value As String)
            myName = Value
        End Set
    End Property

    ' An image of the character
    Public Property Image() As Image Implements ICharacter.Image
        Get
            Return myImage
        End Get
        Set(ByVal Value As Image)
            myImage = Value
        End Set
    End Property

    ' The character's physical strength
    Public Property Strength() As Integer _
                    Implements ICharacter.Strength
        Get
            Return myStrength
        End Get
        Set(ByVal Value As Integer)
            myStrength = Value
        End Set
    End Property

    ' Return a copy of this Character object.
    Public Function Clone() As Object _
                    Implements ICloneable.Clone
        Return Me.MemberwiseClone()
    End Function

    ...
End Class 'Character

' A class for representing hero characters
Public Class Hero
    Inherits Character
    Private myBravery As Integer
```

```vbnet
    Public Property Bravery() As Integer
        Get
            Return myBravery
        End Get
        Set(ByVal Value As Integer)
            myBravery = Value
        End Set
    End Property
End Class 'Hero


' An instance of this class keeps a collection of prototypical
' character object and creates new character objects by copying
' the prototypical objects.
Public Class CharacterManager
    Private characters As New ArrayList()
    Private Shared rand As New Random()


    '
    ' Get a copy of random character from the collection.
    '
    ReadOnly Property RandomCharacter() As Character
        Get
            Dim i As Integer = rand.Next(characters.Count)
            Dim c As Character = CType(characters(i), Character)
            Return CType(c.Clone(), Character)
        End Get
    End Property


    '
    ' Add a prototypical object to the collection.
    '
    Public Sub AddCharacter(ByVal character As Character)
        characters.Add(character)
    End Sub
End Class 'CharacterManager


' This class loads character objects and adds them to the
' the CharacterManager.
'
Class CharacterLoader
    Private mgr As CharacterManager

    'cm - The CharacterManager this object will work with.
    Sub New(ByVal cm As CharacterManager)
        mgr = cm
    End Sub

    ' Load character objects from the specified file.
    ' Since failure only affects the rest of the program to
    ' the extent that new character objects are not loaded,
    ' we need not throw any exceptions.
```

```
Function loadCharacters(ByVal fname As String) As Integer
    Dim formatter As New BinaryFormatter()
    Dim reader As Stream = File.OpenRead(fname)
    Dim objectCount As Integer = 0 ' Number of objects loaded
    ' If construction of InputStream fails, just return
    Try
        While True
            Dim o As Object = formatter.Deserialize(reader)
            If TypeOf o Is Character Then
                mgr.AddCharacter(CType(o, Character))
                objectCount += 1
            End If
        End While
    Finally
        If reader IsNot Nothing Then
            reader.Close()
        End If
    End Try
    Return objectCount
End Function 'loadCharacters

End Class 'CharacterLoader
```

RELATED PATTERNS

Composite: The Prototype pattern is often used with the Composite pattern. The composite is used to organize prototype objects.

Abstract Factory: The Abstract Factory pattern can be a good alternative to the Prototype pattern if the dynamic changes that the Prototype pattern allows to the prototypical object palette are unneeded.

`PrototypeBuilder` classes may use the Abstract Factory pattern to create a set of prototypical objects.

Façade: The client class commonly acts as façade that separates the other classes that participate in the Prototype pattern from the rest of the program.

Factory Method: The Factory Method pattern can be an alternative to the Prototype pattern when the palette of prototypical objects never contains more than one object.

Decorator: The Prototype pattern is often used with the Decorator pattern to compose prototypical objects.

Singleton

This pattern was previously described in [GoF95].

SYNOPSIS

The Singleton pattern ensures that only one instance of a class is created. All objects using an instance of the class use the same instance.

CONTEXT

Suppose that you are designing part of an e-commerce framework to manage monetary amounts. A monetary amount is made up of a number and a currency. You decide there will be a class whose primary responsibility is to create objects to encapsulate a monetary amount. It will also be responsible for converting monetary amounts from one currency to another. You decide to call this class MonetaryAmountFactory.

The initial implementation of the MonetaryAmountFactory class will have a small set of currencies hard-wired. However, because the class will eventually be required to support more currencies and the currencies that countries use may change occasionally, you anticipate that the class will eventually be driven by data from a database table.

The fact that the MonetaryAmountFactory class will eventually involve the management of external data raises some issues regarding the design of the Monetary AmountFactory class. You want to be sure that clients of the MonetaryAmount Factory class all use the same set of currencies. You also want to avoid fetching multiple copies of the currency table, since that is a pure waste of memory.

Figure 4.16 shows the organization of the MonetaryAmountFactory class. The constructor for the MonetaryAmountFactory class is private. This prevents another class from directly creating an instance of the MonetaryAmountFactory class. Instead, to get an instance of the MonetaryAmountFactory class, other classes must call its getInstance function. The getInstance function is a shared function that always returns the same instance of the MonetaryAmountFactory class. The instance it returns is the instance referred to by its private shared variable my Instance.

The rest of the MonetaryAmountFactory class's functions are responsible for creating monetary amounts and converting monetary amounts from one currency to another. Since the MonetaryAmountFactory class will have only one instance, all of its clients will use the same instance. Only one copy of the currency tables will be needed.

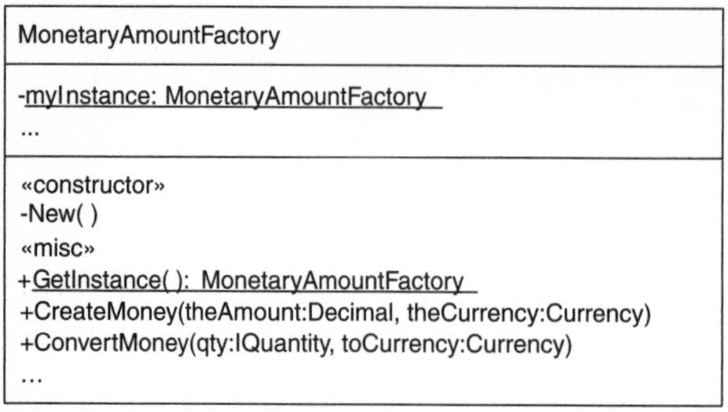

```
┌─────────────────────────────────────────────────────┐
│ MonetaryAmountFactory                                │
├─────────────────────────────────────────────────────┤
│ -myInstance: MonetaryAmountFactory                   │
│ ...                                                  │
├─────────────────────────────────────────────────────┤
│ «constructor»                                        │
│ -New( )                                              │
│ «misc»                                               │
│ +GetInstance( ): MonetaryAmountFactory               │
│ +CreateMoney(theAmount:Decimal, theCurrency:Currency)│
│ +ConvertMoney(qty:IQuantity, toCurrency:Currency)    │
│ ...                                                  │
└─────────────────────────────────────────────────────┘
```

Figure 4.16   Monetary Amount Factory

FORCES

☺ There must be at least one instance of a class. Even if the functions of your class use no instance data or only shared data, you may need an instance of the class for a variety of reasons. For example, you may want to access the class indirectly through an interface.

☺ There should be no more than one or instance of a class. This may be the case because you want to have only one source of some information. For example, you may want to have a single object that is responsible for generating a sequence of serial numbers.

☺ The one instance of a class must be accessible to all clients of that class.

☹ An object is cheap to create but takes up a lot of memory or continuously uses other resources during its lifetime.

SOLUTION

The Singleton pattern is relatively simple, since it only involves one class. The organization of this class is shown in Figure 4.17.

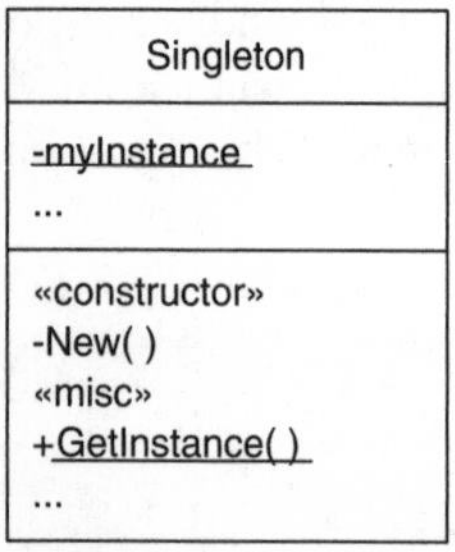

```
┌─────────────────────┐
│      Singleton      │
├─────────────────────┤
│ -myInstance         │
│ ...                 │
├─────────────────────┤
│ «constructor»       │
│ -New( )             │
│ «misc»              │
│ +GetInstance( )     │
│ ...                 │
└─────────────────────┘
```

Figure 4.17   Singleton

A singleton class has a shared variable that refers to the one instance of the class. This instance is created when the class is loaded into memory. You should implement the class in a way that prevents other classes from creating additional instances. That means ensuring that all of the class's constructors are private.

To access the one instance of a singleton class, the class provides a shared method, typically called `GetInstance` or `GetClassname`, which returns a reference to the one instance of the class.

IMPLEMENTATION

Though the Singleton pattern involves a relatively simple solution, there are a surprising number of subtleties in its implementation.

Private Constructor: To enforce the nature of a singleton class, you must code the class in a way that prevents other classes from directly creating instances of the class. A way to accomplish this is to declare the class's constructors private. Be careful to declare at least one private constructor. If a class does not declare any constructors, then the compiler automatically generates a default public constructor.

Lazy Instantiation: A common variation on the Singleton pattern occurs in situations where the instance of a singleton may not be needed. You do not know if the program will need to use the singleton instance until the first time that the `GetInstance` function is called. In situations like this, postpone creation of the instance until the first call to `GetInstance`.

Allowing More than One Instance: Another variation on the Singleton pattern stems from the fact that it has a class's instantiation policy encapsulated in the class itself. Because the instantiation policy is encapsulated in the class's `GetInstance` function, it is possible to vary the creation policy. Some possible policies are to have `GetInstance` alternately return one of two instances or to periodically create a new instance for `GetInstance` to return.

This sort of situation can come up when you are using small fixed individual objects to represent external resources, and you want to balance the load between them. When you generalize this to an arbitrary or variable number of objects, you get the Object Pool pattern.

Making Copies of a Singleton: A singleton object is usually intended to be the only instance of its class. Even in the case that you allow more than one instance of a singleton object, you generally want to ensure that creation of singleton objects is entirely under the control of the singleton class's `GetInstance` object. This means that you don't want any other classes making copies of a singleton object.

One consequence of this is that a singleton class should not implement the `System.ICloneable` interface or provide any other way for other classes to make a copy of its instance.

Serialization is a mechanism for converting the contents of objects into a stream of bytes or Extensible Markup Language (XML). Deserialization is a mechanism for converting a stream of bytes or XML created by serialization to objects that have the same contents as the original objects.

Serialization can be used to copy objects, but copying is not usually the intended use of serialization. The two most common uses for serialization are:

- Serialization is used to make objects persistent by writing them to a file as a stream of bytes. This allows persisted objects with the same contents to be re-created later on.

- Serialization is used to support remote procedure calls using Simple Object Access Protocol (SOAP). SOAP uses serialization to pass argument values to remote procedure calls and also to pass the return value back to a remote caller.

Both of these uses are things that you will generally not want to do with a singleton object. In general, singleton objects should not be included in a serialized stream of objects. You can ensure this by never directly serializing a singleton object and by not having any classes save a reference to a singleton object in its instance variables. Instead, have clients of a singleton class call the singleton class's getInstance methods every time they wants to access a singleton object.

Concurrent GetInstance Calls

If there is any chance that multiple threads may call a singleton class's get Instance method at the same time, then you will need to ensure that the get Instance method does not create multiple instances of the singleton class. Consider the following code:

```
Public Class Foo
    Private Shared myInstance As Foo
    ...
    Public Shared Function GetInstance() As Foo
        If myInstance Is Nothing Then
            myInstance = New Foo()
        End If
        Return myInstance
    End Function
    ...
End Class
```

If two threads call the GetInstance function at the same time and there were no previous calls to the GetInstance function, then both calls will see that the value of myInstance is Nothing, and both calls will create an instance of Foo. To avoid this problem, you can use a SyncLock statement to ensure that only one thread at a time is able to test the value of myInstance. This ensures that only one instance of Foo is created.

When you use a `SyncLock` statement for this purpose, you will normally have it get a lock on the class that contains the `GetInstance` function. Here is what the preceding example would look like with the addition of a `SyncLock` statement:

```
Public Class Foo
    Private Shared myInstance As Foo
    ...
    Public Shared Function GetInstance() As Foo
        SyncLock GetType(Foo)
            If myInstance Is Nothing Then
                myInstance = New Foo()
            End If
        End SyncLock
        Return myInstance
    End Function
    ...
End Class
```

Using a `SyncLock` statement does add a small amount of overhead by getting a lock before it proceeds.

CONSEQUENCES

☺ No more than one instance of a singleton class exists.

☺ The singleton class's `GetInstance` method encapsulates the creation policy for the singleton class. Classes that use a singleton class do not depend on the details of the singleton class's instantiation.

• Other classes that want a reference to the one instance of the singleton class must get that instance by calling the class's `GetInstance` function, rather than by constructing the instance themselves.

☹ Subclassing a singleton class is awkward and results in imperfectly encapsulated classes. In order to subclass a singleton class, you must give it a constructor that is not private. Also, since shared functions cannot be overridden, a subclass of a singleton class must leave its base class's `GetInstance` function exposed.

.NET API USAGE

The `System.DBNull` class is a singleton. The value of its shared `Value` property is the class's single instance.

CODE EXAMPLE

The code example for this pattern comes from the e-commerce mini-framework that appears in Appendix A on this book's Web site. It is an implementation of the class design discussed under the "Context" heading.

The `Currency` class used in this code example is defined in Appendix A. It should not be confused with the Currency type that was supported in older versions of VB.

```vb
' This class is a singleton that is responsible for creating
' Quantity objects to represent monetary amounts.
Public Class MonetaryAmountFactory
    Inherits AbstractAmountFactory


    ' The single instance of this class.
    Private Shared ReadOnly myInstance As MonetaryAmountFactory _
        = New MonetaryAmountFactory()


    Private Shared ReadOnly myConverter As ICurrencyConversion _
        = New HardwiredCurrencyConversion()
    ...
    ' Private constructor to ensure that only this class's GetInstance
    ' method can instantiate this class.
    '
    Private Sub New()
        ...
    End Sub
    ...
    ' Return the single instance of this class.
    Public Shared Function GetInstance() As MonetaryAmountFactory
        Return myInstance
    End Function


    ' Return a Quantity that encapsulates the given amount and
    ' currency.
    Public Function CreateMoney( _
                    ByVal theAmount As Decimal, _
                    ByVal theCurrency As Currency) _
                As IQuantity
        Dim unit As MeasurementUnit _
            = CurrencyToMeasurementUnit(theCurrency)
        Return CreateQuantity(theAmount, unit)
    End Function
    ...
    ' Convert the given Quantity of money to the specified
    ' currency.
    Public Function _
        ConvertMoney(ByVal theQty As IQuantity, _
                    ByVal theCurrency As Currency, _
```

```
                         ByVal theMaxPrecision As Integer, _
                         ByVal time As DateTime) As IQuantity
            ...
        End Function
        ...
    End Class
```

RELATED PATTERNS

You can use the Singleton pattern with many other patterns. In particular, it is often used with the Abstract Factory, Builder, and Prototype patterns.

Cache Management: The Singleton pattern has some similarity to the Cache Management pattern. A Singleton is functionally similar to a Cache that only contains one object.

Object Pool: The Object Pool pattern is for managing an arbitrarily large collection of similar objects rather than just a single object.

Object Pool

This pattern was previously described in [Grand02].

SYNOPSIS

Manage the reuse of objects when a type of object is expensive to create or only a limited number of a kind of object can be created.

CONTEXT

Suppose that you are working for a company that has a large number of legacy mainframe applications it wants to make accessible as ADO.NET data providers. The motivation for this is to make the mainframe data as accessible as to .NET applications as data in SQL Server or any .NET-compatible database.

Creating an ADO.NET data provider involves writing classes that implement a few core interfaces. One of those interfaces is `System.Data.IDbConnection`. Classes that implement the `IDbConnection` interface are responsible for creating a connection with a data source, passing commands to the data source, returning results from the data source, and providing a context for transactions.

You have been given the task of designing the classes that will implement the `IDbConnection` interface.

You anticipate that the most expensive operation that `IDbConnection` object will perform is opening a connection. You expect that opening a connection will be relatively expensive for a few reasons:

- It can take a few seconds to open each connection. Opening a connection can entail establishing a network connection, logging in to the mainframe application, and performing whatever additional navigation and handshaking the application requires before you can start requesting data from it.

- The more connections there are to an application, the more resources are consumed on the mainframe side.

- Each open connection will consume resources on the client, including memory and the CPU cycles needed to maintain the network connection.

Because opening a connection is such an expensive operation, you want classes that implement the IDbConnection interface to reuse an existing connection rather than open a new one, whenever possible. However, you must design implementations of the IDbConnection interface to reuse connections in a way that is transparent to ADO.NET.

Your implementation will use a strategy to manage connections based on the premise that connections opened using the same connection string are interchangeable. So long as a database connection is in a state that allows it to convey a query to the database, it does not matter which connection associated with the same connection string is used. Using this observation, you will design implementations of the IDbConnection interface to have two layers.

A class called Connection will implement the upper layer. ADO.NET will directly use Connection objects. A Connection object's ConnectionString property will identify an application. However, the Connection object will not directly encapsulate a connection. Only while a Connection object is being used to send a command to an application and fetch the result will it be paired with an IConnectionImpl object. IConnectionImpl objects encapsulate an actual connection. This is the lower layer of the implementation.

The Connection class will delegate the responsibility for creating and reusing ConnectionImpl objects to other classes. A class named ConnectionPool will be responsible for maintaining a pool of ConnectionImpl objects that are not currently paired up with a Connection object. A ConnectionImpl object will be created only when a Connection object needs to be paired up with a ConnectionImpl object and the pool of ConnectionImpl objects is empty. The class diagram in Figure 4.18 shows this design.

A Connection object calls the ConnectionPool object's AcquireImpl function when it needs an IConnectionImpl object, passing its connection string. If any ConnectionImpl objects in the ConnectionPool object's collection were created with the same connection string, the ConnectionPool object returns one of those objects. If there are no such IConnectionImpl objects in the ConnectionPool object's collection, then the ConnectionPool object tries to create one and return it. It tries to create an IConnectionImpl object by passing the connection string to the ConnectionFactory object's CreateConnectionImpl function. If it is unable to create a ConnectionImpl object, the ConnectionPool object waits until an existing ConnectionImpl object is returned to the pool by a call to the releaseImpl subroutine and then it returns that object.

The ConnectionPool class is a singleton. There should only be one instance of the ConnectionPool class. The class's constructor is private. Other classes access the one instance of the ConnectionPool class by calling its getInstance function, which is shared.

There are many reasons a `ConnectionPool` object's `AcquireImpl` function may be unable to create a `ConnectionImpl` object. Among those may be a limit on the number of `ConnectionImpl` objects it can create that connect to the same application. The reason for the limit is to be able to guarantee that an application will be able to support a minimum number of clients. Since there will be a maximum number of connections each application can support, limiting the number of connections each client can have to an application allows you to guarantee support for a minimum number of clients.

FORCES

☺   A program may not create more than a limited number of instances of a particular class.

☺   Creating instances of a particular class is sufficiently expensive that creating new instances of that class should be avoided.

☺   A program can avoid creating some objects by reusing objects that it has finished with rather than letting them be garbage collected.

☺   Some instances of a class are interchangeable. If you have multiple instances on hand that meet certain criteria, you can arbitrarily choose one to use for a purpose. It does not matter which one you choose.

☺   Resources can be managed centrally by a single object or in a decentralized way by multiple objects. It is easier to achieve predictable results by managing resources centrally by a single object.

☹   Some objects consume resources that are in short supply. Some objects may consume a lot of memory. Some objects may periodically check to see if some condition is true, thereby consuming CPU cycles and perhaps network bandwidth. If the resources an object consumes are in short supply, then it may be important that the object stops using the resource when the object is not being used.

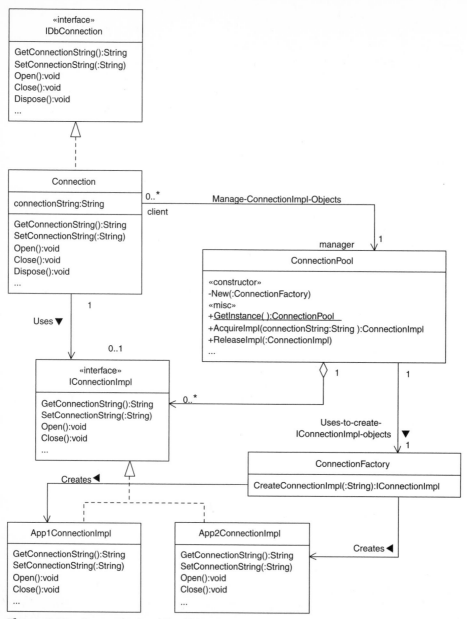

Figure 4.18 ConnectionImpl Pool Management

SOLUTION

If instances of a class can be reused, avoid creating instances of the class by reusing them. The class diagram in Figure 4.19 shows the roles that classes play in the Object Pool pattern.

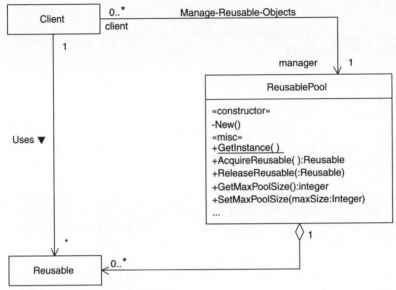

Figure 4.19   Object Pool Pattern

Here are descriptions of the roles classes play in the Object Pool pattern, as shown in Figure 4.19.

Reusable

Instances of classes in this role collaborate with other objects for a limited amount of time, then they are no longer needed for that collaboration. An important characteristic of `Reusable` object is that they are, in some sense, interchangeable. It may be that all `Reusable` objects are interchangeable. An example of this would be objects that control access to phone lines. Assuming that the phone lines they control are all equivalent in the sense that any phone call can be made on any phone line, it does not matter which object is used.

It may be the case that `Reusable` objects having the same value for some property are interchangeable. An example of this is contained in the example under the "Context" heading. In that example, `IConnectionImpl` objects that have the same value for their connection string are interchangeable.

Client

Instances of classes in this role use `Reusable` objects. In many applications of the Object Pool pattern, clients do not interact directly with reusable objects. Instead, they interact with an intermediary that hides the use of the object pool. This is discussed in more detail in the "Implementation" section.

ReusablePool

Instances of classes in this role manage `Reusable` objects for use by `Client` objects. It is desirable to keep all `Reusable` objects that are not currently in use in the same object pool so that they can be managed by one coherent policy. To achieve this, the `ReusablePool` class should be a singleton class. Its constructor(s) are private, which forces other classes to call its `getInstance` function to get the one instance of the `ReusablePool` class.

A `Client` object calls a `ReusablePool` object's `acquireReusable` function when it needs a `Reusable` object. A `ReusablePool` object maintains a collection of `Reusable` objects that are not currently in use. If there are any `Reusable` objects in the pool when the `acquireReusable` function is called, it removes a `Reusable` object from the pool and returns it. If the pool is empty, then the `acquireReusable` method creates a `Reusable` object if it can. If the `acquireReusable` method cannot create a new `Reusable` object, then it waits until a `Reusable` object is returned to the collection.

`Client` objects pass a `Reusable` object to a `ReusablePool` object's `release Reusable` subroutine when they are finished with the object. The `releaseReusable` subroutine returns a `Reusable` object to the pool of `Reusable` objects that are not in use.

In many applications of the Object Pool pattern, there are reasons for limiting the total number of `Reusable` objects that may exist. In such cases, the `ReusablePool` object that creates `Reusable` objects is responsible for not creating more than a specified maximum number of `Reusable` objects. If `ReusablePool` objects are responsible for limiting the number of objects they will create, then the `ReusablePool` class will have a property for specifying the maximum number of objects to be created. That property is indicated in the preceding diagram as `maxPoolSize`.

IMPLEMENTATION

Here are some of the issues to consider when implementing the Object Pool pattern.

Hiding the Object Pool

In many implementations of the Object Pool pattern, you do not want the classes that use the reusable object to be burdened with the details of having to know how to use the object pool in addition to having to know how to use the reusable objects. To organize your design so that clients of reusable objects do not have to be aware of the object pool, you can use the Façade pattern.

The design shown in Figure 4.18 contains an example of this. Client classes (not shown) interact with `Connection` objects. The client classes do not know or need to know that the `Connection` class is just a façade that hides the creation and pooling of the objects that do the real work.

Delegating Object Creation

One of the responsibilities of a class in the `ReusablePool` role is creating new reusable objects when appropriate. It is common for a `ReusablePool` class to delegate the responsibility for creating objects to another class. There are two reasons for doing this:

- If creating the objects is much more complicated than invoking the objects' constructor, then delegating the responsibility for object creation to another class can make the `ReusablePool` class more cohesive.

- Removing the responsibility for object creation from the `ReusablePool` class may result in more opportunities to reuse the `ReusablePool` class.

Ensuring a Maximum Number of Instances

In many cases, the object that manages an object pool is supposed to limit the number of instances of a class that can be created. It is easy for an object to limit the number of objects it creates. However, to robustly enforce a limit on the total number of objects created, the object responsible for managing the object pool must be the only object able to create those objects.

You can ensure that a class is instantiated only by the class that manages the object pool. You can do that by making the managed class's constructor(s) private and implementing the pool management class as a member of the managed class. If you do not have control over the structure of the class whose instances will be managed, you may be able to add that structure to the class through inheritance.

Data Structure

When there is a limit on the number of objects that may be created or just a limit on the size of the object pool, using a simple array is usually the best way to implement the object pool. When there is no limit on the size of the object pool, using an `ArrayList` is an appropriate way to implement the object pool.

Limiting the Size of the Pool

If you do not take any measures to limit the size of an object pool, there may be circumstances in which it will grow to an excessively large size, thereby consuming memory that could be put to better use.

There may be an occasional spike in the number of reusable objects that are needed. Perhaps there are only five to seven objects needed most of the time but occasionally more than 100 are needed. In such situations, it may be wasteful to keep over 100 objects around when 99 percent of the time fewer than 10 objects are needed.

You can manage such a situation by placing a limit on the number of objects that may be kept in an object pool. Such a limit is generally less than the number of objects that the pool will allow to exist at once.

When a pool-managed object is no longer needed, it is released back to the ReusablePool object. If the pool already contains its maximum number of objects, then the released object is not added to the pool. If the object is tying up any external resources, the pool tells the object to release the external resources. Since the object is not added to the pool, the object may become eligible for garbage collection at this time.

Managing Stateful Objects

An assumption that underlies the use of an object pool is that the objects it manages are interchangeable. When a client acquires an object from a pool, it expects the object to be in known state. If it is possible for clients to alter the state of pool-managed objects, there has to be a way for the pool to ensure that its objects return to the expected state. These are the most common ways this is done:

- The pool explicitly resets the state of an object before a client acquires the object. This may not be possible in some cases. For example, once a connection object is closed, it may not be possible for the pool to reopen it. Besides, you really don't want clients closing the connection.

- If your implementation of the Object Pool pattern uses a façade class that hides reusable classes from their clients, then you simply do not provide a way for the façade class to modify the state of reusable objects in a problematic way.

- If you are not using a façade class, you can prevent clients from changing the state of pool-managed objects by using the Decorator pattern. For example, to do this with a connection object, you would create a wrapper object that implements the IDbConnection interface. The wrapper object would delegate all of its functions and subroutines to a real connection object, except for the close subroutine. You would implement the close subroutine so that it does nothing.

CONSEQUENCES

- ☺ Using the Object Pool pattern avoids the creation of objects. It works best when the demand for objects does not vary greatly over time.

- ☺ Keeping the logic to manage the creation and reuse of a class's instances in a separate class from the class whose instances are being managed results in a more cohesive design. It eliminates interactions between the implementation of a creation and reuse policy and the implementation of the managed class's functionality.

CODE EXAMPLE

The code example is a generic implementation of an object pool. Because all the objects in an object pool are supposed to be interchangeable, being able to specify the type of object that will be pooled ensures consistency at the type level.

```
Imports System
Imports System.Collections
Imports System.Threading


' Interface for object pools.
Public Interface IObjectPool(Of objectType)
    ' Number of objects in pool.
    ReadOnly Property Count() As Integer

    ' Returns an object from the pool or Nothing if the pool is empty
    Function GetObject() As objectType

    ' Return an object from the pool.  If the pool is empty
    ' waits until an object is put in the pool.
    Function WaitForObject() As objectType

    ' Return an object to the pool.
    Sub Release(ByVal o As objectType)
End Interface 'IObjectPool


' This is an abstract baseclass for classes that implement the
' IObjectPool class.  It provides common logic for Object
' pools.
Public MustInherit Class AbstractObjectPool(Of objectType)
    Implements IObjectPool(Of objectType)

    ' Because this class is not written to work with a specific
    ' class, it does not know how to create the objects it
    ' manages. Instead, it delegates the responsibility for
    ' creating objects to an object that implements an interface
    ' named ICreation. The ICreation interface is listed towards
    ' the end of this section.
    Private creator As ICreation(Of objectType)

    ' creator - The object that the pool will delegate the
    '     responsibility for creating objects that it will
    '     manage.
    Public Sub New(ByVal creator As ICreation(Of objectType))
        Me.creator = creator
    End Sub

    ' The object to lock to ensure single threaded access to the
    ' pool's data structure.
    Protected MustOverride ReadOnly Property SyncRoot() _
                                                As Object

    ' Return true if it is ok for this object pool to create
    ' another pool-managed object.
    Protected MustOverride Function OkToCreate() As Boolean

    '
    ' Create an object to be managed by this pool.
    '
```

```vb
Protected Overridable Function createObject() As objectType
    Return creator.Create()
End Function 'createObject


' Remove an object from the pool array and return it.
' Return Nothing if the pool is empty
Protected MustOverride Function removeObject() As objectType


' Number of objects in pool.
Public MustOverride ReadOnly Property Count() As Integer _
                        Implements IObjectPool(Of objectType).Count


'
' Return an object from the pool.  If there is no object
' in the pool, one is created unless this object pool has a
' creation policy that prevents creating an object in its
' current state.  If the object cannot be created,
' then this method returns Nothing.
'
Public Function GetObject() As objectType _
    Implements IObjectPool(Of objectType).GetObject
    SyncLock SyncRoot
        Dim o As objectType = removeObject()
        If o IsNot Nothing Then Return o
        If OkToCreate() Then Return createObject()
        Return Nothing
    End SyncLock
End Function 'GetObject


'
' Return an object from the pool.  If there is no object
' in the pool, one is created unless this object pool has a
' creation policy that prevents creating an object in its
' current state.  If the object cannot be created,
' then this method waits until an object becomes
' available for reuse.
'
Public Function WaitForObject() As objectType _
    Implements IObjectPool(Of objectType).WaitForObject
    SyncLock SyncRoot
        Dim o As objectType = removeObject()
        If o IsNot Nothing Then Return o
        If OkToCreate() Then Return createObject()
        Do
            ' Wait until notified that an object has
            ' been put back in the pool.
            Monitor.Wait(SyncRoot)
            o = removeObject()
        Loop While o Is Nothing
        Return o
```

```
          End SyncLock
     End Function 'WaitForObject


     ' Return an object to the pool.
     Public MustOverride Sub Release(ByVal o As objectType) _
                              Implements IObjectPool(Of objectType).Release
End Class


'
' This class limits the number of objects.
'
Public Class SizedObjectPool(Of objectType)
     Inherits AbstractObjectPool(Of objectType)

     ' Because there is a definite limit on the number of objects
     ' this class will allow to be awaiting reuse, this class can
     ' use a simple array to contain them. It uses the instance
     ' variable named count to track the number of objects that are
     ' actually awaiting reuse.
     Private myCount As Integer

     ' This array contains the objects that are waiting to be
     ' reused.  It is managed as a stack.
     Private pool() As objectType

     ' Internal operations are synchronized on this object.
     ' See the discussion of the Internal Lock Object pattern for
     ' a more detailed explanation of lock objects.
     Private lockObject As New Object()

     ' The object to lock to ensure single threaded access to the
     ' pool's data structure.
     Protected Overrides ReadOnly Property SyncRoot() As Object
          Get
               Return lockObject
          End Get
     End Property

     ' Return true if it is ok for this object pool to create
     ' another pool-managed object.
     ' This pool does not have a policy of restricting the number of
     ' objects that it allows to exist at any one time, so this method
     ' always returns true.  If there were such a policy, the result of
     ' this method would depend on whether the number of outstanding
     ' objects was less than some maximum value.
     Protected Overrides Function OkToCreate() As Boolean
          Return True
     End Function
```

```vb
' c - The object that the pool will delegate the
'     responsibility for creating objects that it will manage.
' m - Maximum number of currently unused objects that this
'     object pool may contain at once.
'
Public Sub New(ByVal c As ICreation(Of objectType), ByVal m As Integer)
    MyBase.New(c)
    myCount = 0
    pool = New objectType(m) {}
End Sub


'
' the number of objects in the pool that are
' awaiting reuse.
'
Public Overrides ReadOnly Property Count() As Integer
    Get
        Return myCount
    End Get
End Property


' maximum number of objects that may be in the
' pool awaiting reuse.
Public Property Capacity() As Integer
    Get
        Return pool.Length
    End Get
    Set(ByVal Value As Integer)
        If Value <= 0 Then
            Throw New ArgumentException( _
                "Capacity must be greater than zero:" & Value)
        End If
        SyncLock SyncRoot
            ReDim Preserve pool(Value)
        End SyncLock
    End Set
End Property


' Remove an object from the pool array and return it.
' Return Nothing if the pool is empty
Protected Overrides Function removeObject() As objectType
    If Count > 0 Then
        myCount -= 1
        Return pool(Count)
    End If
    Return Nothing
End Function 'removeObject


'
' Release an object to the Pool for reuse.
'
```

```
' o - The object that is available for reuse.
Public Overrides Sub Release(ByVal o As objectType)
    ' no nulls
    If o Is Nothing Then
        Throw New NullReferenceException()
    End If
    SyncLock SyncRoot
        If Count < Capacity Then
            pool(Count) = o
            myCount += 1
            ' Notify a waiting thread that we have put an
            ' object in the pool.
            Monitor.Pulse(SyncRoot)
        End If
    End SyncLock
End Sub 'Release


End Class 'SizedObjectPool


' Object pool classes delegate the creation of new objects to
' this interface.
Public Interface ICreation(Of objectType)
    ' Return a newly created object
    Function Create() As objectType
End Interface 'ICreation
```

RELATED PATTERNS

Cache Management: The Cache Management pattern manages the reuse of specific or unique instances of a class. The Pool pattern manages and creates instances of a class that can be used interchangeably.

Façade: The Façade pattern is often used to hide from the use of an object pool from the classes that use the reusable objects. The `Connection` class in Figure 4.18 is an example of such a façade object.

Factory Method: The Factory Method pattern can be used to encapsulate the creation logic for objects. However, it does not manage them after their creation.

Singleton: Objects that manage object pools are usually singletons.

Thread Pool: The Thread Pool pattern (discussed in [Grand01]) is a specialized form of the Object Pool pattern.

Lock Object: The lock object pattern may be used in the implementation of the Object Pool pattern.

Layered Architecture: The Object Pool pattern is an application of the Layered Architecture pattern described in [BMRSS96].

CHAPTER 5

Partitioning Patterns

Filter (165)
Composite (175)
Read-Only Interface (187)

A common problem-solving strategy is *divide and conquer*. It involves dividing a complex, difficult to solve problem into simpler, easier to solve problems. The patterns in this chapter provide guidance on how to partition classes and interfaces in ways that make it easier to arrive at a good design.

The Filter pattern describes how to organize computations on a data stream in a flexible way that allows you to mix and match different computations on the same data stream.

The Composite pattern provides guidance in how to organize a hierarchy of objects.

The Read-Only Interface pattern describes how to partition the classes that use an object so that those that should be allowed to modify it, can and those that shouldn't be allowed to, can't.

Filter

This pattern was previously described in [BMRSS96].

SYNOPSIS

Objects that have compatible interfaces but perform different transformations and computations on data streams can be dynamically connected to perform arbitrary operations.

CONTEXT

Suppose that you are designing a program for forensic auditors. Forensic auditors examine the records of a company to find evidence of wrongdoing. They typically work under the authority of a court order, and cannot assume that the staff of the company under investigation will help them understand the data.

Data in databases is, at a low level, self-describing. A database's schema contains at least the names of fields and enough information to know how to access them.

Data in application specific flat files can be difficult to make sense of. If there is no description of the files' format, as is often the case, it is necessary to reverse engineer the files' organization and format.

You have been given the task of creating a program to allow auditors to transform data in files in a variety of ways that may help them make sense of the contents of a flat file. The program should allow an auditor to put files through a sequence of specified transformations, with the idea of transforming the file into a form that the can be understood by one of the auditor's other tools. To implement this requirement, you decide to design a class to encapsulate each kind of transformation.

Because you need to combine transformations in arbitrary ways, you want the organization used to chain transformation objects together to be as simple as possible. One way to accomplish this is to design the transformation classes so that all transformation objects fit together the same way. You accomplish this by designing a common interface for all transformation classes to implement. Figure 5.1 shows this organization.

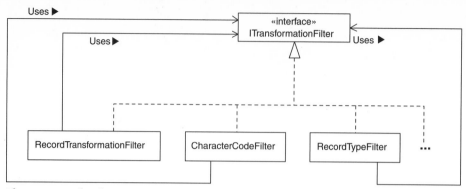

Figure 5.1   File Filters

Because all of the transformation classes implement the same interface, they can be combined in any sequence. This allows auditors to view files with different combination of filters until they see something that they can make sense of.

FORCES

☺ Classes that implement common data transformations and data analyses can be used in a great variety of programs.

☺ You want to perform arbitrary combinations of data transformations and data analyses.

☺ The use of transformation/analysis objects should be transparent to other objects.

SOLUTION

Base a solution on common interfaces and delegation. Organize classes that participate in the Filter pattern as data sources, data sinks, and data filters. Data filter classes perform the transformation and analysis operations.

There are two basic forms of the Filter pattern. In one, data flows as a result of a data sink object calling a method in a data source object. In the other, data flows when a data source object passes data to a method of a data sink object.

Figure 5.2 shows the form of Filter where data sink objects get data by calling methods in data sources. This form of filter is sometimes called a *pull filter*.

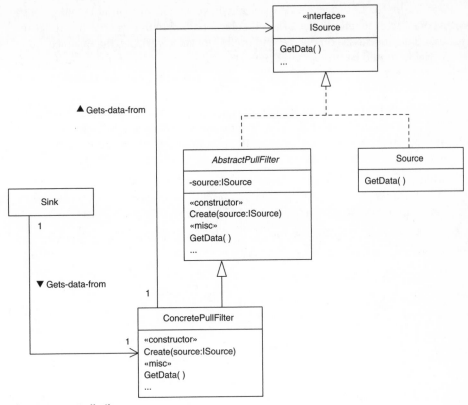

Figure 5.2   Pull Filter

Here are descriptions of how the classes in Figure 5.2 participate in the pull form of the Filter pattern:

ISource: An interface in this role declares one or more methods that return data. Figure 5.2 shows one such method named `GetData`.

Source: A class in this role is primarily responsible for providing data rather than transforming or analyzing it. Classes in this role are required to implement the `ISource` interface.

AbstractPullFilter: A class in this role implements `ISource` and is an abstract base class for classes that transform or analyze data. Its constructor takes an argument that is an `ISource` object. Instances of this class delegate data fetching to the `ISource` object passed to their constructor. Because subclasses of this class inherit the fact that it implements the `ISource` interface, its instances can provide data to other `AbstractPullFilter` objects.

AbstractPullFilter classes typically have an instance variable that is set by a constructor to refer to the ISource object passed to the constructor. To ensure that their subclasses do not depend on this instance variable, the instance variable should be private. AbstractPullFilter classes typically define a GetData method that simply calls the GetData method of the ISource object referred to by the instance variable.

ConcretePullFilter: Classes in this role are a concrete subclass of an Abstract PullFilter class. They override the inherited GetData method to perform appropriate transformation or analysis operations on data it gets by calling the overridden GetData method.

Sink: Instances of classes in this role call the GetData method of an ISource object. Unlike ConcretePullFilter objects, instances of Sink classes use data without passing it on to another AbstractPullFilter object.

Figure 5.3 is a class diagram for the form of Filter where data source objects pass data to methods of data sink objects. This form of filter is sometimes called a *push filter*.

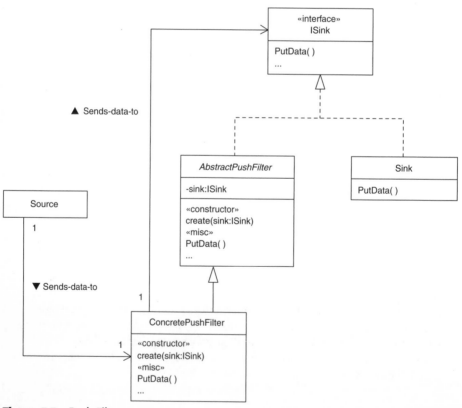

Figure 5.3   Push Filter

ISink: An interface in this role declares one or more methods that take data through their parameters. In Figure 5.3, one such method is indicated in the diagram as `PutData`.

Sink: A class in this role is primarily responsible for receiving and processing data, rather than transforming or analyzing data. Classes in this role are required to implement the `ISink` interface. Data is passed to `Sink` objects by passing the data to the `Sink` object's `PutData` method.

AbstractPushFilter: A class in this role is an abstract base class for classes that transform or analyze data. Its constructor takes an argument that is an `ISink` object. Instances of this class pass data to the `ISource` object that was passed to their constructor. Because subclasses of this class inherit the fact that it implements the `ISink` interface, its instances can accept data from other objects that pass data to `ISink` objects.

`AbstractPushFilter` classes typically have an instance variable that is set by a constructor that refers to the `ISink` object passed to the constructor. However, to ensure their subclasses do not depend on this instance variable, the instance variable should be private. `AbstractPushFilter` classes typically define a `PutData` method that simply calls the `PutData` method of the `SinkIF` object referred to by the instance variable.

ConcretePushFilter: Classes in this role are a concrete subclass of an `AbstractPushFilter` class. They override the `PutData` method that they inherit to perform the appropriate transformation or analysis operations.

Source: Instances of classes in this role call the `PutData` method of an `ISink` object.

IMPLEMENTATION

Filter classes should be implemented without any dependencies on the programs that will use them. A Filter class implementation should not assume which other Filter classes it will be used with. It follows that filter objects should not have side effects and should communicate with each other only through the data that they exchange through method calls.

Making filter classes independent of programs that used them increases their reusability. However, in some cases there can be performance penalties if a filter object is not allowed to use context-specific information. The best design is sometimes a compromise between these considerations. For example, you could define one or more interfaces that declare methods for providing context-specific information to a filter object. If a program detects that a filter object implements one of those interfaces, it can use the interface to provide additional information to the filter.

CONSEQUENCES

☺ The portion of a program that follows the Filter pattern can be structured as a set of sources, sinks, and filters.

☺ Filter objects that do not maintain internal state can be dynamically replaced while a program is running. This property of stateless filters allows dynamic change of behavior and adaptation to different requirements at run time.

• It is quite reasonable for a program to incorporate both forms of the Filter pattern. However, it is unusual for the same class to participate in both forms.

☹ If your design calls for filters to be dynamically added to or removed while processing a data stream, then you will need to design a mechanism to manage this change in a predictable way. In particular, you will need a mechanism to ensure that the program is at an appropriate place in the data stream when it adds or removes filters.

.NET API USAGE

The DirectShow API is used to support streaming media, such as video and audio. The DirectShow model for processing data is an application of the Filter pattern. DirectShow organizes the processing of data streams into building blocks it calls filters. DirectShow filters fall into three different categories:

■ A *source filter* gets raw data for processing from a source such as DVD, Television Card, local file, or camera. Source filters fill the `Source` roll of the Filter pattern.

■ A *transform filter* accepts data from a source filter of another transform filter. The transform filter processes the data in some way and then passes it on to another DirectShow filter. The types of supported transformations include uncompressing data, merging data streams, and so on. Transform filters fill the role of `ConcretePushFilter` in the Filter pattern.

■ A *renderer filter* accepts data from another filter and presents it to the user by displaying images, playing sound, or passing it on to another external device as appropriate. Renderer filters fill the `Sink` roll in the Filter pattern.

All DirectShow filters implement the `IBaseFilter` interface. The `IBaseFilter` interface fills the `ISink` role of the Filter pattern.

The abstract class `CBaseFilter` implements the `IBaseFilter` interface. It is intended to be used as the base class for implanting new DirectShow filters. The `CBaseFilter` class fills the `AbstrctPushFilter` role of the Filter pattern.

CODE EXAMPLE

This is an example of classes that implement the pull form of the Filter pattern. Here are classes that read and filter a stream of bytes:

```
Imports System.IO

'
' This class participates in the Filter pattern as an abstract
' source.
Public Interface IInStream
    'Read bytes and fill an array with those bytes.
    ' array - The array of bytes to fill
    'returns:
    ' If not enough bytes are available to fill the
    ' array then this method returns after having
    ' only put that many bytes in the array.  This
    ' methods returns -1 if the end of the data
    ' stream is encountered.
    '
    Function Read(ByVal array() As Byte) As Integer
End Interface ' interface IInStream


'
' This class implements the IInStream interface and
' participates in the Filter pattern as a source.
' It reads a stream of bytes from a file.
'
Public Class FileInStream
    Implements IInStream
    Private file As FileStream

    ' Constructor(string)
    ' name - The name of the file to read
    Public Sub New(ByVal name As String)
        file = System.IO.File.OpenRead(name)
    End Sub 'New


    '
    ' Read bytes from a file and fill an array with those bytes.
    '
    Public Function Read(ByVal array() As Byte) As Integer _
      Implements IInStream.Read
        Return file.Read(array, 0, array.Length)
    End Function 'Read
End Class ' class FileInStream


'
' This class participates in the Filter
' pattern as an abstract source filter.
'
Public MustInherit Class FilterInStream
    Implements IInStream

    Private inStream As IInStream
```

```
' Constructor(IInStream)
' inStream -  The IInStream object that this object should
' delegate read operations to.
'
Public Sub New(ByVal inStream As IInStream)
    Me.inStream = inStream
End Sub 'New


'

' Read bytes from a stream of bytes and fill an array
' with those bytes.
'
Public Overridable Function Read(ByVal array() As Byte) As Integer _
Implements IInStream.Read
    Return inStream.Read(array)
End Function 'Read
End Class ' FilterInStream
```

Finally, we look at some classes that participate in the Filter pattern as a concrete source filter. The first of these performs the simple analysis of counting the number of bytes it has read.

```
' This class tracks the numbers of bytes read.
Public Class ByteCountInStream
    Inherits FilterInStream
    Private byteCount As Long = 0

    'Constructor
    ' The InStream that this object should delegate
    ' read operations to.
    Public Sub New(ByVal inStream As IInStream)
        MyBase.New(inStream)
    End Sub 'New


    '

    ' Read bytes from a stream of bytes into an array.
    '
    Public Overrides Function Read(ByVal array() As Byte) As Integer
        Dim count As Integer
        count = MyBase.Read(array)
        If count > 0 Then
            byteCount += count
        End If
        Return count
    End Function 'Read


    '

    'The number of bytes that have been read by this object.
    '
```

```
        Public ReadOnly Property Count() As Long
            Get
                Return byteCount
            End Get
        End Property ' Count
    End Class ' ByteCountInStream


    '
    ' This is a filter class that performs
    ' character code translations of a stream of bytes.
    ' This class treats the bytes in a bytes stream as eight bit
    ' character codes and translates them to other character
    ' codes using a translation table.
    '
    Public Class TranslateInStream
        Inherits FilterInStream
        Private translationTable() As Byte

        'Maximum number of bytes to perform character translation on
        Public Shared TransTblLength As Integer = 256
        'Constructor
        ' inStream -
        '     The IInStream object that this object should
        '     delegate read operations to.
        '
        ' table -
        '     An array of bytes used to determine
        '     translation values for character codes.  The
        '     value to replace character code n with is at
        '     index n of the translation table.  If the array
        '     is longer than TransTblLength elements, the
        '     additional elements are ignored.  If the array
        '     is shorter than TransTblLength elements, then
        '     no translation is done on character codes
        '     greater than or equal to the length of the
        '     array.
        '
        Public Sub New(ByVal inStream As IInStream, ByVal table() As Byte)
            MyBase.New(inStream)
            ' Copy translation data to create translation table.
            ReDim Preserve translationTable(TransTblLength)
            Dim len As Integer
            len = System.Math.Min(TransTblLength, table.Length)
            System.Array.Copy(table, translationTable, len)
            For i As Integer = table.Length To TransTblLength - 1
                translationTable(i) = CByte(i)
            Next i
        End Sub 'New
```

```
' Read bytes from a stream of bytes into an array while translating.
'
Public Overrides Function Read(ByVal array() As Byte) As Integer
    Dim count As Integer
    count = MyBase.Read(array)
    For i As Integer = 0 To count - 1
        array(i) = translationTable(array(i))
    Next i
    Return count
End Function 'Read
End Class ' TranslateInStream
```

RELATED PATTERNS

Composite: The Composite pattern can be an alternative to the Filter pattern. It allows for the possibility of routing data through branches of a tree.

Pipe: The Pipe pattern is sometimes an alternative to the Filter pattern and is sometimes used with the Filter pattern.

This book does not contain a chapter for the Pipe pattern. It is described in [BMRSS96]. Like the Filter pattern, the Pipe pattern allows an object that is a data source to send a stream of data to an object that is a data sink. Instead of the movement of data being initiated by the source or the sink object, they operate asynchronously of each other. The data source object puts data in a buffer when it wants to. The data sink gets data from the buffer when it wants to. If the buffer is empty when the data sink tries to get data from it, the data sink waits until there is data in the buffer.

The Pipe pattern can be thought of as a combination of the Filter pattern and the Producer-Consumer pattern, which is described elsewhere in this book.

Decorator: The Filter pattern is a special case of the Decorator pattern, where a data source or data sink object is wrapped to add logic to the handling of a data stream.

Composite

The Composite pattern is also known as the Recursive Composition pattern. The Composite pattern was previously described in [GoF95].

SYNOPSIS

Build complex objects by recursively composing similar objects into a treelike structure. Allow objects in the tree to be manipulated in a consistent manner by requiring all objects in the tree to have a common interface or base class.

The following description of the Composite pattern describes it in terms of recursively building a composite object from other objects. It appears in this partitioning patterns chapter because during the design process, the Composite pattern is often used to recursively decompose a complex object into simpler objects.

CONTEXT

Suppose that you are writing a document-formatting program. It formats characters into lines of text organized into columns that are organized into pages. A document may contain other elements. Columns and pages can contain frames that can contain columns. Columns, frames, and lines of text can contain images. Figure 5.4 shows these relationships:

As you can see, there is a fair amount of complexity in Figure 5.4. Page and Frame objects must know how to handle and combine two kinds of elements. Column objects must know how to handle and combine three kinds of elements. The Composite pattern removes this complexity by allowing these objects to only know how to handle one kind of element. It accomplishes this by insisting that document element classes all implement a common interface. Figure 5.5 shows how you can simplify the document element class relationships by using the Composite pattern.

By applying the Composite pattern, you have introduced a common interface for all document elements and a common base class for all container classes. This reduces the number of aggregation relationships to one. Management of the aggregation is now the responsibility of the `CompositeDocumentElement` class. The concrete container classes (`Document`, `Page`, `Column`, . . .) only need to understand how to combine one kind of element.

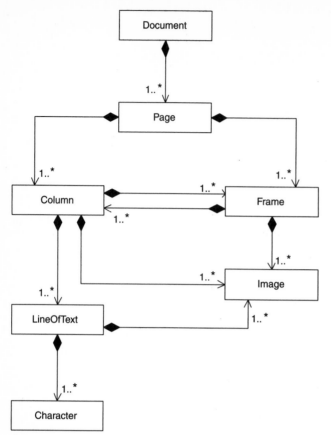

Figure 5.4 Document Container Relationships

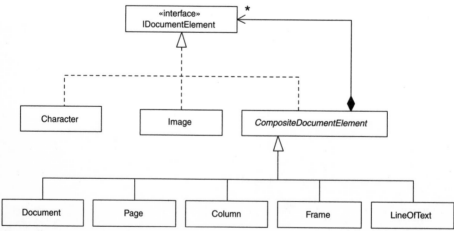

Figure 5.5 Document Composite

FORCES

☺   You have a complex object you want to decompose into a part-whole hierarchy of objects.

☺   You want to minimize the complexity of the part-whole hierarchy by minimizing the number of different kinds of child objects that objects in the tree need to be aware of.

☺   There is no requirement to distinguish between most of the part-whole relationships.

SOLUTION

Minimize the complexity of a composite object organized into part-whole hierarchies by providing an interface to be implemented by all objects in the hierarchy and an abstract base class for all composites in the hierarchy. The generalized class relationships for such an organization are shown in Figure 5.6.

Following are descriptions of the interface and classes that participate in the Composite pattern:

IElement: An interface in the IElement role is implemented by all the objects in the hierarchy of objects that make up a composite object. Composite objects normally treat objects they contain as instances of classes that implement the IElement interface rather than as instances of their actual class.

Element1, Element2, . . .: Instances of these classes are used as leaves in the tree organization.

AbstractComposite: A class in this role is the abstract base class of all composite objects that participate in the Composite pattern. AbstractComposite defines and provides default implementations of methods for managing a composite object's elements. The Add method adds an element to a composite object. The Remove method removes an element from a composite object. The GetChild method returns a reference to an element object of a composite object.

ConcreteComposite1, ConcreteComposite2, and so on: Instances of these are composite objects that use other IElement objects.

Instance of these classes can be assembled in a treelike manner, as shown in Figure 5.7.

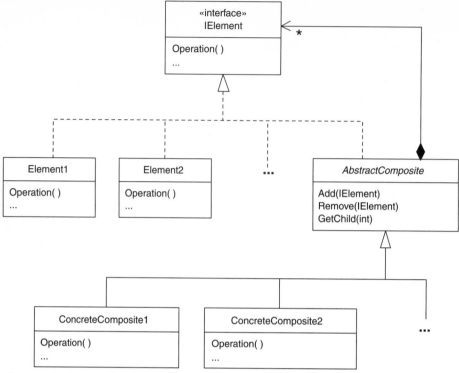

Figure 5.6 Composite Class Relationships

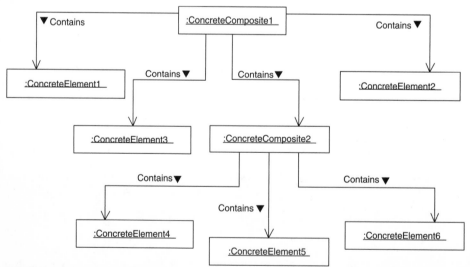

Figure 5.7 Composite Object

Note that you don't need to have an abstract composite class if there is only one concrete composite class.

IMPLEMENTATION

Classes that participate in the Composite pattern may implement some operations by delegating them to an instance's parent object. For example, consider the design shown in Figure 5.5. The `Character` class may have a method named `getFont` that is supposed to return the font to use for rendering the character. If a character does not have a font directly associated with it, then it can use the font associated with its container object as its default font.

The best way to implement functions or subroutines that delegate operations to a parent object with speed and simplicity is to have each instance of `Abstract Composite` contain a reference to its parent. It is important to implement the parent reference in a way that ensures consistency between parent and child. It must always be true that an `IElement` object identifies an `AbstractComposite` object as its parent if, and only if, the `AbstractComposite` identifies the `IElement` object as one of its children. The best way to enforce this is to only modify parent and child references in the `AbstractComposite` class's `add` and `remove` subroutines.

Sharing components among multiple parents using the Flyweight pattern conserves memory. However, shared elements cannot easily maintain parent references.

The `AbstractComposite` class may provide a default implementation of child management for composite objects. However, it is very common for concrete composite classes to override the default implementation.

If a concrete composite object delegates an operation to the objects that constitute it, then caching the result of the operation may improve performance. If a concrete composite object caches the result of an operation, it is important for the objects that constitute the composite to notify the composite object when their state changes so the composite can invalidate its cached values.

CONSEQUENCES

☺ You can access a tree-structured composite object and the objects that constitute it through the `IElement` interface, whether they are simple objects or composite. The structure of the composite does not force other objects to make this distinction.

☺ Client objects of an `AbstractComposite` can simply treat it as an `Abstract Composite`, without being aware of any subclasses of `AbstractComposite`.

☺ If a client invokes a method of an `IElement` object that is supposed to perform an operation and the `IElement` object is an `AbstractComposite` object, it may delegate the operation to the `IElement` objects that constitute it. Similarly, if a client object calls a method of an `IElement` object that is *not* an `AbstractComposite` and the method requires some contextual information, the `IElement` object delegates the request for contextual information to its parent.

- Some elements may implement operations that are unique to the element. For example, under the context heading of this pattern is a design for the recursive composition of a document. At the lowest level, is has a document consisting of character and image elements. It is very reasonable for the character elements of a document to have a `getFont` method. A document's image elements have no need for a `getFont` method. The main benefit of the Composite pattern is to allow the clients of a composite object and the objects that constitute it to be unaware of the specific class of the objects they deal with. To allow other classes to call `getFont` without being aware of the specific class they are dealing with, all the objects that can constitute a document can inherit the `getFont` method from `IDocumentElelement`. In general, when applying the Composite pattern, the interface in the `IElement` role declares specialized methods if they are needed by any `ConcreteComposite` class.

A principle of object-oriented design is that specialized methods should only appear in classes that need them. Normally, a class should have methods that provide related functionality and form a cohesive set. Putting a specialized method in a general-purpose class rather than the specialized class makes the general-purpose class less cohesive. The unrelated method is inherited by subclasses of the general-purpose class that are unrelated to the method.

Because simplicity through ignorance of class is the basis of the Composite pattern, when applying the Composite pattern it is okay to sacrifice high cohesion for simplicity. This is an exception to a widely accepted rule, based on experience. Try it, you'll like it.

- ☹ The Composite pattern allows any `IElement` object to be a child of an `AbstractComposite`. If you need to enforce a more restrictive relationship, you will have to add type-aware code to `AbstractComposite` or its subclasses. This reduces the value of the Composite pattern.

.NET USAGE

The .NET framework includes a set of classes that implement the XML document object model (DOM). These classes are used to represent an XML document as a tree of objects.

The `System.Xml.XmlNode` class fills both the `IComponent` and `Abstract Composite` roles. Instances of its concrete subclasses, such as `System.Xml.Xml Document`, `System.Xml.XmlElement`, and `System.Xml.XmlCharacterData`, are arranged in a treelike manner to represent the content and structure of an XML document.

CODE EXAMPLE

The example of the applying the Composite pattern is a more detailed version of the document related classes that appeared under the "Context" heading. Figure 5.8 shows some methods that were left out of Figure 5.6.

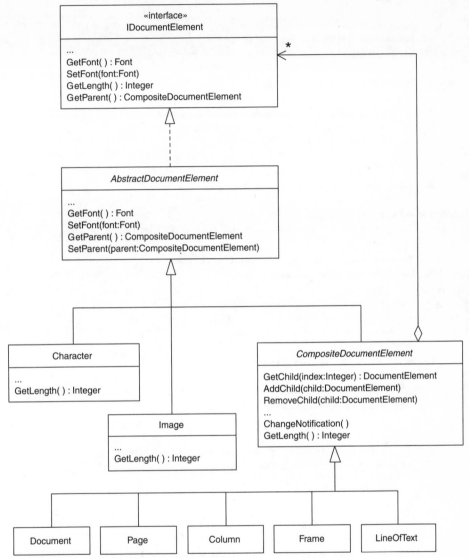

Figure 5.8   Detailed Document Composite

As you look through the following code, you will see that the Font property is an example of subroutines/functions/properties that consult an object's parent object. The Length property gathers information from an object's children and caches it for later use. The ChangeNotification subroutine is used to invalidate cached information.

There is also an abstract class named AbstractDocumentElement. This abstract class contains common logic for managing fonts and parents.

```
Imports System.Drawing

' This interface defines properties and methods
' for all classes that make up a document must implement.
'

Public Interface IDocumentElement
    ' This object's parent or Nothing if parentless
    Property Parent() As CompositeDocumentElement
    ' The Font associatiated with this object
    Property Font() As System.Drawing.Font


    ' The number of characters that this object
    ReadOnly Property Length() As Integer


End Interface 'IDocumentElement
' This class contains the common logic for managing fonts and parents
'

Public MustInherit Class AbstractDocumentElement
    Implements IDocumentElement


    ' This is the font associated with this object.  If the
    ' font variable is Nothing, then this object's font will be
    ' inherited through the container hierarchy from an
    ' enclosing object.
    Private mFont As System.Drawing.Font


    ' This object's container
    Private mParent As CompositeDocumentElement


    ' This object's parent.  If no parent, will be Nothing
    Public Property Parent() As CompositeDocumentElement _
        Implements IDocumentElement.Parent


        Get
            'Return this object's parent or Nothing if it has no parent.
            Return mParent
        End Get
        Set(ByVal Value As CompositeDocumentElement)
            ' Set this object's parent.
            mParent = Value
        End Set
    End Property


    '
    ' The Font associatiated with this object.  If
    ' there is no Font associated with this object, then
    ' provide the Font associated with this object's parent.
    ' If there is no Font associated with this object's
    ' parent then provide Nothing.
    '
```

```
        Public Property Font() As System.Drawing.Font _
            Implements IDocumentElement.Font
        Get
            If mFont IsNot Nothing Then
                Return mFont
            ElseIf mParent IsNot Nothing Then
                Return mParent.Font
            Else
                Return Nothing
            End If
        End Get
        Set(ByVal Value As System.Drawing.Font)
            Me.mFont = Value
        End Set
    End Property


    ' The number of characters that this object contains.
    Public MustOverride ReadOnly Property Length() As Integer _
    Implements IDocumentElement.Length


End Class 'AbstractDocumentElement

' This class is the abstract baseclass of all document elements that
' contain other document elements.
Public MustInherit Class CompositeDocumentElement
    Inherits AbstractDocumentElement
    ' Collection of this object's children
    Private children As New System.Collections.ArrayList()


    '
    ' The cached value from the previous call to Length
    ' or -1 to indicate that charLength does not contain a
    ' cached value.
    Private cachedLength As Integer = -1


    ' Accessor for child objects of this object.
    Default Public ReadOnly Property Item(ByVal index As Integer) As
IDocumentElement
        Get
            Return CType(children(index), IDocumentElement)
        End Get
    End Property


    '
    ' Make the given IDocumentElement a child of this object.
    '
    Public Sub Add(ByVal child As IDocumentElement)
        SyncLock children
            SyncLock child
                children.Add(child)
```

```
                    CType(child, AbstractDocumentElement).Parent = Me
            End SyncLock
        End SyncLock
        changeNotification()
    End Sub 'Add
```

The AddChild and RemoveChild subroutines both contain a SyncLock statement to get a lock on the given child. This is because these methods modify both the container and its child.

```
    Public Sub Remove(ByVal child As AbstractDocumentElement)
        SyncLock children
            SyncLock child
                If Me Is child.Parent Then
                    child.Parent = Nothing
                End If
                children.Remove(child)
            End SyncLock
        End SyncLock
        changeNotification()
    End Sub 'Remove


    ' A call to this method means that one of this object's
    ' children has changed in a way that invalidates whatever
    ' data this object may be caching about its children.
    Sub changeNotification()
        cachedLength = -1
        If Parent IsNot Nothing Then
            Parent.changeNotification()
        End If
    End Sub 'changeNotification


    ' The number of characters that this object contains.
    Public Overrides ReadOnly Property Length() As Integer
        Get
            Dim len As Integer = 0
            For i As Integer = 0 To children.Count - 1
                Dim thisChild As AbstractDocumentElement
                thisChild = CType(children(i), AbstractDocumentElement)
                len += thisChild.Length
            Next i
            cachedLength = len
            Return len
        End Get
    End Property
End Class 'CompositeDocumentElement


'The Image class is an example of a class that implements a
'method so other classes that constitute a document do not need
'to treat the Image class specially. Its GetCharLength method
```

```
'always returns 1, so that an image can be treated a just a big
'character.
Public Class Image
    Inherits AbstractDocumentElement

    Public Overrides ReadOnly Property Length() As Integer
        Get
            Return 1
        End Get
    End Property
End Class 'Image
```

The other classes in the class diagram that are subclasses of Composite
DocumentElement do not have any features that are interesting with respect to the
Composite pattern. In the interest of brevity, just one of them is shown here:

```
Public Class Page
    Inherits CompositeDocumentElement
    '...
End Class 'Page
```

RELATED PATTERNS

Chain of Responsibility: The Chain of Responsibility pattern can be combined
with the Composite pattern by adding child to parent links so that children can
get information from an ancestor without knowing which ancestor the information came from.

Visitor: You can use the Visitor pattern to encapsulate operations in a single
class that would otherwise be spread across multiple classes.

Read-Only Interface

The Read-Only interface pattern was first described as a pattern in [LL01].

SYNOPSIS

An object is supposed to be modified by some of its clients, but not by others. Ensure that clients that are not supposed to modify an object don't modify the object by forcing the clients to access the object through an interface that does not include any subroutines, functions, or properties to modify the object.

CONTEXT

You are designing software to be part of a building security system. Part of its job is to monitor the state of physical sensors that detect the opening and closing of doors, the temperature of rooms, and other such things. The sensors send messages to a computer running the security software. The software may update a screen or take other actions as a result of receiving messages. Figure 5.9 shows these interactions.

Figure 5.9 shows two top-level interactions. Both interactions begin with a sensor whose software implements an interface named `ISensor`. In the first interaction, a temperature sensor delivers a temperature to a `SensorController` object in the monitoring software. In the second interaction, a sensor transmits a change in the state of a door (open, closed, locked . . .). All sensors send data to the `SensorController` object. The `SensorController` object is responsible for determining the identity and type of the sensor that sent data. It passes the data to the object in the monitoring program that corresponds to the sensor that sent the data.

Each data object, such as the `DoorData` or `TemperatureData` (shown in Figure 5.9), corresponds to a sensor. It contains the data most recently received from the sensor to which it corresponds. When a data object receives new data, it notifies registered handler objects that there is new data. Any object can be a handler object if it implements the appropriate interface. Handler objects are generally responsible for displaying the most current information received from a sensor or for notifying other objects if the values in some data objects meet specified conditions.

This collaboration requires the `SensorController` object to update the contents of data objects. However, you don't want handler objects to update the contents of data objects. One way to ensure that no programmer makes the mistake of coding a handler object to update a data object is to insist that handler objects access data objects through an interface that does not include functions, subroutines, or properties to modify the contents of a data object. Figure 5.10 shows a relevant part this organization.

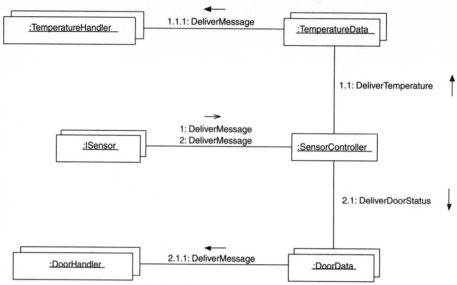

Figure 5.9   Security Controller Collaborations

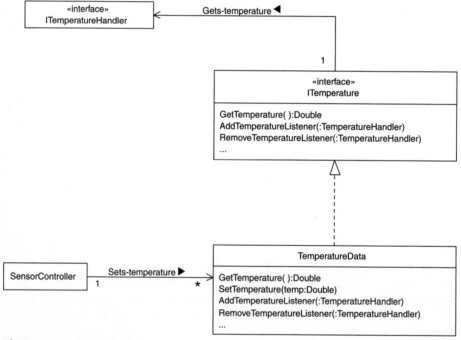

Figure 5.10   Data Interface

In Figure 5.10, the `SensorController` class uses the `TemperatureData` class directly. It is able to set the temperature value in `TemperaturData` objects by calling their `SetTemperature` method.[1] `ITemperatureHandler` objects are able to get the temperature value from a `TemperaturData` object because the `GetTemperature` method is declared in the `ITemperature` interface. However, `Temperature Listener` objects cannot modify the temperature value in a `TemperatureData` object because they access `TemperatureData` objects through the `ITemperature` interface; the `ITemperature` interface does not declare the `SetTemperature` method.

FORCES

☺ There is a class whose instances you want some other classes to be able to modify but not others.

☺ You want instances of a class to be modified by instances of classes in a different assembly. This means that making the methods that modify the class's instances `Friend` accessible will not be a useful way to limit which classes can call them.

☹ You are in a position to force a class's clients to accesses the class through an interface you specify. This will generally be the case if you are designing the class and its clients. It may not be practical in a number of situations. The client classes may be third-party software. You may be in a maintenance situation where you don't want to change the interface that client classes use.

☹ This pattern is useful to protect against programming mistakes. However, by itself, it is not helpful in protecting against malicious programming practices.

SOLUTION

Provide read-only access to a mutable object by requiring objects to access the mutable object through an interface that does not include any subroutines, functions, or properties for modifying the object. This organization is shown in Figure 5.11.

---

[1]The design for the `ITemperature` interface includes a `GetTemperature` method, which is most obviously implemented as a `ReadOnly` property named `Temperature`. Because the interface declares the `Temperature` property to be `ReadOnly`, the `TemperatureData` class must implement the `Temperature` property as a `ReadOnly` property. For this reason, `TemperatureData` objects have a separate `SetTemperature` method to set the value of their `Temperature` property.

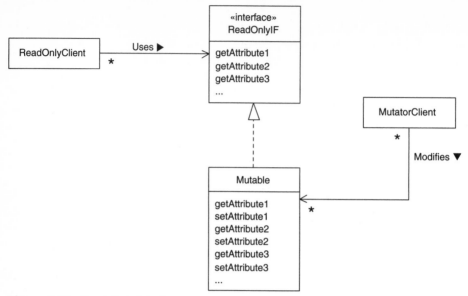

Figure 5.11   Read-Only Interface

Following are descriptions of the roles classes and interfaces play in the Read-Only interface pattern:

Mutable: A class in this role has functions and subroutines to get and set the values of its attributes. It also implements the `IReadOnly` interface.

IReadOnly: An interface in this role has the same `Get` methods as the `Mutable` class, which implements the interface. However, the interface does not include any methods that could cause a `Mutable` object to modify its contents.

MutatorClient: Classes in this role use the `Mutable` class directly and may call its methods that modify the state of a `Mutable` object.

ReadOnlyClient: Classes in this role access the `Mutable` class through the `IReadOnly` interface. Classes that access the `Mutable` class through the `IReadOnly` interface are not able to access methods that modify `Mutable` objects.

IMPLEMENTATION

If you just want to make a single method of a class available to some of its clients, in some circumstances it is more convenient to use a delegate than an interface.

Classes that provide read-write properties cannot directly implement a read-only interface because a read-write property cannot implement a `ReadOnly` property. This difficulty can be overcome by using the adapter pattern. This involves writing another class that implements the read-only interface by delegating the work of its properties, functions and subroutines to the original class.

Classes that have `ReflectionPermission` permission can use reflection to discover and access nonpublic members of a class. If you are concerned about malicious classes trying to bypass a read-only interface, ensure that none of the classes using the read-only interface have the `ReflectionPermission` permission.

CONSEQUENCES

☺ Using the Read-Only Interface pattern prevents programming mistakes that would result in classes being able to modify objects that they should not be able to modify.

☹ The Read-Only Interface pattern does not prevent objects from being improperly modified as a result of malicious programming.

CODE EXAMPLE

The code example for this pattern is some code that implements part of the design shown under the "Context" heading:

```
' The temperature event handler
Public Delegate Sub EventHandler(ByVal o As Object, _
                                 ByVal e As System.EventArgs)


' Temperature data object
Public Class TemperatureData
    Implements ITemperature

    Private mTemperature As Double

    Public ReadOnly Property Temperature() As Double _
        Implements ITemperature.Temperature
        Get
            Return mTemperature
        End Get
    End Property

    Public Sub SetTemperature(ByVal value As Double)
        mTemperature = value
        FireTemperature()
    End Sub

    Private Event handlers As EventHandler
    ' Event handler for temperature events

    Public Sub AddEventHandler(ByVal h As EventHandler) _
      Implements ITemperature.AddEventHandler
        AddHandler handlers, h
    End Sub ' AddHandler
```

```
Public Sub RemoveEventHandler(ByVal h As EventHandler) _
  Implements ITemperature.RemoveEventHandler
    RemoveHandler handlers, h
End Sub ' RemoveHandler


'Send a TemperatureEvent to all registered
'TemperatureListener objects.
Private Sub FireTemperature()
    Dim evt As New TemperatureEvent()
    RaiseEvent handlers(Me, evt)
End Sub 'FireTemperature
End Class 'TemperatureData


' Temperature event class
Public Class TemperatureEvent
    Inherits System.EventArgs
End Class 'TemperatureEvent
```

SensorController objects set the temperature in a TemperatureData object by setting its Temperature property. No other class is supposed to set the Temperature property. To enforce this, other classes access TemperatureData objects through the ITemperature interface.

```
' A readonly interface for accessing the Temperature object
Public Interface ITemperature
    ' The temperature reading encapsulated in this object.
    ReadOnly Property Temperature() As Double
    Sub AddEventHandler(ByVal h As EventHandler)
    Sub RemoveEventHandler(ByVal h As EventHandler)
End Interface 'ITemperature
```

Notice that the ITemperature interface does not have the Temperature set accessor, and no SetTemperature method.

RELATED PATTERNS

Interface: The Read-Only Interface pattern uses the Interface pattern.

Adapter: The Adapter pattern may be used to implement the Read-Only Interface pattern for classes that have read-write properties.

Structural Patterns

Adapter (195)
Iterator (205)
Bridge (213)
Façade (225)
Flyweight (233)
Dynamic Linkage (245)
Virtual Proxy (255)
Decorator (265)
Cache Management (273)

The patterns in this chapter describe common ways that different types of objects can be organized to work with each other.

The Adapter pattern describes how an object can have a client that expects it to implement a particular interface, even though it does not implement the interface.

The Iterator pattern describes how an object can access the contents of a collection of objects without knowing the structure or class of the collection.

The Bridge pattern describes how to manage parallel hierarchies of abstractions and implementations.

The Façade pattern describes how to hide the complexity of using a group of related objects behind a single object.

The Flyweight pattern describes how to avoid having multiple instances of an object consuming memory by sharing instances that contain common values.

The Dynamic Linkage pattern describes how to dynamically add classes to a program at run time.

The Virtual Proxy pattern describes how to postpone the creation of objects in a way that is transparent to their clients.

The Decorator pattern describes how to dynamically augment or modify the behavior of existing objects.

The Cache Management pattern describes how to avoid creating similar objects multiple times by reusing the object that was previously created.

Adapter

This pattern was previously described in [GoF95].

SYNOPSIS

An adapter class implements an interface known to its clients and provides access to an instance of a class not know to its clients. An adapter object provides the functionality promised by an interface without its clients having to assume what class is being used to implement the interface.

CONTEXT

Suppose that you are writing a function that copies an array of objects. The function is supposed to filter out objects that do not meet certain criteria, so the copied array may not contain all the elements in the original array. To promote reuse, you want the function to be independent of the filtering criteria being used. You can do this by defining an interface that declares a function that the array copier can call to find out if it should include a given object in the new array.

In Figure 6.1, an `ArrayCopier` class delegates to the `ICopyFilter` interface the decision to copy an element from the old array to the new array. If the `IsCopyable` function returns true for an object, then the object is copied to the new array.

This solution solves the immediate problem of allowing the copy criteria used by `ArrayCopier` objects to be encapsulated in a separate object without having to be concerned about what the object's class is. However, this solution presents another problem.

Sometimes the logic needed for filtering is in a function of the objects being filtered. If these objects do not implement the `ICopyFilter` interface, then the `ArrayCopier` object cannot directly ask these objects if they should be copied. However, the `Array Copier` object can indirectly ask the filtered objects if they should be copied, even if they do not implement the `ICopyFilter` interface.

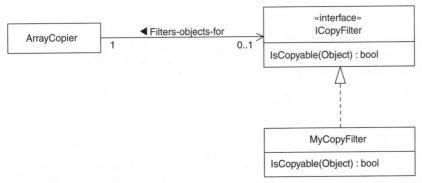

Figure 6.1   Simple Copy Filter

Suppose that a class called Document has a function called IsValid that returns a Boolean result. You want an ArrayCopier object to use the result of IsValid to filter a copy operation. Because Document does not implement the ICopyFilter interface, an ArrayCopier object cannot directly use a Document object for filtering. Another object that does implement the ICopyFilter interface cannot independently determine if a Document object should be copied to a new array. It does not work because it has no way to get the necessary information without calling the Document object's IsValid function. The answer is for that object to call the Document object's IsValid function, resulting in the solution shown in Figure 6.2.

In this solution, the ArrayCopier object, as always, calls the IsCopyable function of an object that implements the ICopyFilter interface. In this case, the object is an instance of the DocumentCopyFilterAdapter class. The DocumentCopyFilter Adapter class implements the IsCopyable function by delegating the call to the Document object's IsValid function.

FORCES

☺ You want to use a class that calls functions or subroutines through an interface, but you want to use it with a class that does not implement the interface. Modifying the class to implement the interface is not an option either because:

- You do not have the source code for the class.

- The class is a general-purpose class, and it would be inappropriate for it to implement an interface for a specialized purpose.

☺ You want to dynamically determine which of another object's functions and subroutines an object calls without the object having knowledge of the other object's class.

☺ You want a class to call a function of another class without having any dependencies on the class that the function belongs to. You want to arrange this in a type-safe way that minimizes the likelihood of calling an inappropriate function.

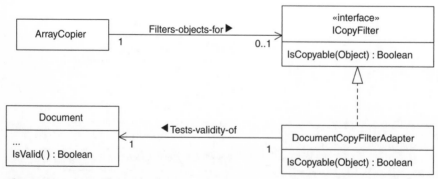

Figure 6.2   Copy Filter Adapter

Suppose that you have a class that calls a function through an interface. You want an instance of this class to call a function of an object that does not implement the interface. You can arrange for the instance to make the call through an adapter object that implements the interface by delegating the calls to a function of the object that doesn't implement the interface. The diagram in Figure 6.3 shows how this works.

Here are the roles that the classes and interface play in Figure 6.3:

Client: A class in this role calls a function or subroutine of another class through an interface to avoid assuming the actual class that implements the function or subroutine.

ITarget: An interface in this role declares a function or subroutine that the client class calls.

Adapter: A class in this role implements the `ITarget` interface. It implements the functions and subroutines that the `Client` calls by delegating the calls to a function or subroutine of the `Adaptee` class, which does not implement the `ITarget` interface.

Adaptee: A class in this role does not implement the `ITarget` interface, but has a function or subroutine that the `Client` class wants to call.

It is possible for an `Adapter` class to do more than simply delegate a function or subroutine call. It may perform some transformation on the arguments. It may provide additional logic to hide differences between the intended semantics of the interface's function or subroutine and the actual semantics of the `Adaptee` class's function or subroutine. There is no limit to how complex an adapter class can be. So long as the essential purpose of the class is as an intermediary for function or subroutine calls to one other object, you can consider it to be an adapter class.

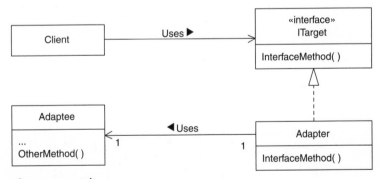

Figure 6.3 Adapter

IMPLEMENTATION

Implementing the adapter class is rather straightforward. You pass a reference to the Adaptee object as a parameter to the adapter object's constructor or to one of its functions or subroutines. This allows the Adapter object to be used with any instance or possibly multiple instances of the Adaptee class. The following example illustrates this:

```
Public Class CustomerBillToAdapter
    Implements IAddress
    Private myCustomer As Customer

    Public Sub New(ByVal customer As Customer)
        myCustomer = customer
    End Sub

    '
    ' Get/Set the first line of the street address.
    '
    Public Property Address1() As String _
      Implements IAddress.Address1
        Get
            Return myCustomer.BillToAddress1
        End Get
        Set(ByVal value As String)
            myCustomer.BillToAddress1 = value
        End Set
    End Property

    '
    ' Get/Set the second line of the street address.
    '
    Public Property Address2() As String _
      Implements IAddress.Address2
        Get
            Return myCustomer.BillToAddress2
        End Get
        Set(ByVal value As String)
            myCustomer.BillToAddress2 = value
        End Set
    End Property

    '
    ' Get/Set the city.
    '
    Public Property City() As String _
      Implements IAddress.City
        Get
            Return myCustomer.BillToCity
        End Get
```

```
      Set(ByVal value As String)
          myCustomer.BillToCity = value
      End Set
   End Property
   ...
```

CONSEQUENCES

☺ The `Client` and `Adaptee` classes remain independent of each other.

☺ You can use an adapter class to determine which of an object's functions and subroutines another object calls. For example, you may have a class whose instances are GUI controls that display and edit addresses. This class fetches and stores addresses by calling functions and subroutines defined by an interface named `IAdress`. To make use of the interface you define adapter classes. The class in the preceding example, `CustomerBillToAdapter`, allows GUI controls to access a `Customer` object's bill-to address through the `IAdress` interface. You may decide to write a similar class named `CustomerShip ToAdapter`, which allows GUI controls to access a `Customer` object's ship-to address through the `IAddress` interface. The difference between the two adapter classes is that they call different functions and subroutines of the `Customer` class. The class of the adapter you provide to the GUI controls determines the functions and subroutines of the `Customer` class that they call.

In cases where there are only individual functions and subroutines to call, an alternative to writing multiple adapter classes is to pass delegates to the adapter object's constructor.

☹ The Adapter pattern adds indirection to a program. Like any other indirection, it contributes to the difficulty in understanding the program.

CODE EXAMPLE

Here are listings of the `IAdress` interface `Customer` and `CustomerShipToAdapter` classes discussed under the "Context" heading.

```
' Classes that contain editable street address information implement
' this interface.
Public Interface IAddress
    ' Get/Set the first line of the street address.
    Property Address1() As String

    ' Get/Set the second line of the street address.
    Property Address2() As String

    ' Get/Set the city.
    Property City() As String
```

```vb
' Get/Set the state.
Property State() As String

' Get/Set the postal code
Property PostalCode() As String
End Interface 'IAddress

' Instances of this class represent a customer
Public Class Customer
    ...

    ' the first line of ship-to street address.
    Private myShipToAddress1 As String

    ' the second line of ship-to street address.
    Private myShipToAddress2 As String

    ' ship-to city.
    Private myShipToCity As String

    ' ship-to state.
    Private myShipToState As String

    ' ship-to postal code
    Private myShipToPostalCode As String

    ' the first line of bill-to street address.
    Private myBillToAddress1 As String

    ' the second line of bill-to street address.
    Private myBillToAddress2 As String

    ' bill-to city.
    Private myBillToCity As String

    ' bill-to state.
    Private myBillToState As String

    ' bill-to postal code
    Private myBillToPostalCode As String

    ' Get/Set the first line of ship-to street address.
    Public Property ShipToAddress1() As String
        Get
            Return myShipToAddress1
        End Get
        Set(ByVal value As String)
            myShipToAddress1 = value
        End Set
    End Property
```

```
' Get/Set the second line of ship-to street address.
Public Property ShipToAddress2() As String
    Get
        Return myShipToAddress2
    End Get
    Set(ByVal value As String)
        myShipToAddress2 = value
    End Set
End Property

' Get/Set ship-to city.
Public Property ShipToCity() As String
    Get
        Return myShipToCity
    End Get
    Set(ByVal value As String)
        myShipToCity = value
    End Set
End Property

' Get/Set ship-to state.
Public Property ShipToState() As String
    Get
        Return myShipToState
    End Get
    Set(ByVal value As String)
        myShipToState = value
    End Set
End Property

' Get/Set ship-to postal code
Public Property ShipToPostalCode() As String
    Get
        Return myShipToPostalCode
    End Get
    Set(ByVal value As String)
        myShipToPostalCode = value
    End Set
End Property

' Get/Set the first line of bill-to street address.
Public Property BillToAddress1() As String
    Get
        Return myBillToAddress1
    End Get
    Set(ByVal value As String)
        myBillToAddress1 = value
    End Set
End Property
```

```vb
    ' Get/Set the second line of bill-to street address.
    Public Property BillToAddress2() As String
        Get
            Return myBillToAddress2
        End Get
        Set(ByVal value As String)
            myBillToAddress2 = value
        End Set
    End Property


    ' Get/Set bill-to city.
    Public Property BillToCity() As String
        Get
            Return myBillToCity
        End Get
        Set(ByVal value As String)
            myBillToCity = value
        End Set
    End Property


    ' Get/Set bill-to state.
    Public Property BillToState() As String
        Get
            Return myBillToState
        End Get
        Set(ByVal value As String)
            myBillToState = value
        End Set
    End Property


    ' Get/Set bill-to postal code
    Public Property BillToPostalCode() As String
        Get
            Return myBillToPostalCode
        End Get
        Set(ByVal value As String)
            myBillToPostalCode = value
        End Set
    End Property
End Class 'Customer


Public Class CustomerBillToAdapter
    Implements IAddress
    Private myCustomer As Customer

    Public Sub New(ByVal customer As Customer)
        myCustomer = customer
    End Sub


    ' Get/Set the first line of the street address.
    Public Property Address1() As String _
      Implements IAddress.Address1
```

```vb
      Get
            Return myCustomer.BillToAddress1
      End Get
      Set(ByVal value As String)
            myCustomer.BillToAddress1 = value
      End Set
    End Property


    ' Get/Set the second line of the street address.
    Public Property Address2() As String _
      Implements IAddress.Address2
      Get
            Return myCustomer.BillToAddress2
      End Get
      Set(ByVal value As String)
            myCustomer.BillToAddress2 = value
      End Set
    End Property


    ' Get/Set the city.
    Public Property City() As String _
      Implements IAddress.City
      Get
            Return myCustomer.BillToCity
      End Get
      Set(ByVal value As String)
            myCustomer.BillToCity = value
      End Set
    End Property


    ' Get/Set the state.
    Public Property State() As String _
      Implements IAddress.State
      Get
            Return myCustomer.BillToState
      End Get
      Set(ByVal value As String)
            myCustomer.BillToState = value
      End Set
    End Property


    ' get/set the postal code
    Public Property PostalCode() As String _
      Implements IAddress.PostalCode
      Get
            Return myCustomer.BillToPostalCode
      End Get
      Set(ByVal value As String)
            myCustomer.BillToPostalCode = value
      End Set
    End Property ' class CustomerBillToAdapter
End Class 'CustomerBillToAdapter
```

RELATED PATTERNS

Façade: The Adapter class provides an object that acts as an intermediary for function or subroutine calls between a client object and *one other* object not known to the client objects. The Façade pattern provides an object that acts as an intermediary for function or subroutine calls between its client object and *multiple* objects not known to the client objects.

Iterator: The Iterator pattern is a specialized form of the Adapter pattern for sequentially accessing the contents of a collection of objects.

Proxy: The Proxy pattern, like the Adapter pattern, uses an object that is a surrogate for another object. However, a Proxy object has the same interface as the object for which it is a surrogate.

Strategy: The Strategy pattern is structurally similar to the Adapter pattern. The difference is in the intent. The Adapter pattern allows a Client object to carry out its originally intended purpose by calling functions and subroutines of objects that implement a particular interface. The Strategy pattern provides objects that implement a particular interface for the purpose of altering or determining the behavior of a Client object.

Iterator

This pattern was described previously in [GoF95].

SYNOPSIS

The Iterator pattern defines an interface that declares functions and subroutines for sequentially accessing the objects in a collection. A class that accesses a collection only through such an interface is independent of the class that implements the interface and the class of the collection.

CONTEXT

Suppose that you are writing classes to browse inventory in a warehouse. There will be a user interface that allows a user to see the description, quantity on hand, location, and other information about each inventory item.

The inventory browsing classes will be part of a customizable application. For this reason, they must be independent of the actual class that provides collections of inventory items. To provide this independence, you design an interface to allow the user interface to sequentially access a collection of inventory items without being aware of the actual collection class being used. The class diagram in Figure 6.4 shows the relevant part of the design.

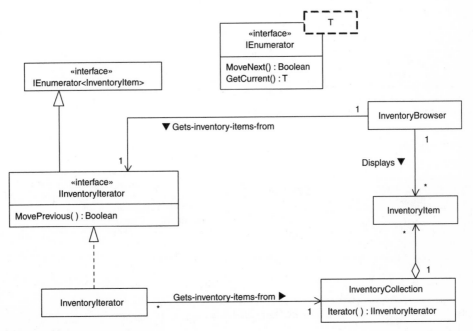

Figure 6.4 Inventory Iterator

In Figure 6.4, the user interface classes that constitute the inventory browser are shown as the composite class `InventoryBrowser`. An instance of the `Inventory Browser` class is asked to display `InventoryItem` objects in the collection encapsulated by an `InventoryCollection` object. The `InventoryBrowser` object does not directly access the `InventoryCollection` object. Instead, it is given an object that implements the `IInventoryIterator` interface. The `IInventoryIterator` interface defines functions to allow an object to sequentially fetch the contents of a collection of `InventoryItem` objects.

FORCES

☺ A class needs access to the contents of a collection without being dependent on the class that implements the collection.

☺ When accessing a remote collection that is very large, creating a local copy of the collection may consume an excessive amount of memory.

☺ A class needs a uniform way of accessing the contents of multiple collections.

☺ Visual Basic .NET's `For Each` statement is specially designed to support collection classes that implement the `IEnumerable` interface.

SOLUTION

The class diagram in Figure 6.5 shows the organization of the classes and interfaces that participate in the Iterator pattern.

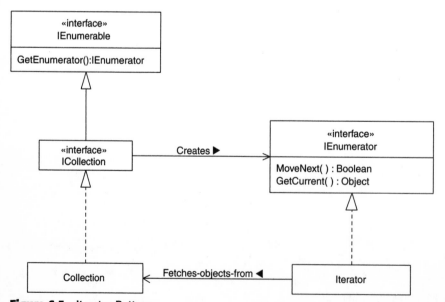

Figure 6.5 Iterator Pattern

Here are descriptions of the roles that classes and interfaces play in the organization shown in Figure 6.5:

Collection: A class in this role encapsulates a collection of objects or values.

IEnumerator: An interface in this role defines functions and subroutines to sequentially access objects encapsulated by a `Collection` object. Often the interface in this role is or inherits `System.Collections.IEnumerator`.

Iterator: A class in this role implements an `IEnumerator` interface. Its instances provide sequential access to the contents of the `Collection` object associated with an `Iterator` object.

ICollection: `Collection` classes normally take responsibility for creating their own `Iterator` objects. It is convenient to have a consistent way to ask a `Collection` object to create an `Iterator` object. To provide this consistency, all `Collection` classes implement an `ICollection` interface that inherits a function for creating `Iterator` objects from the `IEnumerable` interface.

IEnumerable: An interface in this role defines a function that create and returns a `Iterator` object. Often the interface in this role is or inherits `System. Collections.IEnumerable`.

IMPLEMENTATION

Generics

Iterator classes that implement the `System.Collections.IEnumerator` interface have a read-only property named `Current` to get objects from a collection. The type of the `Current` property is `Object`. This works well for collections of objects that are of different types. It is inconvenient for collections that contain a particular kind of object. Collections that contain a particular kind of object are more common than collections that contain no particular kind of object.

To access a member of an object returned by the `Current` property, you need to cast the object to a more specialized type. This is an extra bit of code that adds overhead and is another opportunity for programmers to add bugs.

Using the generic form of the interface (`System.Collections.Generic. IEnumerator`), you get a `Current` property whose type is the type of objects actually in the collection. This saves some programmer effort and runtime overhead. If the iterator class implements the generic form of the `IEnumerator` interface, the collection should implement the generic form of the `IEnumerable` interface (`System. Collections.Generic.IEnumerable`).

Additional Functions

The IIterator interface shown under the "Solution" heading has a minimal set of functions. It is common for IIterator interfaces to define additional functions and subroutines when they are useful and the underlying collection classes support them. In addition to functions for testing the existence of and fetching the next collection element, the following sorts of functions are common:

- Test for the existence of and fetch the previous collection element.
- Move to the first or last collection element.
- Get the number of elements in the traversal.

Multiple Orderings

Sometimes, there may be a need to traverse a collection in more than one order. For example, it may be necessary to traverse a collection of people in order of name or Social Security number. To do this with iterators, you need different kinds of iterators. If you only need a few different kinds of iterators, the simplest way for clients of the collection class to get an iterator object is to have a different function to get each kind of iterator. If there are more than a few different kinds of iterators, it may be simpler to have one function that takes arguments that describe the kind of iterator it should return.

The most common variation in the order that iterators traverse a collection is forward and backward. By having iterators that go in opposite directions, the client of the iterator does not need to have different logic for going forward and backward.

Null Iterator

A *null iterator* is an iterator that returns no objects. Its HasNext function always returns false. Null iterators are usually implemented as a simple class that implements the appropriate IIterator interface. The use of null iterators can simplify the implementation of collection classes and other iterator classes by removing the need for some code to handle the special case of a null traversal. Though this is different than the null object pattern, the underlying principle is the same: Reduce the number of possible execution paths.

Modification to the Underlying Collection

Modifying a collection object while an iterator is traversing its contents can cause problems. If no provisions are made for dealing with such modifications, an iterator may return an inconsistent set of results. The potential inconsistencies include skipping objects or returning the same object twice.

A simple way to handle this is to consider an iterator to be invalid after its underlying collection is modified. You can implement this by having a collection class's functions and subroutines increment a counter when they modify the collection. Iterator objects can detect changes to their underlying collection by noticing a difference between the current change count and the value of the change count when the iterator was created. If an iterator object's function notices that the underlying collection has changed, it can throw an exception.

A more robust way of handling modifications to an underlying collection is to ensure that the iterator returns a consistent set of results. There are a number of ways to accomplish this. Though making a full copy of the underlying collection works in most cases, it is usually the least desirable technique because it is the most expensive in terms of both time and memory.

CONSEQUENCES

☺ It is possible to access a collection of objects without knowing the source of the objects.

☺ By using multiple iterator objects, it is simple to have and manage multiple traversals at the same time.

☺ A collection class may provide different kinds of iterator objects to traverse the collection in different ways. For example, a collection class that maintains an association between key objects and value objects may have a function for creating iterators that traverse just the key objects and a function for creating iterators that traverse just the value objects.

.NET API USAGE

The .NET Framework defines the IEnumerator interface, which fills the IIterator role for many classes. The .NET Framework also defines an interface called IEnumerable. Many classes that have a function to create an IEnumerator object implement the IEnumerable interface. The IEnumerable interface fills the ICollection role of the Iterator pattern.

CODE EXAMPLE

The design discussed under the context heading is a good organization for the problem discussed there. However, it does not take full advantage of the support that .NET supplies for collections. In particular, .NET has support for collections that can be used to advantage. Figure 6.6 shows this improved design.

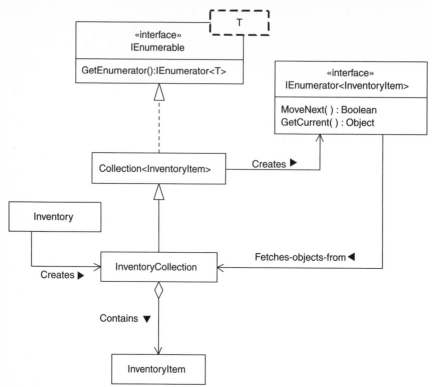

Figure 6.6 Iterator Pattern

For a code example, we will look at some skeletal code that implements the design shown in Figure 6.5. Here is a listing of the InventoryCollection class:

```
Imports System.Collections.Generic

' track a collection of inventory items
Public Class InventoryCollection
    Inherits List(Of InventoryItem)
End Class 'InventoryCollection
```

As you can see, InventoryCollection is a very simple specialization of the Collection class.

The Inventory class uses an Iterator to access the items in the Inventory Collection. The use of the iterator is implicit in the For Each statement. The follow skeletal listing shows the relevant portion of the Inventory class.

```
Imports System.Collections.Generic

Public Class Inventory
    Private MyItems As InventoryCollection
    Private RetailValues As Dictionary(Of InventoryItem, Decimal)
    ...

    Public Function TotalRetailValue() As Decimal
        Dim Total As Decimal
        For Each item As InventoryItem In MyItems
            Total += RetailValues(item)
        Next
        Return Total
    End Function
End Class
```

To round out this code example, here is a skeletal listing of the `InventoryItem` class:

```
' Instances of this class describe an inventory item
Public Class InventoryItem
    Private myItemNumber As String
    ...
    Public Property ItemNumber() As String
        Get
            Return myItemNumber
        End Get
        Set(ByVal value As String)
            myItemNumber = value
        End Set
    End Property

    Public Overrides Function GetHashCode() As Integer
        Return ItemNumber.GetHashCode
    End Function
End Class 'InventoryItem
```

RELATED PATTERNS

Adapter: The Iterator pattern is a specialized form of the Adapter pattern for sequentially accessing the contents of collection objects.

Factory Method: Some collection classes may use the Factory Method pattern to determine what kind of iterator to instantiate.

Null Object: Null iterators are sometimes used to implement the Null Object pattern.

Bridge

This pattern was previously described in [GoF95].

SYNOPSIS

The Bridge pattern is useful when there is a hierarchy of abstractions and a corresponding hierarchy of implementations. Rather than combining the abstractions and implementations into many distinct classes, the Bridge pattern implements the abstractions and implementations as independent classes that can be combined dynamically.

CONTEXT

Suppose that you need to provide classes to access physical sensors for control applications. These are devices such as scales, speed-measuring devices, and location-sensing devices. What these devices have in common is that they perform a physical measurement and produce a number. One way these devices differ is in the type of measurement that they produce.

- The scale produces a single number based on a measurement at a single point in time.
- The speed-measuring device produces a single measurement that is an average over a period of time.
- The location-sensing device produces a stream of measurements.

This suggests that these devices can be supported by three classes shown in Figure 6.7 that support these different measurement techniques.

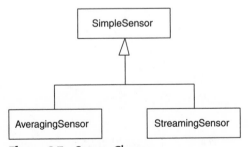

Figure 6.7   Sensor Classes

The three classes shown in Figure 6.7 provide clean abstractions that apply to many more types of sensors than the three that inspired them. There are other kinds of sensors that produce simple measurements, time-averaged measurements, and streams of measurements. You would like to be able to reuse these classes with other kinds of sensors. A difficulty in achieving such reuse is that the details of communicating with sensors from different manufacturers vary. Suppose that the software you are writing will need to work with sensors from two manufacturers called Eagle and Hawk. You could handle this problem by having manufacturer-specific classes, as shown in Figure 6.8.

The problem with this solution is not just that it does not reuse classes for simple, averaging, and streaming sensors. Because it exposes differences between manufacturers to other classes, it forces other classes to recognize differences between manufacturers and therefore be less reusable. The challenge here is to represent a hierarchy of abstractions in a way that keeps the abstractions independent of their implementations.

A way to accomplish this is by adding some indirection that shields a hierarchy of classes that support abstractions from classes that implement those abstractions. Have abstraction classes access implementation classes through a hierarchy of implementation interfaces that parallels the abstraction hierarchy, as shown in Figure 6.9.

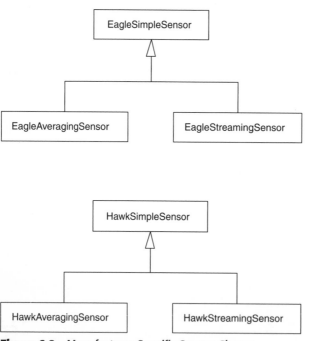

Figure 6.8 Manufacturer-Specific Sensor Classes

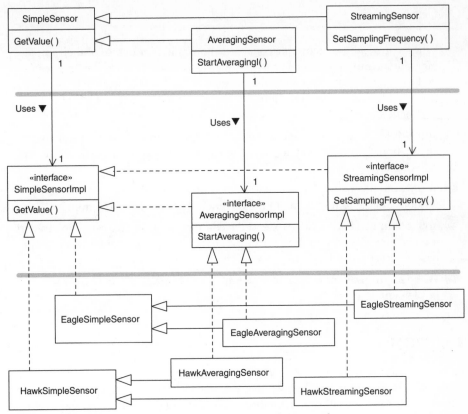

Figure 6.9   Independent Sensor and Sensor Manufacturer Classes

The solution shown in Figure 6.9 divides the problem into three hierarchies separated by horizontal gray lines.

- On the top, there is a hierarchy of manufacturer-independent sensor classes on the top.

- On the bottom, there are parallel hierarchies of manufacturer-specific classes.

- In the middle, there is a parallel hierarchy of interfaces that allow the manufacturer-independent classes to be independent of any manufacturer-specific classes.

Any logic that is common to a type of sensor will go in a manufacturer-independent class. Logic that is specific to a manufacturer will go in a manufacturer-specific class.

Most of the logic in this example is for handling exceptional conditions. An example of such a condition is when a simple sensor detects an out-of-range value too large for it to measure. Manufacturer-independent handling for that condition could be to translate that to a predetermined maximum value for the application. Manufacturer-specific handling for that condition might require not considering any readings from the sensor to be valid until a certain amount of time has elapsed after the end of the out-of-range condition.

FORCES

☺ When you combine hierarchies of abstractions and hierarchies of their implementations into a single class hierarchy, classes that use those classes become tied to a specific implementation of the abstraction. Changing the implementation used for an abstraction should not require changes to classes that use the abstraction.

☺ You would like to reuse logic common to different implementations of an abstraction. The usual way to make logic reusable is to encapsulate it in a separate class.

☺ You would like to be able to create a new implementation of an abstraction without having to reimplement the common logic of the abstraction.

☺ You would like to be able to extend the common logic of an abstraction by writing one new class rather than writing a new class for each combination of the base abstraction and its implementation.

☺ When appropriate, multiple abstractions should be able to share the same implementation.

SOLUTION

The Bridge pattern allows classes corresponding to abstractions to be separate from classes that implement those abstractions. You maintain a clean separation by having abstraction classes access implementation classes through interfaces organized in a hierarchy that parallels the inheritance hierarchy of the abstraction classes (see Figure 6.10).

Figure 6.10 shows the roles that classes and interfaces play in the Bridge pattern. Here are descriptions of these roles:

Abstraction: This class represents the top-level abstraction. It is responsible for maintaining a reference to an object that implements the `AbstractionImpl` interface, so that it can delegate operations to its implementation. If an instance of the `Abstraction` class is also an instance of a subclass of the `Abstraction` class, then the instance will refer to an object that implements the corresponding subinterface of the `AbstractionImpl` interface.

SpecializedAbstraction: This role corresponds to any subclass of the `Abstraction` class. For each such subclass of the `Abstraction` class, there is a corresponding subinterface of the `AbstractionImpl` interface. Each `SpecializedAbstraction` class delegates its operations to an implementation object that implements the `SpecializedAbstractionImpl` interface that corresponds to the `SpecializedAbstraction` class.

AbstractionImpl: This interface defines functions and subroutines for all low-level operations that an implementation for the `Abstraction` class must provide.

SpecializedAbstractionImpl:. This corresponds to a subinterface of `AbstractionImpl`. Each `SpecializedAbstractionImpl` interface corresponds to a `SpecializedAbstraction` class and defines functions and subroutines for the low-level operations needed for an implementation of that class.

Impl1, Impl2: These classes implement the `AbstractionImpl` interface and provide different implementations for the `Abstraction` class.

SpecializedImpl1, SpecializedImpl2: These classes implement one of the `SpecializedAbstractionImpl` interfaces and provide different implementations for a `SpecializedAbstraction` class.

Figure 6.10 shows the abstraction implementation interfaces having the same functions and subroutines as the corresponding abstraction classes. This is a presentational convenience. It is possible for abstraction implementation interfaces to have different functions and subroutines than the corresponding abstraction classes.

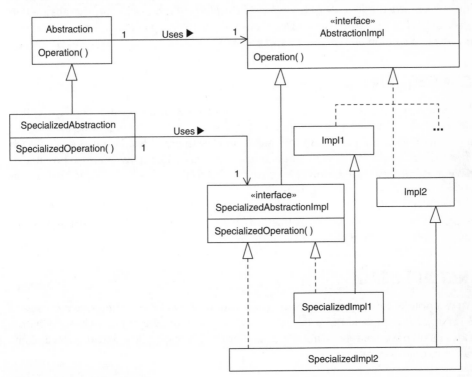

Figure 6.10   Bridge Pattern

IMPLEMENTATION

One issue that always must be decided when implementing the Bridge pattern is how to create implementation objects for each abstraction object. The most basic decision to make is whether abstraction objects will create their own implementation objects or delegate the creation of their implementation objects to another object.

Having the abstraction objects delegate the creation of implementation objects is usually the best choice. It preserves the independence of the abstraction and implementation classes. If abstraction classes are designed to delegate the creation of implementation objects, the design usually uses the Abstract Factory pattern to create the implementation objects.

However, if there are only a small number of implementation classes for an abstract class and the set of implementation classes is not expected to change, then having the abstraction classes create their own implementation objects is a reasonable optimization.

A related decision is whether an abstraction object will use the same implementation object throughout its lifetime. As usage patterns or other conditions change, it may be appropriate to change the implementation object an abstraction object uses. If an abstraction class directly creates its own implementation objects, it is reasonable to directly embed the logic for changing the implementation object in the abstraction class. Otherwise, you can use the Decorator pattern to encapsulate the logic for switching implementation objects in a wrapper class.

CONSEQUENCES

The Bridge pattern keeps classes that represent an abstraction independent of the classes that supply an implementation for the abstraction. The abstraction and its implementations are organized into separate class hierarchies. You can extend each class hierarchy without directly impacting another class hierarchy. It is also possible to have multiple implementation classes for an abstraction class or multiple abstraction classes using the same implementation class.

Classes that are clients of the abstraction classes do not have any knowledge of the implementation classes, so an abstraction object can change its implementation without any impact on its clients.

.NET API USAGE

An example of the Bridge pattern is the streaming I/O classes. The `MemoryStream`, `BufferedStream`, and `FileStream` classes inherit from the `Stream` class. Each provides its own way of representing of a sequence of bytes. Yet, the consumers can simply treat them as streams.

EXAMPLE

For an example of the Bridge pattern, we will look at some code to implement the sensor-related classes that were discussed under the "Context" heading. We will assume that the objects that represent sensors and their implementation are created by a Factory Method. The Factory Method object will know what sensors are available, what objects to create to provide access to a sensor, and will create those objects when access to a sensor is first requested.

Here is the code for the `SimpleSensor` class that plays the role of abstraction class:

```
' Instances of this class are used to represent all kinds of sensors.
' Instances of subclasses of this class represent specialized kinds of
' sensors.
Public Class SimpleSensor
    ' A reference to the object that implements operations specific to
    ' the actual sensor device that this object represents.
    Private myImpl As SimpleSensorImpl

    ' This constructor is intended to be called by a factory method
    ' object that is in the same package as this class and the
    ' classes that implement its operations.
    '
    ' impl - The object that implements the sensor type-specific
    '         operations this object will provide.
    Public Sub New(ByVal impl As SimpleSensorImpl)
        myImpl = impl
    End Sub

    ' This allows subclasses of this class to get the reference
    ' to the implementation object.
    Friend ReadOnly Property Impl() As SimpleSensorImpl
        Get
            Return myImpl
        End Get
    End Property

    ' Return the value of the sensor's current measurement.
    Public ReadOnly Property CurrentMeasure() As Integer
        Get
            Return myImpl.CurrentMeasure
        End Get
    End Property
End Class 'SimpleSensor
```

As you can see, the `SimpleSensor` class is simple. It does little more than delegate its operations to an object that implements the `SimpleSensorImpl` interface. Here is the `SimpleSensorImpl` interface:

```
' All objects that implement operations for SimpleSensor objects must
' implement this interface.
Public Interface SimpleSensorImpl
    '
    ' Return the value of the sensor's current measurement.
    '
    ReadOnly Property CurrentMeasure() As Integer
End Interface 'SimpleSensorImpl
```

Some subclasses of the `SimpleSensor` class maintain the same simple structure. Following is code for the `AveragingSensor` class. Instances of the `Averaging Sensor` class represent sensors that produce values that are the average of measurements made over a period of time.

```
' Instances of this class are used to represent sensors that produce
' values that are the average of measurements made over a period of
' time.
Public Class AveragingSensor
    Inherits SimpleSensor


    ' This constructor is intended to be called by a factory method
    ' object that is in the same package as this class and the the
    ' classes that implement its operations.
    ' impl - The object that implements the sensor type-specific
    '        operations this object will provide.
    Public Sub New(ByVal impl As AveragingSensorImpl)
        MyBase.New(impl)
    End Sub


    ' Averaging sensors produce a value that is the average of
    ' measurements made over a period of time.  That period of time
    ' begins when this method is called.
    Public Sub BeginAverage()
        CType(Impl, AveragingSensorImpl).BeginAverage()
    End Sub
End Class 'AveragingSensor
```

As you can see, the `AveragingSensor` class is also very simple, delegating its operations to the implementation objects that it is using. Here is its corresponding implementation interface:

```
' All objects that implement operations for AveragingSensor objects must
' implement this interface.
Public Interface AveragingSensorImpl
    Inherits SimpleSensorImpl
    ' Averaging sensors produce a value that is the average of
    ' measurements made over a period of time.  That period of time
    ' begins when this method is called.
    Sub BeginAverage()
End Interface 'AveragingSensorImpl
```

It is reasonable for subclasses of the `SimpleSensor` class to be more complex and provide additional services of their own. The `StreamingSensor` class delivers a stream of measurements to objects registered to receive the measurements. It delivers each measurement by passing the measurement to a delegate. It does not place any requirements on how long calls to the delegate may take before returning. There is merely an expectation that it will return in a reasonable amount of time. On the other hand, the implementation objects used with instances of the `StreamingSensor` class may need to deliver measurements at a steady rate or lose them. In order to avoid losing measurements, instances of the StreamingSensor class buffer measurements that are delivered to it, while it asynchronously delivers those measurements to other objects. Here is code for the StreamingSensor class:

```
Imports System
Imports System.Threading
Imports System.IO
Imports System.Collections


'
' Instances of this class are used to represent sensors that produce
' a stream of measurement values.
'
Public Class StreamingSensor
    Inherits SimpleSensor
    Implements StreamingSensorListener

    Private consumer As StreamReader ' stream for incoming measurement values
    Private listeners As New ArrayList() ' aggregate listeners here
    Private queue As Queue

    ' queue for available measurements
    '
    ' Constructed by a factory method
    ' object that is in the same package as this class and the
    ' classes that implement its operations.
    '
    ' i - The object that implements the sensor type-specific
    '     operations this object will provide.
    '
    ' r - a stream reader to use for reading the sensor data
    '
    Public Sub New(ByVal i As StreamingSensorImpl, ByVal r As StreamReader)
        MyBase.New(i)
        consumer = r
        queue = New Queue() ' allocate a queue for this instance
        ' start a thread to deliver measurement values
        ThreadPool.QueueUserWorkItem(AddressOf Me.DeliverValues)
    End Sub


    ' Streaming sensors produce a stream of measurement values.  The
    ' stream of values is produced with a frequency no greater than
    ' the given number of times per minute.
    '
    Public WriteOnly Property SamplingFrequency() As Integer
        Set(ByVal value As Integer)
```

```vb
                    ' delegate this to the implementation object
                    CType(Impl, StreamingSensorImpl).SamplingFrequency = value
            End Set
    End Property


    '
    ' StreamingSensor objects deliver a stream of values to
    ' interested objects by passing each value to the object's
    ' EnQueueMeasurement method.  The delivery of values is done
    ' using its own thread and is asynchronous of everything else.
    '
    ' value - The measurement value being delivered.
    Public Sub EnqueueMeasure(ByVal value As Integer) _
    Implements StreamingSensorListener.EnqueueMeasure
        queue.Enqueue(value)
    End Sub


    '
    ' Remove the current item from the sensor queue
    '
    Public Function DequeueMeasure() As Integer
        Return CInt(queue.Dequeue())
    End Function



    '
    ' Is there an entry available in the sensor queue
    '
    Public Function IsMeasureAvailable() As Boolean
        Return queue.Count > 0
    End Function


    '
    ' This method asynchronously removes measurement values from the
    ' pipe and delivers them to registered listeners.
    '
    Private Sub DeliverValues(ByVal o As Object)
        While True
            Dim s As String = consumer.ReadLine()
            If s Is Nothing Then
                Return
            End If
            Dim value As Integer
            Try
                value = Convert.ToInt32(s)
            Catch e As System.FormatException
                Return ' ignore bad values
            Catch e As System.OverflowException
                Return ' ignore overflow values
            End Try
```

```
        EnqueueMeasure(value)
    End While
End Sub 'DeliverValues

End Class 'StreamingSensor
```

In order for the `StreamingSensor` class to deliver a measurement to an object, the object must implement the `StreamingSensorListener` interface. It delivers measurements by passing them to the `processMeasurement` subroutine that the `StreamingSensorListener` interface declares. The `StreamingSensor` class also implements the `StreamingSensorListener` interface. Implementation objects deliver measurements to instances of the `StreamingSensor` class by calling its `processMeasurement` subroutine.

Finally, here is the implementation interface that corresponds to the `Streaming Sensor` class:

```
' All objects that implement operations for StreamingSensor objects must
' implement this interface.
'
Public Interface StreamingSensorImpl
    Inherits SimpleSensorImpl
    '
    ' Streaming sensors produce a stream of measurement values.  The
    ' stream of values is produced with a frequency no greater than
    ' the given number of times per minute.
    '
    WriteOnly Property SamplingFrequency() As Integer
    '
    ' This property is set by an object than represents the
    ' streaming sensor abstraction so that this object can perform a
    ' call-back to that object to deliver measurement values to it.
    '
    WriteOnly Property StreamingSensorListener() As StreamingSensorListener
End Interface 'StreamingSensorImpl
```

RELATED PATTERNS

Layered Architecture: The Bridge design pattern is a way of organizing the entities identified using the Layered Architecture pattern (described in [BMRSS96]) into classes.

Abstract Factory: The Abstract Factory pattern can be used by the Bridge pattern to decide which implementation class to instantiate for an abstraction object.

Decorator: The Decorator pattern can be used to dynamically select the implementation object that an abstraction object delegates an operation to.

Façade

This pattern was previously described in [GoF95].

SYNOPSIS

The Façade pattern simplifies access to a related set of objects by providing one object that all objects outside the set use to communicate with the set.

CONTEXT

Consider the organization of classes to support the creation and sending of e-mail messages. The classes may include the following:

- A `MailMessageBody` class, whose instances will contain message bodies
- An `Attachment` class, whose instances will contain message attachments that can be attached to a `MailMessageBody` object
- A `MailMessageHeader` class, whose instances will contain header information (to, from, subject . . .) for an e-mail message
- A `MailMessage` class, whose instances will tie together a `MailMessage Header` object and a `MailMessageBody` object
- A `Security` class, whose instances can be used to add a digital signature to a message
- A `MailMessageSender` class, whose instances are responsible for sending `MailMessage` objects to a server that is responsible for delivering the e-mail to its destination or another server

Figure 6.11 is a class diagram showing the relationships between these classes and a client class:

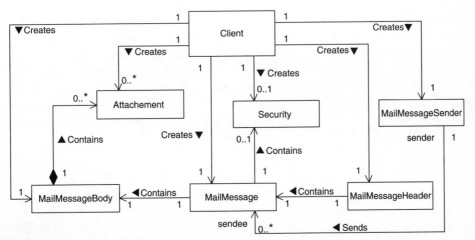

Figure 6.11   E-Mail Creation

As you can see, working with these e-mail classes adds complexity to a client class. To use these classes, a client must know of at least these six of them, the relationships between them, and the order in which it must create instances of the classes. If every client of these classes must take on this additional complexity, it makes the e-mail classes more difficult to reuse.

The Façade pattern is a way to shield clients of classes like these e-mail classes from their complexity. It works by providing an additional reusable object that hides most of the complexity of working with the other classes from client classes. Figure 6.12 is a class diagram showing this more reusable organization.

In this new scheme, the portion of the `Client` class responsible for interacting with the e-mail classes has been refactored into a separate reusable class. Client classes now need only be aware of the `MailMessageCreator` class. Furthermore, the internal logic of the `MailMessageCreator` class can shield client classes from having to create the parts of an e-mail message in any particular order.

FORCES

☺ There are many dependencies between classes that implement an abstraction and their client classes. The dependencies add noticeable complexity to clients.

☺ You want to simplify client classes, because simpler classes result in fewer bugs. Simpler clients also mean less work is required to reuse the classes that implement the abstraction.

☺ You are designing classes to function in cleanly separated layers. You want to minimize the number of classes that are visible from one layer to the next.

SOLUTION

Figure 6.13 is a class diagram showing the general structure of the Façade pattern. The client object interacts with a `Façade` object that provides necessary functionality by interacting with the rest of the objects. If there is some additional functionality needed by only some clients, instead of providing it directly, the `Façade` object may provide a function to access another object that does provide the functionality.

It is not necessary for a `Façade` class to act as an impenetrable barrier separating client classes from the classes that implement an abstraction. It is sufficient, and sometimes better, for a `Façade` class to merely be a default way of accessing the functionality of the classes that implement an abstraction. If some clients need to directly access abstraction-implementing classes, then the `Façade` class should facilitate this with a function that returns a reference to the appropriate implementation object.

The point of the `Façade` class is to allow simple clients, not require them.

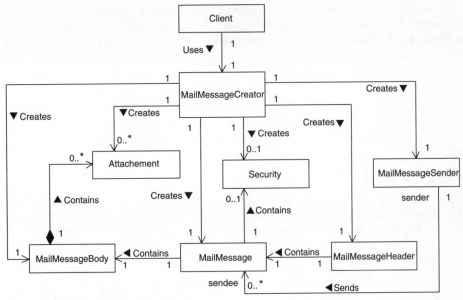

Figure 6.12   Reusable E-Mail Creation

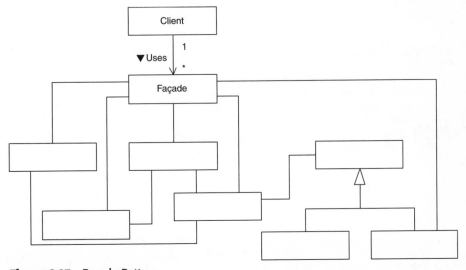

Figure 6.13   Façade Pattern

IMPLEMENTATION

A Façade class should provide a way for client objects to obtain a direct reference to an instance of abstraction-implementing classes that client objects may need to know about. However, there may be some abstraction-implementing classes that client classes have no legitimate reason to know about. These classes should be hidden from client classes.

Sometimes you want to vary the implementation classes that a façade object uses to accommodate variations on the abstraction being implemented. For example, returning to the e-mail example under the context heading, you may need a different set of classes to create MIME (Multipurpose Internet Mail Extensions)–, MAPI (Messaging Application Programming Interface)–, or Notes-compliant messages. Different sets of implementation classes usually require different `Façade` classes. You can hide the use of different `Façade` classes from client classes by applying the Interface pattern. Define an interface that all `Façade` classes for e-mail creation must implement. Then have client classes access the `Façade` class through an interface rather than directly.

CONSEQUENCES

☺ Interposing a façade class between the classes that implement an abstraction and their clients simplifies client classes by moving dependencies from client classes to the façade class. Clients of façade objects do not need to know about any classes behind the façade.

☺ Because the Façade pattern reduces or eliminates the coupling between a client class and the classes that implement an abstraction, it may be possible to change the classes that implement the abstraction without any impact on the client class.

.NET API USAGE

No implementations of the Façade pattern are visible externally. However, it is used internally in the implementation of several classes.

EXAMPLE

Below is code for the `MailMessageCreator` class shown in the class diagram under the "Context" heading. Instances of the `MailMessageCreator` class are used to create and send e-mail messages. It is shown here as a typical example of a `Façade` class.

```
Imports System.Collections

'
' Instances of this class are used to create and send e-mail messages.
' It assumes that an e-mail message consists of a message body and zero or
' more attachments. The content of the message body must be provided as
' either a String object or an object that implements an interface called
' RichText.  Any kind of an object can be provided as the content of an
' attachment.
'
```

```
Public Class MailMessageCreator
    ' Enum to indicate the type of message to create
    Public Enum MailMessageType As Integer
        MIME
        MAPI
        NOTES
        BANYAN
    End Enum

    Private myHeaderFields As New Hashtable()
    Private myMailMessageBody As RichText
    Private myAttachments As New ArrayList()
    Private mySignMailMessage As Boolean
    Private myMailMessageType As MailMessageType


    '
    ' Constructor to create a MailMessageCreator object that will create an
    ' e-mail message and send it to the given address.  It will attempt to
    ' infer the type of message to create from the "to" address.
    '
    ' sendTo - The address that this object will send a message to.
    ' from - The address that the message will say it is from.
    ' subject - The subject of this message.
    '
    Public Sub New(ByVal sendto As String, ByVal from As String, ByVal
subject As String)
        MyClass.New(sendto, from, subject, InferMailMessageType(sendto))
    End Sub


    '
    ' Constructor to create a MailMessageCreator object that will create an
    ' e-mail message and send it to the given address.
    '
    ' sendTo - The address that this object will send a message to.
    ' from - The address that the message will say it is from.
    ' subject -  The subject of this message.
    ' type -  The type of message to create.
    '
    Public Sub New(ByVal sendto As String, ByVal from As String, _
                ByVal subject As String, ByVal type As MailMessageType)
        myHeaderFields("to") = sendto
        myHeaderFields("from") = from
        myHeaderFields("subject") = subject
        myMailMessageType = type
    End Sub

    ...
```

```vbnet
' The contents of the message body.
Public Sub SetMailMessageBody(ByVal value As String)
    MailMessageBody = New RichTextString(value)
End Sub


' The contents of the message body.
Public WriteOnly Property MailMessageBody() As RichText
    Set(ByVal Value As RichText)
        Me.myMailMessageBody = Value
    End Set
End Property


' Add an attachement to the message
' attachment - the object to attach to the message
Public Sub AddAttachment(ByVal attachment As Object)
    myAttachments.Add(attachment)
End Sub


' Flag whether this message should be signed.  The default is false.
Public WriteOnly Property SignMailMessage() As Boolean
    Set(ByVal Value As Boolean)
        mySignMailMessage = Value
    End Set
End Property


' Set the value of a header field.
' name - The name of the field to set the value of
' value - The value to set the field to.
Public Sub SetHeaderField(ByVal name As String, ByVal value As String)
    myHeaderFields(name.ToLower()) = value
End Sub


' Send the message
Public Sub Send()
    Dim body As New MailMessageBody(myMailMessageBody)
    For i As Integer = 0 To myAttachments.Count - 1
        body.AddAttachment(New Attachment(myAttachments(i)))
    Next i
    Dim header As New MailMessageHeader(myHeaderFields)
    Dim msg As New MailMessage(header, body)
    If mySignMailMessage Then
        msg.Security = CreateSecurity()
    End If
    CreateMailMessageSender(msg)
End Sub 'Send
```

```
      '
      ' Infer a message type from a destination e-mail address.
      ' address - an e-mail address.
      Private Shared Function InferMailMessageType(ByVal address As
   String) As MailMessageType
          Dim type As MailMessageType = MailMessageType.MIME
          ...
          Return type
      End Function 'InferMailMessageType


      '
      ' Create a Security object appropriate for signing this message.
      '
      Private Function CreateSecurity() As Security
          Dim s As Security = Nothing
          ...
          Return s
      End Function 'CreateSecurity


      '
      ' Create a MailMessageSender object appropriate for the type of
      ' message being sent.
      '
      Private Sub CreateMailMessageSender(ByVal msg As MailMessage)
      End Sub 'CreateMailMessageSender


      ...
   End Class 'MailMessageCreator
```

The Façade pattern places no demands on the classes that the Façade class uses. Since they contain nothing that contributes to the Façade pattern, their code is not shown.

RELATED PATTERNS

Interface: The Interface pattern can be used with the Façade pattern to allow different façade classes to be used without client classes being aware of the different façade classes.

Adapter: The Adapter pattern allows client classes to treat a single object that does *not* implement an interface as an object which *does* implement the interface. The Façade pattern can be used to allow client classes to treat a group of objects as a single object that implements a particular interface.

Flyweight

This pattern was previously described in [GoF95].

SYNOPSIS

If instances of a class that contain the same information can be used interchangeably, the Flyweight pattern allows a program to avoid the expense of multiple instances that contain the same information by sharing one instance.

CONTEXT

Suppose that you are writing a word processor. Figure 6.14 is a class diagram showing some classes you might use to represent a document.

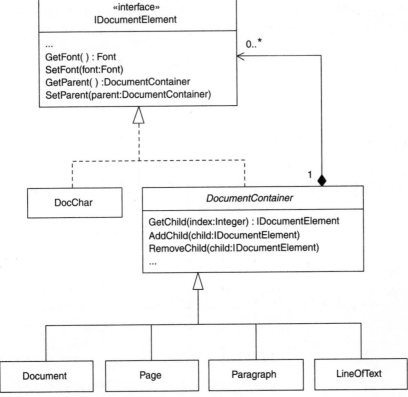

Figure 6.14   Document Representation Classes

This class organization includes the following classes:

- The IDocumentElement interface is implemented by all classes used to represent a document. All subclasses of the DocumentContainer class inherit the abstract Font property.

- An instance of the DocChar class is used to represent each character in a document.

- The DocumentContainer class is the base class of the container classes Document, Page, Paragraph, and LineOfText.

You can specify the font of each character by setting the Font property of the DocChar object that represents it. If the character's font is unspecified, then it uses its container's font. If its container's font has not been set, then the container uses its container's font, and so on.

Given this structure, one document that is a few pages long might contain tens of Paragraph objects that contain a few hundred LineOfText objects and thousands or tens of thousands of DocChar objects. Clearly, using this design will result in a program that uses a lot of memory to store DocChar objects.

It is possible to avoid the memory overhead of those many DocChar objects by having only one instance of each distinct DocChar object. The classes in Figure 6.14 use a DocChar object to represent each character in a document. To represent, "She saw her father" a LineOfText object uses DocChar objects, as shown in Figure 6.15.

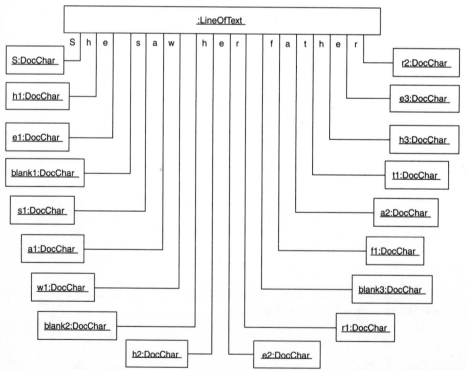

Figure 6.15 Unshared Character Objects

As you can see, the characters 'h', 'e', ' ', 'a' and 'r' are used multiple times. In an entire document, all the characters typically occur many times. It is possible to reorganize the objects so that one DocChar object is used to represent all occurrences of the same character. Figure 6.16 shows this organization.

To make the sharing of DocChar objects work, the DocChar objects cannot have any intrinsic attributes that are not common to every place the object is referenced. An intrinsic attribute is an attribute whose value is stored with the object. This is distinct from an extrinsic attribute, whose value is stored outside the object it applies to.

The class organization shown in Figure 6.14 shows a DocChar class whose instances can have an intrinsic font attribute. Those DocChar objects that do not have a font stored intrinsically use the font of their paragraph.

To make the sharing of DocChar objects work, classes must be reorganized so DocChar objects that have their own font store them extrinsically. The class diagram in Figure 6.17 includes a CharacterContext class whose instances store extrinsic attributes for a range of characters.

In this organization, the DocCharFactory class is responsible for providing a DocChar object that represents a given character. Given the same character to represent, a DocCharFactory object's getDocChar function will always return the same DocChar object. All the concrete classes are subclasses of the DocumentContainer class, except for the DocChar class. This means that the DocChar class does not have an intrinsic font attribute. If the user wants to associate a font with a character or range of characters, then the program creates a CharacterContext object, as shown in Figure 6.18. The objects shown in Figure 6.18 are a representation of a line of text that looks like this:

She saw *her* father

Because the word "her" is italicized, a character context is created for just the letters in that word so that there is a place to specify the font.

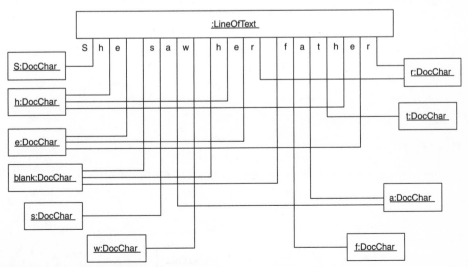

Figure 6.16 Shared Character Objects

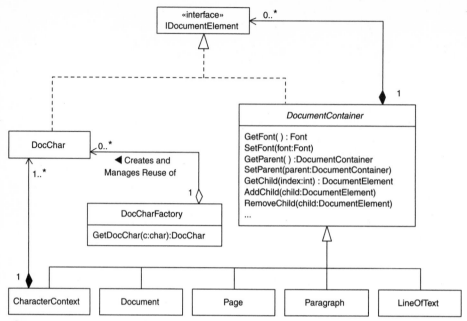

Figure 6.17 Document Shared Representation Classes

FORCES

☺ You have an application that uses a large number of similar objects.

☺ You want to reduce the memory overhead of having a large number of similar objects.

☺ The program does not rely on the object identity of the similar objects. The only important distinction between these objects is the value(s) that they contain.

☺ Representing similar things with similar objects to represent each thing takes more memory than representing similar things with the same object. The more things that can be represented with the same object, the greater the memory savings.

SOLUTION

Figure 6.19 shows the general organization of classes for the Flyweight pattern.

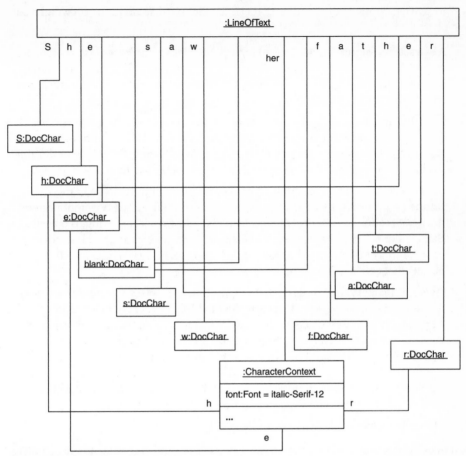

Figure 6.18   Font in CharacterContext

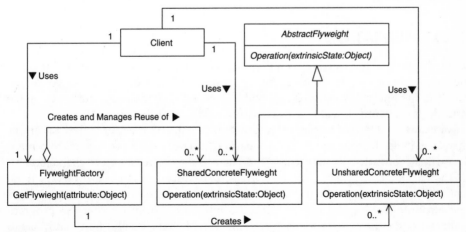

Figure 6.19   Flyweight Pattern

Here are descriptions of the roles that classes that participate in the Flyweight pattern play:

AbstractFlyweight: The AbstractFlyweight class is the base class of all other flyweight classes. It defines the properties, functions and subroutines common to flyweight classes. These properties, functions and subroutines require access to extrinsic state information.

SharedConcreteFlyweight: Instances of classes in this role are sharable objects. If they contain any intrinsic state, it must be common to all the entities they represent. For example, the sharable DocChar objects from the example under the Context heading have the character that they represent as their intrinsic state.

UnsharedConcreteFlyweight: Instances of classes that participate in the UnsharedConcreteFlyweight role are not sharable. The Flyweight pattern does not require the sharing of objects. It just allows object sharing. If objects that cannot be shared are instances of the AbstractFlyweight class, they will be instances of different subclasses of the AbstractFlyweight class than objects that can be shared.

FlyweightFactory: Instances of FlyweightFactory classes provide instances of the AbstractFlyweight class to client objects. If a client object asks a FlyweightFactory object to provide an instance of an UnsharedConcrete Flyweight class, then it simply creates the instance. However, if a client object asks a FlyweightFactory object to provide an instance of a Shared ConcreteFlyweight class, it first checks to see if it previously created a similar object. If it did, then it provides the previously created object to the client. Otherwise, it creates a new object and provides that to the client.

Client: Instances of classes in this role use flyweight objects.

If there is only one class in the SharedConcreteFlyweight role, it may be unnecessary to have any classes in the role of AbstractFlyweight or Unshared ConcreteFlyweight.

IMPLEMENTATION

There is a tradeoff to make between the number of attributes you make extrinsic and the number of flyweight objects needed at run time. The more attributes you make extrinsic, the fewer flyweight objects will be needed. The more attributes you make intrinsic, the less time it will take objects to access their attributes.

For example, in the document representation example, if the user makes a range of characters italic, the program creates a separate CharacterContext object to contain the extrinsic font attribute for the DocChar objects that represent those characters. An alternative would be to allow the font attribute to be intrinsic to DocChar objects. If the font attribute is intrinsic, then DocChar objects will spend less time accessing their font attribute. Letting the font attribute be intrinsic also means that the program will need a DocChar object for each combination of character and font that it has to represent.

CONSEQUENCES

☺ Using shared flyweight objects can drastically reduce the number of objects in memory. There is a price to pay for the reduced memory consumption:

- The Flyweight pattern makes a program more complex. The major sources of additional complexity are providing flyweight objects with their extrinsic state and managing the reuse of flyweight objects.

- The Flyweight pattern can increase the run time of a program because it takes more effort for an object to access extrinsic state than intrinsic state.

☺ Usually, it is possible to distinguish between entities by the objects that represent them. The Flyweight pattern makes this impossible, because it uses one object to represent multiple entities.

☺ Shared flyweight objects cannot contain parent pointers.

☺ Because of the complexity that the Flyweight pattern adds and the constraints it places on the organization of classes, the Flyweight pattern should be considered an optimization to be used only after the rest of a design is worked out.

.NET API USAGE

The common language run time uses the Flyweight pattern to manage the String objects used to represent string literals. If there is more than one string literal in a program that consists of the same sequence of characters, it uses the same String object to represent all of those string literals.

The String class's Intern function is responsible for managing the String objects used to represent string literals.

EXAMPLE

The following is some of the code that implements the design in Figure 6.17. Some of the classes don't contain any code of interest with respect to the Flyweight pattern, so code for those classes is not presented. For example, there is no code of interest in the IDocumentElement interface. The DocumentContainer class defines some functions and subroutines inherited by all of the container classes that are used to represent a document.

```
Imports System.Collections
Imports System.Drawing
'
' Instances of this class are composite objects that contain
' DocumentElement objects.
'
```

```
Public MustInherit Class DocumentContainer
    Inherits DocumentElement
    ' Collection of this object's children
    Private children As New ArrayList()

    ' This is the font associated with this object.  If the font
    ' variable is Nothing, then this object's font will be inherited
    ' through the container hierarchy from an enclosing object.
    Private myFont As Font

    Private myParent As DocumentContainer ' this object's container

    '
    ' the child objects of this object
    '
    Default Public ReadOnly Property Item(ByVal index As Integer) As
DocumentElement
        Get
            Return CType(children(index), DocumentElement)
        End Get
    End Property

    '
    ' Make the given DocumentElement a child of this object.
    '
    Public Sub Add(ByVal child As DocumentElement)
        SyncLock child
            children.Add(child)
            If TypeOf child Is DocumentContainer Then
                CType(child, DocumentContainer).Parent = Me
            End If
        End SyncLock
    End Sub  ' Add(DocumentElement)

    '
    ' Make the given DocumentElement NOT a child of this object.
    '
    Public Sub Remove(ByVal child As DocumentElement)
        SyncLock child
            If TypeOf child Is DocumentContainer Then
                If Me Is CType(child, DocumentContainer).Parent Then
                    CType(child, DocumentContainer).Parent = Nothing
                End If
            End If
            children.Remove(child)
        End SyncLock
    End Sub ' Remove(DocumentElement)

    '
    ' object's parent or Nothing if it has no parent.
    '
```

```
    Public Property Parent() As DocumentContainer
        Get
            Return myParent
        End Get
        Set(ByVal value As DocumentContainer)
            myParent = value
        End Set
    End Property


    '
    ' the Font associatiated with this object.  If there is no
    ' Font associated with this object, then return the Font associated
    ' with this object's parent. If there is no Font associated
    ' with this object's parent the return Nothing.
    '
    Public Property Font() As Font
        Get
            If myFont IsNot Nothing Then
                Return myFont
            ElseIf Parent IsNot Nothing Then
                Return Parent.Font
            Else
                Return Nothing
            End If
        End Get
        Set(ByVal value As Font)
            Me.myFont = value
        End Set
    End Property


    . . .
End Class 'DocumentContainer
```

The members shown for the DocumentContainer class manage the state of all the document container classes including the CharacterContext class. Using these inherited functions and subroutines, the CharacterContext class is able to manage the extrinsic state of DocChar objects even though it doesn't declare any of its own functions or subroutines for that purpose. Following is the code for the DocChar class that represents characters in a document.

```
Imports System


'
' Instances of this class represent a character in a document.
'
Friend Class DocChar
    Inherits DocumentElement
    Private character As Char
```

```vb
' Constructor for a character
' c - the character that this object represents.
Friend Sub New(ByVal c As Char)
    character = c
End Sub


...


'
' the character that this object represents
'
Protected Friend Overridable ReadOnly Property TheChar() As Char
    Get
        Return character
    End Get
End Property


'
' a unique value that determines where it is stored
' internally in a hash table.
'
Public ReadOnly Property HashCode() As Integer
    Get
        Return Convert.ToInt32(TheChar)
    End Get
End Property


'
' Redefine equals so that two DocChar objects are considered
' equal if they represent the same character.
'
Public Overloads Function Equals(ByVal o As Object) As Boolean
    If o Is Nothing Or Not (TypeOf o Is DocChar) Then
        Return False
    End If
    Return CType(o, DocChar).TheChar = TheChar
End Function ' Equals(Object)


'
' Always override GetHashCode if you override Equals
'
Public Overrides Function GetHashCode() As Integer
    Return Convert.ToInt32(TheChar)
End Function ' GetHashCode
End Class 'DocChar
```

Last, here is the code for the DocCharFactory class, which is responsible for the sharing of DocChar objects:

```
Imports System
Imports System.Collections


'
' Instances of this class are responsible for managing instances of the
' DocChar class.
'
Friend Class DocCharFactory
    Private myChar As New MutableDocChar()
    Private docCharPool As New Hashtable()


    '
    ' Return a DocChar object that represents the given character.
    ' c  - The character to be represented.
    '
    Function GetDocChar(ByVal c As Char) As DocChar
        myChar.TheChar = c
        Dim thisChar As DocChar = DirectCast(docCharPool(myChar), DocChar)

        If thisChar Is Nothing Then
            thisChar = New DocChar(c)
            docCharPool(thisChar) = thisChar
        End If
        Return thisChar
    End Function 'GetDocChar


    '
    ' To allow lookups of DocChar objects in a Hashtable or simillar
    ' collection, we will need a DocChar object that represents the
    ' same character as the DocChar object we want to find in the
    ' collection.  Creating a DocChar object to perform each lookup
    ' would largely defeat the purpose of putting the DocChar objects
    ' into the collection.  That purpose is to avoid creating a
    ' DocChar object for each character to be represented and instead
    ' use one DocChar object to represent every occurence of a
    ' character.
    '
    ' An alternative to creating a DocChar object for each lookup is
    ' to reuse the same DocChar object, changing the character that
    ' it represents for each lookup.  The problem with wanting to
    ' change the character that a DocChar object represents is that
    ' DocChar objects are immutable.  There is no way to change the
    ' character that a DocChar object represents.
    '
    ' A way to get around that problem it by using this private
    ' subclass of DocChar that does provide a way to change the
    ' character it represents.
    '
```

```
Private Class MutableDocChar
    Inherits DocChar
    Private character As Char


    '
    ' Constructor
    '
    Public Sub New()
        MyBase.New(Convert.ToChar(0)) ' It doesn't matter what we
pass to base.
    End Sub


    '
    ' the character that this object represents.
    '
    Public Shadows Property TheChar() As Char
        Get
            Return character
        End Get
        Set(ByVal value As Char)
            character = value
        End Set
    End Property
End Class 'MutableDocChar


End Class 'DocCharFactory
```

RELATED PATTERNS

Composite: The Flyweight pattern is often combined with the Composite pattern to represent the leaf nodes of a hierarchical structure with shared objects.

Factory Method: The Flyweight pattern uses the Factory Method pattern to create new flyweight objects.

Cache Management: The implementation of a `FlyweightFactory` class may use a cache.

Immutable: Shared flyweight objects are often immutable.

Dynamic Linkage

SYNOPSIS

Allow a program, upon request, to load and use arbitrary classes that implement a known interface.

CONTEXT

Suppose that you are writing software for a new kind of smart food processor that can be fed raw ingredients, and by slicing, dicing, mixing, boiling, baking, frying, and stirring is able to produce cooked, ready-to-eat food. On a mechanical level, the new food processor is a very sophisticated piece of equipment. However, a crucial part of the food processor is a selection of programs to prepare different kinds of foods. A program that can turn flour, water, yeast, and other ingredients into different kinds of bread is very different from a program that can stir-fry shrimp to exactly the right texture. The food processor will be required to run a great variety of programs to produce a great variety of foods. Because of the large variety of programs that will be required, it is not possible to build them all into the food processor. Instead, the food processor will load its programs from a CD-ROM or similar medium.

In order for these dynamically loaded programs and the food processor's operating environment to work with each other, they will need a way to call each other's properties, functions and subroutines. The class diagram in Figure 6.20 shows an arrangement of classes and interfaces to allow this:

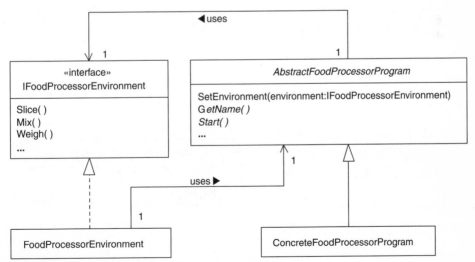

Figure 6.20   Food Processor Program Class Diagram

The organization shown in Figure 6.20 allows an object in the food processor environment to call properties, functions and subroutines of the top-level object in a food processor program by calling the properties, functions and subroutines of its base class. It also allows the top-level object to call the functions and subroutines of the food processor environment object through the `IFoodProcessorEnvironment` interface that it implements. Figure 6.21 is a collaboration diagram showing these interactions.

Figure 6.21 shows the initial steps that occur when the food processor's operating environment is asked to run a program:

1.1　The environment gets the `ConstructorInfo` object that is associated with a given program name in a `Hashtable` object that is used as a recipe dictionary.

1.2　The environment uses the `ConstructorInfo` object to create an instance of the program's top-level class.

1.3　The environment sets the `program` object's `environment` property reference to refer to the environment. Passing this reference to the program allows the program to call the environment's properties, functions and subroutines.

1.4　The environment gets the program's name from the program.

1.5　The environment displays the program's name.

1.6　The environment starts the program running.

　　1.61　The program weighs its ingredients.

　　1.62　The program mixes its ingredients.

The program continues executing additional steps that are beyond the scope of the drawing.

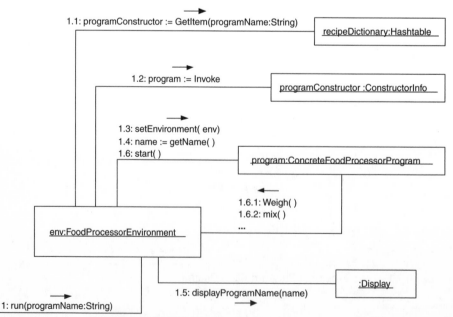

Figure 6.21　Food Processor Collaboration

FORCES

☺ A program must be able to load and use arbitrary classes that it has no prior knowledge of.

☺ Instances of a loaded class must be able to call back to the program that loaded it.

☻ Adding classes to a program that the program was not distributed with poses a security risk. There is also a risk of a version mismatch between the class and the program.

SOLUTION

Figure 6.22 is a class diagram showing the roles of interfaces and classes that participate in the Dynamic Linkage pattern.

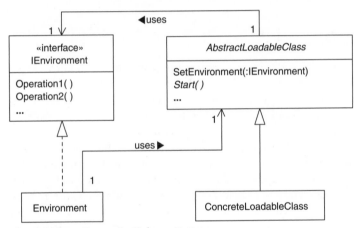

Figure 6.22 Dynamic Linkage Pattern

Here are descriptions of the roles classes and interfaces play in the Dynamic Linkage pattern.

IEnvironment: An interface in this role declares the environment's properties, functions and subroutines that a loaded class can call.

Environment: A class in this role is part of the environment that loads a ConcreteLoadableClass class. It implements the IEnvironment interface. A reference to an instance of this class is passed to instances of the Concrete LoadableClass class, so that they can call the functions and subroutines of the Environment object declared by the IEnvironment interface.

AbstractLoadableClass: Any class that is the top-level class of a food processor program must be a subclass of a class in the `AbstractLoadableClass` role. A class in this role is expected to declare a number of other, usually abstract, functions, subroutines, and properties, in addition those that are shown. Here is a description.

- There should be a write-only property with a name like `Environment`, which allows instances of subclasses of `AbstractLoadableClass` to be passed a reference to an instance of a class that implements the `IEnvironement` interface. The purpose of this is to allow `Abstract LoadableClass` objects to call the functions and subroutines of an `Environment` object.

- The environment calls another subroutine, typically named `start`, to tell an instance of a loaded class to start doing whatever it is supposed to be doing.

ConcreteLoadableClass. Classes in this role are subclasses of `Abstract LoadableClass` that can be dynamically loaded.

IMPLEMENTATION

The Dynamic Linkage pattern, as presented, requires the environment to know about the `AbstractLoadableClass` class and the loaded class to know about the `IEnvironment` interface. In cases where less structure is needed, other mechanisms for interoperation are possible. Other mechanisms usually involve a naming convention and the use of reflection to discover classes and their members.

Another requirement of the Dynamic Linkage pattern is that the `Environment` class somehow knows the name of a class that it wants to load. The mechanism for discovering the name varies with the application. In some cases, names may be hardwired. For the food processor example, a reasonable mechanism would be for a CD or other distribution medium to contain a directory of programs. The food processor would display the directory of programs as a menu, allowing the user to pick one.

Incompatible Classes

Some implementations of the Dynamic Linkage pattern may need to deal with the possibility of incompatible versions of the same class being used by different dynamically loaded classes. For example, suppose that programs for making lasagna sheets and wonton wrappers come on different CDs and both use a helper class named `Fu`. However, the two classes named `Fu` are incompatible. Suppose that the food processor first runs the lasagna program and then tries to run the wonton wrapper program. If the wonton wrapper class is given the lasagna `Fu` class when it is loaded, it will not work.

A strategy for avoiding this problem is to ensure that all of the supporting classes that are implicitly dynamically loaded along with an explicitly dynamically loaded class are not used by any other explicitly dynamically loaded class. You can implement that strategy by using a different AppDomain object for each dynamically loaded class. For example, some browsers use a different class loader for loading different applets. This prevents classes loaded as part of one program from being used as part of another.

Security Risk

A program that dynamically loads classes and calls their functions and subroutines poses some security risks. You would like to assume that the loaded classes will behave as intended and be generally well behaved. However, there is a possibility that this will not be the case. Here are some of the potential risks:

- The class may do something that denies the use of the environment for other purposes. One of its functions or subroutines that is supposed to return in a reasonable amount of time may never return. If the environment is multi-threaded, the class may consume CPU cycles, memory, or other resources that are needed for other purposes.

- The class may do something that violates the integrity of its environment. This can take many forms.

A detailed description of how to deal with these issues is beyond the scope of this book. Here are a few high-level remarks to get you started in the right direction.

The first issue to resolve is the size of the security risk in question. If the likelihood of anything going wrong is sufficiently low or the consequences are sufficiently low, then it is not worth taking any measures to lessen the likelihood or consequences of a security problem. However, if the likelihood or consequences are sufficiently great, then it is worth taking all possible measures.

The next issue is to determine the level of code access security (CAS) that you may wish to confer on a particular class. Remember that in the .NET Framework architecture, that the same security level is applied to all the classes within an assembly. Using a combination of CAS and strong named assemblies, you can assure that a class has been created by a known provider and restrict its level of access to only the level necessary for the job at hand.

A longer reading of the .NET Framework documentation on "Key Security Concepts" and "Code Access Security" will help determine the appropriate tradeoff levels. We also recommend [LLMP02].

Correctly using the mechanisms provided by the security architecture will make it unlikely that classes from sources that you do not trust will be able to do things that they are not supposed to do.

CONSEQUENCES

- ☺ Subclasses of the AbstractLoadableClass class can be dynamically loaded.

- ☺ The operating environment and the loaded classes do not need any specific foreknowledge of each other.

- Dynamic linkage increases the total amount of time it takes for a program to load all the classes it uses. However, it does have the effect of spreading out, over time, the overhead of loading classes. This can make an interactive program seem more responsive. The Virtual Proxy pattern can be used for this purpose.

⊗ Using the Dynamic Linkage pattern poses a security risk.

.NET API USAGE

The most obvious usage of the Dynamic Linkage pattern is ASP.NET. Classes extend from System.Web.Forms, and the ASP.NET environment itself, request fields, and so on, are accessible through its interfaces.

CODE EXAMPLE

The example is the code that implements the food processor design shown under the "Context" heading. First, here is the interface for the food processor environment:

```
'
' Food processor programs call methods of classes that implement this
' interface.
'
Public Interface FoodProcessorEnvironmentIF
    '
    ' Make a slice of food of the given width.
    ' width - The width of the slice to make.
    '
    Sub Slice(ByVal width As Integer)


    '
    ' Mix food at the given speed.
    ' speed - The speed to mix at.
    '
    Sub Mix(ByVal speed As Integer)


    '
    ' Weigh food.
    ' returns - the wieght in ounces.
    '
    ReadOnly Property Weight() As Double
End Interface 'FoodProcessorEnvironmentIF
```

Here is the abstract class that is the base class for all top-level program classes:

```
'
' Top level classes of food processor are subclasses of this class
'
Public MustInherit Class AbstractFoodProcessorProgram
```

```
    Private myEnvironment As FoodProcessorEnvironmentIF
        '
    ' The food processor environment passes a reference to itself to
    ' this method. That allows instances of subclasses of this class
    ' to call the methods of the food processor environement object
    ' that implements the FoodProcessorEnvironmentIF interface.
    '
    Public Property Environment() As FoodProcessorEnvironmentIF
        Get
            Return myEnvironment
        End Get
        Set(ByVal value As FoodProcessorEnvironmentIF)
            myEnvironment = Value
        End Set
    End Property


        '
    ' the name of this food processing program object.
        '
    Public MustOverride ReadOnly Property Name() As String


        '
    ' A call to this method tells a food processing program to start
    ' doing whatever it is supposed to be doing.
        '
    Public MustOverride Sub Start()


    ...


End Class 'AbstractFoodProcessorProgram
```

Here is the class that is responsible for the food processor environment being able to run programs: It uses a `ClassLoader` object to manage the classes that it loads.

```
Imports System
Imports System.Reflection
Imports System.IO


    '
' Food processor programs call methods of classes that implement this
' interface.
    '
Public Class FoodProcessorEnvironment
    Implements FoodProcessorEnvironmentIF


        '
    ' Make a slice of food of the given width.
    ' width - The width of the slice to make.
        '
```

```vb
Public Sub Slice(ByVal width As Integer) _
        Implements FoodProcessorEnvironmentIF.Slice
    ...
End Sub


'
' Mix food at the given speed.
' speed - The speed to mix at.
'
Public Sub Mix(ByVal speed As Integer) _
        Implements FoodProcessorEnvironmentIF.Mix
    ...
End Sub


'
' The wieght in ounces
'
Public ReadOnly Property Weight() As Double _
        Implements FoodProcessorEnvironmentIF.Weight
    Get
        Dim w As Double = 0.0
        ...
        Return w
    End Get
End Property


' Run the named program.
' assemblyName - the name of the assembly containing the program.
' programName - the name of the program to run.
Public Sub Run(ByVal assemblyName As String, ByVal programName As
String)
    Dim a As System.Reflection.Assembly
    Try
        a = System.Reflection.Assembly.LoadFrom(assemblyName)
    Catch ex As Exception
        ' Not found
        ...
        Return
    End Try ' try
    Dim program As AbstractFoodProcessorProgram
    Try
        program = CType(a.CreateInstance(programName),
AbstractFoodProcessorProgram)
    Catch ex As Exception
        ' Unable to run
        ...
        Return
    End Try
    program.Environment = Me
    display(program.Name)
    program.Start()
End Sub 'Run
```

```
        Private Sub display(ByVal s As String)
            ...
        End Sub 'display

End Class 'FoodProcessorEnvironment
```

Finally, here is sample code for a top-level program class:

```
'
' Top level classes of food processor are subclasses of this class
'
Public Class ConcreteFoodProcessorProgram
    Inherits AbstractFoodProcessorProgram
    '
    ' Return the name of this food processing program object.
    '
    Public Overrides ReadOnly Property Name() As String
        Get
            Return "Chocolate Milk"
        End Get
    End Property


    '
    ' A call to this method tells a food processing program to start
    ' doing whatever it is supposed to be doing.
    '
    Public Overrides Sub Start()
        Dim weight As Double = Environment.Weight
        If weight > 120.0 And weight < 160.0 Then
            Environment.Mix(4)
        End If
        ...
    End Sub 'Start

End Class 'ConcreteFoodProcessorProgram
```

RELATED PATTERNS

Virtual Proxy: Implementations of the Virtual Proxy pattern sometimes use the Dynamic Linkage pattern to load the class that it needs to create its underlying object.

Protection Proxy: The Protection Proxy pattern (described in [Grand01]) is sometimes used with the Dynamic Linkage pattern to minimize security risks.

Virtual Proxy

This pattern was previously described in [Larman01].

SYNOPSIS

If an object is expensive to instantiate and may not be needed, it may be advantageous to postpone its instantiation until it is clear the object is needed. The Virtual Proxy pattern hides from its clients the fact that an object may not yet exist by having them access the object indirectly through a proxy object. The proxy object implements the same interface as the object that may not exist. This technique of delaying the instantiation of an object until it is actually needed is sometimes called *lazy instantiation*.

CONTEXT

Suppose that you are part of a team that has written a large application for a company that operates a chain of home improvement warehouses. The application is designed to be launched through a Web site that allows people to buy everything the warehouses sell. The purpose of the application is to supplement the catalog of merchandise with a variety of assistants to allow customers to decide just what they need. These assistants include:

- A kitchen cabinet assistant that allows a customer to design a set of kitchen cabinets and then automatically order all of the pieces necessary to assemble the cabinets

- An assistant to determine how much lumber a customer needs to build a wood deck

- An assistant to determine the quantity of broadloom carpet needed for a particular floor plan and the best way to cut it

There are more assistants, but they are not the point of this discussion. The point is that the application is very large. Due to its size, it takes an unacceptably long amount of time to download the application over a modem connection.

One way to reduce the time needed to download the application is not to download any assistants until they are needed. The Virtual Proxy pattern provides a way to postpone downloading part of an application in a way that is transparent to the rest of the application. The idea is that instead of having the rest of the application directly access the classes that constitute an assistant, they will access those classes indirectly through a proxy class. The proxy classes are specially coded so that they don't contain any static references[1] to the class they are a proxy for. This means that when the proxy classes are loaded, there are no references to the class they are a proxy for. If the rest of the application refers only to the proxies and not to the classes that implement assistants, the application will not automatically load the assistants.

When a proxy's property, function or subroutine is called, it first ensures that the classes that implement the assistant are loaded and instantiated. It then calls the corresponding function or subroutine through an interface. Figure 6.23 is a class diagram showing this organization:

Figure 6.23 shows the main portion of the application referring to a `Cabinet AssistantProxy` class that implements the `ICabinetAssistant` interface. The main portion of the application contains no references to the classes that implement the cabinet assistant. When they are needed, the `CabinetAssistantProxy` class ensures that the classes that implement the cabinet assistant are loaded and instantiated. The code that accomplishes this is listed under the "Code Example" heading.

FORCES

☺ There is a class that is very time-consuming to instantiate.

☺ It may not always be necessary to instantiate the class.

☺ If there are a number of classes whose instances will not be needed until an indefinite amount of time has passed, instantiating them all at once may introduce a noticeable delay in the program's response. Postponing their instantiation until they are needed may spread out the time that the program spends instantiating them and appear to make the program more responsive.

☺ Managing the delayed instantiation of classes should not be a burden placed on the class's clients. Therefore, the delayed instantiation of a class should be transparent to its clients.

---

[1]By static reference, I mean a reference to a class that a compiler will recognize at compile time. For example

```
Dim myFoo as Foo
```

is an example of a static reference to a class named Foo. Contrast this static reference to Foo with this example:

```
Type fooType = Type.GetType("Foo")
```

In this example the compiler sees a string that happens to contain the name of a class. The string is not recognized as the name of a class until run time, when the GetType method is called.

☹ Sometimes, the best way to ensure the good performance of a program is to prolong its initialization, so that all objects that are expensive to instantiate are created when the program starts. This can avoid having to spend time initializing things later on.

SOLUTION

Figure 6.24 is a class diagram showing the organization of classes that participate in the Virtual Proxy pattern.

Following is an explanation of the roles played by the interface and classes of the Virtual Proxy pattern.

Service

A `Service` class supplies the top-level logic for a service that it provides. When you create an instance of it, it creates the other objects that it needs. These other classes are indicated in the diagram as `ServiceHelper1`, `ServiceHelper2`...

Client

A class in this role uses the service provided by the `Service` class. `Client` classes never directly use a `Service` class. Instead, they use a `ServiceProxy` class that provides the functionality of the `Service` class. Not directly using a `Service` class keeps client classes insensitive to whether or not the instance of the `Service` class that `Client` objects indirectly use already exists.

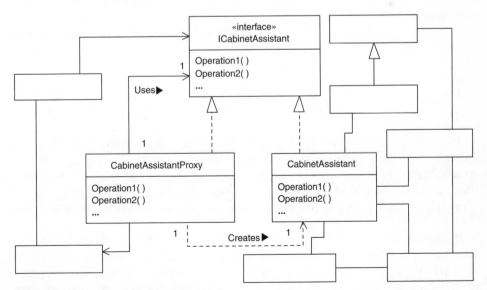

Figure 6.23 Cabinet Assistant Proxy

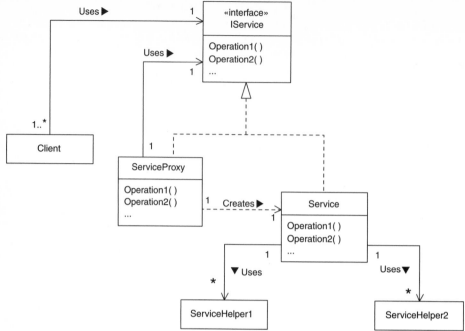

Figure 6.24 Virtual Proxy Pattern

ServiceProxy

The purpose of the `ServiceProxy` class is to delay creating instances of the `Service` class until they are actually needed.

A `ServiceProxy` class provides indirection between `Client` classes and a `Service` class. The indirection hides from `Client` objects the fact that when a `ServiceProxy` object is created, the corresponding `Service` object does not exist, and the `Service` class may not even have been loaded.

A `ServiceProxy` object is responsible for creating the corresponding `Service` object. A `ServiceProxy` object creates the corresponding `Service` object the first time it is asked to perform an operation that requires the existence of the `Service` object.

A `ServiceProxy` class is specially coded to obtain access to the `Service` class through a dynamic reference. Usually, classes reference other classes through static references. A static reference simply consists of the name of a class appearing in an appropriate place in some source code. When a compiler sees that kind of reference, it generates output that causes the other class to automatically be loaded along with the class that contains the reference.

The Virtual Proxy pattern prevents the loading of the `Service` class and related classes along with the rest of the program by ensuring that the rest of the program does not contain any static references to the `Service` class. Instead, the rest of the program refers to the `Service` class through the `ServiceProxy` class, and the `Service` Proxy class refers to the `Service` class through a dynamic reference.

A dynamic reference consists of a function or subroutine call that passes a string, containing the name of a class, to a function that loads the class if it isn't loaded and returns a reference to the class. Typically, the function call is to the static function `Type.GetType`. Because the name of the class only appears inside of a string, compilers are not aware that the class will be referenced and so they do not generate any output that causes that class to be loaded.

IService

A `ServiceProxy` class creates an instance of the `Service` class through property, function or subroutine calls that do not require static references to the `Service` class. A `ServiceProxy` class also calls properties, functions and subroutines of the `Service` class without having any static references to the `Service` class. It calls properties, functions and subroutines of the `Service` class by taking advantage of the fact that the `Service` class implements the `IService` interface.

The `IService` interface declares all the properties, functions and subroutines that the `Service` class implements and are needed by the `ServiceProxy` class. A `ServiceProxy` object treats the reference to the `Service` object it creates as a reference to an `IService` object. The `Service` class uses static references to the `IService` interface to call properties, functions and subroutines of `Service` objects. No static references to the `Service` class are required.

IMPLEMENTATION

Shared Service Objects

The solution assumes that when a `ServiceProxy` object is first asked to perform an operation, it creates a `Service` object and then continuously has the `Service` object associated with it. However, if the `Service` object consumes a lot of memory or another resource while it exists, it may be a bad thing to have as many `Service` objects as you have `ServiceProxy` objects.

If the `Service` objects are not stateful and are interchangeable, then consider using the Object Pool pattern to minimize the number of `Service` objects that you create. The idea is that when a `ServiceProxy` object needs a `Service` object to perform an operation, it gets the `Service` object from an object pool. When the `Service` object finishes the requested operation, the `ServiceProxy` object returns it to the object pool. This allows you to have many `ServiceProxy` objects but only a few `Service` objects.

Deferred Class Loading

In many cases, the class accessed through a virtual proxy uses other classes that the rest of the program does not use. Because of this relationship, these classes are not loaded until after the class accessed by the virtual proxy is loaded. If it is important that these classes not be loaded until the class accessed by the virtual proxy is loaded, then a problem may occur when the program is in the maintenance phase of its life cycle. A maintenance programmer may add a direct reference to one of those classes without realizing the performance implications. Unless the quality control testing for the program includes performance tests, the problem is likely to go unnoticed until the program's users complain.

You can lessen the likelihood of this happening by making the relationship between the classes explicit. You can make the relationship explicit by putting the classes in question in an assembly with only the class used by the proxy being public and visible outside the assembly. Figure 6.25 shows this organization.

CONSEQUENCES

☺ Classes accessed by the rest of a program exclusively through a virtual proxy are not loaded until they are needed.

☺ Objects accessed through a virtual proxy are not created until they are needed.

☺ Classes that use the proxy do not need to be aware of whether the `Service` class is loaded, of whether an instance of it exists, or that the class even exists.

● All classes other than the proxy class must access the services of the `Service` class indirectly through the proxy. This is critical. If just one class accesses the `Service` class directly, then the `Service` class will be loaded before it is needed. This is a quiet sort of bug. It generally affects performance but not function, so it is hard to track down.

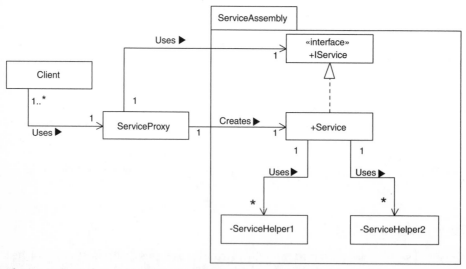

Figure 6.25   Relationship Made Explicit by Using a UML Package

CODE EXAMPLE

To conclude the example begun under the "Context" heading, here is some of the code that implements the cabinet assistant and its proxy. First, the relevant code for the CabinetAssistant class:

```vbnet
'
' This is a skeletal example of a service class that is used by a
' virtual proxy.  The notworthy aspect of this class is that it
' implements an interface that is written to declare the methods of this
' class rather than the other way around.
'
Public Class CabinetAssistant
    Implements ICabinetAssistant

    '
    ' constructor
    '
    Public Sub New(ByVal s As String)
        ...
    End Sub ' Constructor(String)

    Public Sub Operation1() _
     Implements ICabinetAssistant.Operation1
        ...
    End Sub 'Operation1

    Public Sub Operation2() _
     Implements ICabinetAssistant.Operation2
        ...
    End Sub 'Operation2

End Class ' CabinetAssistant
```

The ICabinetAssistant interface simply declares the functions and subroutines defined by the CabinetAssistant class:

```vbnet
'
' This is an example of an interface implemented by a service providing
' class that declares all of its methods that a virtual proxy will need
' to call.
'
Public Interface ICabinetAssistant
    Sub Operation1()
    Sub Operation2()
End Interface 'ICabinetAssistant
```

Finally, here is code for the CabinetAssistantProxy class, where all interesting things happen:

```vb
Imports System
Imports System.Reflection


'
' This class is an example of a virtual proxy.
'
Public Class CabinetAssistantProxy
    Private assistant As ICabinetAssistant = Nothing
    Private myParam As String ' for assistant object's constructor


    '
    ' Constructor
    '
    Public Sub New(ByVal s As String)
        myParam = s
    End Sub


    '
    ' Get the the CabinetAssistant object that is used to implement
    ' operations.  This method creates it if it did not exist.
    '
    ReadOnly Property CabinetAssistant() As ICabinetAssistant
        Get
            If assistant Is Nothing Then
                Try
                    ' get the type handle
                    Dim t As Type = Type.GetType("CabinetAssistant")
                    ' build the parameter types of the constructor we want
                    Dim types() As Type = {GetType(String)}
                    ' get the info handle for the constructor
                    Dim ci As ConstructorInfo = _
                        t.GetConstructor(BindingFlags.Instance Or
BindingFlags.Public, _
                        Nothing, types, Nothing)
                    ' create the array of objects for the constructor
parameters
                    Dim p() As Object = {myParam}
                    ' get the virtual instance for this type
                    assistant = CType(ci.Invoke(p), ICabinetAssistant)
                Catch
                End Try
                If assistant Is Nothing Then
                    ' deal with failure to create CabinetAssistant object
                    Throw New ApplicationException()
                End If
            End If
            Return assistant
        End Get
    End Property
```

```
    Public Sub Operation1()
        CabinetAssistant.Operation1()
    End Sub 'Operation1

    Public Sub Operation2()
        CabinetAssistant.Operation2()
    End Sub 'Operation2

End Class 'CabinetAssistantProxy
```

RELATED PATTERNS

Façade: The Façade pattern can be used with the Virtual Proxy pattern to minimize the number of proxy classes that are needed.

Proxy: The Virtual Proxy pattern is a specialized version of the Proxy pattern.

Object Pool: You can use the Object Pool pattern to allow many `ServiceProxy` objects to share and reuse a small number of `Service` objects.

Decorator

The Decorator pattern is also known as the Wrapper pattern. This pattern was previously described in [GoF95].

SYNOPSIS

The Decorator pattern extends the functionality of an object in a way that is transparent to its clients, by implementing the same interface as the original class and delegating operations to the original class.

CONTEXT

Suppose that you are responsible for maintaining the software for a security system that controls physical access to a building. Its basic architecture is that a card reader or other data entry device captures identifying information and passes the information to the object that controls a door. If the object that controls the door is satisfied with the information, it unlocks the door. Figure 6.26 is a collaboration diagram showing this.

Suppose that you need to integrate this access control mechanism with a surveillance system. A surveillance system typically has more cameras connected to it than it has TV monitors. Most of the TV monitors cycle through images from different cameras. They show a picture from each camera for a few seconds and then move on to the next camera for which the monitor is responsible. There are rules about how the surveillance system is supposed to be set up to ensure its effectiveness. For this discussion, the relevant rules are:

- At least two cameras cover each doorway connected to the access-control system.

- Each monitor is responsible for not more than one camera that covers an access-controlled doorway. The reason for this is that if there are multiple cameras viewing a doorway, then the failure of a single monitor should not prevent the images from all of the cameras on that doorway from being seen.

The specific integration requirement is that when an object that controls a door receives a request for the door to open, the monitors responsible for the cameras pointed at the doorway display that doorway. Your first thought about satisfying this requirement is that you will enhance a class or write some subclasses. Then you discover the relationships shown in Figure 6.27.

Figure 6.26   Basic Physical Access Control

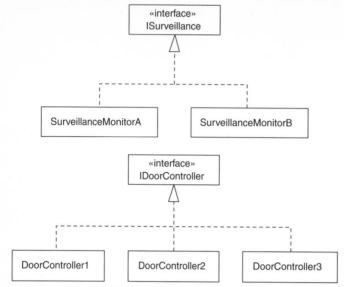

Figure 6.27 Security System Classes

There are three different kinds of doors installed and two different kinds of surveillance monitors in use. You could resolve the situation by writing two subclasses of each of the door controller classes, but you would rather not have to write six classes. Instead, you use the Decorator pattern to solve the problem by delegation rather than inheritance.

You write two new classes called `DoorControllerWrapperA` and `Door ControllerWrapperB`. The organization of these classes is shown in Figure 6.28. Both these classes implement the `IDoorController` interface. They inherit the implementation of the `IDoorController` interface from their abstract base class `AbstractDoorControllerWrapper`.

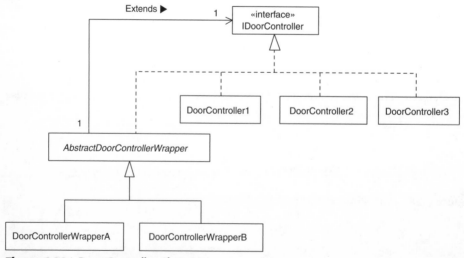

Figure 6.28 Door Controller Classes

The `AbstractDoorControllerWrapper` class implements all the functions and subroutines of the `DoorController` interface with implementations that simply call the corresponding function or subroutine of another object that implements the `DoorController` interface. The `DoorControllerA` and `DoorControllerB` classes are concrete wrapper classes. They extend the behavior of the `RequestOpen` implementation that they inherit to also ask a surveillance monitor to display its view of that doorway. Figure 6.29 is a collaboration diagram showing this.

This approach allows doorways viewed by multiple cameras to be handled by simply putting multiple wrappers in front of the `IDoorController` object.

FORCES

☺ There is a need to extend the functionality of a class, but there are reasons not to extend it through inheritance.

☺ There is the need to dynamically extend the functionality of an object and possibly also to withdraw the extended functionality.

SOLUTION

Figure 6.30 is a class diagram showing the general structure of the Decorator pattern.

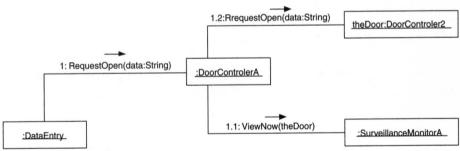

Figure 6.29   Door Surveillance Collaboration

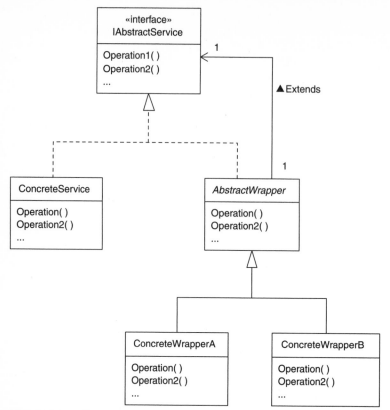

Figure 6.30 Decorator Pattern

Here are descriptions of the roles that classes and interfaces play in the Decorator pattern.

> **IAbstractService:** An interface in this role is implemented by all service objects that may potentially be extended through the Decorator pattern. Classes whose instances can be used to dynamically extend classes that implement the IAbstractService interface must also implement the IAbstractService interface.

> **ConcreteService:** Classes in this role provide the basic functionality that is extended by the Decorator pattern.

> **AbstractWrapper:** The abstract class in this role is the common base class for wrapper classes. Instances of this class take responsibility for maintaining a reference to the IAbstractService object that ConcreteWrapper objects delegate to.

> This class also normally implements all properties, functions and subroutines declared by the IAbstractService interface, so they simply call the like-named property, function, or method of the IAbstractService object that the

wrapper object delegates to. This default implementation provides exactly the behavior needed for properties, functions, or subroutines whose behavior is not being extended.

ConcreteWrapperA, ConcreteWrapperB . . . : These concrete wrapper classes extend the behavior of the properties, functions and subroutines they inherit from the `AbstractWrapper` class in whatever way is needed.

IMPLEMENTATION

Most implementations of the Decorator pattern are simpler than the general case. Here are some of the common simplifications.

If there is only one `ConcreteService` class and no `AbstractService` class, then the `AbstractWrapper` class may be a subclass of the `ConcreteService` class.

If there will be only one concrete wrapper class, then there is no need for a separate `AbstractWrapper` class. You can merge the `AbstractWrapper` class' responsibilities with the concrete wrapper class. It may also be reasonable to dispense with the `AbstractWrapper` class if there will be two concrete wrapper classes, but no more than that.

CONSEQUENCES

☺ The Decorator pattern provides more flexibility than inheritance. It allows you to dynamically alter the behavior of individual objects by adding and removing wrappers. Inheritance, on the other hand, determines the nature of all instances of a class statically.

☺ By using different combinations of a few different kinds of wrapper objects, you can create many different combinations of behavior. To create many different kinds of behavior with inheritance requires that you define that many different classes.

• Using the Decorator pattern generally results in fewer classes than using inheritance. One on hand, having fewer classes simplifies the design and implementation of programs. On the other hand, using the Decorator pattern usually results in more objects. The larger number of objects can make debugging more difficult, especially since the objects tend to look mostly alike.

☹ The flexibility of wrapper objects makes them more error prone than inheritance. For example, it is possible to combine wrapper objects in ways that do not work, or to create circular references between wrapper objects.

☹ One last difficulty associated with using the Decorator pattern is that it makes using object identity to identify service objects difficult, since it hides service objects behind wrapper objects.

CODE EXAMPLE

The code example for the Decorator pattern is code that implements some of the door controller classes shown in diagrams under the "Context" heading. Here is an implementation of the `IDoorController` interface:

```
' All classes that control doors must implement this interface.
'
Public Interface IDoorController
    '
    ' Ask the door to open if the given key is acceptable.
    ' key - A data string presented as a key to open the door.
    '
    Sub RequestOpen(ByVal key As String)


    '
    ' close the door
    '
    Sub Close()
End Interface 'IDoorController
```

Here is the `AbstractDoorControllerWrapper` class that provides default implementations to its subclasses for the subroutine declared by the `IDoorController` interface:

```
' This is the superclass of all DoorController wrappers.
'
Public MustInherit Class AbstractDoorControllerWrapper
    Implements IDoorController
    Private wrappee As IDoorController

    '
    ' Constructor
    ' wrappee - The DoorController object that this object will delegate to.
    '
    Public Sub New(ByVal wrappee As IDoorController)
        Me.wrappee = wrappee
    End Sub


    '
    ' Ask the door to open if the given key is acceptable.
    '
    ' key - A data string presented as a key to open the door.
    Public Sub RequestOpen(ByVal key As String) _
     Implements IDoorController.RequestOpen
        wrappee.RequestOpen(key)
    End Sub
```

```
'
' close the door
'
Public Sub Close() _
 Implements IDoorController.Close
    wrappee.Close()
End Sub
```

End Class 'AbstractDoorControllerWrapper

Finally, here is a subclass of the `AbstractDoorControllerWrapper` class that extends the default behavior by asking a monitor to display the image from a named camera:

```
'
' Instances of this class are wrapper objects that request a type A
' surveillance monitor to display the image of a particular program.
'
Public Class DoorControllerWrapperA
    Inherits AbstractDoorControllerWrapper

    Dim camera As String                  ' name of camera that views
this doorway
    Dim monitor As SurveillanceMonitorIF ' monitor for camera.

    '
    ' Constructor
    ' wrappee - The DoorController object that this object will delegate to.
    ' camera - The name of a camera that views this door.
    ' monitor - The monitor to ask to view camera's image.
    Public Sub New(ByVal wrappee As IDoorController, _
                   ByVal camera As String, _
                   ByVal monitor As SurveillanceMonitorIF)
        MyBase.New(wrappee)
        Me.camera = camera
        Me.monitor = monitor
    End Sub

    '
    ' Ask the door to open if the given key is acceptable.
    ' key - A data string presented as a key to open the door.
    Public Overloads Sub RequestOpen(ByVal key As String)
        monitor.ViewNow(camera)
        MyBase.RequestOpen(key)
    End Sub

End Class
```

RELATED PATTERNS

Delegation: The Decorator pattern is a structured way of applying the Delegation pattern.

Filter: The Filter pattern is a specialized version of the Decorator pattern that focuses on manipulating a data stream.

Strategy: The Decorator pattern can be used to arrange for things to happen before or after the properties, functions and subroutines of another object are called. If you want to arrange for things to happen in the middle of calls to properties, functions, or subroutines, consider using the Strategy pattern.

Template Method: The Template Method pattern is another alternative to the Decorator pattern that allows variable behavior in the middle of a function or subroutine call instead of before or after it.

Cache Management

SYNOPSIS

The Cache Management pattern allows fast access to objects that would otherwise take a long time to access. It involves keeping a copy of objects that are expensive to construct. The object may be expensive to construct for any number of reasons, such as requiring a lengthy computation or being fetched from a database.

CONTEXT

Suppose that you are writing a program that allows people to fetch information about products in a catalog. Fetching all of a product's information can take a few seconds because it may have to be gathered from multiple sources. Keeping a product's information in the program's memory allows the next request for the product's information to be satisfied more quickly, since it is not necessary to spend the time to gather the information.

Keeping information in memory that takes a relatively long time to fetch into memory, for quick access the next time it is needed, is called *caching*. The large number of products in the catalog makes it infeasible to cache information for all the products in memory. What can be done is to keep information for as many products as feasible in memory. Products guessed to be the most likely to be used are kept in memory so they are there when needed. Products guessed to be less likely to be used are not kept in memory. Deciding which and how many objects to keep in memory is called *cache management*.

Figure 6.31 shows how cache management would work for the product information example.

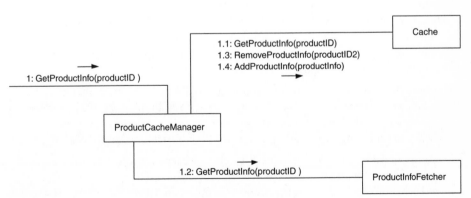

Figure 6.31   Product Cache Management Collaboration

1. A product ID is passed to a `ProductCacheManager` object's `getProduct-Info` function.

    1.1 The `ProductCacheManager` object's `getProductInfo` function attempts to retrieve the product description object from a `Cache` object. If it successfully retrieves the object from the cache, it returns the object.

    1.2 If it was unable to retrieve the product description object from the cache, it calls a `ProductInfoFetcher` object's `getProductInfo` function to fetch the product description.

    1.3 Many cache managers implement a policy to limit the number of objects in a cache, because keeping too many objects in the cache can be wasteful or even counterproductive. If the cache manager decides that the retrieved object should be stored in the cache but the cache already contains as many objects as it should, the cache manager will avoid increasing the number of objects in the cache. It does this by picking a product description object to remove from the cache and passes its product ID to the `Cache` object's `removeProductInfo` subroutine.

    1.4 Finally, if the cache manager had decided that the fetched object should be stored in the cache, it calls the `Cache` object's `addProductInfo` subroutine.

FORCES

☺ There is a need to access an object that takes a long time to construct or fetch. Typical reasons for an object's construction being expensive are that its contents must be fetched from external sources or that it requires a lengthy computation. The point is that is takes substantially longer to construct the object than to access the object once it is cached in internal memory.

☺ When the number of objects that are expensive to construct is small enough that they can all fit comfortably in local memory, then keeping all of the objects in local memory will provide the best results. This guarantees that if access to one of these objects is needed again, it will not be necessary to incur the expense of constructing the object again.

☺ If very many expensive-to-construct objects will be constructed, then they may not all fit in memory at the same time. If they do fit in memory, they may use memory that will later be needed for other purposes. Therefore, it may be necessary to set an upper bound on the number of objects cached in local memory.

☺ An upper bound on the number of objects in a cache requires an enforcement policy. The enforcement policy will determine which fetched objects to cache and which to discard when the number of objects in the cache reaches the upper bound. Such a policy should attempt to predict which objects are most and least likely to be used in the near future.

☺ Some objects reflect the state of something outside of the program's own memory. The contents of such objects may not be valid after the time that such objects are created.

SOLUTION

Figure 6.32 shows the general structure of the Cache Management pattern.

Here are descriptions of classes that participate in the Cache Management pattern and the roles that they play:

Client: Instances of classes in this role delegate the responsibility of obtaining access to specified objects to a CacheManager object.

ObjectKey: Instances of the ObjectKey class identify the object to be fetched or created.

CacheManager: Client objects request objects from a CacheManager object by calling its FetchObject function. The argument to the FetchObject function is an ObjectKey object that identifies the object to fetch. The FetchObject function works by first calling the Cache object's FetchObject function. If that fails, it calls the ObjectCreater object's CreateObject function.

ObjectCreater: ObjectCreater objects are responsible for creating objects that are not in the cache.

Cache: A Cache object is responsible for managing a collection of cached objects. Given an ObjectKey object, a Cache object quickly finds the corresponding cached object. The CacheManager object passes an ObjectKey object to the Cache object's FetchObject function to get a cached object from the cache. If the FetchObject function does not return the requested object, the CacheManager object asks the ObjectCreater object to create it. If the ObjectCreater object returns the requested object, the Cache object passes the returned object to this object's AddObject subroutine. The AddObject subroutine adds the object to the cache if this is consistent with its cache management policy. The AddObject subroutine may remove an object from the cache to make room for the object it is adding to the cache.

IMPLEMENTATION

Structural Considerations

If you are designing both the CacheManager class and the ObjectCreator class, they should implement a common interface. Client objects should access Cache Manager objects through the common interface. This is to make the use of a cache transparent to Client objects. If they implement a common interface, then Client objects are using an object that implements the same interface whether caching is being used or not.

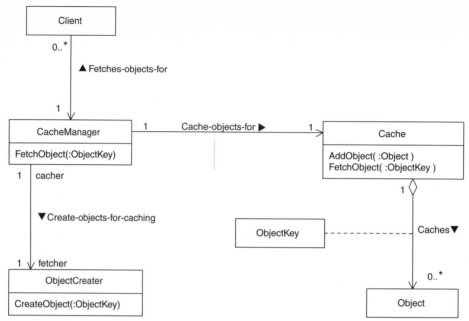

Figure 6.32 Cache Management Pattern

The reason that such an interface is not indicated in the "Solution" section as part of this pattern is that classes in the ObjectCreator role are often designed before caching becomes a consideration. Because of this, ObjectCreator objects often do not implement any suitable interface, and the effort required to have them implement such an interface is generally not expended.

Implementation of the Cache

Implementing the Cache Management pattern involves making some potentially complex choices. Making optimal choices can involve much statistical analysis, queuing theory, and other sorts of mathematical analysis. However, it is usually possible to produce a reasonable implementation by being aware of what the choices are and experimenting with different solutions.

The most basic decision to make when implementing the Cache Management pattern is how to implement the cache itself. The considerations for picking a data structure for the cache are:

- It must be able to quickly find objects when given their ObjectKey.
- Since search operations will be done more frequently than addition or removal, searching should be as fast as or faster than those operations.
- Since we expect frequent additions and removal of objects, the data structure must not make these operations a lot more expensive than search operations.

A hash table satisfies these needs. When implementing in .NET, a cache is usually implemented using an instance of the System.Collections.Hashtable class.

Performance-Tuning a Cache

The remaining implementation issues relate to *performance tuning*. Performance tuning is not something to spend time on until after your program is functioning correctly. In the design and initial coding stages of your development effort, make some initial decisions about how to deal with these issues and then ignore them until you are ready to deal with performance-related issues.

The simplest way of measuring the effectiveness of caching is to compute a statistic called its *hit rate*. The hit rate is the percentage of object fetch requests that the cache manager satisfies with objects stored in the cache. If every request is satisfied with an object from the cache, then the hit rate is 100 percent. If no request is satisfied, then the hit rate is 0 percent. The hit rate depends largely on how well the implementation of the Cache Management pattern matches the way that objects are requested.

There is always a maximum amount of memory that you can afford to devote to a cache. This means that you will have to set a limit on the objects that can be in the cache. If the potential set of objects available for collection in a cache is small, you don't have to impose an explicit limit. Most problems are not so conveniently self-limiting.

Specifying in advance a maximum amount of memory to devote to a cache is difficult since you may not know in advance how much memory will be available or how much memory the rest of your program will need. Enforcing a limit on the amount of memory a cache can use is especially difficult in .NET because there is no definite relationship between an object and the amount of physical memory that it occupies.

An alternative to specifying and enforcing a limit that measures memory is to simply count objects. Object counting is a workable alternative to measuring actual memory usage if the average memory usage for each object is a reasonable approximation of the memory usage for each object. Counting objects is very straightforward, so you can simplify things by limiting the contents of a cache to a certain number of objects. Of course, the existence of a limit on the size of a cache raises the question of what should happen when the size of the cache reaches the maximum number of objects and another object is created. At that point, there is one more object than the cache is supposed to hold. The cache manager must then discard an object.

The selection of which object to discard is important, because it directly affects the hit rate. On one hand, if the discarded object is always the next one requested then the hit rate will be 0 percent. On the other hand, if the object discarded will not be requested before any other object in the cache, then discarding that object has the least negative impact on the hit rate. Clearly, making a good choice of which object to discard requires a forecast of future object requests.

In some cases, it is possible to make an educated guess about which objects a program will need in the near future, based on knowledge of the application domain. In the most fortunate cases, it is possible to predict with high probability that a specific object will be the next one requested. In those cases, if the object is not already in the cache, it may be advantageous to asynchronously create it immediately rather than wait for the program to request it. This technique is called *prefetching* the object.

In most cases, the application domain does not provide enough clues to make such precise forecasts. However, there is a usage pattern that turns up in so many cases that it is the basis for a good default strategy for deciding which object to discard: The more recently a program has requested an object, the more likely it is to request the object again. The strategy based on this observation is always to discard the least recently used object in the cache. People often abbreviate this "least recently used" strategy as LRU.

One way to keep track of how recently each object in the cache has been used is to associate a timestamp with each object in the cache. The timestamps would indicate when each object in the cache was last used. This turns out to be a relatively slow way to keep track of which object in the cache is least recently used, because the cache manager has to search through all the timestamps to find the oldest.

A way to avoid having to search through timestamps is to have a collection that has the objects in the cache in the order from least recently used to most recently used. This avoids having to a search for the least recently used object. The least recently used object will always be the first object in the collection. Since keeping objects ordered in a collection is the best way to keep track of which is the least recently used object, the next decision to make is what kind of collection is best for this purpose.

.NET includes a collection class named `System.Collections.ArrayList`. The `ArrayList` class is the most commonly used class for keeping a collection of objects in an arbitrary order. The `ArrayList` class is a reasonable choice for keeping track of which is the least recently used object in a cache. However the `ArrayList` class is not the most efficient choice. The problem has to do with how much work is required to keep the object in an `ArrayList` in order from least recently used to most recently used.

To keep objects in an `ArrayList` in order of how recently they have been used, there are three steps to perform every time an object in the cache is used:

1. The index of the object must be found by searching through the `ArrayList`. On average, half of the `ArrayList` will need to be searched to find the right object.

2. The object is removed from the `ArrayList`. Because this leaves a hole in the `ArrayList`, the hole needs to be filled. To fill the hole, every object in the `ArrayList` that has a higher index than the object being used is moved to an index one lower than where it was before the object was used. On average, half of the objects in the `ArrayList` will need to be moved to fill the hole.

3. The object is added back to the `ArrayList` at the end of the `ArrayList`. This step always takes the same short amount of time.

The `ArrayList` class's `Remove` function performs the first two steps. Having a method that does this for us makes it easy to program. The problem is that the amount of time it takes is proportionate to the length of the `ArrayList`. If the number of objects in a cache will be in the thousands or higher, it is worth using a collection class that is more complicated to program but allows the most recently used object to be moved to the end of the collection in a fixed amount of time, no matter how big the cache is.

For the code example for the Interface and Abstract Class pattern, we presented a type of collection called a doubly linked list. Objects in a doubly linked list have a reference to the next and previous object in the list. Removing an object from a doubly linked list just involves changing the references in the next and previous object so that they refer to each other rather than to the removed object. Removing an object from a doubly linked list always takes the same short amount of time. This makes using a doubly linked list an improvement over an `ArrayList`.

Just using a doubly linked list makes removing an object from the collection fast. All by itself, it does not eliminate the need for having to search through the collection to find the object to be removed.

A way to eliminate the search is to use a `Hashtable` to find the right object in the doubly linked list. This `Hashtable` would use the same objects as keys that are used to find objects in the cache. Its values would be the nodes of the doubly linked list. Figure 6.33 shows these details.

At this point, the implementation technique for determining the least recently used object is rather good. All searching has been eliminated. There is one last improvement to be made. The detailed design in Figure 6.33 shows two associations between the `Hashtable` class and other classes. Both of these associations involve exactly the same keys. To implement this, we would need two `Hashtable` objects. Every time a key is added to or removed from one `Hashtable` object, the same key must be added or removed from the other `Hashtable` object. This seems like duplicated work.

Looking carefully at Figure 6.33, we see that we can simplify the design so that it uses only one `Hashtable` object. Because of the other associations we have added to support tracking the least recently used object, the association labeled `Caches` is no longer needed.

Figure 6.34 shows the simplified detailed design. There is an implementation of this design in the code example for this pattern. In this simplified design, the cache first uses the `Hashtable` to find the `DoublyLinkedNode`. The `DoublyLinkedNode` refers to the cached object.

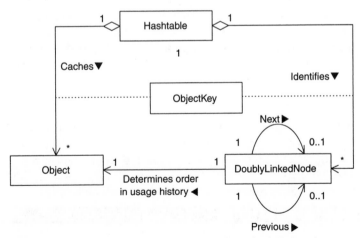

Figure 6.33   Hashtable for Finding Doubly Linked List Nodes

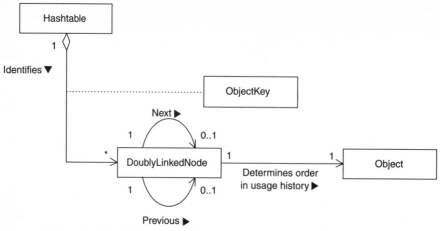

Figure 6.34   Simplified Design Needing Only One Hashtable

Now let's take a look at setting a numeric limit on the number of objects in a cache. A mathematical analysis can give a precise value to use for the maximum number of objects that may be placed in a cache. It is unusual to do such an analysis for two reasons. The first is that the mathematical analysis involves probability and queuing theory that is beyond the knowledge of most programmers. The other reason is that such an analysis can be prohibitively time-consuming. The number of details that need to be gathered about the program and its environment can be prohibitively large. However, you can usually arrive at a reasonable cache size empirically.

Begin by adding code to your `CacheManager` class to measure the hit rate as the number of object requests satisfied from the cache divided by the total number of object requests. You can then try running with different limits on the object size. As you do that, you will be looking for two things. The most important thing to look out for is that if the cache is too large it can cause the rest of your program to fail or slow down. The program can fail by running out of memory. If the program is garbage collected, as most .NET programs are, it can slow down waiting for the garbage collector to finish scavenging memory for new objects. If the program is running in a virtual memory environment, a large cache can cause excessive paging.

Suppose that you want to tune a program that uses a cache. You run the program, under otherwise identical conditions, with different maximum cache sizes set. Let's say that you try values as large as 6,000. At 6,000 you find that the program takes three times as long to run as at 4,000. This means that 6,000 is too large. Suppose that the hit rate you got at the other values was as demonstrated in the following table.

MAX CACHE SIZE	HIT RATE
250	20%
500	60%
1000	80%
2000	90%

MAX CACHE SIZE	HIT RATE
3000	98%
4000	100%
5000	100%

Clearly, there is no need to allow the cache to be larger than 4,000 objects since that achieves a 100 percent hit rate. Under the conditions that you ran the program, the ideal cache size is about 4,000. If the program will be run only under those exact conditions, then no further tuning may be needed. Many programs will be run under other conditions. If you are concerned that your program will be run under other conditions, you may want to use a smaller cache size to avoid problems under conditions where less memory is available. The number you pick will be a compromise between wanting a high hit rate and wanting a small cache size. Since lowering the cache size to 3,000 reduces the hit rate to 98 percent, 3,000 might be an acceptable cache size. If a 90 percent hit rate is good enough, then 2,000 is an acceptable cache size.

If it is not possible to achieve a high hit rate with available memory and creating the objects is sufficiently expensive, then consider using a secondary cache. A secondary cache is typically a disk file that is used as a cache. The secondary cache takes longer to access than the primary cache that is in memory. However, if it takes sufficiently less time to fetch objects out of a local disk file than it would to create them again from their original source, then it can be advantageous to use a secondary cache.

The way that you use a secondary cache is to move objects from the primary cache to the secondary cache instead of discarding the objects when the primary cache is full.

GetHashCode( )

The efficient operation of a cache requires that a `Hashtable` is able to quickly find objects. The `Hashtable` relies on classes of the objects it contains having a good implementation of the `GetHashCode` method. Every class inherits the `GetHashCode` method from the `Object` class.

If the `GetHashCode` method of every object in a `Hashtable` returns a different value, then the `Hashtable` will find objects by comparing them with only one object. If multiple objects in the `Hashtable` have a `GetHashCode` method that returns the same value, then the `Hashtable` may have to compare an object that is looking for to all the objects whose `GetHashCode` method that returns the same value.

CONSEQUENCES

Sometimes applications of the Cache Management pattern are added to the design of a program after the need for a performance optimization has been discovered. This is usually not a problem because the impact of the Cache Management pattern on the rest of a program is minimal. If access to the objects in question is already implemented using the Virtual Proxy pattern, an implementation of the Cache Management pattern can be inserted into the proxy class with no modification to other classes.

☺ The primary consequence of using the Cache Management pattern is that a program spends less time fetching objects from expensive sources.

☹ When objects are created with data from an external source, another consequence of using the Cache Management pattern is that the cache may become inconsistent with the original data source. The consistency problem breaks down into two separate problems that can be solved independently of each other. Those problems are *read consistency* and *write consistency*.

- Read consistency means that the cache always reflects updates to information in the original object source. If the objects being cached are stock prices, then the prices in the object source can change and the prices in the cache will no longer be current.

- Write consistency means that the original object source always reflects updates to the cache.

- To achieve absolute read or write consistency for objects in a cache with the original object source requires a mechanism to keep them synchronized. Such mechanisms can be complicated to implement and add considerable execution time. They generally involve techniques such as locking and optimistic concurrency, which are beyond the scope of this volume. Some patterns in [Grand01] deal with these issues. They are mentioned under the "Related Patterns" heading at the end of this pattern.

- If it is not feasible to achieve absolute read or write consistency, you may be able to settle for relative consistency. Relative consistency does not guarantee that the contents of a cache always appear to match the original object source. Instead, the guarantee is that if an update occurs in the cache or the original data source, the other will reflect the update within some specified amount of time.

CODE EXAMPLE

Suppose that you are writing software for an employee timekeeping system. The system consists of timekeeping terminals and a timekeeping server. The terminals are small boxes mounted on the walls of a place of business. When an employee arrives at work or leaves work, the employee notifies the timekeeping system by running his or her ID card through a timekeeping terminal. The terminal reads the employee's ID on the card and acknowledges the card by displaying the employee's name and options. The employee then selects an option to indicate that he or she is starting work, ending work, going on break, or other options. The timekeeping terminals transmit these timekeeping events to the timekeeping server. At the end of each pay period, the business's payroll system gets the number of hours each employee worked from the timekeeping system and prepares paychecks.

The exact details an employee sees will depend on an employee profile that a terminal receives from the timekeeping server. The employee profile will include the employee's name, the language in which to display prompts for the employee, and any special options that apply to the employee.

Most businesses assign their employees a fixed location in the business place to do their work. Employees with a fixed work location will normally use the timekeeping terminal nearest to their work location. To avoid long lines in front of timekeeping terminals, it is recommended that the terminals be positioned so that fewer than 70 employees with fixed work locations will use the same timekeeping terminal.

A substantial portion of the acquisition cost of the timekeeping system will be the cost of the terminals. To keep their cost down, the timekeeping terminals will have a minimal amount of memory. However, to keep response time down, we will want the terminals to cache employee profiles so that most of the time they will be able to respond immediately when presented with an employee's ID card. This means that you will have to impose a maximum cache size that is rather modest. A reasonable basis for an initial maximum cache size is the recommendation that the terminals be positioned so that no more than 70 employees with fixed work locations use the same terminal. Based on this, we come up with an initial cache size of up to 80 employee profiles.

The reason for picking a number larger than 70 is that under some situations more than 70 employees may use the same timekeeping terminal. Sometimes one part of a business will borrow employees from another part of a business when they experience a peak workload. Also, there will be employees, such as maintenance staff, that float from one location to another.

Figure 6.35 is a class diagram that shows how the Cache Management pattern is applied to this problem.

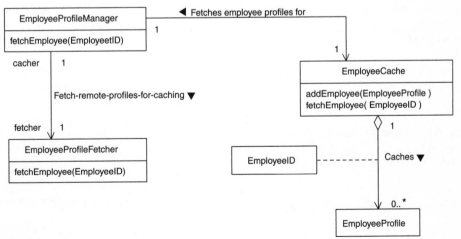

Figure 6.35 Timekeeping Cache Management

Here is the code that implements the timekeeping terminal's cache management. First, here is the code for the `EmployeeProfileManager` class:

```
'
' Instances of this class retrieve the EmployeeProfile associated
' with an EmployeeID.
'
Public Class EmployeeProfileManager
    Private cache As New EmployeeCache()
    Private server As New EmployeeProfileFetcher()


    ' Fetch an employee profile for the given employee id from the
    ' internal cache or timekeeping server if the profile is not
    ' found in the internal cache.
    '
    ' id - the employee's id
    ' returns - the employee's profile or Nothing if the employee's
    '           profile is not found on the timekeeping server.
    '
    Function FetchEmployee(ByVal id As EmployeeID) As EmployeeProfile
        Dim emp As EmployeeProfile = cache.FetchEmployee(id)
        If emp Is Nothing Then            ' if profile not in cache try
server
            emp = server.FetchEmployee(id)
            If emp IsNot Nothing Then    ' Got the profile from the server
                cache.AddEmployee(emp)   ' put profile in the cache
            End If
        End If
        Return emp
    End Function 'FetchEmployee

End Class 'EmployeeProfileManager
```

The logic in the `EmployeeProfileManager` class is straightforward conditional logic. The logic of the `EmployeeCache` class is more intricate, since it manipulates a data structure to determine which employee profile to remove from the cache before adding an employee profile to a full cache. It also uses a doubly linked list in the way discussed under the "Implementation" heading.

```
Imports System.Collections


'
' Instances of this class are responsible for maintaining a cache of
' objects for a CacheManager object.
'
Public Class EmployeeCache
    ' We use a linked list to determine the least recently used
    ' employee profile.  The cache itself is implemented by a
```

```
' Hashtable object. The Hashtable values are linked list
' objects that refer to the actual EmployeeProfile object.
Private cache As New Hashtable()

' This is the list that refers to the most/least
' recently used EmployeeProfile.
Private list As New DoublyLinkedList()

' The maximum number of EmployeeProfile objects that may be in the
' cache.
Private MAX_CACHE_SIZE As Integer = 80

' The number of EmployeeProfile objects currently in the cache.
Private currentCacheSize As Integer = 0

' Objects are passed to this method for addition to the cache.
' However, this method is not required to actually add an object
' to the cache if that is contrary to its policy for what object
' should be added.  This method may also remove objects already in
' the cache in order to make room for new objects.
'
' emp - The employeeProfile that is being proposed as an addition to
    the cache.
'
Public Sub AddEmployee(ByVal emp As EmployeeProfile)
    Dim id As EmployeeID = emp.ID

    If cache(id) Is Nothing Then ' if profile not in cache
        ' Add profile to cache, making it the most recently used.
        Dim node As CachedEmployeeNode
        If currentCacheSize >= MAX_CACHE_SIZE Then
            ' remove least recently used EmployeeProfile from
            ' the cache
            node = CType(list.RemoveFirst(), CachedEmployeeNode)
            cache.Remove(node)
        Else
            node = New CachedEmployeeNode()
        End If
        ' put the now most recently used profile in the cache
        node.CachedEmployee = emp
        list.AddLast(node)
        cache(id) = node
        currentCacheSize += 1
    Else  ' profile already in cache
        ' AddEmployee shouldn't be called when the object is already
        ' in the cache.  Since that has happened, do a fetch so
        ' that so object becomes the most recently used.
        FetchEmployee(id)
    End If ' if cache(id) Is Nothing
End Sub 'AddEmployee
```

```
'
' Return the EmployeeProfile associated with the given EmployeeID
' the cache or Nothing if no EmployeeProfile is associated with the
' given EmployeeID.
' id - the EmployeeID to retrieve a profile for.
Public Function FetchEmployee(ByVal id As EmployeeID) As
EmployeeProfile
    Dim employeeNode As CachedEmployeeNode = _
        CType(cache(id), CachedEmployeeNode)
    If employeeNode Is Nothing Then
        Return Nothing
    End If
    ' Move employeeNode to the end of the list to indicate
    ' it is most recently used.
    employeeNode.Remove()
    list.AddLast(employeeNode)
    Return employeeNode.CachedEmployee
End Function 'FetchEmployee


End Class 'EmployeeCache
```

Here is the EmployeeProfile and the EmployeeID classes.

```
Imports System.Globalization

'
' Instances of this class contain employee profile information
'
Public Class EmployeeProfile
    Private myId As EmployeeID ' Employee Id
    Private myLocale As CultureInfo ' Language Preference
    Private mySupervisor As Boolean
    Private myName As String      ' Employee name


    '
    ' Constructor
    ' id - Employee Id
    ' locale - The CultureInfo of the employee's language of choice.
    ' supervisor - true if this employee is a supervisor.
    ' name - Employee's name
    Public Sub New(ByVal id As EmployeeID, ByVal locale As CultureInfo, _
                ByVal supervisor As Boolean, ByVal name As String)
        Me.myId = id
        Me.myLocale = locale
        Me.mySupervisor = supervisor
        Me.myName = name
    End Sub 'New


    ' Return the employee's ID
    Public ReadOnly Property ID() As EmployeeID
```

```
        Get
            Return myId
        End Get
    End Property


    ' the CultureInfo indicating Employee's preferred language
    Public ReadOnly Property Locale() As CultureInfo
        Get
            Return myLocale
        End Get
    End Property


    '
    ' Return true if the employee is a supervisor.
    '
    Public Function IsSupervisor() As Boolean
        Return mySupervisor
    End Function

End Class 'EmployeeProfile

'
' Instances of this class identify an employee.
'
Public Class EmployeeID
    Private id As String


    '
    ' constructor
    '
    ' id - A string containing the employee ID.
    Public Sub New(ByVal id As String)
        Me.id = id
    End Sub


    '
    ' Returns a hash code value for this object.
    '
    Public Overrides Function GetHashCode() As Integer
        Return id.GetHashCode()
    End Function 'GetHashCode


    '
    ' Return true if the given object is an employee id that is equal to this
    ' one.
    ' o - The object to compare with this one.
    Public Overloads Function Equals(ByVal o As Object) As Boolean
        ' check for Nothing and correct type
        If (o Is Nothing) Or (TypeOf o Is EmployeeID) Then
            Return False
```

```
        End If
        Return id.Equals(CType(o, EmployeeID).id)
    End Function 'Equals


    '
    ' Return the string representation of this EmployeeID.
    '
    Public Overrides Function ToString() As String
        Return id
    End Function

End Class 'EmployeeID
```

The following classes are the implementation of the doubly linked list. This next class is a specialization of a general-purpose class to implement a node in a doubly linked list.

```
Friend Class CachedEmployeeNode
    Inherits AbstractDoubleLink

    ' Reference to a cached object
    Private myObject As EmployeeProfile

    Friend Property CachedEmployee() As EmployeeProfile
        Get
            Return myObject
        End Get
        Set(ByVal Value As EmployeeProfile)
            myObject = Value
        End Set
    End Property
End Class
```

The following classes implement the application-independent portion of the doubly linked list:

```
' Class to manage a doubly linked list of IDoubleLink objects.
Public Class DoublyLinkedList
    Private myFirstNode As IDoubleLink
    Private myLastNode As IDoubleLink

    ' The first node of the doubly linked list.
    Public ReadOnly Property FirstNode() As IDoubleLink
        Get
            Return myFirstNode
        End Get
    End Property

    ' The last node of the doubly linked list.
    Public ReadOnly Property LastNode() As IDoubleLink
        Get
```

```
            Return myLastNode
        End Get
    End Property


    ' Add an IDoubleLink object to the beginning of the list.
    Public Sub AddFirst(ByVal node As IDoubleLink)
        If myFirstNode Is Nothing Then
            myLastNode = node
        Else
            myFirstNode.PrevNode = node
            node.NextNode = myFirstNode
        End If
        myFirstNode = node
        node.ListObject = Me
    End Sub


    ' Add an IDoubleLink object to the end of the list.
    Public Sub AddLast(ByVal node As IDoubleLink)
        If myLastNode Is Nothing Then
            myFirstNode = node
        Else
            myLastNode.NextNode = node
            node.PrevNode = myLastNode
        End If
        myLastNode = node
        node.ListObject = Me
    End Sub


    ' Remove the first object in the list.
    Public Function RemoveFirst() As IDoubleLink
        Dim prevFirstNode As IDoubleLink = myFirstNode

        If myFirstNode IsNot Nothing Then
            If myFirstNode.NextNode Is Nothing Then
                myLastNode = Nothing
            Else
                myFirstNode.NextNode.PrevNode = Nothing
            End If
            myFirstNode.ListObject = Nothing
            myFirstNode = myFirstNode.NextNode
        End If

        Return prevFirstNode
    End Function


    ' Remove the last object in the list.
    Public Function RemoveLast() As IDoubleLink
        Dim prevLastNode As IDoubleLink = myLastNode

        If myLastNode IsNot Nothing Then
            If myLastNode.PrevNode Is Nothing Then
                myFirstNode = Nothing
```

```vb
            Else
                myLastNode.PrevNode.NextNode = Nothing
            End If
            myLastNode.ListObject = Nothing
            myLastNode = myLastNode.PrevNode
        End If

        Return prevLastNode
    End Function
End Class


' defines the properties to be implemented for an IDoubleLink
'
Public Interface IDoubleLink
    ' The previous member of the Doubly linked list this
    ' object belongs to or Nothing.
    Property PrevNode() As IDoubleLink

    ' The next member of the Doubly linked list this
    ' object belongs to or Nothing.
    Property NextNode() As IDoubleLink

    ' Add the given IDoubleLink object to the doubly linked list
    ' after this object.
    Sub InsertAfter(ByVal newNode As IDoubleLink)

    ' Add the given IDoubleLink object to the doubly linked list
    ' before this object
    Sub InsertBefore(ByVal newNode As IDoubleLink)

    ' Remove this object from the doubly linked list.
    Sub Remove()

    ' The DoublyLinkedList object that this list node is under.
    Property ListObject() As DoublyLinkedList
End Interface 'IDoubleLink

' This class implements the IDoubleLink interface
Public MustInherit Class AbstractDoubleLink
    Implements IDoubleLink

    ' The DoublyLinkedList object that this object is under
    Private myListObject As DoublyLinkedList

    ' The previous member of the Doubly linked list this
    ' object belongs to or Nothing.
    '
    Private myPrevious As IDoubleLink

    ' The next member of the Doubly linked list this
    ' object belongs to or Nothing.
```

```
'
Private myNext As IDoubleLink


' The previous member of the Doubly linked list this
' object belongs to or Nothing.
'
Public Property PrevNode() As IDoubleLink Implements IDoubleLink.PrevNode
    Get
        Return myPrevious
    End Get
    Set(ByVal Value As IDoubleLink)
        myPrevious = Value
    End Set
End Property



'
' The next member of the Doubly linked list this
' object belongs to or Nothing.
'
Public Property NextNode() As IDoubleLink Implements IDoubleLink.NextNode
    Get
        Return myNext
    End Get
    Set(ByVal Value As IDoubleLink)
        myNext = Value
    End Set
End Property


' Add the given IDoubleLink object to the doubly linked list
' after this object.
Public Sub InsertAfter(ByVal newNode As IDoubleLink) _
                        Implements IDoubleLink.InsertAfter
    If (Me.NextNode Is Nothing) And (ListObject IsNot Nothing) Then
        ListObject.RemoveLast()
    Else
        newNode.NextNode = Me.NextNode
        newNode.PrevNode = Me
        If Me.NextNode IsNot Nothing Then
            Me.NextNode.PrevNode = newNode
        End If
        Me.NextNode = newNode
    End If
End Sub


' Add the given IDoubleLink object to the doubly linked list
' before this object
Public Sub InsertBefore(ByVal newNode As IDoubleLink) _
                        Implements IDoubleLink.InsertBefore
    If (Me.PrevNode Is Nothing) And (ListObject IsNot Nothing) Then
        ListObject.RemoveFirst()
```

```
        Else
            newNode.PrevNode = Me.PrevNode
            newNode.NextNode = Me
            If Me.PrevNode IsNot Nothing Then
                Me.PrevNode.NextNode = newNode
            End If
            Me.PrevNode = newNode
        End If
    End Sub


    ' Remove this object from the doubly linked list.
    Public Sub Remove() Implements IDoubleLink.Remove
        If NextNode IsNot Nothing Then
            NextNode.PrevNode = PrevNode
        End If
        If PrevNode IsNot Nothing Then
            PrevNode.NextNode = NextNode
        End If
    End Sub


    ' The DoublyLinkedList object that this object is under.
    Public Property ListObject() As DoublyLinkedList _
                            Implements IDoubleLink.ListObject
        Get
            Return myListObject
        End Get
        Set(ByVal Value As DoublyLinkedList)
            myListObject = Value
        End Set
    End Property
End Class 'AbstractDoubleLink
```

RELATED PATTERNS

Façade: The Cache Management pattern uses the Façade pattern.

Template Method: The Cache Management pattern uses the Template Method pattern to keep its Cache class reusable across application domains.

Virtual Proxy: The Cache Management pattern is often used with a variant of the Virtual Proxy pattern to make the cache transparent to objects that access object in the cache.

Object Replication: The Object Replication pattern (described in [Grand01]) describes some issues related to maintaining cache consistency.

Optimistic Concurrency: The Optimistic Concurrency pattern (described in [Grand01]) describes a technique that can sometimes be used to manage cache consistency with superior performance.

Ephemeral Cache Item: The Ephemeral Cache Item pattern (described in [Grand01]) describes the management of caches with relative consistency.

Behavioral Patterns

Chain of Responsibility (295)
Command (305)
Little Language (317)
Mediator (343)
Snapshot (355)
Observer (373)
State (383)
Strategy (395)
Null Object (401)
Template Method (407)
Visitor (415)
Hashed Adapter Object (427)

The patterns in this chapter are used to organize, manage and combine behavior. Most of them fall into these general categories:

- Patterns that organize a behavior requesting client's use of a behavior.
- Patterns that organize the relationship between a behavior requesting client and behavior providing object.
- Patterns that organize the implementation of a behavior.

The Hashed Adapter Objects pattern is the lowest level pattern that organizes a client's use of behaviors. The Hashed Adapter Objects pattern allows a variable behavior to be selected in a way that is faster than a long chain of if statements. The Command pattern allows sequences of behavior to be recorded or manipulated. The Little Language pattern allows higher level organization of behavior by using scripts to orchestrate behavior.

The Observer pattern is the simplest of the patterns that organize the relationship between a behavior-requesting client and a behavior-providing object. The Observer pattern allows client objects to work with behavior-providing objects while they have only minimal knowledge of each other. The Chain of Responsibility allows behavior-providing objects to decide among themselves which one will handle a particular request for a behavior.

The Template Method pattern uses inheritance to organize variations in a behavior's implementation using a fill-in-the-blanks metaphor. The Strategy pattern allows the implementation of a behavior to be varied dynamically at run time. The Null Object State is a refinement to the Strategy pattern that allows a behavior to conditionally not be performed without introducing an additional execution path. If the implementation of multiple classes would be complicated by dependencies between their instances, the Mediator pattern can be used to simplify their implementation. The Visitor pattern allows the implementation of a behavior to be driven by the contents of a complex data structure, while minimizing the behavior-providing class's awareness of the data structure and also minimizing the data structure's awareness of the behavior.

The Snapshot pattern allows the state of a program to be saved and later restored to what it previously was.

Chain of Responsibility

This pattern was previously described in [GoF95].

SYNOPSIS

The Chain of Responsibility pattern allows an object to send a command without knowing what object or objects will receive it or what they will do with it. It accomplishes this by passing the command to a chain of objects that is typically part of a larger structure. Each object in the chain may handle the command, pass the command to the next object in the chain or do both.

CONTEXT

Suppose that you are writing software to monitor a security system. Physically, the security system consists of sensing devices (motion detectors, smoke detectors and so on) that transmit status information to a computer. The computer's job is to log all status information, maintain a display showing current status information and transmit alarms in the event of an emergency.

One goal for the monitoring software is that it should be highly scalable. It should work for a small retail store, an office building, a warehouse, or a multibuilding complex. This goal has implications for the way you design the monitoring software.

To keep things simple, your monitoring program should instantiate an object for every sensor it will monitor. This provides a simple way to model each sensor's state. To ensure scalability, an object responsible for an individual sensor should not assume anything about its environment, except that it is at the bottom level of a hierarchical organization.

The organization will include objects corresponding to real-world things such as rooms, areas, floors, and buildings. Directly modeling the real world provides a straightforward way to display the status of different parts of buildings. It also allows the interpretation of a sensor's state to be based on its environment. For example, if the temperature of a closed room exceeds 180°F, then you may want the fire sprinklers in just that room to turn on. If the temperature in an open area of a warehouse exceeds 150°F you may want to turn on the fire sprinklers over that area and the adjacent areas. In contrast, if the temperature in a freezer exceeds 30°F, you may want to sound an alarm to let people know that that freezer is getting too warm.

In all these cases, the object that models a sensor does not decide what to do about the sensor's state. Instead, it delegates the decision to an object at a higher level in the hierarchy that has more contextual knowledge. Such objects either decide what to do about a notification or pass it on to the object that is organizationally above it.

Figure 7.1 shows an example of objects organized in this hierarchical way.

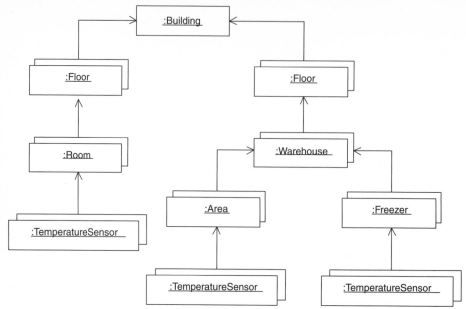

Figure 7.1 Physical Security Object Organization

For example, when a `TemperatureSensor` object contained in an area of a warehouse receives a notification of the current temperature from the physical sensor, it passes that notification to the `Area` object that contains it. Rather than decide the significance of the temperature, it passes the notification to the `Warehouse` object that contains the `Area` object. The `Warehouse` object determines the meaning of the temperature. If the temperature is above 150°F, the `Warehouse` object decides that there is a fire. It turns on the sprinklers in the area that notified it and the surrounding areas. The `Warehouse` object does not pass on the temperature notification.

FORCES

☺ You want an object to be able to send a command to another object without specifying the receiver. The sending object does not care which object handles the command, only that an object will receive the command and may handle it.

☺ You want the receivers of a command to be able to handle the command without having to know anything about the object that sent the command.

☺ More than one object may be able to receive and handle a command; the sending object needs a way to prioritize among the receivers without knowing anything about them.

☺ The objects you may want to potentially handle commands are organized into a structure that can serve to prioritize the potential handlers of a command.

SOLUTION

Figure 7.2 is a class diagram that shows the organization of the Chain of Responsibility pattern.

Here are explanations of the roles these classes play in the Chain of Responsibility pattern:

> **CommandSender:** Instances of a class in this role send commands to the first object in a chain of objects that may handle the command. The object that receives the command must implement the ICommandHandler interface. CommandSender objects send a command by calling the first ICommand Handler object's PostCommand subroutine.

> **ICommandHandler:** All objects in a chain of objects that may handle a command must implement an interface in this role. It defines a function and a subroutine.

> - It defines a HandleCommand function to handle whatever commands an implementing class is expected to handle. The HandleCommand function returns true if it handled a command or false if it did not.

> - It defines a PostCommand subroutine that calls the HandleCommand function. If the HandleCommand function returns false and there is a next object in the chain, it calls the next object's PostCommand subroutine. If the HandleCommand function returns true, it means there is no need to pass the command on to the next object in the chain.

> **AbstractCommandHandler:** Classes in this role are abstract classes that implement the PostCommand subroutine. This provides the convenience of a common implementation of PostCommand for classes in the ConcreteCommandHandler role. It is very unusual for classes to want anything other than the default logic for the PostCommand subroutine. Classes in the CommandSender role refer to objects in a chain of responsibility only through the ICommandHandler interface and not as instances of the AbstractCommandHandler class. The AbstractCommandHandler class is an implementation detail. Though unusual, it is possible for classes that implement the ICommandHandler interface to not be subclasses of the AbstractCommandHandler class.

> **ConcreteCommandHandler1, ConcreteCommandHandler2 . . .:** Instances of classes in this role are objects in a chain of objects that can handle commands.

Typically, CommandHandler objects are part of a larger structure. This is the case in the example shown in Figure 7.1.

IMPLEMENTATION

In many cases, the objects that constitute a chain of responsibility are part of a larger structure. The chain of responsibility is formed through some links in the larger structure. When links to form a chain of responsibility do not already exist, you must add properties to the classes to create links that form a chain of responsibility.

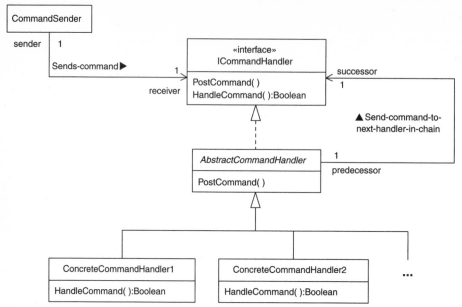

Figure 7.2 Chain of Responsibility Pattern

A decision to make, whenever implementing the Chain of Responsibility pattern, is how to pass commands to and through the chain of objects. There are two basic ways. One way is to encapsulate each kind of command in a single object that can be passed to a single `PostCommand` subroutine. The other way is to have as many different types of `PostCommand` subroutines and `HandleCommand` functions as there are different types of information associated with commands.

Passing commands in a single object is often the better choice. The amount of time it takes to create a command object will generally be *roughly* three times the cost of passing the individual parameters to a function or subroutine. However, the cost of propagating a command through a chain of objects may be reduced since there is only one parameter to be passed. Also, passing commands in a single object usually results in less code.

On the other hand, passing the information that constitutes a command through separate parameters saves the cost of object creation at the cost of additional parameter passing. If you know the chain of objects will be short, passing a command as multiple parameters can be the better choice.

Because the intent of the Chain of Responsibility pattern is similar to event handling, people sometimes look for a way to use .NET delegates in the implementation of Chain of Responsibility. Because each call to a `ConcreteCommandHandler` object involves deciding whether or not to also call the next object in the chain, .NET delegates are not helpful in implementing the Chain of Responsibility pattern.

CONSEQUENCES

☺ The Chain of Responsibility pattern reduces coupling between the object that sends a command and the object that handles the command. The sender of a command does not need to know what object will actually handle the command. It merely needs to be able to send the command to the object at the head of the chain of responsibility.

☺ The Chain of Responsibility pattern allows flexibility in deciding how to handle commands. Decisions about which object will handle a command can be varied by changing which objects are in the chain of responsibility or changing the order of the objects in the chain of responsibility.

• The Chain of Responsibility pattern does not guarantee that every command will be handled. Commands that are not handled are ignored.

☹ If the number of objects in a chain becomes large, there can be efficiency concerns about the amount of time that it takes a command to propagate through the chain. A high percentage of commands that are not handled exacerbates the problem, because commands that are not handled propagate through the full length of the chain.

.NET API USAGE

An example of the Chain of Responsibility pattern used within the .NET class libraries is the .NET Remoting ChannelSink architecture. When sending (ClientChannelSink) or receiving (ServerChannelSink) messages you can provide your own chain of channel sinks, which can operate on the send/receive or request/response message pair.

The HTTP (Hypertext Transfer Protocol) runtime in ASP.NET also uses the Chain or Responsibility pattern.

CODE EXAMPLE

Continuing the physical security example, Figure 7.3 shows the classes used in the physical security example.

In Figure 7.3, classes that extend the Sensor class call the Notify subroutine they inherit to report a measurement to the object responsible for handling its measurements. Classes that inherit the AbstractSecurityZone class are responsible for handling measurements from the appropriate kind of Sensor object.

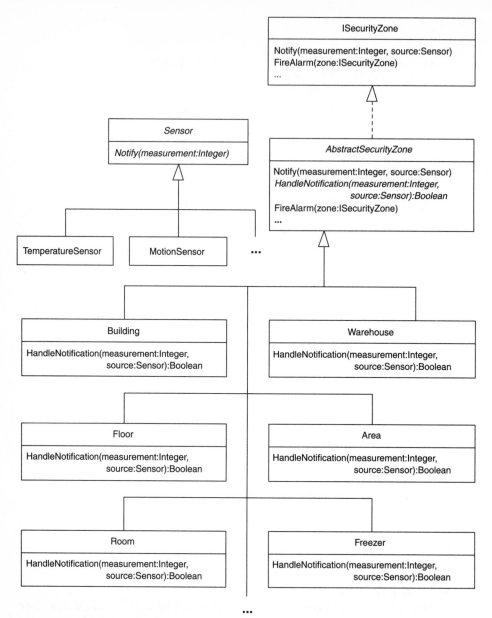

Figure 7.3 Physical Security Classes

The following is some code for the classes shown in Figure 7.3. First, here is code for the TemperatureSensor class. Notice that the TemperatureSensor class does nothing with a reading from a temperature sensor but pass it on.

```
' Instances of this class model the state of a temperature sensor.
Public Class TemperatureSensor
    Inherits Sensor
    Private myZone As SecurityZone = Nothing

    ' The security zone that this sensor's is part of.
    Public Property Zone() As SecurityZone
        Get
            Return myZone
        End Get
        Set(ByVal Value As SecurityZone)
            myZone = Value
        End Set
    End Property 'Zone

    ' When the temperature sensor associated with this object
    ' observes a different temperature this method is called.
    '
    ' measurement - The new temperature.
    Public Overrides Sub Notify(ByVal measurement As Integer)
        Zone.Notify(measurement, Me)
    End Sub 'Notify
End Class 'TemperatureSensor
```

All classes that model security zones implement the ISecurityZone interface:

```
' Classes used to model a kind of security zone implement this
' interface.
Friend Interface ISecurityZone
    '
    ' This method is called to notify this security zone of a
    ' change in a sensor measurement.
    '
    ' measurement - The new measurement
    ' mySensor - The object that models the sensor that produced the
    '            measurement.
    '
    Sub Notify(ByVal measurement As Integer, ByVal mySensor As Sensor)

    '
    ' This method is called by a child zone to report a fire.
    ' It is expected that the child zone has turned on
    ' sprinklers or taken other appropriate measures to control
    ' the fire within the child zone. The purpose of this method
    ' is to be overridden by other subclasses so that it can
    ' take any necessary actions outside of the child zone.
    '
    Sub FireAlarm(ByVal zone As SecurityZone)
End Interface 'ISecurityZone
```

Here is the code for the `SecurityZone` class, which is the base class of all classes that form the chains of responsibility in this example:

```
' This is the base class for all classes that are used to model a kind
' of security zone.
Public MustInherit Class SecurityZone
    Implements ISecurityZone
    Private myParent As SecurityZone = Nothing


    '
    ' Return this object's parent zone.
    '

    Public ReadOnly Property Parent() As SecurityZone
        Get
            Return myParent
        End Get
    End Property
    '
    ' This method is called to notify this security zone of a change in
    ' a sensor measurement.
    '

    ' measurement - The new measurement
    ' mySensor - The object that models the sensor that produced
    '            the measurement.
    '
    '

    Public Sub Notify(ByVal measurement As Integer, ByVal mySensor As Sensor) _
    Implements ISecurityZone.Notify
        If Not HandleNotification(measurement, mySensor) _
            And myParent IsNot Nothing Then
            myParent.Notify(measurement, mySensor)
        End If
    End Sub 'Notify


    '
    ' This method is called by the notify method so that this
    ' object can have a chance to handle measurements.
    '

    Public MustOverride Function HandleNotification( _
        ByVal measurement As Integer, ByVal sensor As Sensor) As Boolean


    '
    ' This method is called by a child zone to report a fire.  It is
    ' expected that the child zone has turned on sprinklers or taken
    ' other appropriate measures to control the fire within the child
    ' zone. The purpose of this method is to be overridden by other
    ' subclasses so that it can take any necessary actions outside of
    ' the child zone.
    '
```

```
    Public Overridable Sub FireAlarm(ByVal zone As SecurityZone) _
    Implements ISecurityZone.FireAlarm
        ' Turn on sprinklers
        '...
        If myParent IsNot Nothing Then
            myParent.FireAlarm(zone)
        End If
    End Sub 'FireAlarm
End Class 'SecurityZone
```

Here are the subclasses of `SecurityZone` that were discussed under the "Context" heading:

```
'
' Instances of this class are used to represent an open area
' in a warehouse, an office building or retail floor.
'
Public Class Area
    Inherits SecurityZone

    ' This method is called by the notify method so that this
    ' object can have a chance to handle measurements.
    Public Overrides Function HandleNotification( _
        ByVal measurement As Integer, ByVal sensor As Sensor) As Boolean
        If TypeOf sensor Is TemperatureSensor Then
            If measurement > 150 Then
                FireAlarm(Me)
                Return True
            End If
        End If
        Return False
    End Function 'HandleNotification
End Class 'Area
'
' Instances of this class are used to represent a warehouse.
'
Public Class Warehouse
    Inherits SecurityZone

    '
    ' This method is called by the notify method so that this
    ' object can have a chance to handle measurements.
    '
    Public Overrides Function HandleNotification( _
      ByVal measurement As Integer, ByVal sensor As Sensor) As Boolean
        Return False
    End Function 'HandleNotification
```

```
'
' This method is called by a child zone to report a fire.
' It is expected that the child zone has turned on
' sprinklers or taken other appropriate measures to control
' the fire within the child zone. The purpose of this method
' is to be overridden by other subclasses so that it can
' take any necessary actions outside of the child zone.
'

Public Overrides Sub FireAlarm(ByVal zone As SecurityZone)
    If TypeOf zone Is Area Then
        ' Turn on sprinklers in surrounding areas
        '...
        ' Don't call base.FireAlarm because that will turn on the
        ' sprinkler for the whole warehouse.
        If Not (Parent Is Nothing) Then
            Parent.FireAlarm(zone)
        End If
        Return
    End If
    MyBase.FireAlarm(zone)
End Sub 'fireAlarm
End Class 'Warehouse
```

RELATED PATTERNS

Composite: When the chain of objects used by the Chain of Responsibility pattern is part of a larger structure, the larger structure is usually built using the Composite pattern.

Command: The Chain of Responsibility pattern makes the particular object that executes a command indefinite. The Command pattern makes the object that executes a command explicit and specific.

Template Method: When the objects that make up a chain of responsibility are part of a larger organization built using the Composite pattern, the Template Method pattern is often used to organize the behavior of individual objects.

Command

This pattern was previously described in [GoF95].

SYNOPSIS

Encapsulate commands in objects so that you can control their selection, their sequencing, queue them, undo them, and otherwise manipulate them.

CONTEXT

Suppose that you want to design a word processing program so that it can undo and redo commands. A way to accomplish this is to materialize each command as an object with do and undo functions. The class diagram for this is shown in Figure 7.4.

When you tell the word processor to do something, instead of directly performing the command, it creates an instance of the class that corresponds to the command. It passes all necessary information to the instance's constructor. For example, when commanded to insert one or more characters, it creates an InsertStringCommand object. It passes, to the object's constructor, the position in the document to make the insertion and the string to insert at that position.

Once the word processor has materialized a command as an object, the command can be processed as an object that implements the ICommand interface, without concern for its class or the command it encapsulates. The word processor calls the object's DoIt subroutine to execute the command. The word processor also puts the command object in a data structure that allows the word processor to maintain a history of executed commands. Maintaining a command history allows the word processor to undo commands in the reverse order that they were issued by calling their Undo subroutines.

FORCES

☺ You need to control the sequencing, selection, or timing of command execution.

☺ You need to manage the undo and redo of commands.

☺ You need to maintain a persistent log of commands executed. You can generate such a log by enhancing command objects so that their DoIt and UndoIt subroutines generate log entries. Since you can use a persistent log to back out the effects of previously executed commands, a persistent log can be incorporated into a transaction management mechanism to allow commands to be undone if a transaction is aborted.

SOLUTION

Figure 7.5 is a class diagram that shows classes that participate in the Command pattern.

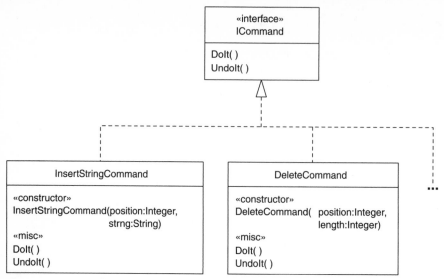

Figure 7.4   Do and Undo Class Diagram

Here are explanations of the roles that interfaces and classes play in the Command pattern:

ICommand: An interface in this role is implemented by classes that encapsulate commands. It minimally defines a `DoIt` subroutine that other classes call to execute the encapsulated command. If undo support is required, the interface also defines an `UndoIt` subroutine that undoes the effects of the last call to the `DoIt` subroutine.

ConcreteCommand: Classes in this role are concrete classes that encapsulate a specific command. Other classes invoke the command through a call to the class's `DoIt` subroutine. The undo logic for the command is invoked through a call to the class's `UndoIt` subroutine.

The object's constructor normally supplies any parameters that the command requires. Most commands require at least one parameter, which is the object that the command acts on. For example, a command to save an object to disk normally requires that the object to be saved is passed to the command object's constructor.

Invoker: A class in this role creates concrete command objects if it needs to invoke a command. It may call a command object's `DoIt` subroutine or leave that for the `CommandManager` object to do.

CommandManager: A `CommandManager` class is responsible for managing a collection of command objects created by an `Invoker` object. The specific responsibilities of a `CommandManager` class can include managing the undo and redo of commands, sequencing commands, and scheduling commands.

`CommandManager` classes are usually independent of the applications in which they are used and can be very reusable.

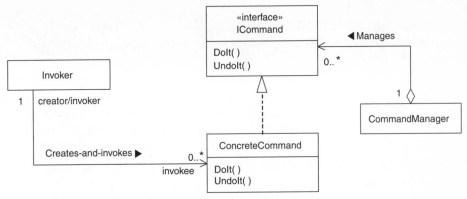

Figure 7.5 Command Pattern

IMPLEMENTATION

There are a few issues to consider when implementing the Command pattern. The first and most important is to decide what commands will be. If the commands are issued by a user interface that provides user-level commands, then a very natural way to identify concrete command classes is to have a concrete command class for each user-level command. If you stick with this strategy and there are any particularly complex user commands, then there will be equally complex command classes. To avoid putting too much complexity in one class, you may want to implement more complex user-level commands as a sequence of ICommand objects.

If the number of external or user-level commands is very large, then you might follow the strategy of implementing external or user-level commands with combinations of command objects. This strategy may allow you to implement a large number of external commands with a smaller number of command classes.

Undo/Redo

Another implementation issue to consider is the capture of state information necessary to undo commands. In order to be able to undo the effects of a command, you must save enough of the state of the objects it operates on to be able to restore that state.

There may be commands that are impractical to undo because they involve saving an excessive amount of state information. For example, a global search and replace command may sometimes involve changing so much information that keeping all of the original information would take up a prohibitive amount of storage. There may be commands that can never be undone because it is not possible to restore the state that those commands change. Commands that involve the deletion of files often fall into this category.

The CommandManager object should be aware when a command is executed that is not undoable. There are a number of reasons for this:

- Suppose that a `CommandManager` object is responsible for the initial execution of commands. If it is aware that a command will be undoable before it is executed, then it can provide a common mechanism for warning a user that an undoable command is about to be executed. When it warns a user, it can also offer the user the option of not executing the command.

- Keeping a command history for undo purposes consumes memory and sometimes other resources. After executing a command that cannot be undone, any command history that is available can be disposed of. Keeping the command history after executing a command that is not undoable is a waste of resources.

- Most user interfaces for programs that have an undo command have a menu item for users to issue an undo command. A good user interface avoids surprising users. Responding to an undo command with a notification that the last command was not undoable surprises a user who expected an undo command to be carried out. A way to avoid this surprise is for the command manager object to enable or disable the undo menu to reflect whether the last executed command was undoable or not undoable.

You can simplify the pattern if you do not need to support undo operations. If no undo support is required, then the `ICommand` interface does not need to define an `undoIt` subroutine.

Avoid User Interface Dependencies

There is a common extension to the Command pattern used when commands are issued by a user interface. The purpose of the extension is to avoid tying user interface components to a specific command object or even requiring user interface components to know about any concrete command classes. The extension consists of embedding the name of a command in user interface components and using a factory method object to create the command objects, as shown in Figure 7.6.

In the organization shown in Figure 7.6, GUI component classes refer to the name of the command they invoke, rather than to the class that implements the command or an instance of it. They invoke commands indirectly by passing the command's name to a factory object that creates an instance of the appropriate concrete command class.

Invoking commands through a command factory provides a layer of indirection that can be very useful. The indirection allows multiple command-issuing objects to transparently share the same command object. More importantly, the indirection makes it easier to have user-customizable menus and toolbars.

Programs commonly create commands in response to events such as keystroke or selecting a menu item. Some programs use events to represent commands. This is usually a bad idea, since changes to the user interface can imply changes to the commands that the user interface invokes. Also it ties commands to the design of the user interface.

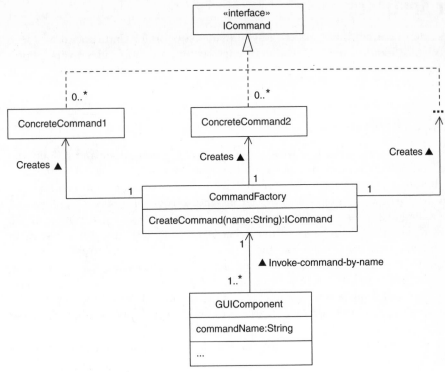

Figure 7.6   Command Factory

CONSEQUENCES

☺ The object that invokes a command is not the same object that executes a command. This separation provides flexibility in the timing and sequencing of commands. Materializing commands as objects means that they can be collected, delegated to, and otherwise manipulated like any other kind of object.

☺ Being able to collect and control the sequencing of commands means that you can use the Command pattern as the basis of a mechanism that supports keyboard macros. This is a mechanism that records a sequence of commands and allows them to be replayed later. The Command pattern can also be used to create other kinds of composite patterns.

☺ Adding new commands is usually easy because it does not break any dependencies.

.NET API USAGE

The Windows Forms `TextBoxBase` class provides support for Undo operations, such that both the `TextBox` and `RichTextBox` controls support undo and redo operations. Note that each implementation provides its own implementations of Redo, while being able to reuse the `TextBoxBase` implementation of `Undo`.

CODE EXAMPLE

The example of commands in a word processor that can be undone and redone presented under the "Context" heading continues here. Figure 7.7 is a collaboration diagram that shows the normal collaboration that creates and executes commands.

Figure 7.7 shows an object creating an instance of the `InsertStringCommand` class, passing to its constructor the document to insert a string into, the string to insert, and the position at which to insert the string. After initializing the `InsertString Command` object, the constructor calls the `CommandManager` object's `invokeCommand` subroutine. The `invokeCommand` subroutine calls the `InsertStringCommand` object's `DoIt` subroutine, which does the actual string insertion. If the `DoIt` function returns true, indicating that the command was successful and can be undone, then the `CommandManager` object adds the `InsertStringCommand` object to its command history.

Here is some code that implements this. First is the `ICommand` interface, which is implemented by all of the concrete command classes in this example:

```
'
' This interface is implemented by classes that encapsulate
' commands for a word processor.
'

Public Interface ICommand
    '
    ' Perform the command encapsulated by this object.
    '
    ' returns - true if sucessful and can be undone.
    Function DoIt() As Boolean


    '
    ' Undo the last invocation of doIt.
    '
    ' return true if the unndo was successful
    Function UndoIt() As Boolean
End Interface 'ICommand
```

Here is source for a concrete class that implements the `ICommand` interface:

```
'
' Command to insert a string into a document.
'
```

```vb
Public Class InsertStringCommand
    Implements ICommand
    Private myDocument As Document ' The document to insert into
    Private str As String ' The string to insert
    Private position As Integer ' The position to insert at


    '
    ' Constructor
    '
    ' theDocument - The document to insert into
    ' position - The position to insert at
    ' s - The string to insert
    Public Sub New(ByVal theDocument As Document, _
                   ByVal position As Integer, ByVal s As String)
        myDocument = theDocument
        Me.position = position
        Me.str = s
        CommandManager.GetInstance().InvokeCommand(Me)
    End Sub


    '
    ' Perform the command encapsulated by this object.
    '
    ' returns true if this call to doCommand was successful and
    ' can be undone by a call to undoCommand.
    Public Function DoIt() As Boolean _
        Implements ICommand.DoIt
        Try
            myDocument.InsertStringCommand(position, str)
        Catch
            Return False
        End Try
        Return True
    End Function 'DoIt


    '
    ' Undo the command encapsulated by this object.
    '
    ' returns - true if undo was successful
    Public Function UndoIt() As Boolean _
        Implements ICommand.UndoIt
        Try
            myDocument.DeleteCommand(position, str.Length)
        Catch
            Return False
        End Try
        Return True
    End Function
End Class 'InsertStringCommand
```

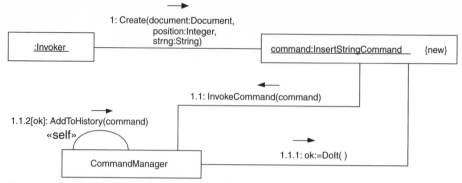

Figure 7.7 Word Processor Command Collaboration

The basic structure of most other classes that implement the ICommand interface is similar. Notable exceptions are the classes for undo and redo commands, which are shown later in this section.

Following is source for the CommandManager class, which is responsible for managing the execution of commands. More specifically, for the purposes of the word processing program, instances of this class are responsible for maintaining a command history for undo and redo. Notice the special handling for undo and redo.

```
'
' Instances of this class are responsible for managing the
' execution of commands.  More specifically, for the purposes
' of this word processing program, instances of this class are
' responsible for maintaining a command history for undo and
' redo.
'
Public Class CommandManager
    ' The single instance of this command.
    Private Shared myInstance As New CommandManager()

    ' The maximum number of command to keep in the history
    Private maxHistoryLength As Integer = 100

    Private history As New ArrayList()
    Private redoList As New ArrayList()


    '
    ' Returns the instance of this class.
    '
    Public Shared Function GetInstance() As CommandManager
        Return myInstance
    End Function 'GetInstance

    ' Private constructor to prevent other classes from
    ' instantiating this class.
    Private Sub New()
    End Sub 'New
```

```
'
' Invoke a command and add it to the history. If the command
' object's doIt method was previously called, then it is
' expected to return false.
'
Public Sub InvokeCommand(ByVal command As ICommand)
    Dim cmdType As Type = CObj(command).GetType()
    Dim uType As Type = GetType(UndoAttribute)
    Dim undoAttr As Attribute
    undoAttr = Attribute.GetCustomAttribute(cmdType, uType)
    If undoAttr IsNot Nothing Then
        undo()
        Return
    End If
    Dim rType As Type = GetType(RedoAttribute)
    Dim redoAttr As Attribute
    redoAttr = Attribute.GetCustomAttribute(cmdType, rType)
    If redoAttr IsNot Nothing Then
        redo()
        Return
    End If
    If command.DoIt() Then
        ' doIt returned true, which means it can be undone
        addToHistory(command)
    Else ' command cannot be undone
        history.Clear()
    End If
    ' After a command that is not an undo or a redo, ensure that
    ' the redo list is empty.
    If redoList.Count > 0 Then
        redoList.Clear()
    End If
End Sub 'InvokeCommand


' Undo the most recent command in the commmand history.
Private Sub undo()
    If history.Count > 0 Then
        ' If there are commands in the history
        Dim undoCommand As ICommand
        undoCommand = CType(history(0), ICommand)
        history.RemoveAt(0)
        undoCommand.UndoIt()
        redoList.Insert(0, undoCommand)
    End If
End Sub 'undo


' Redo the most recently undone command
Private Sub redo()
    If redoList.Count > 0 Then
        ' If the redo list is not empty
        Dim redoCommand As ICommand
        redoCommand = CType(redoList(0), ICommand)
```

```
            redoList.RemoveAt(0)
            redoCommand.DoIt()
            history.Insert(0, redoCommand)
        End If
    End Sub 'redo


    ' Add a command to the command history.
    Private Sub addToHistory(ByVal command As ICommand)
        history.Insert(0, command)
        ' If size of history has exceded maxHistoryLength, remove
        ' the oldest command from the history
        If history.Count > maxHistoryLength Then
            history.RemoveAt((history.Count - 1))
        End If
    End Sub 'addToHistory
End Class 'CommandManager
```

Notice that the CommandManager class does not actually use the command classes that represent the undo and redo classes. It just checks if their instances have the Undo or Redo attributes. Here is the source for UndoAttribute:

```
'
' This is attribute indicates that a command object is an undo
' command.
'
<AttributeUsage(AttributeTargets.Class, Inherited:=True)> _
Public Class UndoAttribute
    Inherits Attribute

End Class
```

The source for the RedoAttribute class is similar.

The reason for using these attributes is to keep the CommandManager class independent of specific undo and redo classes. Because the CommandManager class is responsible for managing undo and redo, all that classes representing undo and redo need to do is let a CommandManager object know that it should undo or redo the last command. It is preferable for it to do this in a way that does not require the Command Manager class to expose any of its special logic. This implies a mechanism that allows a CommandManager object to ask if it needs to perform an undo or redo, rather than being told. Being able to determine if an object has the Undo or Redo attributes allows a CommandManager object to ask if it should perform an undo or redo without having to know anything about the class that has the attribute.

Finally, here is source for the UndoCommand class. The RedoCommand class is very similar.

```
'
' Instances of this class represent undo commands.
'
<Undo()> Public Class UndoCommand
    Implements ICommand
```

```
'
' This implementation of doIt does not actually do anything.
' The logic for undo is in the CommandManager class.  A
' CommandManager object knows that it is supposed to invoke
' its undo logic when it sees an instace of this class
' because this class implments the Undo interface.  The Undo
' interface is a semantic interface that is used to mark a
' class as representing an undo command.
'

Public Function DoIt() As Boolean _
    Implements ICommand.DoIt
    ' This method should never be called
    Throw New System.NotImplementedException()
End Function


'
' This implementation of undoIt does not actually do
' anything.  Undo commands are not undone.  Instead a redo
' command is issued.
'

Public Function UndoIt() As Boolean _
    Implements ICommand.UndoIt
    ' This method should never be called
    Throw New System.NotImplementedException()
End Function

End Class 'UndoCommand
```

Because there should never be a reason to call the functions of this class, they always throw an exception.

RELATED PATTERNS

Factory Method: The Factory Method pattern is sometimes used to provide a layer of indirection between a user interface and command classes.

Little Language: You can use the Command pattern to help implement the Little Language pattern. You can also use the Little Language pattern to implement commands.

Marker Interface: You can use the Marker Interface pattern with the Command pattern to implement undo/redo processing.

Snapshot: If you want to provide a coarse-grained undo mechanism that saves the entire state of an object rather than a command-by-command account of how to reconstruct previous states, you can use the Snapshot pattern.

Template Method: The Template Method pattern can be used to implement the top-level undo logic of the Command pattern.

Little Language

The Little Language pattern is based on the Interpreter pattern documented in [GoF95] and the notion of little languages popularized by Jon Bentley [Bentley86]. You can find more sophisticated techniques for designing and implementing languages in [ASU86].

SYNOPSIS

Suppose that you need to solve many similar problems, and you notice that the solutions to these problems can be expressed as different combinations of a small number of elements or operations. The simplest way to express solutions to these problems may be to define a little language. Common types of problems you can solve with little languages are searches of common data structures, creation of complex data structures and formatting of data.

CONTEXT

Suppose that you need to write a program that searches a collection of files to find files that contain a given combination or combinations of words. You don't want to have to write a separate program for each search. Instead, you can define a little language that allows users to describe combinations of words and then write one program that finds files that contain a combination of words specified in the little language.

Though you could use regular expressions to specify the words to be searched for, you want to design a little language that will be easier for people to use with little or no training.

The definition of a language usually consists of two parts. The *syntax* of a language defines the words and symbols that make up the language and how they may be combined. The *semantics* of a language defines the meaning of the words, symbols, and their combinations that make up the language.

You usually define the syntax of a language by writing a grammar. A grammar is a set of rules that define the sequences of characters that make up the words and symbols of the language. A grammar also contains rules that define how you can combine the words and symbols of the language to form larger constructs.

The precise definition of the semantics of a large language can be very complicated and lengthy. However, for a little language a few simple paragraphs of explanation may be good enough.

Let's return to the idea of defining a little language to define combinations of words. One way to define a little language is to first create a few examples of what the language should look like. Then you can generalize from the examples to a complete definition.

Following this plan, consider some things that will be useful to say in a little language for specifying combinations of words. The most basic thing is to be able to specify a combination that consists of just a single word. The most obvious way to specify that is by simply writing the word like this:

```
bottle
```

You will also want to be able to specify combinations of words that don't contain a word. A simple way of doing that is to precede the word you don't want in combinations by the word "not" like this:

```
not box
```

This specifies all combinations of words that do not contain the word "box".

Using words like "not" to mean something other than a word that can be part of a combination makes those words special. Words like that are called *reserved words*, because they are reserved for a special purpose and cannot be used the way that other words can be used. If you treat the word "not" as a reserved word, that means that you cannot specify a combination of words that contains the word "not" by just writing the word "not". As you read further in this discussion, you will see that there are reasons to treat other words as reserved words. This suggests that it will be useful to have a way to indicate a combination of words that contains any arbitrary word, sequence of words, or punctuation. A way of indicating a combination of arbitrary words and punctuation is to enclose the sequence of words in quotation marks like this:

```
"Yes, not the"
```

The next level of complexity is to specify combinations of two words. Obviously, the syntax for a combination of two words must allow you to specify which words are in the combination. Since there are different ways to combine words, the syntax for specifying combinations of two words must also provide for specifying how the words are combined. One way to do that is to write one word of the combination, followed by a special word that indicates how the words are combined, followed by the second word of the combination. For example, you could write

```
bottle or jar
```

to indicate combinations of words that contains at least one of the words "bottle" or "jar".

You will need additional words to indicate other ways to combine two words:

- Use the word "and" to indicate combinations of words that contain both words.

- Use the word "near" to indicate combinations that include the two words occurring within 25 words of each other.

If you wanted to combine the reserved word "and" with the reserved word "not" to indicate a combination of words that contains "garlic" but not "onions", it would be reasonable to write

```
garlic and not onions
```

These examples cover most of the things you will need to describe combinations involving two words. When you go beyond two words, you will need to deal with additional issues. It seems clear that

```
red and "pickup truck" and broken
```

means combinations of words that contain all three of the word "red", the phrase "pickup truck" and the word "broken". When you mix different ways of combining words, the meaning becomes ambiguous. Does

```
turkey or chicken and soup
```

mean combinations of words that contain the word "turkey" or both of the words "chicken" and "soup"? Does it mean combinations of words that contain the word "soup" and at least one of the words "chicken" or "turkey"? One way to resolve this ambiguity is to require the use of parentheses to specify the order in which the logical connectors in a combination are used. To specify the first interpretation you could write

```
turkey or (chicken and soup)
```

To specify the second interpretation, you could write

```
(turkey or chicken) and soup
```

Most people don't like being forced to write parentheses, so a rule that resolves the ambiguity without parentheses is desirable. A common type of rule used in language definitions to resolve this sort of ambiguity is called a *precedence rule*.

A precedence rule is a rule that assigns a different precedence to the different operations that occur in a language. Its use is to provide a way of deciding the order of operations. Operations with a higher precedence are done before operations with a lower precedence. Suppose that you assign the following precedence values:

near	3
and	2
or	1

Given those precedence values, the meaning of

```
mansion or big near house and rich
```

would be combinations of words that include the word "mansion" or both the words "rich" and "big", with the word "big" occurring within 25 words of the word "house". If we were to add parenthesis, it would be the same as

```
mansion or ((big near house) and rich)
```

Before you try to design any classes to make sense out of this little language, it is important to write a grammar that defines the syntax of the language. This will provide a clear specification from which to code. There are a few different strategies for organizing a grammar. The strategy used in this example is a top-down strategy. This means starting with the top-level construct in the language, a combination, and deciding all of the lower-level constructs that can constitute it until the grammar is complete.

Above the level of individual characters, the constructs that make up a grammar are called tokens. The tokens in a grammar are classified as either terminal tokens or non-terminal tokens. Terminal tokens correspond to a contiguous sequence of characters. The word in a combination such as

```
fence
```

is a terminal token, as are parentheses and quoted strings. Higher-level constructs that are defined in terms of terminal tokens are called non-terminal tokens. A combination is a non-terminal token.

In most little languages, including this word combination language, terminal tokens may be separated by white-space characters that do not contribute to the meaning of the language.

The rules that determine how to recognize sequences of characters as terminal tokens are called lexical analysis rules. The rules that determine how to recognize non-terminal tokens as sequences of terminal and non-terminal tokens are called productions.

The notation used here for writing productions is called Backus-Naur Form, or more commonly BNF. In BNF, terminal tokens and non-terminal tokens are written using different fonts to distinguish them. This book indicates terminal tokens like this:

quoted_string

This book indicates non-terminal tokens like this:

combination

A production consists of a non-terminal token and a sequence of terminal and non-terminal tokens that can be recognized as that first non-terminal. Here is an example of a production:

combination (**word**

This production says that a combination non-terminal token can consist of just a word terminal token.

If there are multiple sequences of tokens that can be recognized as a non-terminal, then there will be multiple productions for that non-terminal. There will be one production for each sequence that can be recognized as that non-terminal. For example, the following set of productions specifies the syntax for combinations that do or don't contain a particular word:

```
combination ( word
combination ( not word
```

The technique you use to specify that a non-terminal token should be recognized from an indefinitely long sequence of tokens is recursion. Here is a set of productions that captures most of the syntax of the preceding examples:

```
combination ( simpleCombination
combination ( simpleCombination or combination
combination ( simpleCombination and combination
combination ( simpleCombination near combination
simpleCombination ( word
simpleCombination ( not word
simpleCombination ( ( combination )
```

Notice that three of the four productions for combination are directly recursive. These three productions could have been written with combination as the first non-terminal token and simpleCombination as the second non-terminal token. Either way, they would match the same sequences of tokens. However, for the implementation technique shown later in this section for turning productions into code, it makes a difference. For the technique we will discuss, it is always best to write productions as shown, in a right-recursive way. What we mean by right-recursive is that when there is a choice about where to put a recursion in a production, we choose to put the recursion as far to the right as we can.

Though this set of productions does not capture all the details of this word combination language, it captures enough that we can work through an example. We will examine how to use these productions to recognize this string as a combination:

```
fox and not brown
```

The string we are trying to recognize begins with a word token. This matches the production

```
simpleCombination ( word
```

That leaves us having recognized this much of the string:

```
---
fox and not brown
```

The line over the string shows how much of the string has been recognized. This is what we have recognized:

```
simpleCombination

    _
  word

    _
  fox
```

In other words, what we have recognized is a `simpleCombination` token that consists of a **word** token that is the word "fox". Four productions begin with `simple Combination`. One of these productions is

```
combination ( simpleCombination
```

This gives us a choice of matching this production with what we have already recognized or trying to match a longer production. When faced with this type of choice, we always try to match a longer production. If we are unable to match a longer production, then we back up and match the shorter production.

The next token in the string is an **and** token. There is one production for `combination` that begins with `simpleCombination` followed by **and**:

```
combination ( simpleCombination and combination
```

In order to finish matching the string to this production, we will need to recognize the rest of the string as a `combination`.

The next token in the string is a **not** token. Looking at the productions for `combination`, we see that `combination` can begin with a `simpleCombination`. There is a production for `simpleCombination` that begins with a **not** token. Now we are trying to finish matching the production

```
simpleCombination ( not word
```

so that we can finish matching

```
combination ( simpleCombination and combination
```

We have recognized this much of the string:

```
-----------
fox and not brown
```

The next token is a `word` token. This means that we have successfully matched the productions that we were tying to match. Since it also exhausts the content of the string, we have recognized the entire string as a `combination` with this internal structure:

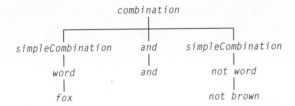

This tree structure that was constructed while parsing the string is called a parse tree. For most languages, the implementation is simpler and faster if it first builds a parse tree data structure and then uses the parse tree to drive subsequent actions.

As mentioned before, the set of productions we used to work through the preceding example does not capture all the details of the word combination language. It does not allow a combination to include quoted strings. It also does not capture precedence rules for and, near or or.

There is another nuance that will be helpful to add to the productions. The previous set of productions uses the same non-terminal token to match the token sequences word and not word. This means that after we have built the parse tree, the same type of object will represent both kinds of sequences. It will simplify the interpretation of the parse tree and make it faster if it is possible to determine which type of sequence an object represents just by looking at its type. You can accomplish this by having productions that recognize those sequences as two different non-terminals.

Here is the final set of productions that captures the precedence rules and recognizes the additional non-terminals:

```
combination ( orCombination
orCombination ( andCombination or orCombination
orCombination ( andCombination
andCombination ( nearCombination and andCombination
andCombination ( nearCombination
nearCombination ( simpleCombination near nearCombination
nearCombination ( simpleCombination
simpleCombination ( ( orCombination )
simpleCombination ( wordCombination
simpleCombination ( notWordCombination
wordCombination ( word
wordCombination ( quoted_string
notWordCombination ( not word
notWordCombination ( not quoted_string
```

You may notice that if you use these productions to parse a string, creating a parse tree node object for each non-terminal, you will have more parse tree node objects than were produced by the previous set of productions. Here is the parse tree that would be produced by parsing the same string as in the previous example,

```
fox and not brown
```

and using the preceding productions to create a parse tree node object for each non-terminal:

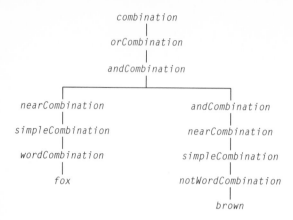

Notice that this parse tree contains many nodes that do not add anything useful to the tree. Without losing any information, this parse tree could be simplified to this:

Before you write any code, you should decide which productions are purely organizational in nature and which productions provide useful information. A parser should only produce parse tree nodes that provide information.

The preceding discussion covers the basics of writing productions to recognize tokens. Now let's consider how to define lexical rules that determine how to recognize terminal tokens from sequences of characters.

In many little languages, the lexical rules are sometimes simple enough that you can adequately define them by a natural language set of descriptions, like this:

- White space consists of one or more consecutive space, tab, new-line or carriage-return characters. White space can be used to separate terminal tokens. It has no other significance and is discarded.

- An and token consists of this sequence of three letters: a, n, d,

Where this approach does not seem adequate, you may prefer a more precise approach based on regular expressions. Regular expressions are a way of specifying how to match a sequence of characters. For example, the regular expression

```
[0-9]+
```

matches a sequence of one or more digits. There are a variety of regular expression notations you can use. The regular expression notation used in this section to define the lexical rules for the word combination language is explained in Table 7.1. It should be sufficiently expressive for most little languages.

Table 7.1 Regular Expression Language

REGULAR EXPRESSION	WHAT IT MATCHES
c	Matches the character c if c is not one of the following special characters.
.	Matches any character.
^	Matches the beginning of a line or a string.
$	Matches the end of a line or string.
[s]	Matches a character that is in a set of characters and character ranges. For example, [aeiou] matches a lowercase vowel. [A-Za-z_] matches an uppercase or lowercase letter or an underscore.
[^s]	Matches a character that is *not* in a set of characters and character ranges. For example, [^0-9] matches a character that is not a digit. The ^ is treated specially only right after the [. For example, [+^] matches a plus sign or a circumflex.
\G	This does not match any characters. It is useful when a regular expression is used at progressive positions in a string, such as when we want to recognize the next token in a string. If a regular expression begins with \G, then it only matches character sequences that begin at the position in the string that the matching operation started. This is different from ^ because ^ only matches character sequences that start at the beginning of a line.
\b	This does not match any characters. It matches the boundary (beginning or end) of a word.
\c	Matches the character c even if c is a special character. Use \\ to match the \ character.
r*	Matches zero or more occurrences of the regular expression r.
r+	Matches one or more occurrences of the regular expression r.
r?	Matches zero or one occurrences of the regular expression r.
Rx	Matches what the regular expression r matches followed by what the regular expression x matches.
(r)	Matches what the regular expression r matches. For example, (xyz)* matches zero or more occurrences of the sequence xyz.
r|x	Matches any string that matches the regular expression r or the regular expression x. For example, (abc)|(xyz) matches the sequence abc or the sequence xyz.
r{m,n}	Matches at least m occurrences but no more than n occurrences of regular expression r.

Table 7.2 shows a set of lexical rules for the word combination language. In the first column is a regular expression. The second column contains the name of the terminal token, if any, that is recognized when the regular expression is matched. When a parser needs to find the next terminal token in its input, it will try the regular expressions in the order in which they appear until it finds one that matches the input. If no regular expression matches the input then the parser knows that something is wrong with the input.

When a regular expression matches the input, if there is a terminal token in the second column, then the parser recognizes that token and processes it according to whatever production it is trying to match. If there is no terminal token in the second column, then the input that the regular expression matches is discarded, and the parser begins again with the first regular expression.

Table 7.2 Lexical Rules for the Word Combination Language

`+`	
`[Oo][Rr]`	`Or`
`[Aa][Nn][Dd]`	`And`
`[Nn][Ee][Aa][Rr]`	`Near`
`[Nn][Oo][Tt]`	`Not`
`[a-zA-Z0-9]+`	`word`
`\(`	`(`
`\)`	`)`
`"([^"]*("")*)*"`	`quoted_string`

Now we have specified the syntax of the word combination language. In the process of specifying the syntax, we have also discussed the semantics of the language sufficiently. The next thing to do is to design the classes. Figure 7.8 shows the classes necessary to implement the word combination language.

Figure 7.8 shows a `Stream` class. Instances of the `LexicalAnalyzer` class read characters of a word combination from an instance of the `Stream` class. An instance of the `Parser` class reads tokens from an instance of the `LexicalAnalyzer` class by calling its `NextToken` function. The diagram indicates that the `NextToken` function returns a `TerminalToken` object. However, the diagram does not include a `TerminalToken` class. If it did, the `TerminalToken` class would be an abstract class that defines no functions, subroutines, or variables. Each subclass of the `Terminal Token` class would correspond to a different terminal token. The subclasses of the `TerminalToken` class would define no functions or subroutines and either no variables or one variable containing the string recognized as that terminal token. These would be very lightweight objects, encapsulating only the type of terminal token that the object represents and in some cases a string. Implementations of the Little Language pattern do not usually bother to encapsulate these pieces of information. Implementations of the `LexicalAnalyzer` class usually provide these pieces of information as unencapsulated pieces of information.

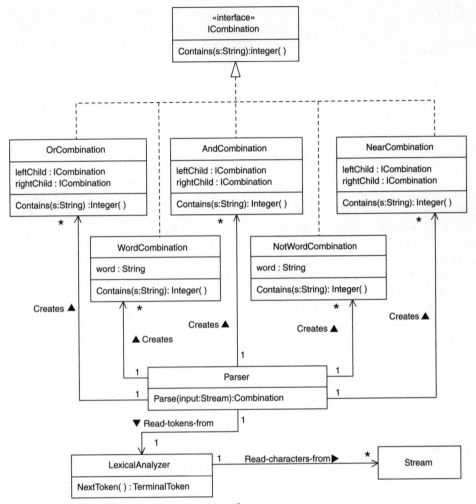

Figure 7.8 Word Combination Language Classes

As a `Parser` object gets tokens from a `LexicalAnalyzer` object, it creates `ICombination` objects, organizing them into a parse tree.

All classes that are instantiated to create parse tree nodes implement the `ICombination` interface. The `ICombination` interface declares a function named `Contains`. The `Contains` function takes a string as its argument and returns an array of `Integer`. Classes implement the `Contains` function to determine if a string meets the requirements of the particular class for containing the desired combination of words. If the string does contain the required combination of words, it passes back an array of `Integer` values that are the offsets in the string of words that satisfied the combination. If the string does not contain the required combination of words, the `Contains` function returns Nothing.

FORCES

☺ You need to identify, create, or format similar kinds of data using many different combinations of a moderate number of operations.

☺ A straightforward representation of combinations of operations can provide adequate performance.

SOLUTION

The Little Language pattern begins with the design of a little language that can specify combinations of operations needed to solve a specific type of problem. The design of a little language specifies its syntax using productions and lexical rules as described under the "Context" heading. The semantics of a little language are usually specified informally by describing what the constructs of the language do using English or another natural language.

Once you have defined a little language, the next step is to design the classes you will use to implement the language. Figure 7.9 is a class diagram showing the organization of classes that participate in the Little Language pattern.

Here are explanations of the roles these classes play in the Little Language pattern:

Client: An instance of a class in this role runs a little language program, feeding it whatever data it needs and using the little program's results. The client creates an instance of the Parser class to parse programs it supplies through Stream objects. The Parser object's Parse function returns an INonterminal object to the Client object. This object is the root of a parse tree. The Client object calls the INonterminal object's execute subroutine to run the program.

Lexical Analyzer: When a Parser object's parse function is called, it creates a LexicalAnalyzer object to read characters from the Stream object that was passed to it. The LexicalAnalyzer object reads characters from the Stream object, recognizes terminal tokens using its lexical rules, and returns these tokens to the Parser class when it calls the LexicalAnalyzer object's Next Token function. The NextToken function returns the next terminal token it finds in the input.

Parser: A Client object creates an instance of the Parser class and then calls the Parser object's Parse function to parse input from Stream objects by matching tokens in the input against the productions of the grammar. The Parse function builds a parse tree as it matches the productions and returns a reference to the parse tree's root to the Client object.

INonterminal: An interface in this role is implemented by all classes whose instances can be parse tree nodes. A Client object calls its Execute subroutine to execute the program.

ConcreteNonterminal1, ConcreteNonterminal2 . . .: Instances of classes in these roles are used as parse tree nodes.

TerminalToken: This abstract class defines no variables or functions or subroutines. Its subclasses correspond to the terminal tokens that the `Lexical Analyzer` class recognizes.

Stream: An instance of the `System.IO.Stream` class can be used to read a stream of characters.

IMPLEMENTATION

Some people feel that it is better to implement a parser by spreading most of its logic through multiple classes that correspond to non-terminal tokens or even productions. A common reason given to explain this organization is that it is somehow more object-oriented. However, it is a less maintainable organization for parsers than the one described previously. There are two reasons for this:

1. Spreading the parsing logic over a number of classes results in less cohesive classes that are difficult to understand. The parser for little languages is usually small enough that people can understand it in its entirety. Spreading the parsing logic over multiple classes makes it much more difficult to understand in its entirety.

2. If a parser is too big to understand in its entirety, then it is big enough that its implementation would be worth changing to use a tool that automatically generates the parser from productions. All available tools that are known to the author of this book generate a parser as a single class or as one main class with some helper classes. If there are other tools that generate a parser as multiple classes, it is very likely that the organization of those classes will be different from any manually generated organization.

   If a parser is manually organized as many classes, switching to an automatically generated parser will involve fixing classes that break because they refer to a defunct class of the manually generated parser. Manually generating a parser as multiple classes can make it more difficult to migrate to an automatically generated parser.

Most subclasses of `TerminalToken` do not contain any functions, subroutines, or variables. Subclasses of `TerminalToken` that do contain variables usually contain just one variable whose value is the substring of the input that the class's instances match. Because subclasses of `TerminalToken` contain so little information, most implementations of the Little Language pattern do not bother using `TerminalToken` or its subclasses. Instead, they pass the type of token that the lexical analyzer recognized and the corresponding string from the lexical analyzer to the parser without encapsulating them in an object.

Parsers build parse trees from the bottom up. The root of a parse tree corresponds to at least as much of the program source as all of its children put together. As a parser parses its input, it creates small parse trees. It joins the small parse trees into larger parse trees with a common root as it recognizes larger and larger constructs. When the parser is done, there is just one big parse tree.

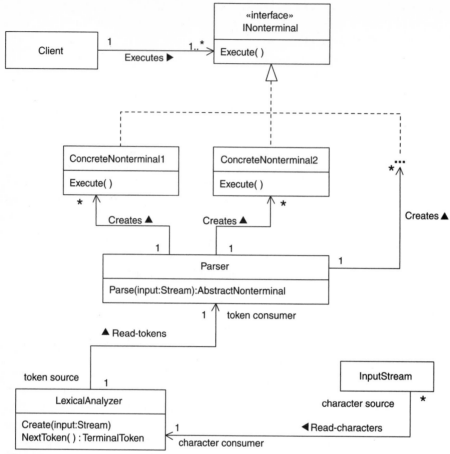

Figure 7.9 Little Language Pattern Classes

The .NET framework includes classes that support the use of regular expressions. These are in the System.Text.RegularExpressions namespace. The classes in that namespace most relevant to lexical analysis are Regex and Match.

Many optimizations and design subtleties that are important to full-service languages are not important to little languages. The point is that the techniques described in this pattern are not sufficient for designing or implementing larger languages like VB or C#.

CONSEQUENCES

☺ The Little Language pattern allows users to specify different combinations of operations. It is almost always easier to design and implement a little language than it is to design and implement a graphical user interface that provides as much flexibility and expressiveness as a little language. On the other hand, most users find the graphical user interface easier to use.

- A language is a form of user interface. Like any user interface, you learn what it makes easy and not so easy to use by using it and watching other people use it.

- A Parser class is usually implemented by writing private functions that mostly correspond to non-terminal tokens. This organization is easy to understand, and grammar changes are easy to implement, so long as the grammar remains relatively small. If the language gets too large, this organization becomes unmanageable.

For larger and full-service languages, there are different and more sophisticated design and implementation techniques. Tools exist that can automatically generate Parser and LexicalAnalyzer classes from productions and lexical rules. There are other tools that assist in the building and simplification of parse trees.

.NET API USAGE

The ToString function of classes that implement the IFormattable.Format interface use the Little Language pattern. The ToString function is passed a string that contains a description of a format in a little language. Each implementing class has its own little language.

Because of the flat structure of these little languages, their parsers do not generate a parse tree, but rather an array of objects.

CODE EXAMPLE

The first code example is the lexical analyzer. It uses .NET's regular expression classes to help it recognize tokens.

```
Imports System.Text.RegularExpressions


'
' This class contains the logic to perform lexical analysis
' for the word combination language.
'
Public Class LexicalAnalyzer
    Private cur As Integer = -1
    Private input As System.IO.TextReader
    Private lastToken As Id
    Private tokenString As String
    Private Shared ReadOnly whitespaceRegex As Regex = New Regex("\G[ ]*")
    Private Shared ReadOnly orRegex As Regex _
        = New Regex("\Gor\b", RegexOptions.IgnoreCase)
    Private Shared ReadOnly andRegex As Regex _
        = New Regex("\Gand\b", RegexOptions.IgnoreCase)
    Private Shared ReadOnly nearRegex As Regex _
        = New Regex("\Gnear\b", RegexOptions.IgnoreCase)
    Private Shared ReadOnly notRegex As Regex _
        = New Regex("\Gnot\b", RegexOptions.IgnoreCase)
```

```vbnet
Private Shared ReadOnly quotedStringRegex As RegEx _
    = New Regex("\G""([^""]*(""""")*)*""", RegexOptions.IgnoreCase)
Private Shared ReadOnly wordRegex As RegEx = New Regex("[a-z0-9]+")


' constants to identify the type of the last recognized token.
Public Enum Id
    ' unexpected character found
    InvalidChar = -1
    ' No tokens recognized yet
    NoToken = 0
    ' Or token
    [Or] = 1
    ' And token
    [And] = 2
    ' Near token
    Near = 3
    ' Not token
    [Not] = 4
    ' Word token
    Word = 5
    ' Left Paren token
    LeftParen = 6
    ' Right Paren token
    RightParen = 7
    ' Quoted String token
    QuotedString = 8
    ' End of file
    Eof = 9
End Enum 'Id


' Constructor
' r - The input stream that contains the input to
'     be lexed.
Public Sub New(ByVal r As System.IO.TextReader)
    input = r
End Sub


'

' The string recognized as word token or the body of a quoted string.
'

Public ReadOnly Property StringValue() As String
    Get
        Return tokenString
    End Get
End Property


Private line As String = Nothing
```

```
      Private Sub ResetStrs()
          line = input.ReadLine()
          cur = 0
      End Sub


    '
    ' Return the type of the next token.  For word and quoted
    ' string tokens, the string that the token represents can be
    ' fetched by calling the StringValue function.
    '
    Public Function NextToken() As Id
        Dim m As Match
        Do
            If cur < 0 Or cur >= line.Length Then
                ResetStrs()
            End If
            If line Is Nothing Then
                lastToken = Id.Eof
                Return Id.Eof
            End If
            m = whitespaceRegex.Match(line, cur)
            cur += m.Length
        Loop While cur >= line.Length

        m = orRegex.Match(line, cur)
        If m.Success Then
            lastToken = Id.Or
            tokenString = m.Value
            cur += m.Length
            Return lastToken
        End If

        m = andRegex.Match(line, cur)
        If m.Success Then
            lastToken = Id.And
            tokenString = m.Value
            cur += m.Length
            Return lasttok
        End If

        m = nearRegex.Match(line, cur)
        If m.Success Then
            lastToken = Id.Near
            tokenString = m.Value
            cur += m.Length
            Return lasttok
        End If

        m = notRegex.Match(line, cur)
        If m.Success Then
            lastToken = Id.Not
            tokenString = m.Value
```

```
            cur += m.Length
            Return lasttok
        End If


        If line(cur) = "("c Then
            lastToken = Id.LeftParen
            tokenString = "("
            cur += 1
            Return Id.LeftParen
        End If

        If line(cur) = ")"c Then
            lastToken = Id.RightParen
            tokenString = ")"
            cur += 1
            Return Id.RightParen
        End If

        m = quotedStringRegex.Match(line, cur)
        If m.Success Then
            lastToken = Id.QuotedString
            tokenString = m.Value
            cur += m.Length
            Return lasttok
        End If

        m = wordRegex.Match(line, cur)
        If m.Success Then
            lastToken = Id.Word
            tokenString = m.Value
            cur += m.Length
            Return lasttok
        End If

        ' Did not find anything we are expecting
        lastToken = Id.NoToken
        tokenString = line.Substring(cur)
        cur = line.Length
        Return lastToken
    End Function 'NextToken
End Class 'LexicalAnalyzer
```

The parser implementation uses a technique called *recursive descent*. A recursive descent parser has functions that correspond to non-terminal tokens defined by grammar productions. The functions call each other in roughly the same pattern that the corresponding grammar productions refer to each other. Where there is recursion in the grammar productions, there is generally recursion in the functions. One important exception is when the recursion is a self-recursion through the rightmost token in a production, like this:

```
orCombination ( andCombination or orCombination
```

Translating this in the obvious way into a self-recursive function produces a function that performs a self-recursion as the last thing it does before it returns. That type of recursion is a special case called *tail recursion*. What is special about tail recursion is that you can always change a tail recursion into a loop. In the following code for the `Parser` class, you will see that functions corresponding to non-terminals defined in a self-recursive way implement the self-recursion using a loop.

```
'
' Instances of this class parse the word combination little language.
'
Public Class Parser
    Private lexer As LexicalAnalyzer ' lexical analyzer that parser uses
    Private token As LexicalAnalyzer.Id

    '
    ' This method parses a word combination that it reads from
    '  a given input stream.
    '
    ' input - An input stream that this method will
    '         read the source for a word combination from.
    ' return - A combination object that is the root of the parse
    '          tree produced by the parse.
    Public Function Parse(ByVal input As System.IO.StreamReader) As
ICombination
        lexer = New LexicalAnalyzer(input)
        Dim c As ICombination = orCombination()
        Expect(LexicalAnalyzer.Id.Eof)
        Return c
    End Function 'Parse

    ' Parse an orCombination
    Public Function orCombination() As ICombination
        Dim c As ICombination = andCombination()
        While token = LexicalAnalyzer.Id.Or
            c = New OrCombination(c, andCombination())
        End While
        Return c
    End Function 'orCombination

    ' Parse an andCombination
    Public Function andCombination() As ICombination
        Dim c As ICombination = nearCombination()
        While token = LexicalAnalyzer.Id.And
            c = New AndCombination(c, nearCombination())
        End While
        Return c
    End Function 'andCombination
```

```vb
' parse a nearCombination
Public Function nearCombination() As ICombination
    Dim c As ICombination = simpleCombination()
    While token = LexicalAnalyzer.Id.Near
        c = New NearCombination(c, simpleCombination())
    End While
    Return c
End Function 'nearCombination


' parse a simpleCombination
Public Function simpleCombination() As ICombination
    If token = LexicalAnalyzer.Id.LeftParen Then
        nextToken()
        Dim c As ICombination = orCombination()
        Expect(LexicalAnalyzer.Id.RightParen)
        Return c
    End If
    If token = LexicalAnalyzer.Id.Not Then
        Return notWordCombination()
    Else
        Return wordCombination()
    End If
End Function 'simpleCombination


' parse a wordCombination
Public Function wordCombination() As ICombination
    If token <> LexicalAnalyzer.Id.Word And _
       token <> LexicalAnalyzer.Id.QuotedString _
    Then
        ' print error message and throw SyntaxException
        Expect(LexicalAnalyzer.Id.Word)
    End If
    Dim c As New WordCombination(lexer.StringValue)
    nextToken()
    Return c
End Function 'wordCombination


' parse a wordCombination
Public Function notWordCombination() As ICombination
    Expect(LexicalAnalyzer.Id.Not)
    If token <> LexicalAnalyzer.Id.Word And _
       token <> LexicalAnalyzer.Id.QuotedString _
    Then
        ' print error message and throw SyntaxException
        Expect(LexicalAnalyzer.Id.Word)
    End If
    Dim c As New NotWordCombination(lexer.StringValue)
    nextToken()
    Return c
End Function 'notWordCombination
```

```
' Get the next token from the lexer.
Public Sub nextToken()
    token = lexer.NextToken()
End Sub 'nextToken
```

The remainder of the `Parser` class is a subroutine called `Expect` and a helper function for `Expect` called `TokenName`. The `Expect` subroutine issues an error message if the current terminal token is not the type of token passed to the `Expect` subroutine. If the token is the expected kind of token, then the `expect` subroutine reads the next token from the lexical analyzer.

Most recursive descent parsers have a subroutine similar to `Expect`, and it is often called `Expect`.

```
'
' Complain if the current token is not the specified kind of
' token.
'
Public Sub Expect(ByVal t As LexicalAnalyzer.Id)
    If token <> t Then
        Dim msg As String = "found " & token.ToString() & _
            " when expecting " & t.ToString()
        Throw New System.ApplicationException(msg)
    End If
    nextToken()
End Sub 'Expect
End Class 'Parser
```

There is an obvious relationship between the productions of the formal grammar and the preceding code for the `Parser` class. Because the relationship between the two is so obvious, you may feel tempted to skip writing the formal grammar and just define your little language with code. Skipping the formal grammar is usually a bad idea for the following reasons:

- Without a formal grammar, there is no precise way to communicate the definition of your language to other people without having them read your source code.

- As the syntax for languages becomes larger or more complex, so does the parser for the language. As the parser becomes more complex, the code becomes cluttered with necessary details, and the relationship between the code and the grammar it implements becomes less obvious.

- Over time, languages often evolve, gaining new features. When trying to make changes to a language that has no formal grammar, you may find it difficult to distinguish between changes to the language's grammar and changes to its implementation.

The next piece of code in this example is the `ICombination` interface, which is an interface implemented by all parse tree objects:

```
'
' This interface is implemented by all classes whose instances
' can be part of a parse tree.
'
Public Interface ICombination

    '
    ' If the given string contains the words that this
    ' ICombination object requires, this method returns an
    ' array of ints.  In most cases, the array contains the
    ' offsets of the words in the string that are required by
    ' this combination.  However, if the array is empty, then
    ' all the words in the string satisfy the combination.  If
    ' the given string does not contain the words that this
    ' Combination object requires, then this method returns
    ' Nothing.
    '
    ' s - The string that this method will search
    '       for the words it requires.
    Function Contains(ByVal s As String) As Integer()
End Interface 'ICombination
```

Notice that the functions of Combination and its subclasses relate almost exclusively to the execution of combinations. There is almost no code related to the manipulation of the objects in the parse tree. Some larger languages require additional analysis of a program after it is parsed, in order to turn it into an executable form. For such languages, a parse tree is an intermediate form for a program, distinct from its executable form. The Little Language pattern assumes that a language is simple enough that you can use a parse tree for both purposes.

Here is the source for NotWordCombination, which is the simplest subclass that implements ICombination:

```
'
' Instances of this class represent an NotWordCombination
' non-terminal token.
'
Public Class NotWordCombination
    Implements ICombination
    Private word As String

    ' constructor
    ' word - The word that this combination requires
    '         in a string
    Public Sub New(ByVal word As String)
        Me.word = word
    End Sub


    '
    ' If the given string contains the word that this NotWordCombination
    ' object requires, this method returns an array of the offsets where
    ' the word occurs in the string.  Otherwise, this method returns
    ' an empty array of Integers.
```

```
'
' s - The string that this method will search for
'       the word it requires.
Public Function Contains(ByVal s As String) As Integer() _
 Implements ICombination.Contains
    If s.IndexOf(word) >= 0 Then
        Return Nothing
    End If
    Return New Integer() {}
End Function
End Class 'NotWordCombination
```

The `WordCombination` class is similar. The main difference is that it contains logic to return an array of the offsets of all of the occurrences in a given string of the word associated with a `WordCombination` object.

The classes that represent logical operators, `OrCombination`, `AndCombination`, and `NearCombination` are more complex. They are responsible for combining the results of two child `ICombination` objects. Here is source code for `AndCombination` and `OrCombination`:

```
'
' Instances of this class represent an AndCombination
' non-terminal token.
'
Public Class AndCombination
    Implements ICombination
    Private leftChild, rightChild As ICombination

    'constructor
    ' left - This object's left child.
    ' right - This object's right child.
    Public Sub New(ByVal left As ICombination, ByVal right As ICombination)
        leftChild = left
        rightChild = right
    End Sub


    ' This method returns an array of the offsets of the words
    ' in the given string that satify both of this
    ' AndCombination object's children.  However, if all the
    ' words in the given string satisfy both of this object's
    ' children, it returns an empty array.  Otherwise, this
    ' method returns Nothing.
    '
    ' s - The string that this method will search for
    '       the words it requires.
    Public Function Contains(ByVal s As String) As Integer() _
     Implements ICombination.Contains
        Dim leftResult As Integer() = leftChild.Contains(s)
        Dim rightResult As Integer() = rightChild.Contains(s)
```

```
If leftResult Is Nothing Or rightResult Is Nothing Then
    Return Nothing
End If
If leftResult.Length = 0 Then
    Return rightResult
End If
If rightResult.Length = 0 Then
    Return leftResult
End If
' Sort the results so that they can be compared and merged
Array.sort(leftResult)
Array.sort(rightResult)

' Count common offsets to find out if there are common
' offsets and how many there will be.
Dim commonCount As Integer = 0
Dim l As Integer = 0
Dim r As Integer = 0

Do While l < leftResult.Length And r < rightResult.Length
    If leftResult(l) < rightResult(r) Then
        l += 1
    ElseIf leftResult(l) > rightResult(r) Then
        r += 1
    Else
        commonCount += 1
        l += 1
        r += 1
    End If
Loop
If commonCount = 0 Then
    Return Nothing ' There are no common results
End If
' merge common results
Dim myResult(commonCount) As Integer
commonCount = 0
l = 0
r = 0
While l < leftResult.Length And r < rightResult.Length
    If leftResult(l) < rightResult(r) Then
        l += 1
    ElseIf leftResult(l) > rightResult(r) Then
        r += 1
    Else
        myResult(commonCount) = leftResult(l)
        commonCount += 1
        l += 1
        r += 1
    End If
End While
```

```
            Return myResult
        End Function 'Contains
    End Class 'AndCombination
    '
    ' Instances of this class represent an OrCombination non-terminal
    ' token.
    '
    Public Class OrCombination
        Implements ICombination
        Private leftChild, rightChild As ICombination

        ' constructor
        ' left - This object's left child.
        ' right - This object's right child.
        Public Sub New(ByVal left As ICombination, ByVal right As ICombination)
            leftChild = left
            rightChild = right
        End Sub


        '
        ' If the some of the words in the given string are the
        ' words that either of this Combination's object's children
        ' require, this method returns an array of the offsets of
        ' the words in the string.  If all of the words in the
        ' given string are the words required by one of this
        ' object's children, then this method returns an empty
        ' array of ints.  Otherwise, this method returns Nothing.
        '
        ' s - The string that this method will search for
        '     the words it requires.
        Public Function Contains(ByVal s As String) As Integer() _
         Implements ICombination.Contains
            Dim leftResult As Integer() = leftChild.Contains(s)
            Dim rightResult As Integer() = rightChild.Contains(s)
            If leftResult Is Nothing Then
                Return rightResult
            End If
            If rightResult Is Nothing Then
                Return leftResult
            End If
            If leftResult.Length = 0 Then
                Return rightResult
            End If
            If rightResult.Length = 0 Then
                Return leftResult
            End If ' create array of combined results
            Dim myResult() As Integer
            myResult = New Integer(leftResult.Length + rightResult.Length) {}
```

```
            System.Array.Copy(leftResult, 0, myResult, 0, _
                            leftResult.Length)
            System.Array.Copy(rightResult, 0, myResult, _
                            leftResult.Length, rightResult.Length)
        Return myResult
    End Function
End Class 'OrCombination
```

RELATED PATTERNS

Composite: A parse tree is organized with the Composite pattern.

Visitor: The Visitor pattern allows you to encapsulate the logic for simple manipulations of a parse tree in a single class.

Mediator

This pattern was previously described in [GoF95]

SYNOPSIS

The Mediator pattern uses one object to coordinate state changes between other objects. It puts the logic to manage state changes of other objects in one class, instead of distributing the logic over the other classes. This results in a more cohesive implementation of the logic and decreased coupling between the other classes.

CONTEXT

The Mediator pattern addresses a problem that commonly occurs in dialog boxes. Suppose that you have to implement a dialog box that looks like the one in Figure 7.10, in order to specify information to reserve a banquet room in a hotel.

The purpose of the dialog in Figure 7.10 is to provide information to reserve a banquet room in a hotel. The requirements of the dialog give rise to a number of dependencies between the dialog's objects.

- The OK button and the list of foods are initially disabled. Also the list of foods is initially empty.

- The start time must be at least three hours earlier than the end time. The controls that are used to select the start and end times are `DateTimePicker` objects. `DateTimePicker` objects are capable of selecting times on any date, but these need to be constrained to pick times on the same date as the selected data.

- When a user selects a radio button, the list of foods becomes enabled and populated. Some foods suitable for table service are not suitable for buffets, so it is not possible to display the list of foods until this selection is made. The selection of foods in will also vary by the time of day.

- When at least one food is selected and the duration of the banquet is at least three hours, the OK button is enabled.

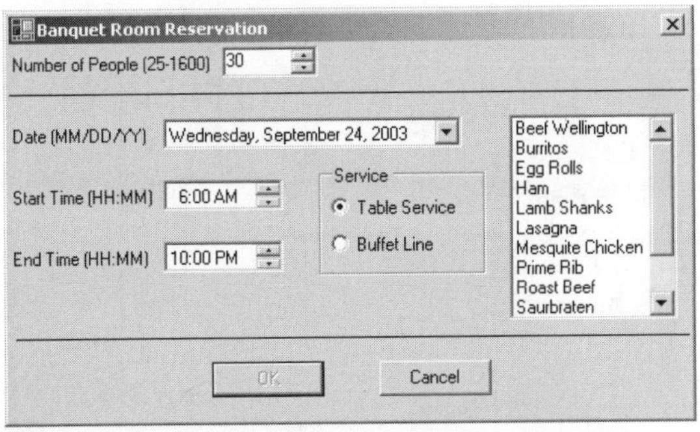

Figure 7.10   Banquet Room Dialog

If each object in the dialog takes responsibility for the dependencies it is associated with, the result is a highly coupled set of objects with low cohesion. Figure 7.11 shows the relationships between the objects.

In the interest of simplifying Figure 7.11, association names, role names, and multiplicity indicators have been left out of the diagram. The point of the diagram is the number of links. As you can see, most of the objects are involved in multiple dependencies. Some are involved in as many as five. A large portion of the time it will take to implement the dialog will be spent coding the dependency links.

The logic for dependency handling is spread out over seven objects. Because of this, the dialog will be difficult to maintain. When a maintenance programmer works on the dialog, he/she will see only a small piece of the dependency handling. Since it will be difficult to understand the details of the dependency handling as a whole, maintenance programmers will not take the time to do it. When programmers maintain code they do not fully understand, the maintenance takes more time and is often of poor quality.

Clearly, reorganizing these objects in a way that minimizes the number of connections and gathers the dependency handling into one cohesive object is a good thing. It is an improvement that will save programmer time and produce more robust code. This is what the Mediator pattern is about. Instead of each object individually managing the dependencies it has with other objects, you use another object that consolidates all of the dependency handling. In this arrangement, each of the other objects has only one dependency connection.

Figure 7.12 shows the dialog's objects organized with an additional object to centrally manage dependencies.

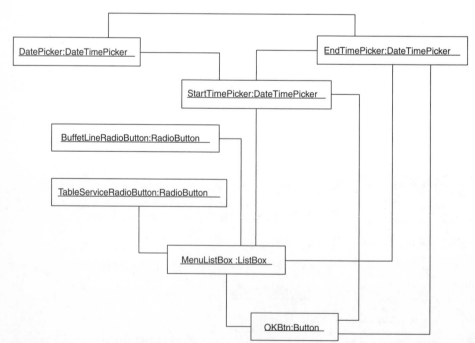

Figure 7.11 Decentralized Dependency Management

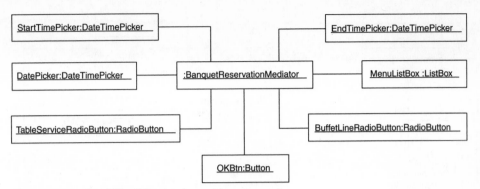

Figure 7.12   Centralized Dependency Management

In addition to making the implementation easier to code and maintain, the design shown in Figure 7.12 is easier to understand.

FORCES

☺ You have a set of related objects and most of the objects are involved in multiple dependency relationships.

☺ You find yourself defining subclasses so that individual objects will be able to participate in dependency relationships.

☺ Classes are difficult to reuse because their basic function is entwined with dependency relationships.

SOLUTION

Figure 7.13 shows how classes and interfaces participate in the Mediator pattern in the general case.

Here are explanations of the roles these classes and delegates play in the Mediator pattern:

Colleague1, Colleague2 . . .

Instances of classes in these roles have state-related dependencies. There are two types of dependencies.

■ One type of dependency requires an object to get approval from other objects before making specific types of state changes.

■ The other type of dependency requires an object to notify other objects after it has made specific types of state changes.

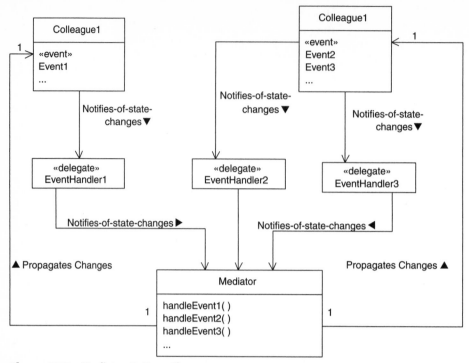

Figure 7.13 Mediator Pattern Classes

Both types of dependencies are handled in a similar way. Instances of `Colleague1`, `Colleague2` . . . are associated with a `Mediator` object. When they need to notify other objects about a state change, they call a subroutine of the `Mediator` object through a delegate. The `Mediator` object's subroutine takes care of the rest.

EventHandler1, EventHandler . . .

Delegates in this role allow the `Colleague1`, `Colleague2` . . . classes to achieve a higher level of reuse. They do this by allowing these classes to be unaware that they are working with a `Mediator` object. The `Colleague` classes use these delegates to deliver events in response to state notifications. The `Colleague` classes only know that they are sending events. The have no direct knowledge of the `Mediator` class.

Mediator

Instances of classes in the `Mediator` role have logic to process state change notifications from `Colleague1`, `Colleague2` . . . objects. `Mediator` classes have one or more subroutines that `Colleague1`, `Colleague2` . . . objects call through delegates to inform a `Mediator` object of state changes.

A `Mediator` object responds to a state change notification by performing whatever logic is appropriate. For proposed state changes, this typically includes indicating approval or disapproval of the change. For notification of completed state changes, this typically includes propagating the notification to other objects.

`Mediator` classes have subroutines that can be called to associate them with `Colleague1, Colleague2 . . .` objects. These subroutines are indicated in the diagram as `registerColleague1, registerColleague2 . . .` They are passed an appropriate `Colleague` object and generally add the `Mediator` object as a handler for relevant events from the `Colleague` object.

IMPLEMENTATION

In many cases, one object is responsible for creating all of the `Colleague` objects and their `Mediator` object. This object acts as a container for the objects that it creates. When a single object is responsible for creating all of the `Colleague` objects and their `Mediator` object, the `Mediator` class is usually declared as a private member of the class. Limiting the visibility of a `Mediator` class increases the robustness of the program.

You will have to make some decisions when you implement the `Mediator` pattern. One decision is whether mediator objects will maintain their own internal model of the state of `Colleague` objects or fetch the state of each object when it needs to know the object's state.

If you take the first approach, then the Mediator object begins by assuming the initial state of the `Colleague` objects that it is responsible for. It will have an instance variable for each `Colleague` object. A `Mediator` object sets the initial value of each of these instance variables to be what it expects the initial state of the corresponding `Colleague` object to be. When a `Colleague` object notifies the `Mediator` object that its state has changed, the `Mediator` object changes the values of its instance variables to match the new state. After the `Mediator` object updates its instance variable, it uses the values of its instance variables to make whatever decisions it needs to make.

If you take the second approach, the `Mediator` object does not try to model the state of `Colleague` objects. Instead, when a `Colleague` object notifies it of a state change, the `Mediator` object makes decisions by fetching the state of each `Colleague` object it must base its decisions on.

When most people first try to implement the Mediator pattern, they think of the first approach. However, in most cases the second approach is the better choice.

The disadvantage to having `Mediator` objects model the state of `Colleague` objects is that it is possible for it to be wrong about the state of a `Colleague` object. To get a `Mediator` object to correctly model the state of `Colleague` objects requires it to have additional code that mimics the logic of `Colleague` objects. If a maintenance programmer later modifies one of the `Colleague` classes, the modification may mysteriously break the `Mediator` class.

The advantage of the second approach is its simplicity. The `Mediator` object can never be wrong about the state of a `Colleague` object. That makes it easier to implement and maintain. However, if fetching the complete state of `Colleague` objects is too time-consuming, then the approach of having the `Mediator` object model the state of `Colleague` objects may be more practical.

Recursive Events

A mediator object may change the state of some object in response to an event that it handles. In some cases, the changes that a mediator object makes to other objects may cause the other objects to fire an event.

You generally do not want mediator objects processing events that are fired as a result of a mediator object's own actions. One way to prevent that from happening is to use the Balking pattern by writing the mediator class's events like this:

```
Private busy As Boolean

' Enforce all invariant relationships between components
' in the form.
Private Sub EnforceInvariants()
    SyncLock Me
        If busy Then
            Return
        End If
        busy = True
    End SyncLock
    Try
        ...
    Finally
        busy = False
    End Try
End Sub
```

This subroutine detects recursive calls by first testing and then setting the value of the busy variable. It wraps the recursion test in a SyncLock statement to allow for the possibility of concurrent events. It handles concurrent events by using the Balking pattern. If it is already handling another event, it cannot handle another event immediately, so it ignores the event.

You may wonder why we would decide to ignore an event rather than just wait to process it. The reason is that in a GUI interface, you must assume that for every user-initiated event, the user expects a particular result. The result that the user expects is often influenced by what the user sees in the interface. If events overlap, that means that the user has clicked, typed or otherwise initiated an event without seeing the result of the previous event.

If the result of the previous event is not what the user expects, the user will be surprised. In many situations, the user will be less surprised if an event is ignored than if it has a different effect than the user expects.

CONSEQUENCES

☺ Most of the complexity involved in managing dependencies is shifted from other objects to the Mediator object. This makes the other objects easier to implement and maintain.

☺ Putting dependency logic for other classes in one mediator class makes it easier for maintenance programmers to find the dependencies.

☺ Using a `Mediator` object usually results in fewer execution paths through the code. This means that less effort is required for exhaustive testing since there are fewer cases to test. The impact of fewer code paths on testing is described in more detail in the discussion of the White Box Testing pattern in [Grand98].

☺ Using a `Mediator` object usually means there is no need to subclass `Colleague` classes just to implement their dependency handling.

☺ `Colleague` classes are more reusable because their core functionality is not entwined with dependency-handling code. Dependency-handling code tends to be specific to an application.

● Putting all the dependency logic for a set of related objects in one place can make understanding the dependency logic easier, up to a point. If a `Mediator` class gets to be too large, then breaking it into smaller pieces can make it more understandable.

☹ Because dependency-handling code is usually application specific, `Mediator` classes are not usually reusable.

CODE EXAMPLE

The code example for the Mediator pattern is the code for a mediator object for the dialog discussed under the "Context" heading. One thing that you may notice about this example is that it is more complex than most of the other examples. This reflects the nature of the Mediator pattern, which is to make all the complexity of event handling the responsibility of `Mediator` classes.

The banquet reservation dialog is implemented as a class named `Banquet ReservationForm`:

```
' Form to collect information for a banquet reservation
Public Class BanquetReservationForm
    ' The default number to set the NumberOfPeopleTextBox
    Public Const PeopleCountDefault As Integer = 30

    ' The minimum number of people for a banquet
    Public Const MinPeopleCount As Integer = 25

    ' The maximum number of people for a banquet
    Public Const MaxPeopleCount As Integer = 1600
```

The preceding constants are used for constraints on the number of people that a banquet can be reserved for. These constraints involve only one component. Since they do not involve dependencies between components, they are not the responsibility of the mediator object.

Constraints that do not involve dependencies between components are installed by a subroutine that handles the Load event:

```
' Perform run-time initialization.
Private Sub BanquetReservationForm_Load(ByVal sender As System.Object, _
                             ByVal e As System.EventArgs) _
  Handles MyBase.Load
    PeopleCountUpDown.Minimum = MinPeopleCount
    PeopleCountUpDown.Maximum = MaxPeopleCount
    PeopleCountUpDown.Text = PeopleCountDefault.ToString

    ' The earliest possible date is tomorrow
    Dim EarliestAllowableDate As DateTime = Today().AddDays(1)
    DatePicker.MinDate = EarliestAllowableDate
    DatePicker.MaxDate = EarliestAllowableDate.AddYears(5)
    DatePicker.Value = EarliestAllowableDate

    Dim mediator As New BanquetReservationMediator(Me)
  End Sub
...
```

The mediator class is implemented as a private member of the dialog's class called BanquetReservationMediator:

```
Private Class BanquetReservationMediator
    ' The minimum duration for a banquet reservation is 3 hours
    Private Shared ReadOnly MinDuration As TimeSpan _
        = New TimeSpan(3, 0, 0) ' 3 hours

    ' The foods available with table service for breakfast.
    Private Shared ReadOnly TableBreakfast As String() _
                        = {"Omlettes", "Bacon", _
                        ...
                        "Eggs Benedict"}

    ' The foods available with table service after breakfast.
    Private Shared ReadOnly TableFood As String() _
                        = {"Roast Beef", "Egg Rolls", _
                        ...
                        "Stuffed Grouper"}

    ' The foods available with buffet service for breakfast.
    Private Shared ReadOnly BuffetBreakfast As String() _
                        = {"Scrambled Eggs", "Bacon", _
                        ...
                        "Fruit Assortment"}

    ' The foods available with buffet service after breakfast.
    Private Shared ReadOnly BuffetFood As String() _
                        = {"Roast Beef", "Egg Rolls", _
```

```
                ...
            "Prime Rib"}
```

The `BanquetReservationMediator` class's constructor wires a subroutine to the relevant events from the `BanquetReservationForm` object's components.

```
' The object whose components this object mediates for.
Private MyForm As BanquetReservationForm

' Constructor
Public Sub New(ByVal theForm As BanquetReservationForm)
    MyForm = theForm
    AddHandler MyForm.StartTimePicker.ValueChanged, _
            AddressOf EventReceived
    AddHandler MyForm.EndTimePicker.ValueChanged, _
            AddressOf EventReceived
    AddHandler MyForm.BuffetLineRadioBtn.CheckedChanged, _
            AddressOf EventReceived
    AddHandler MyForm.TableServiceRadioBtn.CheckedChanged, _
            AddressOf EventReceived
    AddHandler MyForm.MenuListBox.SelectedIndexChanged, _
            AddressOf EventReceived
End Sub

' Handle events by calling EnforceInvariants
Public Sub EventReceived(ByVal sender As Object, ByVal e As
EventArgs)
        EnforceInvariants()
End Sub
```

The constructor wires all these events to the `EventReceived` subroutine. The `EventReceived` subroutine simply enforces all the invariant relationships between the components of the dialog by calling the `EnforceInvariants` subroutine.

The `EnforceInvariants` subroutine is responsible for ensuring that all of the constraints between the components are enforced. It is separate from the `Event Received` subroutine to allow for the possibility of enforcing the constraints in response to something other than an event.

```
Public Sub EnforceInvariants()
    ' Propagate the selected date to the chosen times.
    Dim datePicker As DateTimePicker = MyForm.DatePicker
    Dim startPicker As DateTimePicker = MyForm.StartTimePicker
    Dim endPicker As DateTimePicker = MyForm.EndTimePicker
    Dim startTime As DateTime = startPicker.Value
    Dim endTime As DateTime = endPicker.Value
    startPicker.Value = MergeDateAndTime(datePicker.Value, startTime)
    endPicker.Value = MergeDateAndTime(datePicker.Value, endTime)
```

```
        startPicker.MinDate = BeginningOfDay(datePicker.Value)
        endPicker.MaxDate = EndOfDay(datePicker.Value)
        startPicker.MaxDate = endPicker.Value.Subtract(MinDuration)
        endPicker.MinDate = startPicker.Value.Add(MinDuration)

        ' Translate start time and the selection of buffet or
        ' table(service) into a food menu.
        If MyForm.BuffetLineRadioBtn.Checked Then
            If startTime.Hour <= 8 Or (startTime.Hour <= 9 And _
                                    endTime.Hour <= 12) Then
                MyForm.MenuListBox.DataSource = BuffetBreakfast
            Else
                MyForm.MenuListBox.DataSource = BuffetFood
            End If
            MyForm.MenuListBox.Enabled = True
        ElseIf MyForm.TableServiceRadioBtn.Checked Then
            If startTime.Hour <= 10 Then
                MyForm.MenuListBox.DataSource = TableBreakfast
            Else
                MyForm.MenuListBox.DataSource = TableFood
            End If
            MyForm.MenuListBox.Enabled = True
        Else
            MyForm.MenuListBox.DataSource = Nothing
            MyForm.MenuListBox.Enabled = False
        End If

        ' Determine if the duration of the banquet is acceptable.
        Dim duration As TimeSpan
        duration = endPicker.Value.Subtract(startPicker.Value)
        Dim durationOk As Boolean
        durationOk = (duration > MinDuration)

        ' Determine if the OK button should be enabled.
        MyForm.OKBtn.Enabled = durationOk _
            And MyForm.MenuListBox.Enabled _
            And MyForm.MenuListBox.SelectedItems.Count > 0
    End Sub
```

These are the invariant relationships that the EnforceInvariants subroutine enforces:

- The start time must occur on the selected date. The start time must be no earlier than 00:00. The start time must be no later than three hours before the end time.

- The end time must occur on the selected date. The end time must be no earlier than three hours after the start time. The end time must be no later than 23:59:59.

- The menu list is empty if neither the buffet line button nor table service radio button are checked. The menu list is enabled if, and only if, the buffet button or table radio button is checked. If the menu list is not empty, then its contents will depend on two independent factors. It will be a table service menu if the table service radio button is checked or a buffet line menu if the buffet line button is checked. The menu will be a breakfast menu if the start time is before 8:00 or if the start time is before 9:00 and the end time is before 12:00; otherwise, it will be a standard menu.

■ The OK button is enabled if, and only if, the food list is enabled and one or more foods on the list have been selected and the duration of the banquet is at least three hours.

The requirement that the OK button is enabled if the duration of the banquet is at least three hours is theoretically unnecessary. Because the start and end times are constrained to be at least three hours apart, it should never be possible for the duration of the banquet to be less than three hours. However, this sort of redundancy can be useful for minimizing the consequences of bugs.

The dependencies between the start and end times involve correctly setting six interrelated parameters. It is easy for a bug to be introduced in the implementation of this logic. In fact, my first attempt at writing that section of code allowed the start time to be set as late as 21:00, no matter what the end time was. By having a redundant and simpler constraint on the OK button, it was still impossible for a user to create an invalid banquet reservation, in spite of the bug.

Mediator classes often have friend auxiliary functions or subroutines that supplement the logic of the primary invariant-enforcing subroutine. Putting some of the logic in auxiliary functions or subroutines helps keep the primary invariant-enforcing subroutine down to a manageable size. The rest of this code example shows the supporting functions that are called by the `EnforceInvariants` subroutine.

```
' Combine the year, month and day of one DateTime with
' the hour, minute and second of another.
Private Function MergeDateAndTime(ByVal dateSource As DateTime, _
                ByVal timeSource As DateTime) As DateTime
    Return New DateTime(dateSource.Year, dateSource.Month, _
                dateSource.Day, timeSource.Hour, _
                timeSource.Minute, timeSource.Second)
End Function


' Return the midnight that begins the given day.
Private Function BeginningOfDay(ByVal day As DateTime) As DateTime
    Return New DateTime(day.Year, day.Month, day.Day)
End Function


' Return the midnight that ends the given day.
Private Function EndOfDay(ByVal day As DateTime) As DateTime
    Return New DateTime(day.Year, day.Month, day.Day, 23, 59, 59)
End Function
    End Class ' BanquetReservationMediator
End Class ' BanquetReservationForm
```

RELATED PATTERNS

Low Coupling/High Cohesion: The Mediator pattern is a good example of an exception to the advice of the Low Coupling/High Cohesion pattern [Grand98].

Observer: The Observer pattern is a large portion of .NET's delegation event model. If you want to use the Mediator pattern in a context that you feel .NET's event model is inappropriate, you can substitute the Observer pattern.

Controller: The Controller pattern (described in [Grand98]) is used to determine what object will handle an external event. The Mediator pattern is used to help implement the handling of events.

White Box Testing: Using the Mediator pattern usually results in fewer execution paths through the code. This means that less effort is required to test a program using the White Box Testing pattern described in [Grand98].

Balking: The Balking pattern may be used to prevent a mediator object from responding to events that are fired as a result of the mediator object's own actions.

Snapshot

This pattern is partially based on the Memento pattern documented in [GoF95].

SYNOPSIS

Capture a snapshot of an object's state so its state can be restored later. The object that initiates the capture or restoration of the state does not need to know anything about the state information. It only needs to know that the object whose state it is restoring or capturing implements a particular interface.

CONTEXT

Suppose that you are writing a program to a play a role-playing game. For the purposes of this discussion, the details of the games are not important. What is important is that it is a single-player game. To play the game, a player directs a character to interact with various computer-controlled characters and simulated objects. One way that a game can end is for the character under the player's control to die. Players of the game will not consider this a desirable outcome.

Among the many features planned for the game are two features that involve saving and restoring the state of the game. The program needs these features because playing one of these games to its conclusion can take a few days of nonstop play.

- To allow a player to play the game over multiple short intervals, it must be possible to save the state of the game to a file so that it can be continued later.

- To arrive at the game's conclusion, a player must successfully guide his/her character through many adventures. If the player's character dies before the game is over, the player will have the option of starting the game over from the very beginning. This may be an unattractive option because the player may be well into the game and have played through the earlier portions of the game a number of times. The program will also offer the player the option of resuming the game at an earlier point than when the character died.

  It will do this by saving part of the game's state, including credit for the character's previous experiences and a record of some of the character's possessions. It will perform a partial state save when the player's character has accomplished a major task. As the game proceeds, these checkpoints become part of the game's overall state, needing to be saved when the rest of the state is saved to disk.

Though the game will involve many classes, there are only a few that will share the responsibility for creating these snapshots of the game's state.

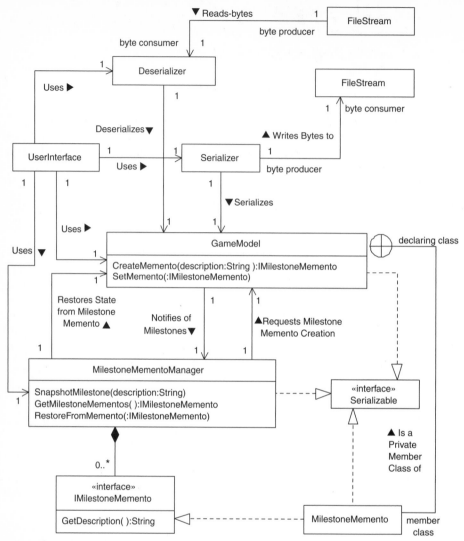

Figure 7.14 Game Snapshot Classes

The classes in Figure 7.14 participate in two distinct state saving mechanisms:

■ There is a mechanism for saving part of a game's state when the player's character achieves a milestone.

■ There is a mechanism for saving and restoring an entire game.

There are two classes in the Figure 7.14 that participate in both mechanisms:

UserInterface: All player-initiated actions come through the UserInterface class. The UserInterface class delivers most of the actions that a player initiates to an instance of the GameModel class. However, player-initiated snapshots of the game follow different routes, which are discussed below.

GameModel: The `GameModel` class is responsible for maintaining the state of the game during play. The `UserInterface` class notifies an instance of the `GameModel` class when the player does something related to the game. The instance of the `GameModel` class determines what the consequences of that action are, modifies the state of the game accordingly and notifies the user interface. An instance of the `GameModel` class may also initiate some actions. It will always report the consequences of any action it initiates to the user interface but will not always report the action itself.

The `UserInterface` class's involvement in making snapshots is to initiate one kind of snapshot and both kinds of restores. Because the `GameModel` class is the top-level class responsible for the state of the game, it is involved in any operation that manipulates the game's state.

These are the other classes and interfaces involved in performing partial state saves and restores.

MilestoneMemento: `MilestoneMemento` is a private class defined by the `GameModel` class. A `GameModel` object creates instances of `Milestone Memento` that contain copies of the values that make up the partial state to be saved. Given a `MilestoneMemento` object, a `GameModel` object can restore itself to the previous state contained in the `MilestoneMemento` object.

IMilestoneMemento: The `MilestoneMemento` class implements this interface. This interface is public. Outside of the `GameModel` class, instances of the `MilestoneMemento` class can be accessed only as instances of the `Object` class or through the `IMilestoneMemento` interface. Neither mode of access allows an object to access the state information encapsulated in `Milestone Memento` objects.

MilestoneMementoManager: The `MilestoneMementoManager` class contributes to the decision to create `MilestoneMemento` objects. It also manages their use after they are created.

Here is how the capture of a game's partial state happens after the player's character has achieved a milestone:

1. A `GameModel` object enters a state indicating that the player's character has achieved one of the game's major milestones.

2. There is a `MilestoneMementoManager` object associated with each `Game Model` object. When the `GameModel` object enters a milestone state, it passes a description of the milestone to the associated `MilestoneMementoManager` object's `snapshotMilestone` subroutine. The player's character may previously have achieved this milestone, died, and then returned to an earlier milestone. If a `MilestoneMemento` object already exists for a milestone, then another `MilestoneMemento` object is not created for the milestone.

3. A `MilestoneMementoManager` object determines if a `MilestoneMemento` object already exists for a milestone by comparing the description string passed to its `snapshotMilestone` subroutine to the descriptions of the `Milestone Memento` objects that already exist. If a `MilestoneMemento` object already exists with the given description, then the `snapshotMilestone` subroutine takes no additional action.

4. If the MilestoneMementoManager object determines that no Milestone
   Memento object already exists for the milestone, then the MilestoneMemento
   Manager object initiates the creation of a MilestoneMemento object to capture the game's partial state at that time. It does this by calling the GameModel
   object's createMemento function, passing it the same description that was
   passed to the MilestoneMementoManager object.

5. The createMemento function returns a freshly created MilestoneMemento
   object. The MilestoneMementoManager object adds the new Milestone
   Memento object to its collection of IMilestoneMemento objects.

When a player's character dies, the UserInterface object offers the player the
option for the character to start from a previously achieved milestone, rather from
the very beginning. It offers the player a list of milestones to choose from by calling the MilestoneMementoManager object's getMilestoneMementos function.
This method returns an array of MilestoneMemento objects that the Milestone
MementoManager object has collected.

If the player indicates that he/she wants the character to start from one of its previously achieved milestones, the UserInterface object passes the corresponding
MilestoneMemento object to the MilestoneMementoManager object's restore
FromMemento subroutine. This subroutine, in turn, calls the GameModel object's
restoreFromMemento subroutine, passing it the chosen MilestoneMemento
object. Using the information in the MilestoneMemento object, the GameModel
object restores its state.

The other snapshot mechanism saves the complete state of the game to a file, including the MilestoneMementoManager object and its collection of Milestone
Memento objects. This mechanism is based on .NET's serialization facility.

If you are unfamiliar with .NET's serialization facility, it is a way to copy the state of
an object to a stream of bytes or XML and then create a copy of the original object from
the contents of the byte stream or XML. There is a somewhat more detailed description
of serialization under the "Implementation" heading of this pattern.

These are the classes involved in saving and restoring a complete snapshot of the
game's state:

Serializer: The Serializer class is responsible for serializing a GameModel
object. It copies the state information of the GameModel object and all other
objects it refers to that are part of the game's state as a byte stream to a file.

FileStream: This is the standard .NET class System.IO.FileStream. It is
used to write a stream of bytes to a file. It is also used to read a stream of bytes
from a file.

Deserializer: The Deserializer class is responsible for reading a serialized
byte stream and creating a copy of the GameModel object and other objects that
were serialized to create the byte stream.

Here is the sequence of events that occurs when the user requests that the game be
saved to a file or restored from a file:

The player tells the user interface that he/she wants to save the game to a file. The UserInterface object creates a Serializer object, passing the name of the file and a reference to the GameModel object to its constructor. The Serializer object creates a BinaryFormatter object and a FileStream object. It uses the Binary Formatter object to serialize the GameModel object and all other game-related objects it refers to a stream of bytes in the file encapsulated by the FileStream object.

When the player wants to restore the game from a file, he/she tells the user interface. The UserInterface object creates a Deserializer object, passing the name of the file and a reference to the GameModel object to its constructor. The Deserializer object creates a BinaryFormatter object and a FileStream object. It uses the BinaryFormatter object to read a serialized byte stream from FileStream object and deserialize the GameModel object and all other game-related objects it refers to from the byte stream.

Most patterns in this book describe only one way to solve a problem. The Snapshot pattern is different. It describes two ways of solving the problem of making a snapshot of an object's state.

FORCES

- ☺ You need to create a snapshot of an object's state and also be able to restore the state of the object.

- ☺ You want a mechanism that saves and restores an object's state to be independent of the object's internal structure, so that the internal structure can change without having to modify the save/restore mechanism.

- ☹ If the implementation of an object is expected to change frequently, maintaining forward or backward compatibility between the implementation that saved some state information and other versions that may use the state information can require a great deal of programming effort.

SOLUTION

The following are two general solutions to the problem of saving a snapshot of an object's state and restoring its state from the snapshot. First is a description of using Memento objects to create a nonpersistent copy of an object's partial state. Then there is a description of how to use serialization to save and restore an object's state. That is followed by a comparison of the two techniques.

Figure 7.15 shows the general organization for objects that use Memento objects to save and restore an object's state.

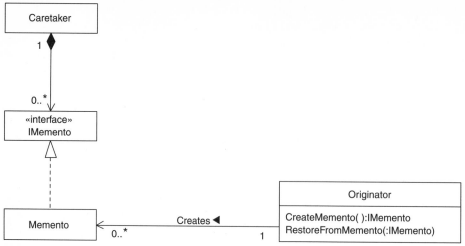

Figure 7.15 Snapshot Using Memento Objects

Here are descriptions of the roles the classes play in the variation of the Snapshot pattern that uses Memento objects:

Originator: A class in this role is a class whose instance's state information is to be saved and restored. When its CreateMemento function is called, it creates a Memento object that contains a copy of the Originator object's state information. Later, you can restore the Originator object's state by passing a Memento object to its RestoreFromMemento subroutine.

Memento: A class in this role is a friend class of the Originator class that implements the IMemento interface. Its purpose is to encapsulate snapshots of an Originator object's state. Only the Originator class should know the specific class(es) that are in this role. Other classes should access instances of the Memento class either as instances of Object or through the IMemento interface.

IMemento: Classes other than the Originator class access Memento objects through this interface. Interfaces in this role may declare no functions or subroutines. If they do declare any functions or subroutines, they should not allow the encapsulated state to be changed. This ensures the consistency and integrity of the state information. Interfaces in this role are designed using the Read-Only Interface pattern.

Caretaker: Instances of classes in this role maintain a collection of Memento objects. After a Memento object is created, it is added to a Caretaker object's collection. When an undo operation is to be performed, a Caretaker object typically collaborates with another object to select a Memento object. After the Memento object is selected, it is typically the Caretaker object that calls the Originator object's RestoreFromMemento function to restore its state.

The other mechanism for creating a snapshot of an object's state is serialization. Serialization is different from most other object-oriented techniques in that it works by violating the encapsulation of the object being serialized. Most, but not necessarily all, of the violation is through .NET's reflection mechanism. This is explained more fully by Figure 7.16 and the following descriptions of roles that classes play in this form of the Snapshot pattern.

Here are descriptions of the roles classes play in the variation of the Snapshot pattern that uses serialization:

Target: An `IFormatter` object converts the state of instances of classes in this role to and from a byte stream. The role of the `Target` object in these activities is passive. The `IFormatter` object does all of the work.

IFormatter: The class in this role implements the standard .NET interface `System.Runtime.Serialization.IFormatter`. It serializes a `Target` object by discovering and accessing a `Target` object's state information and writing the information to a `Stream` with additional information to allow it to restore the state information. It deserializes a target object by creating the object in a special way and setting the values of the object's instance variables from the serialized data. The special way that it creates the target object does not involve calling the target object's constuctors.

The .NET framework includes two classes that implement the `IFormatter` interface.

- `System.Runtime.Serialization.Formatters.Binary.Binary Formatter` is a class that represents serialization data as binary data. This representation of serialized objects is more compact than the XML representation.

- `System.Runtime.Serialization.Formatters.Soap.Soap Formatter` is a class that represents serialization data as XML in a way that is SOAP compliant. This representation is substantially larger that the binary representation. However, this representation has the advantage of interoperability. It can work with remote SOAP-compliant environments that are not .NET based.

Stream: An object in this role is an instance of a subclass of the standard .NET class `System.IO.Stream`. A class in this role is responsible for reading and writing serialized data.

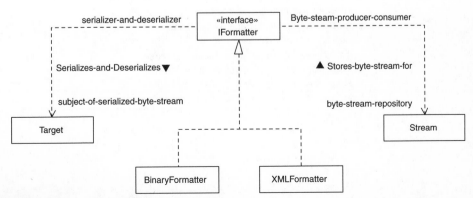

Figure 7.16 Snapshot Using Serialization

Table 7.3 shows some key differences between the two techniques for creating and managing snapshots of an object's state.Table 7.3 Comparison of State Saving by Serialization and Memento Objects

	SERIALIZATION	MEMENTO
Persistence	You can use serialization to save state in a persistent form by serializing it to a file.	Using `Memento` objects does not provide persistence.
Complexity of Implementation	Serialization can be the simpler technique for saving the entire state of an object. This is especially true for objects whose state includes references to other objects whose state must be also be saved.	Using `Memento` objects is often a simpler way to capture part of an object's state.
Object Identity	Absolute object identity is lost unless you supply additional code to preserve it. The default way that serialization restores an object's state is by creating a copy of the object. If the original object contains other objects and there are multiple references to the same object, then the duplicate object will contain references to an identical but distinct object. Among the objects referred to by the restored object, serialization preserves relative object identity.	Object identity is preserved. Using `Memento` objects is a simpler way to restore the state of an object so that it refers to the same object that it referred to before.
Overhead	Using serialization adds considerable overhead to the process of creating a snapshot to be saved in memory. The bulk of the overhead comes from the fact that serialization works through .NET's reflection mechanism and creates new objects when restoring state.	There is no particular overhead associated with using `Memento` objects.
Expertise Required	In cases where you need to make a snapshot of an object's complete state, the classes of all of the objects involved have the `Serializable` attribute and preserving object identity is not important, serialization requires minimal expertise. As situations vary from these constraints, the required level of expertise quickly increases. Some situations may require an in-depth knowledge of serialization internals, reflection and other arcane aspects of .NET.	Using `Memento` objects requires no specialized knowledge.

IMPLEMENTATION

Using Memento objects to make snapshots of an object's state is very straightforward to implement. Using serialization requires additional expertise and sometimes additional complexity. A complete description of serialization is beyond the scope of this book. What follows is a description of some features of serialization relevant to the Snapshot pattern.

An object can be serialized only if its class has the Serializable attribute. To serialize an object, you need either a SOAPFormatter or BinaryFormatter object to perform the serialization. You also need a Stream object that the SOAPFormatter or BinaryFormatter object can use to write the serialized representation of the object. You can create these objects like this:

```
Imports System.IO
Imports System.Runtime.Serialization.Formatters.Binary

Dim outStream as New FileStream("filename.bin", FileMode.Create)
Dim formatter as New BinaryFormatter()
```

The ObjectOutputStream object will write the byte stream it produces to the OutputStream object passed to its constructor.

Once you have created these objects, you can serialize an object by passing it and the Steam to the IFormatter object's Serialize subroutine, like this:

```
formatter.Serialize(outStream, myGameModel)
```

The Serialize method uses .NET's reflection facility to discover the instance variables of the object that myGameModel references. It accesses them and writes their value to outStream in the appropriate format. In this example it would be a binary format. If the IFormatter object were an instance of SOAPFormatter, then the format would be SOAP-compliant XML.

Turning serialization data into an object is called deserialization. To deserialize the contents of a file, you need the same kind of IFormatter object that created the serialization data and a Stream object to read the serialization data. You can create it like this:

```
Dim inStream as Stream
inStream = New FileStream("filename.bin", FileMode.Open)
Dim formatter as New BinaryFormatter()
```

Once you have created these objects, you can deserialize the contents of the file like this:

```
Dim g as GameModel
g = CType(formatter.Deserialize(inStream), GameModel)
```

The Deserialize function is declared to return a reference to an Object. Since you will usually want to treat the object it returns as an instance of a more specialized class, you will usually cast the result of the Deserialize method to the more specialized class.

So far, serialization seems simple. Though there are many situations in which the preceding details are all that you need to know, there are also many situations that are more complex.

The default behavior, when serializing an object, is to also serialize all of the objects it refers to and all of the objects that they refer to, until the complete set has been serialized. Though an object may be an instance of a class that has the `Serializable` attribute, if it refers to an instance of any call that does not have the `Serializable` attribute, any attempt to serialize the object will fail. It will fail when the `IFormatter` object's `Serialize` method calls itself recursively to serialize the object that cannot be serialized and throws an instance of `System.Runtime.Serialization.SerializationException`. There is a way to avoid this problem.

You can specify that the serialization mechanism should ignore some of an object's instance variables. The simplest way to do this is to declare the variable with the `NonSerialized` attribute, like this:

```
<NonSerialized()> Public myStream as Stream
```

Because the serialization mechanism ignores variables that have the `NonSerialized` attribute, it does not matter to the serialization mechanism if a variable with the `NonSerialized` attribute refers to an object that cannot be serialized.

There is another problem that can be solved by declaring some instance variables with the `NonSerialized` attribute. Instances of some classes refer to other objects that refer to many objects that do not need to be saved. Serializing those objects would just add overhead to serialization and deserialization. If the value of an instance variable does not need to be part of an object's serialized state, then declaring the instance variable with the `NonSerialized` attribute avoids the overhead of unnecessarily serializing and deserializing its values.

Declaring instance variables with the `NonSerialized` attribute solves a few problems during serialization. It also creates a problem during deserialization. The serialization data does not contain values for variables with the `NonSerialized` attribute. If you make no other arrangements, after deserialization an object's `NonSerialized` variables will contain the default value for their declared type. For example, `NonSerialized` variables declared with a numeric type will have the value 0. Serialization ignores initializers and normal constructors. Unless it is acceptable for an object to suddenly find its `NonSerialized` variables unexpectedly set to null or zero, this is a problem.

The serialization mechanism allows you to solve this problem by having a class take responsibility for supplying the values of its instance variables to the serialization mechanism and getting the values of its instance variables from the deserialization mechanism. A class takes this responsibility if it implements the `System.Runtime.Serialization.ISerializable` interface.

Classes that implement the `ISerializable` interface must implement its `GetObjectData` subroutine. An implementation of the `GetObjectData` subroutine looks something like this:

```
Public Sub GetObjectData(ByVal info As SerializationInfo, _
                         ByVal context As StreamingContext) _
   Implements ISerializable.GetObjectData
     info.AddValue("myFont", myFont)
     info.AddValue("count", count)
     ...
End Sub 'GetObjectData
```

The main thing this GetObjectData subroutine does is to supply the values of its object's instance variables to the serialization mechanism by calling the SerilaizationInfo parameter's AddValue subroutine. Only the instance variables whose name and value are passed to the AddValue subroutine are serialized.

A GetObjectData subroutine may provide information to the serialization mechanism that does not correspond to any instance variable. This can be useful if you need to provide information to reconstruct an object that cannot be serialized. For example, a FileStream object that is being used to read from a file cannot be serialized. However, you can reconstruct it from the file name and the current file position. The file's name and position would both come from the FileStream object rather than an instance variable.

If a class that implements the ISerializable interface is subclassed, then its subclass must have its own GetObjectData subroutine to serialize its own instance variables. The subclass's GetObjectData subroutine must call the base class's Get ObjectData subroutine, otherwise the base class's instance variables won't be serialized.

The GetObjectData subroutine's StreamingContext parameter can be used to get information that may be useful for a GetObjectData subroutine to deicide what information to provide to the serialization mechanism.

A class that implements the ISerializable interface must also have a special constructor with a signature like this:

```
Protected Sub New(ByVal info As SerializationInfo, _
                  ByVal context As StreamingContext)
     Dim position as Long
     Dim fileName as String
     position = CInt(info.GetValue("size", GetType(Integer)))
     fileName = CStr(info.GetValue("shape", GetType(String)))
     ...
End Sub 'New
```

All classes that implement the ISerializable interface must have an interface with this signature. The deserialization mechanism invokes this constructor. The constructor is expected to initialize all of the class's instance variables from the serialization data that it gets by calling its SerializationInfo argument's GetValue function.

If the class's base class implements the ISerializable interface, then the special constructor must invoke the base class's special constructor.

Here is an example to show how these pieces can fit together:

```
Imports System
Imports System.Runtime.Serialization
Imports System.Runtime.Serialization.Formatters.Binary
Imports System.IO
Imports System.Collections


' This class provides access to text files, fetching a string
' containing the next or previous n lines.
' This class illustrates a serializable class that refers to a
' non-serializable object.  In particular it refers to a FileStream
' that is not serializble.  Since it cannot write the FileStream
' object directly to a file, it saves the file name and the current
' position in the file.
'
<Serializable()> Public Class TextFileReader
    Implements ISerializable

    <NonSerialized()> Private file As FileStream
    Private myFilename As String
    Private stack As FilePositionStack

    '
    ' Construct a TextFileReader that will read from the specified
    ' file.
    '
    ' name - The name of the file to read from.
    Public Sub New(ByVal name As String)
        myFilename = name
        file = New FileStream(myFilename, FileMode.Open)
        stack = New FilePositionStack()
    End Sub 'New


    ' Deserialization constructor
    Public Sub New(ByVal info As SerializationInfo, _
                   ByVal context As StreamingContext)
        myFilename = info.GetString("myFilename")
        Dim pos As Integer = info.GetInt32("position")
        stack = CType(info.GetValue("stack", _
            GetType(FilePositionStack)), FilePositionStack)
        file = New FileStream(myFilename, FileMode.Open)
        file.Seek(pos, SeekOrigin.Begin)
    End Sub 'New


    Public Function readLine() As String
        Dim r As New StreamReader(file)
        Dim line As String = r.ReadLine()
        If line IsNot Nothing Then
            file.Position += line.Length ' update current position
```

```vbnet
        End If
        Return line
End Function 'readLine


' returns a string containing the next n lines of text in the file
Public Function GetNext(ByVal n As Integer) As String
    Dim lines As String = ""
    For i As Integer = n To -1 Step -1
        stack.SavePosition(file)
        Dim line As String = readLine()
        If line Is Nothing Then
            If lines.Length > 0 Then
                Return lines
            Else
                Throw New ApplicationException("No lines found")
            End If
        End If
        lines += line & vbCrLf
    Next i
    Return lines
End Function 'GetNext


'
' Return a string containing the n lines of text preceding the n
' lines before the files current position. If there aren't that
' many lines before the current position then this method returns
' the first n lines in the file.
'
Public Function GetPrevious(ByVal n As Integer) As String
    For i As Integer = n * 2 To -1 Step -1
        stack.RestorePosition(file)
    Next i
    Return GetNext(n)
End Function 'GetPrevious


'
' Name of the text file associated with this object.
'
Public ReadOnly Property FileName() As String
    Get
        Return myFilename
    End Get
End Property


'
' Save this object in the named file.
'
' name - The name of the file
Public Sub Save(ByVal name As String)
    Dim s As Stream = System.IO.File.Open(name, FileMode.Create)
    Dim f As New BinaryFormatter()
```

```
        f.Serialize(s, Me)
        s.Close()
    End Sub

    '
    ' Retrive a TextFileReader object from the named file.
    '
    ' name - The name of the file
    Public Shared Function Restore(ByVal name As String) As TextFileReader
        Dim s As Stream = System.IO.File.Open(name, FileMode.Open)
        Dim f As New BinaryFormatter()
        Dim r As TextFileReader = CType(f.Deserialize(s), TextFileReader)
        s.Close()
        Return r
    End Function 'Restore

    '
    ' this methods overrides the default serialization logic in order
    ' to write information that will allow the FileStream object
    ' referenced by the variable file to be reconstructed during
    ' deserialization.
    '
    Public Sub GetObjectData(ByVal info As SerializationInfo, _
                             ByVal context As StreamingContext) _
      Implements ISerializable.GetObjectData
        info.AddValue("filename", FileName)
        info.AddValue("position", file.Position)
        info.AddValue("stack", stack)
    End Sub 'GetObjectData

    ' This class implements a stack of file positions.
    <Serializable()> Friend Class FilePositionStack
        Private stack As Stack

        Friend Sub New()
            stack = New Stack()
        End Sub 'New

        ' Push a file position on the stack.
        Friend Sub SavePosition(ByVal file As FileStream)
            stack.Push(file.Position)
        End Sub 'SavePosition

        ' Pops a file position off the stack.
        Friend Sub RestorePosition(ByVal file As FileStream)
            file.Seek(CInt(stack.Pop()), SeekOrigin.Begin)
        End Sub 'RestorePosition
    End Class 'FilePositionStack
End Class 'TextFileReader
```

This class is called `TextFileReader`. It has an instance variable named `file` that refers to a `FileStream` object. The `FileStream` class does not have the `Serializable` attribute. For instances of `TextFileReader` to be successfully serialized and deserialized, it is not sufficient that the `TextFileReader` class has the `Serializable` attribute. It must also

- Prevent its reference to a `FileStream` object from being serialized.

- Add additional information to the serialized byte stream so that it is possible to reconstruct the `FileStream` object.

- Provide logic to allow the `FileStream` object to be reconstructed during deserialization.

To prevent its reference to a `FileStream` object from being serialized, the `TextFileReader` class declares its `file` variable to have the `NonSerialized` attribute.

To reconstruct the original object's `FileStream` object, the `TextFileReader` class implements the `ISerializable` interface. Its implementation of the `ISerializable` interface's the `GetObjectData` subroutine provides the `FileStream` object's `Name` and `Position` properties in place of the `FileStream` object. This is sufficient information to reconstruct the `FileStream` object when a `TextFileReader` object is deserialized. This method reads the file position that was written to the serialized byte stream and passes it to the new `RandomAccessFile` object's `seek` method.

Another issue you may need to deal with is the fact that deserialization creates a new object. In situations like the role-playing game described under the "Context" heading, this can be inconvenient. The inconvenience is that other objects already refer to the existing object. To modify their references to refer to the new object would be to involve those objects in the details of another object's deserialization. The simplest way to deal with this problem is by having all of the references to the object in question be indirect. Returning to the design of the game, what you would do there is to make the association between `GameModel` objects and their state indirect.

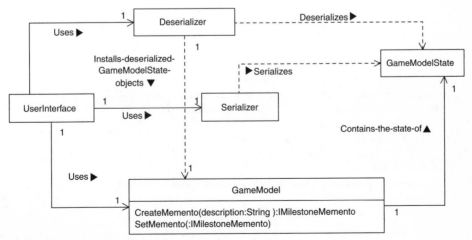

Figure 7.17   GameModelState as a Separate Class

Figure 7.17 shows this addition to the game design from Figure 7.14. There is a GameModelState class that contains the current state of the game. The User Interface class still interacts with the GameModel class. When the state of the game is to be saved, a Serializer object serializes the current GameModelState object. When the state of the game is to be restored, a Deserializer object creates a new GameModelState object that the GameModel object uses in place of the existing GameModelState object.

CONSEQUENCES

☺ Both forms of the Snapshot pattern keep a lot of the complexity of saving and restoring an object's state out of its class.

☹ The Snapshot pattern is not very suitable for undoing a fine-grained sequence of commands. Making many snapshots of an object can consume a prohibitive amount of storage. Capturing the changes to an object's state (the Command pattern) may be more efficient.

CODE EXAMPLE

The following is some of the code to implement the design discussed under the "Context" heading. First is the code for the GameModel class, which is very central to any state-saving operation:

```
Imports System
Imports System.Runtime.Serialization
Imports System.Runtime.Serialization.Formatters.Binary
Imports System.IO
Imports System.Collections


'
' Instances of this class model the state of a game.
' Each game will use only one instance of this class, which it will get
' by calling this class' getGameModel method.
'
<Serializable()> Public Class GameModel
    Private Shared theInstance As New GameModel()
    Private mementoManager As MilestoneMementoManager

    ' This constructor is private to force other classes to call this
    ' class's GetGameModel method to get an instance of it.
    Private Sub New()
        mementoManager = New MilestoneMementoManager(Me)
    End Sub 'New
```

```
        '
        ' This method returns the single instance of this class that other
        ' classes will use.
        '
        Public Shared Function GetGameModel() As GameModel
            Return theInstance
        End Function
        ...
    End Class 'GameModel
```

The point of the preceding portion of the GameModel class is to make the Game
Model class a singleton class. By making its constructor private, other classes are
unable to use its constructor. That forces them to get an instance of the GameModel
class by calling its getGameModel method.

The remaining portions of the GameModel class related to the Snapshot pattern are
involved in the management of memento objects.

```
    '
    ' Instances of this class contain a snapshot of this object's state.
    '
    Public Class MilestoneMemento
        Implements IMilestoneMemento

        ' constructor
        ' d - The reason this object is being created.
        Public Sub New(ByVal d As String)
            Me.myDescription = d
        End Sub 'New

        Private myDescription As String

        ' Description of why this memento was created.
        Public ReadOnly Property Description() As String _
         Implements IMilestoneMemento.Description
            Get
                Return myDescription
            End Get
        End Property ' The following variables are set by a GameModel object

        Private myMementoManager As MilestoneMementoManager

        ' game model manager
        Public Property MementoManager() As MilestoneMementoManager
            Get
                Return myMementoManager
            End Get
            Set(ByVal Value As MilestoneMementoManager)
                myMementoManager = Value
            End Set
        End Property
    End Class 'MilestoneMemento
```

RELATED PATTERNS

Command: The Command pattern allows state changes to be undone on a command-by-command basis without having to make a snapshot of an object's entire state after every command.

Read-Only Interface: Interfaces in the IMemento role are designed using the Read-Only Interface pattern.

Observer

The Observer pattern is very well known and widely used. Since it was originally documented, patterns have evolved. It is important to know about the Observer pattern when working with existing designs that use it.

The .NET Delegation Event Model is a superior choice for new designs. It produces designs that are more reusable. A number of CASE and programming tools provide assistance for the construction and use of classes designed to work with the Delegation Event Model.

The Observer pattern was previously described in [GoF95].

SYNOPSIS

Allow objects to dynamically register dependencies between objects, so that an object will notify those objects that are dependent on it when its state changes.

CONTEXT

Suppose that you work for a company that manufactures smoke detectors, motion sensors, and other security devices. To take advantage of new market opportunities, your company plans to introduce a new line of devices. These devices will be able to send a signal to a security card that can be installed in most computers. The hope is that companies that make security-monitoring systems will integrate these devices and cards with their systems. To make it easy to integrate the cards with monitoring systems, you have been given the task of creating an easy-to-use application program interface (API).

The API must allow your future customers to easily integrate their programs with it so their programs will receive notifications from the security card. It must work without forcing the customers to alter the architecture of their existing software. All that the API may assume about the customer's software is that one or more objects will have a method that should be called when a notification is received from a security device. Figure 7.18 is a design for the API.

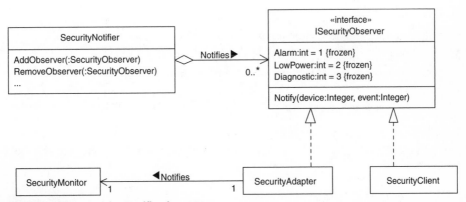

Figure 7.18 Security Notification API

Instances of the `SecurityNotifier` class receive notifications from the security card. They, in turn, notify objects that previously requested to receive notifications. Only objects that implement the `ISecurityObserver` interface can be registered with a `SecurityNotifier` object to receive notifications from it. An `ISecurityObserver` object becomes registered to receive notifications from a `SecurityNotifier` object when it is passed to the `SecurityNotifier` object's `AddObserver` subroutine. Passing it to the `SecurityNotifier` object's `RemoveObserver` subroutine ends the `ISecurityObserver` object's registration to receive notifications.

A `SecurityNotifier` object passes a notification to an `ISecurityObserver` object by calling its `Notify` subroutine. The parameters it passes to its `Notify` subroutine are a number that uniquely identifies the security device that the original notification came from and a number that specifies the type of notification.

The remaining classes in the diagram are not part of the API. They are classes that would already exist or be added to potential customers' monitoring software. The class indicated in the diagram as `SecurityClient` corresponds to any class a customer adds to his or her monitoring software that implements the `SecurityObserver` interface. Customers may add such classes to their monitoring software to process notifications from a `SecurityNotifier` object.

The class indicated in the diagram as `SecurityMonitor` corresponds to an existing class in a customer's monitoring software that does not implement the `ISecurity Observer` interface, but does have a subroutine that should be called to process notifications from security devices. The customer is able to have instances of such a class receive notifications without modifying the class. The customer is able to do this by writing an adapter class that implements the `ISecurityObserver` interface so that its `Notify` subroutine calls the appropriate method of the `SecurityMonitor` class.

FORCES

☺ You are implementing two otherwise independent classes. An instance of one will need to notify other objects when its state changes. An instance of the other will need to be notified when an object it has a dependency on changes state. However, the two classes are not specifically intended to work with each other. To promote reuse, one should not have direct knowledge of the other.

☺ You have a one-to-many dependency relationship that may require an object to notify multiple objects when it changes its state.

☹ Some logic is required to route or prioritize notifications. The logic is independent of the sender and recipients of the notifications.

SOLUTION

Figure 7.19 is a class diagram that shows the roles that classes and interfaces play in the Observer pattern.

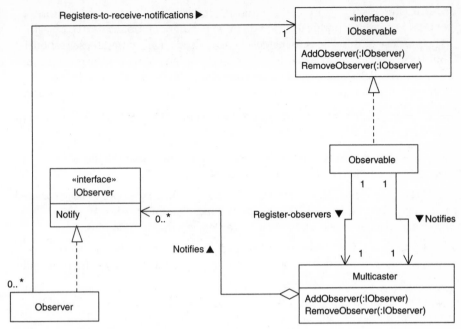

Figure 7.19   Observer Pattern

You will notice that Figure 7.19 is more complicated than Figure 7.16. Figure 7.16 incorporates some simplifications that are described in the Implementation section.

The following are descriptions of roles that the classes and interfaces in the preceding diagram play in the Observer pattern:

IObserver: An interface in this role defines a subroutine that is typically called `Notify` or `Update`. An `Observable` object calls the subroutine to provide a notification that its state has changed, passing it whatever arguments are appropriate. In many cases, a reference to the `Observable` object is one of the arguments that allow the method to know what object provided the notification.

Observer: Instances of classes in this role implement the `IObserver` interface and receive state change notifications from `Observable` objects.

IObservable: `IObservable` objects implement an interface in this role. The interface defines two subroutines that allow `Observer` objects to register and unregister for receiving notifications.

Observable: A class in this role implements the `IObservable` interface. Its instances are responsible for managing the registration of `IObserver` objects that want to receive notifications of state changes. Its instances are also responsible for delivering the notifications. The `Observable` class does not directly implement these responsibilities. Instead, it delegates these responsibilities to a `Multicaster` object.

Multicaster: Instances of a class in this role manage registration of IObserver objects and deliver notifications to them on behalf of an Observable object. The purpose of this role is to increase reuse of code. Delegating these responsibilities to a Multicaster class allows their implementation to be reused by all Observable classes that implement the same IObservable interface or deliver notifications to objects that implement the same IObserver interface.

Figure 7.20 summarizes the collaborations between the objects that participate in the Observer pattern:

1 Objects that implement an IObserver interface are passed to the Add Observer method of an IObservable object.

   1.1 The IObservable object delegates the AddObserver call to its associated Multicaster object. The Multicaster object adds the IObservable object to the collection of IObserver objects that it maintains.

2 The IObservable object labeled o needs to notify other objects that its state has changed. It initiates the notification by calling the Notify subroutine of its associated Multicaster object.

   2.1 The Multicaster object calls the Notify subroutine of each one of the IObserver objects in its collection.

IMPLEMENTATION

You should find implementing this pattern achievable with the following advice.

Observing the Observable

An Observable object normally passes a self-reference as a parameter to an Observer object's Notify subroutine. In most cases, the Observer object needs access to the Observable object's attributes in order to act on the notification. Here are some ways to provide that access:

■ Add properties to the IObservable interface for fetching attribute values. This is usually the best solution. However, it works only if all classes that implement the IObservable interface have a common set of attributes sufficient for Observer objects to act on notifications.

■ You can have multiple IObservable interfaces, with each providing access to enough attributes for an Observer object to act on notifications. To make that work, IObserver interfaces must declare a version of their Notify subroutine for each one of the IObservable interfaces. However, requiring observer objects to be aware of multiple interfaces removes much of the original motivation for having IObservable interfaces. Requiring a class to be aware of multiple interfaces is not much better than requiring it to be aware of multiple classes, so this is not a good solution.

- You can pass attributes that IObserver objects need as parameters to their Notify subroutine. The main disadvantage of this solution is that it requires Observable objects to know enough about IObserver objects to provide them with the correct attribute values. If the set of attributes required by IObserver objects changes, you must modify all the Observable classes accordingly.

- You can dispense with the IObservable interface and pass the Observable objects to IObserver objects as instances of their actual class. This implies overloading the IObserver interface's Notify subroutine, so that there is a Notify subroutine for each Observable class that will deliver notifications to IObserver objects.

The main disadvantage of this approach is that Observer classes must be aware of the Observable classes that will be delivering notifications to its instances and know how to fetch the attributes it needs from them. On the other hand, if only one Observable class will be delivering notifications to Observer classes, then this is the best solution. It adds no complexity to any classes. It substitutes a dependency on a single interface for a dependency on a single class. Then it simplifies the design by eliminating the IObservable interface. The example under the "Context" heading uses this simplified solution.

Eliminating the Multicaster

Another simplification often made to the Observer pattern is to eliminate the Multicaster class. If an Observable class is the only class delivering notifications to objects that implement a particular interface, then there is no need for the reusability a Multicaster class provides. This is the reason that the example under the "Context" heading does not have a class in the Multicaster role. Another reason not to have a Multicaster class is that an Observable object will never have to deliver notifications to more than one object. In this case, the management and delivery of notifications to Observer objects is so simple that a Multicaster class adds more complexity than it removes.

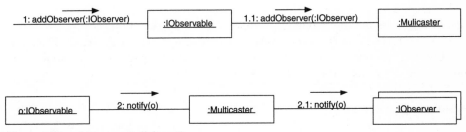

Figure 7.20   Observer Collaboration

Batching Notifications

It may not be necessary or useful to notify Observer objects of every change to an observable object. If this is the case, you can avoid unnecessary notifications by batching state changes and waiting until an entire batch of state changes is complete before delivering notifications. If another object makes changes to an Observable object's state, then providing a single notification for a batch of changes is more complicated. You will have to add a subroutine to the Observable object's class that other objects can call to indicate the beginning of a batch of state changes. When a state change is part of a batch, it should not cause the object to deliver any notifications to its registered observers. You will also have to add a subroutine to the Observable object's class that other objects call to indicate the end of a batch of state changes. When this subroutine is called, if any state changes occurred since the beginning of the batch, the object should deliver notifications to its registered observers.

If multiple objects will initiate changes to an Observable object's state, then determining the end of a batch of changes may be more complicated. A good way to manage this complexity is to add an additional object that coordinates state changes initiated by the other objects and understands their logic well enough to determine the end of a batch of changes. See the description of the Mediator pattern for a more detailed description of how to use one object to coordinate the actions of other objects.

Veto

The Observer pattern is usually used to notify other objects that an object's state has changed. A common variation is to define an alternate IObservable interface that allows objects to request that they receive a notification before an object's state changes. The usual reason for sending state change notifications after a state change is to allow the change to propagate to other objects. The usual reason for sending a notification before a state change is so that other objects can veto a state change. The usual way to implement this is to have an object throw an exception to prevent a proposed state change.

Throwing an exception to veto a change has the virtue that it will usually work even if the person who codes the Observer class does not make any provision for checking for the exception. However, throwing exceptions is more expensive than the Observable class's Notify method returning a result to indicate that the state change should not happen.

Returning a result is more bug prone that throwing an exception because it relies on the person who codes the Observer class remembering to check the result. The additional time it takes to throw an exception is not usually a performance problem, so throwing an exception is the usual way to communicate a veto.

CONSEQUENCES

The Observer pattern allows an object to deliver notifications to other objects without the sender or receiver of the notifications being aware of each other's class.

There are some situations in which the Observer pattern can have unforeseen and undesirable results:

- Delivering notifications can take a long time if an object has a large number of objects to deliver the notification to. That can happen because one object has many observers directly registered to receive its notifications. It can also happen because an object has many indirect observers, since its notifications are cascaded by other objects. You can sometimes lessen the impact of this by making the delivery of notification happen asynchronously in its own thread. However, asynchronous delivery of notifications can introduce its own problems.

- A more serious problem happens if there are cyclic dependencies. Objects call each other's Notify subroutines until the stack overflows. Though serious, the problem can easily be solved by adding an internal flag to one of the classes involved in the cycle that detects a recursive notification.

- If a notification can be delivered asynchronously of other threads, as is the case in the example under the "Context" heading, there are additional consequences to consider. You must ensure that the asynchronous delivery of notifications is done in a way that ensures the consistency of the objects that receive the notifications. It may also be important that notification does not block waiting for another thread for any length of time.

When an observer object receives a notification, it knows which object changed, but it does not know in what way it changed. Avoid requiring an Observer object to determine which attributes of an IObservable object changed. It is simpler for an observer to act on all of an IObservable object's attributes rather than going to the trouble of determining which have changed and then acting on just those.

.NET API USAGE

The .NET event style of processing uses the Observer pattern. Classes whose instances or methods can be event sources, participate in the Observable role. Events participate in the Observer role. All .NET events are multicast capable.

CODE EXAMPLE

Following is code that implements some of the security monitoring design presented under the "Context" heading. The first piece of code is the ISecurityObserver interface. For instances of a class to be able to receive notifications, it must implement the ISecurityObserver interface.

```
'
' The possible kinds of security conditions that can be the reason
' for a notification.
'
Public Enum SecurityCondition As Byte
    Alarm = 1
    LowPower = 2
    Diagnostic = 3
End Enum
```

```
' Classes that implement this interface can register to receive
' security notifications from SecurityNotifier objects.
'
Public Interface ISecurityObserver

    ' This is method is called to deliver a security notification to
    ' this object.
    '
    ' d - A number that identifies the device that originated this
    '     notification.
    ' e - The security condition that is the reason for this
    '     notification.
    '
    Sub Notify(ByVal d As Integer, ByVal e As SecurityCondition)
End Interface 'ISecurityObserver
```

The following piece of code is the `SecurityNotifier` class responsible for delivering the notifications that a computer receives from security devices.

```
Imports System.Collections

'
' When an instance of this class receives a notification from
' a security device, it passes it on to all of its registered
' observers.
'
Public Class SecurityNotifier
    Private observers As New ArrayList()

    ' Add a new observer to this object.
    Public Sub AddObserver(ByVal observer As ISecurityObserver)
        observers.Add(observer)
    End Sub 'AddObserver

    ' Remove an observer from this object
    Public Sub RemoveObserver(ByVal observer As ISecurityObserver)
        observers.Remove(observer)
    End Sub 'RemoveObserver


    ' This method is called when this object needs to pass on a
    ' notification to its registered observers.
    '
    ' d - A number that identifies the device that originated this
    '     notification.
    ' e - The security condition that is the reason for this
    '     notification.
    '
```

```
    Public Sub Notify(ByVal d As Integer, ByVal e As SecurityCondition)
        For Each ThisObserver As ISecurityObserver In observers
            ThisObserver.Notify(d, e)
        Next
    End Sub
End Class 'SecurityNotifier
```

The last class shown here is an adapter class that allows instances of the Security Monitor class to receive notifications, even though the SecurityMonitor class does not implement the ISecurityObserver class.

```
'
' Instances of this class receive a notification from an
' object that is can only deliver it to an object the
' implements the ISecurityObserver interface and
' passes it on to a SecurityMonitor object that does not
' implement ISecurityObserver
'
Public Class SecurityAdapter
    Implements ISecurityObserver

    Private sm As SecurityMonitor

    ' Constructor
    Public Sub New(ByVal sm As SecurityMonitor)
        Me.sm = sm
    End Sub 'New


    '
    ' This is method is called to deliver a security notification to
    ' this object.
    '
    ' d - A number that identifies the device that originated this
    '     notification.
    ' e - The security condition that is the reason for this
    '     notification.
    '
    Public Sub Notify(ByVal d As Integer, ByVal e As SecurityCondition) _
     Implements ISecurityObserver.Notify
        Select Case e
            Case SecurityCondition.Alarm
                sm.SecurityAlert(d)
            Case SecurityCondition.Diagnostic, _
                SecurityCondition.LowPower
                sm.DiagnosticAlert(d)
        End Select
    End Sub
End Class 'SecurityAdapter
```

RELATED PATTERNS

Adapter: The Adapter pattern can be used to allow objects that do not implement the required interface to participate in the Observer pattern by receiving notifications on their behalf.

Delegation: The Observer pattern uses the Delegation pattern.

Mediator: The Mediator pattern is sometimes used to coordinate state changes initiated by multiple objects to an `Observable` object.

Publish-Subscribe: The Publish-Subscribe pattern (described in [Grand98]) is a specialized version of the Observer pattern for delivery of notifications to remote and distributed objects.

State

This pattern was previously described in [GoF95].

SYNOPSIS

Encapsulate the states of an object as discrete objects, each extending a common base class.

CONTEXT

Many objects are required to have a dynamically changing set of attributes called their state. Such objects are called stateful objects. An object's state will usually be one of a predetermined set of values. When a stateful object becomes aware of an external event, its state may change. The behavior of a stateful object is in some ways determined by its state.

For an example of a stateful object, suppose that you are writing a dialog for editing parameters of a program. The dialog will have buttons for specifying the disposition of changes you have made:

- The dialog will have an OK button that saves the parameter values in the dialog to both a file and the program's working values.

- The dialog will have a Save button that saves the parameter values only to a file.

- The dialog will have an Apply button that saves the parameter values only to the program's working values.

- The dialog will have a Revert button that restores the dialog values from the file.

It is possible to design such a dialog to be stateless. If a dialog is stateless, it will always behave the same way. The OK button will be enabled whether or not you have edited the values in the dialog. The Revert button will be enabled even if the user has just reverted the dialog values to the contents of the file. If there are no other considerations, then designing this dialog to be stateless is satisfactory.

In some cases, the dialog's stateless behavior may be a problem. Updating the values of the program's working values may be disruptive. Storing parameter values to a file might take an annoyingly long time if the file is on a remote shared file server.

A way to avoid unnecessary saves to the file or unnecessary setting of the program's working parameter values is to make the dialog stateful so that it will not perform these operations when they are not useful. Instead, it will allow them only when updating the file or working values with values different than what they already contain. Figure 7.21 is a state diagram showing the four states needed to produce this behavior.

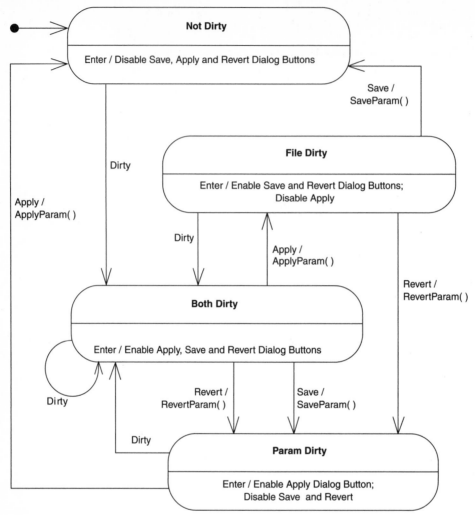

Figure 7.21   Parameter Dialog State Diagram

If you are unfamiliar with state diagrams, here is what Figure 7.21 means:

The solid circle at the top of the diagram shows the dialog's initial state. Since there is no action written on the line leading away from the circle, it means that the dialog goes from its initial state to the state named **Not Dirty**.

Once the dialog has started, its state changes when events happen to it. Events happen when the dialog's buttons are pressed. An event called Dirty happens to the dialog as a consequence of something being done to change the contents of the dialog.

Aside from when the dialog initially goes to the **Not Dirty** state, it changes to a different state only in response to an event. There are four states shown in Figure 7.21. Here are descriptions of the states:

■ On entry into the **Not Dirty** state, the dialog disables its Save, Apply, and Revert buttons. This means that the only event that can happen to a dialog when it is in the **Not Dirty** state is the Dirty event.

If a Dirty event happens when a dialog is in the **Not Dirty** state, it goes to the state named **Both Dirty**.

- When the dialog enters the **Both Dirty** state, it enables its Apply, Save and Revert buttons. While in the **Both Dirty** state, here is what can happen to the dialog's state:

  - If a Dirty event happens to the dialog, it stays in the **Both Dirty** state.

  - If the Apply button is pressed, the dialog calls a subroutine named `Apply Param` and then the dialog goes to the **File Dirty** state.

  - If the Revert Button is pressed, the dialog calls a subroutine named `RevertParam` and then dialog goes to the **Param Dirty** state.

  - If the Save button is pressed, the dialog calls a subroutine named `SaveParam` and then the dialog goes to the **Param Dirty** state.

- When the dialog enters the **File Dirty** state, it enables its Save and Revert buttons; it disables its Apply button. While in the **File Dirty** state, here is what can happen to the dialog's state:

  - If a Dirty event happens to the dialog, it goes to the **Both Dirty** state.

  - If the Revert Button is pressed, the dialog calls a subroutine named `RevertParam` and then dialog goes to the **Param Dirty** state.

  - If the Save button is pressed, the dialog calls a subroutine named `SaveParam` and then the dialog goes to the **Not Dirty** state.

- When the dialog enters the **Param Dirty** state, it enables its Apply button; it disables its Save and Revert buttons. While in the **Param Dirty** state, here is what can happen to the dialog's state:

  - If a Dirty event happens to the dialog, it goes to the **Both Dirty** state.

  - If the Apply Button is pressed, the dialog calls a subroutine named `Apply Param` and then dialog goes to the **Not Dirty** state.

One way to implement the logic for the dialog's state is to have one subroutine to handle events and organize its logic using chains of `If . . . Else` statements. You decide against using this procedural technique because you are concerned that in the long run it might be hard to maintain.

Instead, you decide to implement the state diagram in Figure 7.21 using an object-oriented design. You choose to implement the state diagram using the classes shown in Figure 7.22.

Figure 7.22 shows four classes that correspond to the four states in the state diagram and their common base class. The base class, `DirtyState`, has a public function called `ProcessEvent`. The `ProcessEvent` function takes an event identifier as its argument and returns the next state. It determines the next state by calling the abstract `NextState` function. Each subclass of `DirtyState` overrides the `NextState` function in an appropriate way to determine the next state.

The `DirtyState` class has four static variables to refer to a single instance of each of its four subclasses. The `DirtyState` class also has a static function called `Start`.

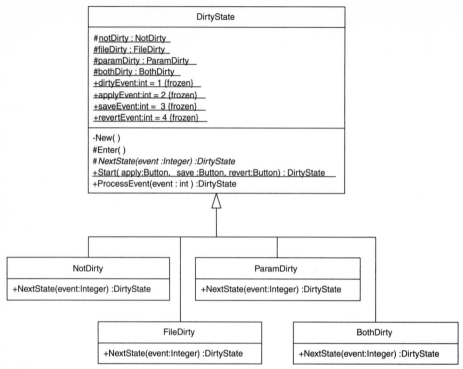

Figure 7.22   DirtyState Class Diagram

The Start function gets things going by creating an instance of each subclass of the DirtyState class and returning the initial state.

The DirtyState class defines a protected subroutine called Enter. A Dirty State object's Enter subroutine is called when it becomes the current state. It is called by the Start function and the ProcessEvent function. The DirtyState class's implementation of the Enter subroutine doesn't do anything. However, subclasses override the Enter method to implement entry actions to be performed when they become the current state.

The DirtyState class defines some constants. These constants identify event codes that are passed to the ProcessEvent function.

FORCES

☺ An object's behavior is determined by an internal state that changes in response to events.

☺ The organization of logic that manages an object's state should be able to scale up to many states without becoming one unmanageably large piece of code.

SOLUTION

Figure 7.23 shows the basic class organization for the State pattern.

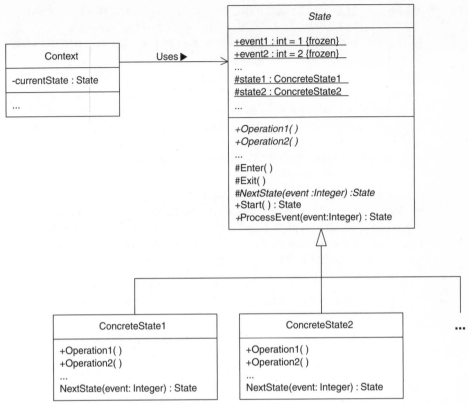

Figure 7.23 State Class Diagram

Here is an explanation of the roles classes play in the State pattern:

Context: Instances of classes in this role exhibit stateful behavior. Instances of `Context` determine their current state by keeping a reference to an instance of a concrete subclass of the `State` class. The subclass of the `State` class determines the state.

State: The `State` class is the superclass of all classes used to represent the state of `Context` objects. A `State` class defines these functions and subroutines.

■ A `State` object's `Enter` subroutine is called when the state that an object represents becomes the current state. The `State` class provides a default implementation of this method that does nothing. It is very common for subclasses of the `State` class to override this method.

■ The `Start` function performs any necessary initialization of state management objects and returns an object corresponding to the client object's initial state. Before it returns the `State` object that represents the initial state, it calls the `State` object's `Enter` function.

■ The `NextState` function is abstract. It takes an argument that indicates the type of the next event and returns the next state. Each concrete subclass of `State` overrides the `NextState` function to determine the correct next state.

- A State object's Exit subroutine is called when the state that the object represents ceases to be the current state. The State class provides a default implementation of this subroutine that does nothing. It is very common for subclasses of the State class to override this subroutine.

- The ProcessEvent function is public. It takes an argument that indicates the type of the next event and returns the new current state. The Process Event function calls the NextState function. If the object that Next State function returns is a different object than the current State object then there is a new current state. In this case, the ProcessEvent function calls the old current state's Exit subroutine and then calls the new current state's Enter subroutine.

- The functions and subroutines Operation1, Operation2 . . . implement operations that behave differently for each state. For example, if an object has states associated with it called On and Off, the implementation for an operation for the On state might do something, and the implementation for the Off state might do nothing. The design of these methods is an application of the Polymorphism pattern described in [Grand98].

The State class defines an Enum of symbolic names for event codes passed to the ProcessEvent function.

Unless a State class has instance variables, there is no need to have more than one instance of it. If there is only one instance of a concrete subclass of State, then the State class will have a shared variable that refers to the instance. Implementations of the ProcessEvent function return the instances referred to by those variables rather than create additional instances.

ConcreteState1, ConcreteState2 . . .: These are concrete subclasses of State. They must implement the Operation1, Operation2 . . . functions and subroutines in an appropriate way. They must also implement the NextState function to determine the appropriate next state for each event. Concrete State classes may override the Enter subroutine and/or Exit subroutine to implement appropriate actions to be perform when entering or exiting a state.

IMPLEMENTATION

No class other than the State class needs to be aware of the subclasses of the State class.

CONSEQUENCES

- ☺ The code for each state is in its own class. This organization makes it easy to add new states without unintended consequences. For this reason, the State pattern works well for small and large numbers of states.

- ☺ To clients of state objects, state transitions appear to be atomic. A client calls the current state's ProcessEvent function. When it returns, the client has its new state.

☺ A procedural implementation of stateful behavior typically involves multiple methods that contain `switch` statements or chains of `If . . . Else` statements for dispatching to state-specific code. These can be large and difficult to understand. Using the State pattern eliminates these `switch` statements or chains of `If . . . Else` statements. It organizes the logic in a more cohesive way that results in classes that have smaller methods.

☺ Using the State pattern results in fewer lines of code and fewer execution paths. This makes it easer to test a program using the White Box Testing pattern described in [Grand98].

☺ State objects that represent nonparametric states can be shared as singletons if there is no need to create a direct instance of the `State` class. In some cases, such as the example shown under the context heading, there is a need to create an instance of the `State` class to provide a set of state objects a way of sharing data. Even in those cases, for each subclass of the `State` class that represents a nonparametric state, there can be a single instance of that class associated with an instance of the `State` class.

• Using the State pattern eliminates the need for code in a method to dispatch to state-specific code. It does not eliminate state-specific `switch` statements that dispatch to a state's handling of an event.

CODE EXAMPLE

Here is code that implements the class diagram shown under the "Context" heading:

```
Imports System.Windows.Forms

Public Class DirtyState
    ' Symbolic constants for events
    Public Enum DirtyState_Events
        DIRTY_EVENT
        APPLY_EVENT
        SAVE_EVENT
        REVERT_EVENT
    End Enum

    ' Symbolic constants for states
    Private Shared myBothDirty As New BothDirty()
    Private Shared myFileDirty As New FileDirty()
    Private Shared myParamDirty As New ParamDirty()
    Private Shared myNotDirty As New NotDirty()

    Private parameters As Parameters
    Private apply, save, revert As Button
```

```
' Having this private constructor prevents classes outside
' of this class from creating an instance of this class.
Private Sub New() ' constructor()
End Sub 'New
```

The DirtyState class's start method initializes the state machine. Its arguments are the Parameters object that the state machine can use to update the program's working values and the buttons that the state machine will enable and disable. The start method returns the initial state.

```
'
' Initialize the state machine and return its initial state.
'
' p The parameters object that this object will work with
' apply The apply button to be enabled/disabled
' save The save button to be enabled/disabled
' revert The revert button to be enabled/disabled
Friend Shared Function Start(ByVal p As Parameters, ByVal apply As Button, _
  ByVal save As Button, ByVal revert As Button) As DirtyState
    Dim d As New DirtyState()
    d.parameters = p
    d.apply = apply
    d.save = save
    d.revert = revert
    myNotDirty.Enter()
    Return myNotDirty
End Function


'
' Respond to a given event with the next state.
' e - An event code
' returns - the next state
Protected Overridable Function NextState(ByVal e As Integer) As DirtyState
    ' This non-overridden method should never be called.
    Throw New System.ApplicationException("Method not overridden")
End Function


'
' Respond to the given event by determining the next
' current state and transitioning to it if it is a
' different state.
'
Public Function ProcessEvent(ByVal e As Integer) As DirtyState
    Dim myNextState As DirtyState = NextState(e)
    If Me Is myNextState Then
        myNextState.Enter()
    End If
    Return myNextState
End Function 'ProcessEvent
```

```
'
' This method is called when this object is becomes the current
  state.
'

Protected Overridable Sub Enter()
End Sub
```

The four concrete subclasses of DirtyState are implemented as private classes.

```
' class to represent state for when the fields of the dialog do not
' match the file or the working parameter values.
Private Class BothDirty
    Inherits DirtyState


    '
    ' Respond to a given event with the next state.
    '
    ' e - An event code
    ' returns - the next state
    Protected Overrides Function NextState(ByVal e As Integer) As
DirtyState
        Select Case e
            Case DirtyState_Events.DIRTY_EVENT
                Return Me
            Case DirtyState_Events.APPLY_EVENT
                If parameters.ApplyParam() Then
                    myFileDirty.Enter()
                    Return myFileDirty
                End If
            Case DirtyState_Events.SAVE_EVENT
                If parameters.SaveParam() Then
                    myParamDirty.Enter()
                    Return myParamDirty
                End If
            Case DirtyState_Events.REVERT_EVENT
                If parameters.RevertParam() Then
                    myParamDirty.Enter()
                    Return myParamDirty
                End If
            Case Else
                Throw New _
                    System.ApplicationException("unexpected event
" & e)
        End Select
        Return Nothing
    End Function 'NextState


    '
    ' This method is called when this object is becomes the current
      state.
```

```vb
        Protected Overrides Sub Enter()
            apply.Enabled = True
            revert.Enabled = True
            save.Enabled = True
        End Sub
    End Class 'BothDirty


    ' class to represent state for when the fields of the dialog match
    ' the working parameter values but not the file.
    Private Class FileDirty
        Inherits DirtyState


        '
        ' Respond to a given event with the next state.
        '
        ' e - An event code
        ' returns - the next state
        Protected Overrides Function NextState(ByVal e As Integer) As
DirtyState
            Select Case e
                Case DirtyState_Events.DIRTY_EVENT
                    myBothDirty.Enter()
                    Return myBothDirty
                Case DirtyState_Events.SAVE_EVENT
                    If parameters.SaveParam() Then
                        myNotDirty.Enter()
                        Return myNotDirty
                    End If
                Case DirtyState_Events.REVERT_EVENT
                    If parameters.RevertParam() Then
                        myParamDirty.Enter()
                        Return myParamDirty
                    End If
                Case Else
                    Throw New _
                        System.ApplicationException("unexpected event
" & e)
            End Select
            Return Nothing
        End Function 'NextState


        '
        ' This method is called when this object is becomes the current
          state.
        '
        Protected Overrides Sub Enter()
            apply.Enabled = False
            revert.Enabled = True
            save.Enabled = True
        End Sub 'Enter
    End Class 'FileDirty
```

```
' class to represent state for when the fields of the dialog match
' the file but not the working parameter values.
Private Class ParamDirty
    Inherits DirtyState

        '
        ' Respond to a given event with the next state..
        '
        ' e - An event code
        ' returns - the next state
        Protected Overrides Function NextState(ByVal e As Integer) As
DirtyState
            Select Case e
                Case DirtyState_Events.DIRTY_EVENT
                    myBothDirty.Enter()
                    Return myBothDirty
                Case DirtyState_Events.APPLY_EVENT
                    If parameters.ApplyParam() Then
                        myNotDirty.Enter()
                        Return myNotDirty
                    End If
                Case Else
                    Throw New System.ApplicationException("unexpected
event " & e)
            End Select
            Return Nothing
        End Function 'NextState


        '
        ' This method is called when this object is becomes the current
          state.
        '
        Protected Overrides Sub Enter()
            apply.Enabled = True
            revert.Enabled = False
            save.Enabled = False
        End Sub
    End Class 'ParamDirty


    '
    ' class to represent state for when the fields of the dialog match
    ' the file and the working parameter values.
    '
    Private Class NotDirty
        Inherits DirtyState

        '
        ' Respond to a given event with the next state..
        '
        ' e - An event code
```

```
                    ' returns - the next state
              Protected Overrides Function NextState(ByVal e As Integer) As
       DirtyState
                    Select Case e
                        Case DirtyState_Events.DIRTY_EVENT
                            myBothDirty.Enter()
                            Return myBothDirty
                        Case Else
                            Throw New _
                                System.ApplicationException("unexpected event
       " & e)
                    End Select
              End Function 'NextState


                    '
                    ' This method is called when this object is becomes the current
                      state.
                    '
              Protected Overrides Sub Enter()
                    apply.Enabled = False
                    revert.Enabled = False
                    save.Enabled = False
              End Sub
          End Class 'NotDirty


       End Class 'DirtyState
```

RELATED PATTERNS

Flyweight: You can use the Flyweight pattern to share state objects.

Mediator: The State pattern is often used with the Mediator pattern when implementing user interfaces.

Singleton: You can implement nonparametric states using the Singleton pattern.

Polymorphism: The design of state-specific operations implemented by concrete state classes follows the Polymorphism pattern discussed in [Grand98].

Strategy

This pattern was previously described in [GoF95].

SYNOPSIS

Encapsulate related algorithms in classes that implement a common interface. This allows the selection of algorithm to vary by object. It also allows one object to vary its selection of algorithm over time.

CONTEXT

Suppose that you have to write a program that displays calendars. A requirement for the program is to able to display sets of holidays celebrated by different nations and different religious groups. The user must be able to specify which sets of holidays to display.

You would like to satisfy the requirement by putting the logic for each set of holidays in a separate class. This will give you a set of small classes to which you could easily add more classes. You want classes that use these holiday classes to be unaware of any specific set of holidays. This brings you to the design shown in Figure 7.24.

Here is how classes in Figure 7.24 work with each other. If a `CalendarDisplay` object has an `IHolidaySet` object to work with, it checks with the `IHolidaySet` object about each day it displays, to find out what holidays fall on that date. Such objects are either an instance of a class like `USHoliday` that identifies a single set of dates or they are an instance of `CompositeHoliday`. The `CompositeHoliday` class is used when the user requests the display of multiple sets of holidays. It is instantiated by passing an array of `Holiday` objects to its constructor.

This arrangement allows a `CalendarDisplay` object to find out what holidays fall on a particular date by just calling an `IHolidaySet` object's `getHolidays` function.

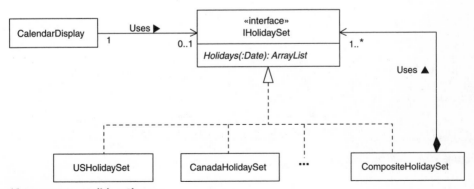

Figure 7.24   Holiday Classes

FORCES

☺ A program must provide multiple variations of an algorithm or behavior.

☺ You need to vary the behavior of each instance of a class.

☺ You need to vary the behavior of objects at run time.

☺ Delegating behavior to an interface allows classes that use the behavior to be unaware of the classes that implement the interface and the behavior.

☺ If a behavior of a class's instances does not vary from instance to instance or over time, then it is simplest for the class to directly contain the behavior or directly contain a static reference to the behavior.

SOLUTION

Figure 7.25 is a class diagram that shows the roles that classes play in the Strategy pattern.

Here are descriptions of the roles that interfaces and classes play in Figure 7.25.

Client: A class in the Client role delegates an operation to an interface. It does so without knowing the actual class of the object it delegates the operation to or how the class implements the operation.

Istrategy: An interface in this role provides a common way to access operations encapsulated by classes that implement the interface.

ConcreteStrategy1, ConcreteStrategy2 . . .: Classes in this role provide alternative implementations of the operation that the client class delegates.

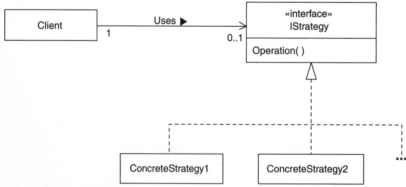

Figure 7.25   Strategy Pattern

The Strategy pattern always occurs with a mechanism for determining the actual ConcreteStrategy object that the client object will use. The selection of a strategy is often driven by configuration information or events. However, the actual mechanism varies greatly. For this reason, no particular strategy-selecting mechanism is included in the pattern.

IMPLEMENTATION

It is common for ConcreteStrategy classes to share some common behavior. You should factor the common behavior that they share into a common base class.

There may be situations where none of the behaviors encapsulated in Concrete Strategy classes are appropriate. A common way to handle a situation like that is for the Client object to have the value Nothing instead of a reference to a Strategy object. This means having to check for Nothing before calling a Strategy object's method. If the structure of the Client object makes this inconvenient, consider using the Null Object pattern.

If the IStrategy interface in a design has only one method, the implementation may be simplified by using a delegate instead of the interface.

CONSEQUENCES

☺ The Strategy pattern allows the behavior of Client objects to be dynamically determined on a per-object basis.

☺ The Strategy pattern simplifies Client classes by relieving them of any responsibility for selecting behavior or implementing alternate behaviors. It simplifies the code for Client objects by eliminating if and switch statements. In some cases, it can also increase the speed of Client objects because they do not need to spend any time selecting a behavior.

.NET API USAGE

The System.Array class has a subroutine named Sort. The purpose of the Sort subroutine is to sort the contents of an array. Sorting objects in an array involves comparing objects to know if they are in the correct order. The default behavior of the Sort subroutine is to compare objects in the array by assuming that they implement the System.IComparable interface and calling their CompareTo function.

You can explicitly provide an alternative strategy for comparing objects in an array by passing it an object that implements the System.Collections.IComparer interface.

CODE EXAMPLE

Here is code that implements the design presented under the "Context" heading. The first listing is for the IHolidaySet interface. The IHolidaySet interface defines a method that returns an array of the names of holidays that fall on a given date. It participates in the Strategy pattern in the IStrategy role.

```
'
' This is implemented by classes that determine if a date is a
' holiday.  Classes that implement this interface will be
' specific to nations or religions.
'
Public Interface IHolidaySet
    '
    ' This method returns a array of strings that describe the holidays
    ' that fall on the given date.  If no holidays fall on the given
    ' date, then this method returns an empty array.
    '
    ' dt - The date to check
    Function Holidays(ByVal dt As DateTime) As String()
End Interface 'IHolidaySet
```

The IHolidaySet interface's getHolidays function returns a zero-length array to indicate that no holiday falls on a date. Returning a zero-length array instead of Nothing means that callers don't have to check for Nothing as a special case. This is less bug prone. This is an application of the Null Object pattern. See the description of the Null Object pattern for a more detailed explanation.

Since an empty array contains no data, it is not necessary for an implementation of the getHolidays function to create a new empty array when it wants to return one. It can always return the same empty array. This is a way to save the expense of creating a zero-length array for every day that is not a holiday.

We give classes that implement the IHolidaySet interface a common abstract base class. This common base class provides a shared empty array that can be used by all implementations of the getHolidays function.

```
'
' Abstract base class for holiday classes
'
Public MustInherit Class AbstractHoliday
    ' Empty array toindicate no holidays
    Public Shared NoHolidays() As String = {}
End Class 'AbstractHoliday
```

Next is a partial listing of the CalendarDisplay class, which participates in the Strategy pattern as a Client class.

```
' Skeletal definition of class to display a calendar
Public Class CalendarDisplay
    Private holiday As IHolidaySet = Nothing
```

```
    ...

    ' Instances of this private class are used to cache information about
    ' dates that are to be displayed.
    Private Class DateCache
        Private Cal As CalendarDisplay
        Private MyDate As DateTime
        Private HolidayStrings() As String

        Public Sub New(ByVal c As CalendarDisplay, ByVal dt As DateTime)
            Cal = c
            MyDate = dt

            If Cal.holiday Is Nothing Then
                HolidayStrings = AbstractHoliday.NoHolidays
            Else
                HolidayStrings = Cal.holiday.Holidays(MyDate)
            End If
        End Sub
    End Class 'DateCache

End Class 'CalendarDisplay
```

Notice that aside from having to handle the possibility of not having any `Holiday` object to work with, the `CalendarDisplay` class is totally unburdened with any details of determining which holidays fall on a date.

The various classes that implement the `IHoliday` interface participate in the Strategy pattern in the `ConcreteStrategy` role. They are not particularly interesting with respect to the Strategy pattern and have this basic structure:

```
'
' This class determines if a particular date is a U.S. holiday.
'
Public Class USHoliday
    Inherits AbstractHoliday
    Implements IHolidaySet

    '
    ' This method returns a array of strings that describe the holidays
    ' that fall on the given date.  If no holidays fall on the given
    ' date, then this method returns an array of length zero.
    '
    ' dt - The date to check
    Public Function Holidays(ByVal dt As DateTime) As String() _
     Implements IHolidaySet.Holidays
        ...
    End Function
End Class 'USHoliday
```

RELATED PATTERNS

Adapter: The Adapter pattern is structurally similar to the Strategy pattern. The difference is in the intent. The Adapter pattern allows a `Client` object to carry out its originally intended purpose by calling a function or subroutine of objects that implement a particular interface. The Strategy pattern provides objects that implement a particular interface for the purpose of altering or determining the behavior of a `Client` object.

Flyweight: If there are many client objects, `ConcreteStrategy` objects may be best implemented as Flyweight objects.

Null Object: The Strategy pattern is often used with the Null Object pattern.

Template Method: The Template Method pattern manages alternate behaviors through subclassing rather than delegation.

Null Object

This pattern was previously described in [Woolf97].

SYNOPSIS

The Null Object pattern provides an alternative to using Nothing to indicate the absence of an object to delegate an operation to. Using Nothing to indicate the absence of such an object requires a test for Nothing before each call to the other object's methods. Instead of using Nothing, the Null Object pattern uses a reference to an object that doesn't do anything.

CONTEXT

You have been given the task of writing classes to encapsulate an enterprise's business rules.[1] Because these classes will be used in a variety of environments, there is a requirement that these objects be able to route warning messages to a dialog box, a log file, other destinations or nowhere at all. A simple way to arrange this is to define an interface called IWarningRouter for routing warning messages and then have the classes you write delegate the routing of warnings to objects that implement that interface, as shown in Figure 7.26.

To handle the situation where warning messages should not be routed anywhere, you could have the variable that would otherwise refer to a WarningRouter object contain Nothing. Using this technique means that a BusinessRule object must first test to see if the variable is Nothing before it can issue a warning message. Depending on the specific business rule class, there may be just one or many places that refer to an IWarningRouter object. There are procedural techniques for limiting the amount of additional complexity implied by those tests for Nothing. However, every call to an IWarningRouter object's methods is an opportunity for someone to forget to put a test for Nothing in the code. Such an omission will cause a NullReference Exception to be thrown at run time.

An alternative to using Nothing to indicate no action is to create a class that implements IWarningRouter and does nothing with a warning message, as shown in Figure 7.27.

---

[1] A business rule is a rule that governs the behavior of a business's information systems. Examples of things determined by such rules are when to reorder stock or when the credit-worthiness of a customer needs to be scrutinized. Business rules change over time, so the implementation of business rules should allow changing them to be as painless as possible.

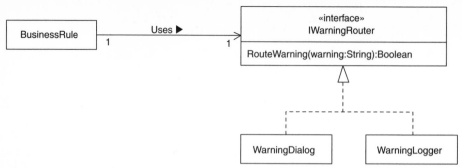

Figure 7.26   WarningRouter Interface

The advantage of having an IgnoreWarning class is that you can use it just like any other class that implements the IWarningRouter interface. It does not require a test for Nothing or any other special logic.

FORCES

☺ A class delegates an operation to another class. The delegating class does not usually care how the other class implements the operation. However, it sometimes does require that the operation be implemented by doing nothing.

☺ You want the class delegating the operation to delegate it in all cases, including the do-nothing case. You do not want the do-nothing case to require any special code.

SOLUTION

Figure 7.28 presents a class diagram that shows the structure of the Null Object pattern.

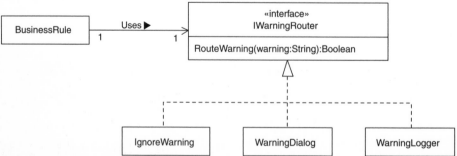

Figure 7.27   Ignore Warning Class

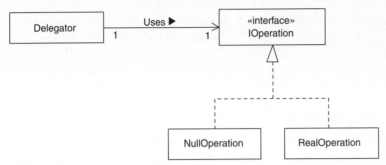

Figure 7.28 Null Object Pattern

Here are descriptions of the roles that classes and interfaces play in the Null Object pattern:

Delegator: A class in this role participates in the Null Object pattern by delegating an operation to an interface or an abstract class. It performs this delegation without having to take responsibility for the operation's do-nothing case. It simply assumes that the object it delegates to will encapsulate the correct behavior, even if the is to do nothing.

In particular, an object in the Delegator role does not need to test for Nothing before invoking methods of the object it is delegating to.

IOperation: A class in the Delegator role delegates an operation to an interface in this role. An abstract class can also fill this role.

RealOperation: Classes in this role implement the operation the Delegator class delegates to the IOperation interface.

NullOperation: Classes in this role provide a do-nothing implementation of the operation that the Delegator class delegates to the IOperation interface.

IMPLEMENTATION

It is often the case that instances of NullOperation classes contain no instance-specific information. When this is the case, you may save time and memory by implementing the NullOperation class as a singleton class.

CONSEQUENCES

☺ The Null Object pattern relieves a class that delegates an operation to another class of the responsibility of implementing the do-nothing version of that operation. This results in simpler code that does not have to test for Nothing before calling the method that implements the delegated operation. It results in more reliable code by eliminating opportunities to create bugs by omitting a test for Nothing from code.

☺ The do-nothing behavior encapsulated by a class in the `NullOperation` role is reusable if there is one consistent do-nothing behavior that works for all `Delegator` classes.

☹ The Null Object pattern increases the number of classes in a program. If there is not already an interface in the `IOperation` role, then the Null Object pattern may introduce more complexity through the introduction of additional classes than it removes by the simplification of code.

CODE EXAMPLE

Following is code that implements the classes presented under the "Context" heading. First is the `IWarningRouter` interface that is implemented by classes that provide environment-appropriate handling for warning messages.

```
'
' This interface is implemented by classes whose instances can be used to
' send warning message to an appropriate destination.
'
Public Interface WarningRouter
    '
    ' This method sends a warning message to whatever destination it
    ' considers appropriate.
    '
    ' returns true if caller should proceed with its current operation.
    Function RouteWarning(ByVal msg As String) As Boolean
End Interface 'WarningRouter
```

Next is some code from the `BusinessRule` class that delegates the handling of warning messages to objects that implement the `IWarningRouter` interface.

```
'
' Baseclass for business rule classes
'
Public Class BusinessRule
    Private warning As WarningRouter = Nothing
    Private expirationDate As System.DateTime = DateTime.MaxValue

    Public Sub New()
        If DateTime.Now > expirationDate Then
            warning.RouteWarning(([GetType]().FullName & " has expired."))
        End If
    End Sub
End Class 'BusinessRule
```

Next is a class that implements the `IWarningRouter` interface by popping up a dialog box that displays the warning message.

```
Imports System.Windows.Forms

Public Class WarningDialog
    Implements WarningRouter


    '
    ' This method sends a warning message to whatever destination it
    ' considers appropriate.
    '
    ' returns true if caller should proceed with its current operation
    Public Function RouteWarning(ByVal warning As String) As Boolean _
     Implements WarningRouter.RouteWarning
        Dim r As DialogResult
        r = MessageBox.Show(warning, "Warning", MessageBoxButtons.OKCancel)
        Return r = DialogResult.OK
    End Function
End Class 'WarningDialog
```

The `WarningDialog` class's `RouteWarning` function returns true if the user clicks the dialog box's OK button or false if the user clicks its Cancel button. The following listing is of the `IgnoreWarning` class. Because it encapsulates do-nothing behavior, its `RouteWarning` method always returns true.

```
Public Class IgnoreWarning
    Implements WarningRouter


    '
    ' This method sends a warning message to whatever destination it
    ' considers appropriate.
    '
    ' returns true if caller should proceed with its current operation
    Public Function RouteWarning(ByVal warning As String) As Boolean _
     Implements WarningRouter.RouteWarning
        Return True
    End Function
End Class 'IgnoreWarning
```

RELATED PATTERNS

Strategy: The Null Object pattern is often used with the Strategy pattern.

Singleton: If instances of a `NullOperation` class contain no instance-specific information, then you may save time and memory by implementing the `NullOperation` class as a singleton class.

Template Method

This pattern was previously described in [GoF95].

SYNOPSIS

Write an abstract class that contains only part of the logic needed to accomplish its purpose. Organize the class so its concrete methods call an abstract method where the missing logic would have appeared. Provide the missing logic in the subclass's methods that override the abstract methods.

CONTEXT

Suppose that you have the task of writing a reusable class for logging users in to an application. In addition to being reusable and easy to use, the tasks of the class will be to:

- Prompt the user for a user id and password.

- Authenticate the user id and password. The result of the authentication operation should be an object. If the authentication operation produces some information needed later as proof of authentication, then the object produced by the authentication operation should encapsulate the information.

- While the authentication operation is in progress, the user should see a changing and possibly animated display that tells the user that authentication is in progress and all is well.

- Notify the rest of the application that login is complete and make the object produced by the authentication operation available to the rest of the application.

Two of these tasks, prompting the user and assuring the user that authentication is in progress, are application independent. Though the strings and images displayed to the user may vary with the application, the underlying logic will always be the same.

The other two tasks, authenticating the user and notifying the rest of the application, are application specific. Every application will have to provide its own logic for these tasks.

The way you organize your Logon class will be a large factor in how easy it is for developers to use. Delegation is a very flexible mechanism. You could simply organize a Logon class so that it delegates the tasks of authenticating the user and notifying the rest of the application. Though this approach gives a programmer a lot of freedom, it does not help guide a programmer to a correct solution.

Programmers are unlikely to make frequent use of your Logon class. This means that when they use it, they will probably not be very familiar with it. Just as it can be easier to fill in the blanks of a preprinted form than to write a document from scratch, giving your Logon class a fill-in-the-blanks organization can guide programmers to the correct use of the Logon class. You can achieve a fill-in-the-blanks organization by defining the Logon class to be an abstract (MustInherit) class that defines abstract (MustOverride) functions and subroutines that correspond to the application-dependent tasks that the programmer must supply code for. To use the Logon class, a programmer must define a subclass of the Logon class. Because the functions, subroutines, and properties corresponding to the tasks that the programmer must code are abstract (MustOverride), a compiler will complain if the programmer does not fill in the blanks by overriding them.

Figure 7.29 presents a diagram that shows the organization of a Logon class and its subclass organized in this way.

The AbstractLogon class has a subroutine called Logon that contains the top-level logic for the top-level task of logging a user onto a program. It calls the abstract function Authenticate and the abstract subroutine NotifyAuthentication to perform the program-specific tasks of authenticating a user and notifying the rest of the program when the authentication is accomplished.

FORCES

☺ You have to design a class for reuse in multiple programs.

☺ The overall responsibility of the class will be the same for all applications. However, portions of its behavior will be different in each program in which it is used.

☺ You can make the class easier for programmers unfamiliar with the class to use by designing it in a way that reminds programmers who use the class to supply logic for all its program-specific responsibilities.

☺ If a class that is not abstract inherits an abstract method but does not override it, then compilers will complain when compiling it.

☺ Designing a class to remind programmers to supply logic for its program-specific responsibilities requires additional effort. If the class is not reused, then the additional effort is wasted.

SOLUTION

Organize reusable logic into an abstract class that calls application-specific logic through place markers in the form of abstract functions and subroutines. To use the abstract class, the programmer must create a subclass that overrides the abstract functions and subroutines with application-specific logic.

Figure 7.30 is a class diagram that shows the organization of the Template Method pattern.

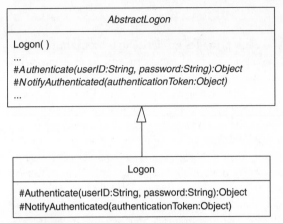

Figure 7.29   Logon Class and Subclass

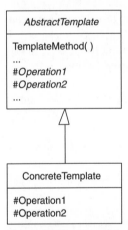

Figure 7.30   Template Method Pattern

Following are descriptions of the roles played by classes in the Template Method pattern:

AbstractTemplate: A class in this role has a concrete function or subroutine that contains the class's top-level logic. This is indicated in the diagram as `TemplateMethod`. It calls other functions and subroutines, defined in the `AbstractTemplate` class as abstract, to invoke lower-level logic that varies with each subclass of the `AbstractTemplate` class.

ConcreteTemplate: A class in this role is a concrete subclass of an `Abstract Template` class. It overrides the abstract functions and subroutines defined by its base class to complete the logic of the `TemplateMethod` method.

IMPLEMENTATION

The basic way an `AbstractTemplate` class provides guidance to a programmer is by forcing him/her to override abstract (`MustOverride`) functions and subroutines with the intention of providing logic to fill in the blanks of its template method's logic. You can add more structure by providing additional functions and subroutines for subclasses to override with supplemental or optional logic. For example, consider a reusable class called `Paragraph` that represents paragraphs in a word processor document.

One of the `Paragraph` class's responsibilities is to determine how to wrap the words it contains into lines that fit within specified margins. The `Paragraph` class has a template method responsible for wrapping the words in a paragraph. Because some word processors allow paragraphs to wrap around graphics, the `Paragraph` class defines an abstract function that the class's word-wrapping logic calls to determine the margins for a line of text. Concrete subclasses of the paragraph class are forced to provide an implementation of the function to determine the margins for each line.

Some word processors include a hyphenation engine that automatically determines where words can be hyphenated. This feature allows longer words to be split between lines so the lines of a paragraph can be of more even lengths. Since not every word processor will require the `Paragraph` class to support hyphenation, it does not make sense for the `Paragraph` class to define an abstract hyphenation function and force subclasses to override it. However, it is helpful for the `Paragraph` class to define a concrete hyphenation function that is called by the word-wrapping logic and does nothing. The point of such a method is that a subclass of `Paragraph` can override the function in those cases where hyphenation needs to be supported.

Functions and subroutines such as those that can be optionally overridden to provide additional or customized functionality are called *hook methods*. To make it easier for a programmer to be aware of the hook methods a class provides, you can apply a naming convention to hook methods. Two of the more common naming conventions for hook methods are to either begin the names of hook methods with the prefix `do-` or end the names of hook methods with the suffix `-Hook`. For example, following those naming conventions, the name of the `Paragraph` class's hyphenation method might be `doHyphenation` or `hyphenationHook`.

CONSEQUENCES

A programmer writing a subclass of an `AbstractTemplate` class is forced to override those methods that must be overridden to complete the logic of the superclass. A well-designed template method class has a structure that provides a programmer with guidance in providing the basic structure of its subclasses.

CODE EXAMPLE

Following is some code that implements the design presented under the "Context" heading. First is the `AbstractLogon` class. It participates in the Template Method pattern in the `AbstractTemplate` role. Its template method is called `Logon`. The `Logon` subroutine puts up a dialog that prompts the user for a user ID and password.

After the user supplies a user ID and password, the Logon subroutine pops up a window telling the user that authentication is in progress. The window stays up while the Logon subroutine calls the abstract function Authenticate to authenticate the user ID and password. If the authentication is successful, it takes down the dialog boxes and calls the abstract subroutine NotifyAuthentication to notify the rest of the program that the user has been authenticated.

```
'
' This is an abstract class for authenticating a user for a program.
'
Public MustInherit Class AbstractLogon
    '
    ' This method authenticates a user.
    '
    ' programName - The name of the program as it
    '               should appear when prompting the user for logon
    Public Sub Logon(ByVal programName As String)
        Dim authenticationToken As Object = Nothing
        Dim logonDialog As New LogonDialog()
        logonDialog.Text = "Log on to " & programName
        While True
            logonDialog.ShowDialog()
            Try
                Dim userId As String = logonDialog.UserId
                Dim password As String = logonDialog.Password
                authenticationToken = Authenticate(userId, password)
                Exit While
            Catch e As Exception
                ' Tell user that authentication failed.
                MessageBox.Show(e.ToString(), _
                    "Authentication Failure", MessageBoxButtons.OK)
            End Try
        End While


        ' Authentication successful
        NotifyAuthentication(authenticationToken)
    End Sub


    '
    ' Authenticate the user based on the supplied user id and password.
    '
    ' userID - the supplied user id
    ' password - the supplied password
    ' returns - An object that encapsulates whatever data is
    '           needed, if any, to prove that the user has been
    '           authenticated
    Protected MustOverride Function Authenticate(ByVal userID As String, _
        ByVal password As String) As Object
```

```
    '
    ' Notify the rest of the program that the user has been
    ' authenticated.
    '
    ' authenticationToken - The object returned by the authenticate
      method
    Protected MustOverride _
    Sub NotifyAuthentication(ByVal authenticationToken As Object)
End Class 'AbstractLogon
```

The `LogonDialog` class implements a dialog to prompt the user for logon information.

```
Public Class LogonDialog
    '
    ' The user ID in this logon dialog.
    '
    Public Property UserId() As String
        Get
            Return UserIdTextBox.Text
        End Get
        Set(ByVal Value As String)
            UserIdTextBox.Text = Value
        End Set
    End Property

    Public Property Password() As String
        Get
            Return PasswordTextBox.Text
        End Get
        Set(ByVal Value As String)
            PasswordTextBox.Text = Value
        End Set
    End Property
End Class
```

Subclasses of the `AbstractLogon` class must override its abstract methods like this:

```
' logon implementation
Public Class Logon
    Inherits AbstractLogon

    ' Perform authentications
    Protected Overrides Function Authenticate(ByVal userID As String, _
      ByVal password As String) As Object
        If userID = "abc" And password = "123" Then
            Return userID
        End If
        Throw New System.ApplicationException("bad userID")
    End Function
```

```
    ' Receive notifications
    Protected Overrides _
    Sub NotifyAuthentication(ByVal authenticationToken As Object)
    End Sub
End Class 'Logon
```

RELATED PATTERNS

Strategy: The Strategy pattern modifies the logic of individual objects at run time. The Template Method pattern modifies the logic of an entire class at compile time.

Visitor

This pattern was previously described in [GoF95].

SYNOPSIS

One way to implement an operation that involves objects in a complex structure is to put logic in each of their classes to support the operation. The Visitor pattern is an alternate way to implement such operations. It avoids complicating the classes of objects in the structure by putting the necessary logic in a separate class. The Visitor pattern also allows the logic to be varied by using different Visitor classes.

CONTEXT

Suppose that you have the assignment of enhancing a word processor to produce a table of contents. From the user's viewpoint, there will be a dialog for specifying information that guides the building of a table of contents. The word processor allows a style name to be associated with each paragraph. The dialog will allow the user to specify which paragraph styles correspond to headings that should appear in the table of contents.

The word processor uses information specified in the dialog to build an internal table. This internal table contains all the information the word processor needs to build a multilevel table of contents. For the rest of this description, the table is referred to as the *internal ToC table*.

Each row of the internal ToC table will include a level number that can correspond to chapter, section, and subsection or any other hierarchical organization the user wants to represent. The rows of the table will also include a paragraph style and other information for formatting the table of contents. If a paragraph style appears in the table, it means that paragraphs with that style are headings whose first line will appear in that level of a table of contents.

In addition to adding the dialog and internal ToC table to the word processor, you will have to add these table-of-contents-related features:

- Generate and insert a table of contents for a single file document into that document.

- Reorganize a single file document into a multifile document, based on a heading level in the internal ToC table.

Since these operations involve manipulating a word processing document, any design for implementing the table of contents features will involve classes that the word processor uses to represent documents. Figure 7.31 shows some classes that the word processor uses to represent documents.

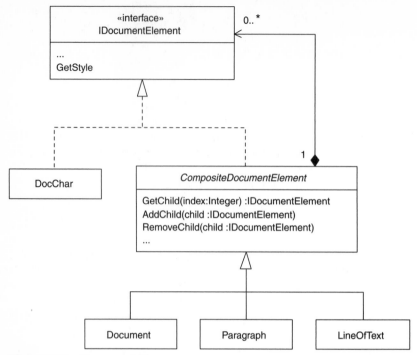

Figure 7.31   Document Classes

The classes that will be of interest to a table-of-contents mechanism are Document, Paragraph and LineOfText. A document contains paragraphs contain lines of text. Any design for generating a table of contents should recognize that Document objects may contain other objects that are not Paragraph objects. It should also recognize that kinds of objects other than Document objects may contain Paragraph objects. Finally, the design should not add complexity to the classes that represent documents.

There are two basic approaches you could take toward implementing the table-of-contents features. One approach is to put the necessary logic in the various classes that represent a document. For reasons discussed in the previous paragraph, this is not a good solution.

The other approach is to put all the logic for each feature in a separate class. When a table-of-contents operation is to be done, the object responsible for the operation examines a Document object and the objects it contains. It looks for Paragraph objects that the Document object directly contains. When it finds Paragraph objects with a style in the internal ToC table driving the table-of-contents operation, it takes the appropriate action. This is the approach shown in Figure 7.32.

Figure 7.32 includes the classes for representing word processing documents that were shown in Figure 7.31. It also includes the following classes:

> **WordProcessor:** The WordProcessor class is responsible for creating and editing the objects that represent a document. It uses the other classes in the diagram to edit a document.

DocumentVisitor: This is an abstract class. Its subclasses explore the objects that constitute a document in order to produce a table of contents or reorganize a document into multiple files. The `DocumentVisitor` class provides logic its subclasses use to navigate among the objects that constitute a document.

The concept is that instances of subclasses of the `DocumentVisitor` class visit the objects that constitute a document, gathering information from each object and then acting on the information.

TOCVisitor: This subclass of the `DocumentVisitor` class is responsible for generating a table of contents. It works by examining each `Paragraph` object directly owned by a `Document` object. When it finds a `Paragraph` object with a style in the internal ToC table, it generates a corresponding table-of-contents entry. The table-of-contents entry uses the contents of the first `LineOfText` object that belongs to the `Paragraph` object.

ReorgVisitor: This subclass of `DocumentVisitor` class is responsible for automatically separating a document into multiple files. It begins by being told to look for paragraphs that correspond to a certain level of organization in a document. It finds this level of organization in the internal ToC table. It fetches the style associated with the level of organization from the table. It then examines all of the `Paragraph` objects that directly belong to a `Document` object. It looks for `Paragraph` objects that have the style it fetched from the table. When it finds a `Paragraph` object with that style, it creates a new `Document` object. It moves the `Paragraph` object that it found, along with all of the `Paragraph` objects immediately following it that are at a lower level of organization to the newly created `Document` object. It writes the new `Document` object and all the paragraph objects now associated with it to a file. It replaces the `Paragraph` objects it moved from the original `Document` object with a new object that contains the name of the file that the moved paragraphs are now stored in.

FORCES

☺ There are a variety of operations that need to be performed on an object structure.

☺ The object structure is composed of objects that belong to different classes.

☺ The types of objects that occur in the object structure do not change often and their connections are consistent and predictable.

SOLUTION

This section contains two versions of the Visitor pattern. The first is an ideal solution that produces a very clean result. Unfortunately, there are many situations for which the ideal solution will not work or will be inefficient. The second version of the Visitor pattern works for a wider range of situations at the expense of introducing additional dependencies between classes.

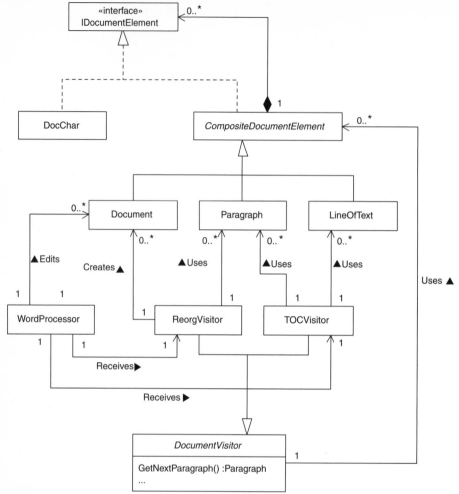

Figure 7.32 Table-of-Contents Classes

Figure 7.33 is a class diagram that shows the roles that classes play in the ideal version of the Visitor pattern.

Here is a description of the roles that classes play in Figure 7.33.

Client: Instances of classes in this role are responsible for manipulating an object structure and the objects that constitute it. They use ConcreteVisitor objects to perform computations on the object structures for which they are responsible.

ObjectStructure: An instance of a class in this role serves as the root object of an object structure. When visiting objects in an object structure, a Visitor object begins with an instance of an ObjectStructure class and then moves on to other objects in the object structure.

It is possible for a class to participate in the Visitor pattern in the Object Structure role and also to participate in the ConcreteElement role as an element of the object structure.

AbstractElement: A class in this role is an abstract base class of the objects that constitute an object structure. It defines an abstract method shown in Figure 7.33 as `accept`. It takes an `AbstractVisitor` object as its argument. Subclasses of an `AbstractElement` class provide an implementation of `accept` that calls a method of the `AbstractVisitor` object and then passes the `Abstract Visitor` object to the `accept` method of other `AbstractElement` objects.

ConcreteElement1, ConcreteElement2 . . .: Instances of classes in this role are elements of an object structure. Computations are done on the objects of an object structure by passing an `AbstractVisitor` object to a `Concrete Element` object's `Accept` subroutine. The `Accept` subroutine passes the `ConcreteElement` object to one of the `AbstractVisitor` object's subroutines so that it can include the `ConcreteElement` object in its computation. When this is done, the `ConcreteElement` object passes the `Abstract Visitor` object to other `ConcreteElement` objects' `Accept` subroutine.

AbstractVisitor: A class in this role is an abstract base class of classes that perform computations on the elements of an object structure. It defines a method for each class that its subclasses will visit, so that their instances can pass themselves to `Visitor` objects to be included in their computations.

ConcreteVisitor1, ConcreteVisitor2 . . .: Instances of classes in this role visit objects that constitute an object structure.

Figure 7.34 is a collaboration diagram that shows more clearly how `Visitor` objects collaborate with object structures.

Figure 7.34 shows the collaboration between a `Visitor` object and the elements of an object structure. After a `Visitor` object is presented to an `ObjectStructure` object, the `ObjectStructure` object passes the `Visitor` object to a `Concrete Element` object's `Accept` subroutine. The `ConcreteElement` object passes itself to the `Visitor` object's `Visit` subroutine to allow the object to include the `Visitor` object in its computation. The `ConcreteElement` object then passes the `Visitor` object to another `ConcreteElement` object so that the `Visitor` object may visit it. The cycle continues on, with the `Visitor` object being passed on to other `Concrete Element` objects. A `ConcreteElement` object may be associated with any number of other `ConcreteElement` objects. It may pass a visitor object to some, all or none of its associated `ConcreteElement` objects.

In this version of the Visitor pattern, the `AbstractElement` objects determine which elements of an object structure a `Visitor` object visits and the order in which it visits them. This works well only if it works for all kinds of `Visitor` objects to follow the same path in visiting elements of an object structure. It has the advantage of keeping `Visitor` classes independent of the structure of the object structure. However, there are situations where this does not work. These situations include:

- Visitors that modify an object structure. The example in the Context section of a visitor object that splits a document into multiple files is such a situation.

- Object structures that are so large that it would add an unacceptable amount of execution time for a `Visitor` to visit every object when it needs to visit only a small subset of the objects in the structure.

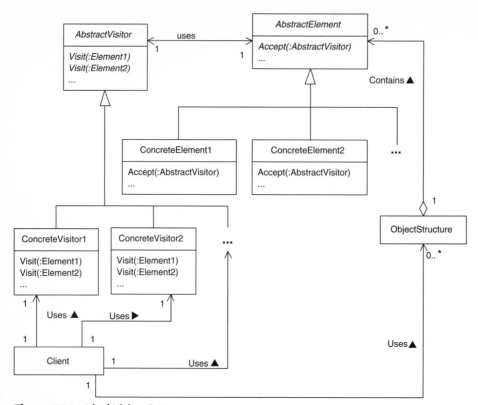

Figure 7.33   Ideal Visitor Pattern

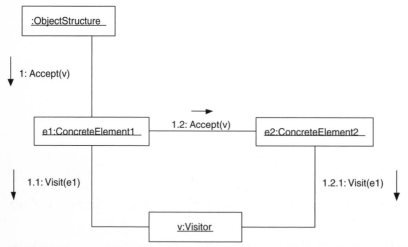

Figure 7.34   Ideal Visitor Collaboration

Figure 7.35 is a class diagram that shows another version of the Visitor pattern. In this version of the Visitor pattern, `Visitor` classes are responsible for navigating their own way through an object structure. Visitors organized in this way are able to modify an object structure or selectively navigate it. The drawback to this organization is that the `Visitor` classes are not as reusable because they have to make assumptions about the structure of an object structure in order to navigate through it.

In this version of the Visitor pattern, the `AbstractElement` class does not contain any methods specifically related to `Visitor` objects. Instead, the `Visitor` class defines methods that its subclasses use to navigate an object structure.

IMPLEMENTATION

When implementing the Visitor pattern, the first decision you will make is whether you can use the ideal version of the pattern. When it is possible, you should use the ideal version of the Visitor pattern because it takes less effort to implement and maintain. When you can't use the ideal version of the Visitor pattern, put as much of the logic as possible for navigating the object structure in the `Visitor` class rather than its subclasses. This will minimize the number of dependencies that `ConcreteVisitor` objects have on the object structure and make maintenance easier.

CONSEQUENCES

☺ The Visitor pattern makes it easy to add new operations on an object structure. Because the `ConcreteElement` classes have no dependencies on `Visitor` classes, adding a new `Visitor` class does not require making changes to an `AbstractElement` class or any of its subclasses.

☺ The Visitor pattern puts the logic for an operation in one cohesive `Concrete Visitor` class. This is easier to maintain than operations that are spread out over multiple `ConcreteElement` classes.

☺ A single `Visitor` object captures the state needed to perform an operation on an object structure. This is easier to maintain and more efficient than the way state information has to be passed as discrete values from one object to another.

☹ Another consequence of the Visitor pattern is the additional work it takes to add new `ConcreteElement` classes. The ideal version of the Visitor pattern requires you to add a new `visit` method to each `ConcreteVisitor` class for each `ConcreteElement` class that you add. For the other version of the Visitor pattern, you may need to change the logic that `Visitor` classes use to navigate the object structure.

☹ A direct consequence of the Visitor pattern is that `ConcreteElement` classes must provide access to enough of their state to allow `Visitor` objects to perform their computations. This may mean that you expose information that would otherwise be hidden by the class' encapsulation.

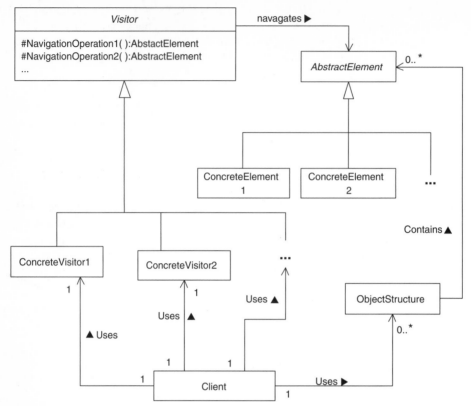

Figure 7.35 Visitor Pattern

CODE EXAMPLE

The following code is for some of the classes presented in the table of contents design under the "Context" heading. First is code for the WordProcessor class that contains top-level logic for a word processor. It is responsible for initiating operations that manipulate documents.

```
' This class contains the top level logic for a word processor
'
Public Class WordProcessor
    ' The doucment currently being editied
    Private activeDocument As Document


    ...


    ' word processor
    Public Sub New(ByVal f As String)
        activeDocument = New Document(f)
    End Sub 'New
```

```
    ' Reorganize a document into subfiles
    Public Sub Reorg(ByVal level As Integer)
        Dim rv As New ReorgVisitor(activeDocument, level)
    End Sub 'Reorg

    ' Build a table of contents
    Public Function BuildToc() As Toc
        Return New TocVisitor(activeDocument).BuildToc()
    End Function 'BuildToc
End Class 'WordProcessor
```

The next listing is for the DocumentVisitor class. The DocumentVisitor class is an abstract base class for classes that implement operations that have to visit many of the objects that constitute a document.

```
'
' Base class for classes that visit objects that make up a
' document and manipulate them.
'
Friend MustInherit Class DocumentVisitor
    ' The document that this object is manipulating
    Private myDocument As Document

    ' This index used to navigate children
    ' of document.
    Private docIndex As Integer = 0

    ' Constructor
    ' document - The Document to be visited
    Friend Sub New(ByVal document As Document)
        myDocument = document
    End Sub

    ' The document that this object is manipulating
    Protected ReadOnly Property Document() As Document
        Get
            Return myDocument
        End Get
    End Property

    ' The next paragraph that is a direct part of the document
    ' being manipulated or Nothing if there is no next paragraph
    Protected ReadOnly Property NextParagraph() As Paragraph
        Get
            Dim myDocument As Document = Document
            While docIndex < myDocument.Count
                Dim docElement As IDocumentElement
                docElement = myDocument.GetChild(docIndex)
                docIndex += 1
                If TypeOf docElement Is Paragraph Then
                    Return CType(docElement, Paragraph)
                End If
```

```
            End While
            Return Nothing
        End Get
    End Property
End Class 'DocumentVisitor
```

The next listing is for the `ReorgVisitor` class, which is responsible for visiting the paragraphs of a document and moving those at a specified level of organization in the table of contents to a separate document.

```
'
' Instances of this class reorganize a document into multiple documents.
'

Friend Class ReorgVisitor
    Inherits DocumentVisitor
    Private levels() As TocLevel

    Friend Sub New(ByVal document As Document, ByVal level As Integer)
        MyBase.New(document)
        Me.levels = document.TocLevels
        Dim p As Paragraph
        p = NextParagraph
        While p IsNot Nothing
            ' ...
            p = NextParagraph
        End While
    End Sub
End Class 'ReorgVisitor
```

As you can see from the preceding listing, the `ReorgVisitor` class concerns itself with `Document` and `Paragraph` objects.

The final listing is for the `TOCVisitor` class. The `TOCVisitor` class is responsible for building a table of contents. It navigates more deeply into a document's object structure, concerning itself with `Document` objects, `Paragraph` objects and `LineOf Text` objects. Its interest in `LineOfText` objects is that a table-of-contents entry will contain the text of the first `LineOfText` object in the paragraph that the table-of-contents entry corresponds to.

```
Imports System.Collections

'
' Instances of this class build a table of contents
'

Friend Class TocVisitor
    Inherits DocumentVisitor
    Private tocStyles As New Hashtable()

    Friend Sub New(ByVal document As Document)
        MyBase.New(document)
        Dim levels As TocLevel() = document.TocLevels
        ' put styles in a hashtable.
```

```
        For i As Integer = 0 To levels.Length - 1
            tocStyles(levels(i).Style) = levels(i)
        Next i
    End Sub 'New

    Friend Function BuildToc() As Toc
        Dim toc As New Toc()
        Dim p As Paragraph
        p = NextParagraph
        While p IsNot Nothing
            Dim styleName As String = p.Style
            If styleName IsNot Nothing Then
                Dim level As TocLevel = CType(tocStyles(styleName), TocLevel)
                If level IsNot Nothing Then
                    Dim firstLine As LineOfText = Nothing
                    For i As Integer = 0 To p.Count - 1
                        Dim e As IDocumentElement = p.GetChild(i)
                        If TypeOf e Is LineOfText Then
                            firstLine = CType(e, LineOfText)
                            Exit For
                        End If
                    Next i
                End If
            End If
            p = NextParagraph
        End While
        Return toc
    End Function 'BuildToc
End Class 'TocVisitor
```

RELATED PATTERNS

Iterator: The Iterator pattern is an alternative to the Visitor pattern when the object structure to be navigated has a linear structure.

Little Language: In the Little Language pattern, you can use the Visitor Pattern to implement the interpreter part of the pattern.

Composite: The Visitor pattern is often used with object structures that are organized according to the Composite pattern.

Hashed Adapter Objects

SYNOPSIS

Dispatch a method call to an adapter object chosen using the content of an arbitrary object. The arbitrary object is used to find the adapter object in a hash table.

CONTEXT

Suppose that a method is required to perform different actions based on an object reference given to the method. The usual technique for implementing this sort of decision is to use a chain of `if` statements or a `switch` statement.

If the number of comparisons that must be made using `if` statements is very large, then the amount of time that it takes to perform the comparisons may be a performance issue. When an object reference must be compared with many other object references, there are faster techniques than using a chain of `if` statements.

We can view the problem as a searching problem. If we put the object references in a data structure, the problem is reduced to selecting a data structure we can search as quickly as possible. The data structure must also allow an additional object to be associated with each object reference. The purpose of the additional object will be to determine what to do when an object reference in the data structure matches a given object reference.

The additional objects will be adapter objects. In other words, the objects will all implement a common interface. The interface will define a function or subroutine that is called when the adapter object is fetched from the data structure. The adapter objects implement the function or subroutine to call another object's function or subroutine that performs the desired action.

The data structure that best meets our needs is a hash table. On average, only about one comparison is required to find an object in a hash table. The drawback to a hash table is that when you fetch objects sequentially from a hash table, the order of the objects is not predictable. Since that is not a problem for this purpose, a hash table seems optimal. The time required to find an object in most other data structures varies with the number of objects in the data structure.

Let's consider a concrete example. Suppose that you are writing a program that has to read and process a file. The file is organized into records. The design of the program requires it to construct an object to encapsulate the contents of each record before using the contents of the record. Figure 7.36 is a class diagram that shows part of the design.

A `FileProcessor` object reads groups of bytes from `FileStream` objects. These groups of bytes are called records. Each record begins with a sequence of 8-bit characters that identify the type of record that it is. The identifying sequence of characters is followed by a `':'` character. What follows that `':'` character varies with the type or record.

`FileProcessor` objects convert each record to a string. `FileProcessor` objects pass the strings to a `RecordFactory` object's `CreateRecord` function. The `Create Record` function returns an instance of a concrete subclass of the `RecordObject` class. The record type determines subclass of `RecordObject`.

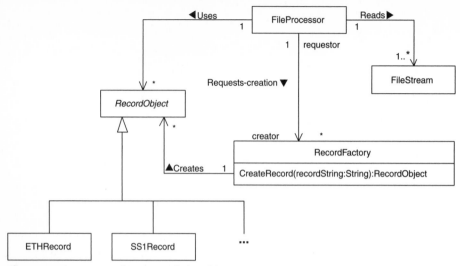

Figure 7.36 Encapsulate Records in Objects

When the time comes to tune your program, you find that it spends a dispropor-tionate amount of time in the `RecordFactory` class's `createRecord` method. You notice that there are over 300 types of records. The test to determine the type of a record is coded as a chain of `if` statements like this:

```
If type = "ETH" Then
    Return New ETHRecord(record)
ElseIf type = "SS1" Then
    Return New SS1Record(record)
. . .
```

You conclude that a lookup in a hash table will be a lot faster than those string com-parisons. The cost of looking up a string in a hash table is typically equivalent to just a few string comparisons. To implement this idea, you add some classes to your design, as shown in the class diagram in Figure 7.37.

In the optimized design in Figure 7.37, classes have been added that correspond to each subclass of `RecordObject`. These classes implement an interface called `IRecordCreator`. An instance of these classes is responsible for creating instances of the corresponding `RecordObject` subclass. A `RecordFactory` object uses objects that implement the `IRecordCreator` interface to create instances of concrete sub-classes of `RecordObject`.

During its initialization, a `RecordFactory` object creates one instance of each class that implements the `IRecordCreator` interface. It associates each of these objects with a string that identifies the record type of the `RecordObject` subclass that the `IRecordCreator` object can instantiate. It delegates the maintenance of these associ-ations to a `Hashtable` object.

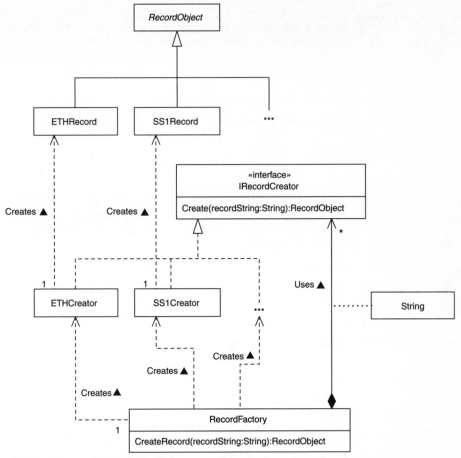

Figure 7.37 Hashed Adapters to Create RecordObjects

A RecordFactory object passes each pair of string and IRecordCreator objects to a Hashtable object's Add subroutine so that each string is a key having the IRecordCreator object as its associated value.

As the program processes a file, it passes strings containing the records it reads to a RecordFactory object's CreateRecord function. The CreateRecord function uses the substring that identifies the record type to get the associated IRecord Creator object from the Hashtable object. The CreateRecord method then makes a polymorphic call to the IRecordCreator object's Create function, passing it the record string. This create method creates and returns an instance of its Record Object class.

The collaboration diagram in Figure 7.38 shows an example of these interactions. It shows what happens when an SS1 record is passed to a RecordFactory object's createRecord method.

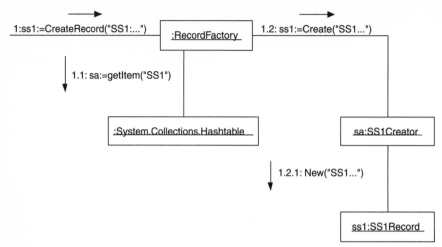

Figure 7.38   Creating an SS1 Record Object

FORCES

☺ There is a large `Select` statement or a long chain of `if` statements that perform `Equals` tests between one object and many other objects; the chain of `if` statements takes a disproportionately large amount of execution time.

☺ An action to be performed is determined by `Equals` tests between a single object and a variable set of other objects.

☺ The set of object-action pairs may grow, shrink, or otherwise vary over time.

☺ A hash table data structure allows a value associated with a key object to be found in an amount of time that is relatively independent of the number of objects in the hash table, provided that certain conditions are met. Hash table data structures are discussed in more detail under the "Implementation" heading.

☹ If there are only a few different objects to be tested, the hash table lookup may take longer than a chain of `if` statements. As with all optimizations, it is best to determine though actual timings whether or not the hash table lookup is faster than a chain of `if` statements.

Even if the chain of `if` statements is long, if one object is chosen much more frequently than the others, it may be possible to achieve better results by putting it at the beginning of an `if` chain.

☹ Though the use of a hash table may result in faster execution, a hash table and adapter classes will consume more memory than a chain of `if` statements.

☹ The sheer number of adapter classes to be created may take a prohibitively long amount of time to code. However, it is often the case that the adapter classes have a strong structural similarity to each other. Sometimes they vary in as few ways as the name of the class and the name of the method that they call.

If they are structurally similar, it is usually possible to automate most of their creation using such tools as editor macros or stand-alone macro processors.

SOLUTION

The givens for the Hashed Adapter Objects pattern are a set of actions and a corresponding set of objects. When an action is to be selected and then performed, the selection is based on called the `Equals` function of the corresponding objects. If one of the corresponding objects is equal to a given object, then the action corresponding to that object is performed. The class diagram in Figure 7.39 shows the organization that the Hashed Adapter Objects pattern provides for handling this.

Here are descriptions of the roles that objects, classes, and interfaces play in the Hashed Adapter Objects pattern:

IAction: An interface in this role defines a function or subroutine, shown in the above diagram as `DoIt`, that a `Client` class can call to get an action performed.

Action: Classes in these roles implement the `IAction` interface and encapsulate a behavior used by a client object. Many of these classes do not directly implement the behavior, but are adapter classes that delegate the behavior to another class that does not implement the `IAction` interface.

ActionKey: Instances of classes in this role are associated with an `Action` object. A `Hashtable` object is usually used to manage the association between `ActionKey` and `Action` objects.

Client: When an instance of a class in this role needs to perform an action associated with an `ActionKey` object, it presents the object to a `Hashtable` object. The `Hashtable` object returns to it an object that implements the `IAction` interface. The `Client` object then calls the `IAction` object's `DoIt` method to perform the needed action.

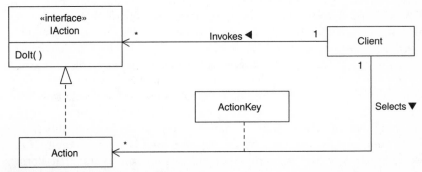

Figure 7.39   Hashed Adapters Classes

IMPLEMENTATION

This pattern has a fairly straightforward implementation.

The Hash Table Data Structure

The most common way to efficiently manage associations between `ActionKey` objects and `Action` objects is to use a `System.Collections.Hashtable` object. A `Hashtable` object encapsulates a hash table data structure. A hash table data structure associates key objects with value objects, so that given that an object that is in the hash table as a key object its associated value object can be found quickly.

The way a hash table data structure works is that when it is given a key object to store or find, it calls the object's `hashCode` function. It uses the value returned by the `GetHashCode` function to determine where in the data structure the object will be stored or looked for. The `GetHashCode` function returns an `Integer` value, so there will generally be more hash code values than there will be places in the data structure. Hash table algorithms resolve this difficulty by associating each place in the data structure with multiple hash code values. That means more than one object may want to be stored in the same place in a hash table. When this actually happens it is called a *collision*.

When there are no collisions, getting the value object associated with a key object involves these steps:

- Call the key object's `GetHashCode` function.
- Look at the place in the data structure where the hash code says that the key object should be if it is in the data structure.
- Determine if the object is there. If an object is in that place in the data structure, determine if it is the same object by calling its `Equals` function.
- If it is there, return the associated value object.

Different hash table algorithms handle collisions differently. However, all techniques for handling collisions require additional searching. Therefore, the time it takes to find something in a hash table is independent of the number of things in the hash table if there are no collisions in the hash table.

It is not generally possible to prevent collisions in a hash table. However, you can arrange for collisions to be unlikely. Usually, the most important thing to control is how full you allow a hash table to get. If a hash table contains more objects than it has places to store them, then it is certain that the hash table contains collisions. As a hash table goes from being 100 percent full to empty, the likelihood that the hash table contains collisions drops from 100 percent to 0. Classes that implement a hash table data structure usually provide a way of specifying an upper bound on how full a hash table may get. If the hash table gets any fuller than that, they enlarge the hash table to keep it within the limit.

The other thing that can affect the performance of hash tables is the quality of the `GetHashCode` functions implemented by the objects stored in the hash table. If the `GetHashCode` function of two different objects returns the same value that storing them both in a hash table will always produce a collision. Therefore, it is important that

`GetHashCode` functions be implemented in a way that makes it unlikely that the `GetHashCode` function of two unequal objects will return the same value.

Alternate Data Structures

There are two reasons for using the Hashed Adapters pattern. One is to efficiently dispatch to a selected action. The other is to have the flexibility to dynamically add and remove actions. When you are using Hashed Adapters for flexibility and you have just a few actions to select from, using a `Hashtable` may not be the most efficient to manage the associations between keys and actions when there are just a few of them. The .NET documentation suggests using a `ListDictionary` for 10 or fewer items. If you are not sure whether it is better to use a `Hashtable` or `ListDictionary`, you might try using a `HybridDictionary`. A `HybridDictionary` uses a `ListDictionary` when there are just a few items, and switches to using a `Hashtable` when there are enough items to justify it.

Another alternative to `Hashtable` that you should consider is `Dictionary<K,V>`. The `Dictionary<K,V>` class is generic, so if you know at design time the types of objects that will be compared, you can use the `Dictionary<K,V>` class to implement the Hashed Adapters pattern in a type safe way.

CONSEQUENCES

☺ If a `Hashtable` class is well tuned, most of the cost of retrieving an action object from a `Hashtable` object will be one call to the given object's `GetHash Code` method and an average of one call to an `ActionKey` object's `Equals` function.

☺ The set of `ActionKey` objects in a `Hashtable` object can be changed during run time, as can the `Action` objects associated with them. That means that the set of objects associated with actions can be varied, as well as the actions associated with those objects.

CODE EXAMPLE

Following are listings of selected portions of the code that implements the design discussed under the "Context" heading. The first is a skeletal listing of a sample subclass of `RecordObject`. This listing shows that the `SS1Record` class, like the other subclasses of `RecordObject`, has a constructor that takes a record string as an argument.

```
'
' Instances of this class encapsulate the information in SS1 records.
'
Public Class Ss1Record
    Inherits RecordObject
```

```
        Public Sub New(ByVal recordString As String)
        End Sub
    End Class 'Ss1Record
```

The adapter classes that are used to create instances of SS1Record and other sub-classes of RecordObject all implement the IRecordCreator interface shown here:

```
    '
    ' Adaptor classes used to create instances of concrete subclasses of
    ' RecordObject implement this interface.
    '
    Public Interface IRecordCreator
        '
        ' Create a RecordObject to encapsulate the given record string.
        '
        Function Create(ByVal recordString As String) As RecordObject
    End Interface 'IRecordCreator
```

Following is a listing of an adapter class that implements the IRecordCreator interface's create method to invoke the constructor of the corresponding subclass of RecordObject.

```
    '
    ' Instances of this class are used to create instances of the SS1Record
    ' class.
    '
    Public Class Ss1Creator
        Implements IRecordCreator

        '
        ' Create a SS1Record to encapsulate the given record string.
        '
        Public Function Create(ByVal recordString As String) As RecordObject _
                    Implements IRecordCreator.Create
            Return New Ss1Record(recordString)
        End Function
    End Class 'Ss1Creator
```

Finally, following is a listing of the RecordFactory class that is responsible for managing the creation of RecordObject objects.

```
Imports System.Collections

Public Class RecordFactory
    Private creators As Hashtable

    ' Constructor
    Public Sub New()
        creators = New Hashtable()
        creators("ETH") = New EthCreator()
```

```
            creators("SS1") = New Ss1Creator()
    End Sub


    ' Create and return an instance of the concrete subclass of
    ' RecordObject that corresponds to the given record type in the
    ' given record string.
    Public Function createRecord(ByVal recordString As String) As
RecordObject
            'get record type
            Dim i As Integer = recordString.IndexOf(":"c)
            If i < 1 Then
                Throw New System.ApplicationException(recordString)
            End If
            Dim recordType As String = recordString.Substring(0, i)

            ' Create the recordObject
            Dim creator As IRecordCreator
            creator = CType(creators(recordType), IRecordCreator)
            If creator Is Nothing Then
                Throw New System.ApplicationException(recordType)
            End If
            Return creator.Create(recordString)
    End Function 'createRecord
End Class 'RecordFactory
```

RELATED PATTERNS

Adapter: The Hashed Adapter Objects pattern uses Adapter objects.

Lookup Table: Both the Hashed Adapter Objects pattern and the Lookup Table pattern (described in [Grand98]) involve the use of an aggregation. However, the aggegation serves a different purpose for each. The Lookup Table pattern uses an aggregation of precomputed results to save the time it will take to compute the results in the future. For the Hashed Adapter Objects pattern, the data structure itself is the source of the time savings.

Polymorphism: When it is possible to select a behavior based on the type of an object, the Polymorphism pattern (described in [Grand98]) produces a simpler result than the Hashed Adapter Objects pattern.

Single Threaded Execution: The Single Threaded Execution pattern is used to coordinate access by multiple threads to the hash table used by the Hashed Adapter Objects pattern.

Strategy: The Hashed Adapter Objects pattern can used to design the selection of strategy objects in the Strategy pattern.

Concurrency Patterns

Single Threaded Execution (439)
Static Locking Order (447)
Lock Object (453)
Guarded Suspension (459)
Balking (467)
Scheduler (471)
Read/Write Lock (483)
Producer-Consumer (493)
Double Buffering (499)
Asynchronous Processing (519)
Future (529)

The patterns in this chapter involve coordinating concurrent operations. These patterns primarily address two types of problems:

1. **Shared resources:** When concurrent operations access the same data or other shared resource, operations may interfere with each other if they access the resource at the same time. To ensure that operations on shared resources execute correctly, the operations must be sufficiently constrained to access their shared resource one at a time. However, if operations are overly constrained, then they may deadlock and not finish executing.

   Deadlock is a situation in which one operation waits for another operation to do something before it proceeds. Because each operation is waiting for the other to do something, they wait forever and never do anything.

2. **Sequence of operations:** If operations are constrained to access a shared resource one at a time, it may be necessary to ensure that they access the shared resource in a particular order. For example, an object cannot be removed from a data structure before it is added to the data structure.

The Single Threaded Execution pattern is the most important pattern in this chapter. Most shared resource issues can be resolved with just the Single Threaded Execution pattern, which ensures that no more than one thread at a time can access a resource. Situations in which the sequence of operations matters are less common. Such situations can be handled using the Scheduler pattern.

When two threads need single-threaded access to multiple objects, they can sometimes deadlock if they are trying to get single-threaded access to the same objects. Using the Static Locking Order pattern is a way to avoid this problem.

When an operation may require exclusive access to multiple resources, using the Lock Object pattern is a way to simplify coordination of access to the multiple resources by locking only one object.

The Guarded Suspension pattern provides guidance on what to do when a thread has exclusive access to a resource and discovers that it cannot complete the operation on that resource because something is not yet ready.

The Balking pattern is useful if an operation must be done either immediately or not at all.

The Read/Write Lock pattern is an alternative to one-at-a-time access if some operations can share the same resource and some operations cannot share.

The Producer-Consumer pattern is useful for coordinating objects that produce a resource with objects that consume the resource.

The Double Buffering pattern is a specialized form of the Producer-Consumer pattern that makes it more likely that resources will be produced before they are needed.

The Asynchronous Processing pattern describes how to avoid waiting for the results of an operation when you don't need to know the result immediately.

The Future pattern describes how to keep classes that invoke an operation from having to know if the operation is synchronous or asynchronous.

Single Threaded Execution

The Single Threaded Execution pattern is also known as Critical Section.

SYNOPSIS

Some functions and subroutines access data or other shared resources in a way that produces incorrect results if concurrent calls access the data or another resource at the same time. The Single Threaded Execution pattern solves this problem by preventing concurrent calls to functions and subroutines from resulting in their concurrent execution.

CONTEXT

Suppose that you are writing software for a system that monitors the flow of traffic on a major highway. At strategic locations on the highway, sensors in the road monitor the number of passing cars per minute. The sensors send information to a central computer. The central computer controls electronic signs located near major interchanges. The signs display messages to drivers, advising them of traffic conditions so that they can select alternate routes.

At the places in the road where sensors measure the flow of cars, there is a sensor for each traffic lane. The sensor in each lane is wired to a controller that totals the number of cars passing that place in the road each minute. The controller is attached to a transmitter that transmits each minute's total to the central computer. Figure 8.1 is a class diagram showing these relationships.

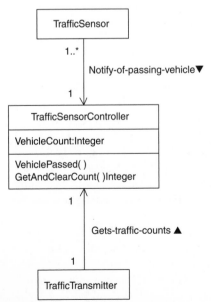

Figure 8.1   Traffic Sensor Classes

Here are descriptions of the classes that appear in Figure 8.1:

TrafficSensor: Each instance of this class corresponds to a physical sensor device. Each time a vehicle passes a physical sensor device, the corresponding instance of the `TrafficSensor` class calls a `TrafficSensorController` object's `VehiclePassed` subroutine. Each `TrafficSensor` object will have its own thread, allowing it to handle inputs from its associated sensor asynchronously of other sensors.

TrafficTransmitter: Instances of this class are responsible for transmitting the number of vehicles that pass a place on the road each minute. A `Traffic Transmitter` object gets the number of vehicles that have passed a place on the road by calling the `GetAndClearCount` function of its corresponding `TrafficSensorController` object. The `TrafficSensorController` object's `GetAndClearCount` function returns the number of vehicles that have passed the sensors since the previous call to the `GetAndClearCount` method.

TrafficSensorController: Instances of the `TrafficSensor` class and the `TrafficTransmitter` class call the functions and subroutines of the `Traffic SensorController` class to update, fetch, and clear the number of vehicles that have passed a place on the road.

It is possible for two `TrafficSensor` objects to call a `TrafficSensor Controller` object's `VehiclePassed` subroutine at the same time. If both calls were to execute at the same time, they would produce an incorrect result. Each call to `VehiclePassed` is supposed to increase the vehicle count by one. Two calls to `VehclePassed` should increase the vehicle count by two. However, if two calls to `VehiclePassed` execute at the same time, the vehicle count is incremented by one instead of two. Here is the sequence of events that would occur if both calls executed at the same time:

1. Both calls fetch the same value of `vehicleCount` at the same time.

2. Both calls add one to the same value.

3. Both calls store the same value in `vehicleCount`.

Clearly, allowing more than one call to `vehiclePassed` to execute at the same time will result in undercounting vehicles. A slight undercount of vehicles is not a serious problem for this application. However, there is a similar problem with more serious consequences.

A `TrafficTransmitter` object periodically calls a `TrafficSensor Controller` object's `GetAndClearCount` function. The `GetAndClearCount` function fetches the value of the `TrafficSensorController` object's `vehicleCount` variable and then sets it to zero. If `vehiclePassed` and `GetAndClearCount` are called at the same time, it creates a situation called a *race condition*.

A race condition is a situation whose outcome depends on the order in which concurrent operations finish. If `GetAndClearCount` finishes last, it sets the value of the `vehicleCount` variable to zero, wiping out the result of the call to `VehiclePassed`. This is just another way for small undercounts to happen. However, the problem is more serious if `VehiclePassed` finishes last.

If VehiclePassed finishes last, it replaces the zero set by GetAndClearCount with a value one greater than the value it fetched. This means the next call to Get AndClearCount will return a value that includes vehicles counted before the previous call to GetAndClearCount. Vehicles may be double counted, triple counted, or worse!

An overcount like this could be large enough to convince the central computer that a traffic jam is starting. It will respond to this sort of situation by displaying messages on electronic signs suggesting that drivers follow alternate routes. An error like this could cause a traffic jam!

A simple way to avoid these problems is to require that no more than one thread at a time executes a TrafficSensorController object's VehiclePassed subroutine or GetAndClearCount function. You can indicate this design decision by indicating that the concurrency of these methods is guarded: In a UML drawing, indicating that a method's concurrency is guarded is equivalent to specifying that it should be implemented in VB.NET with its entire body inside of a SyncLock statement. This is shown in Figure 8.2.

Any number of threads may call the guarded methods of the same object at the same time. However, only one thread at a time is allowed to execute the object's guarded methods. While one thread is executing an object's guarded methods, other threads wait until the thread is finished executing the object's guarded methods. When the thread is finished, a waiting thread is arbitrarily selected to execute the object's guarded methods next. This ensures single-threaded execution of an object's guarded methods.

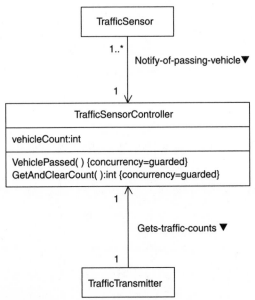

Figure 8.2 Synchronized Traffic Sensor Classes

FORCES

☺ A class has methods or properties that update or set instance or class variables.

☺ A method manipulates external resources that support only one operation at a time.

☺ The class's methods may be called concurrently by different threads.

☺ No time constraint requires a method to execute immediately when it is called.

SOLUTION

Ensure that operations that cannot correctly be performed concurrently are not performed concurrently. Accomplish this by making methods that should not be executed concurrently guarded. Figure 8.3 shows the general case.

The class in Figure 8.3 has two kinds of methods. It has unguarded methods named `SafeOp1`, `SafeOp2`, . . . that can safely execute concurrently. It has guarded methods named `UnsafeOp1`, `UnsafeOp2` . . . that are unsafe if executed concurrently. When different threads call the guarded methods of a `Resource` object at the same time, only one tread at a time is allowed to execute the methods. The rest of the threads wait for that thread to finish.

IMPLEMENTATION

Guarded methods are implemented in VB.NET by wrapping the body of the methods in a `SyncLock` statement, like this:

```
Private lockObject As New Object
Public Sub foo()
    SyncLock lockObject
        ...
    End SyncLock
End Sub
```

It may take longer to call guarded methods than unguarded methods. Consider the collaboration diagram in Figure 8.4.

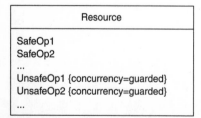

Figure 8.3 Single Threaded Execution Pattern

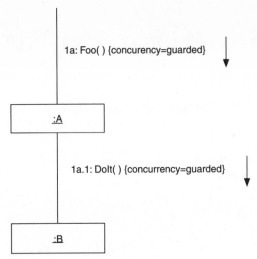

Figure 8.4 Lock Factoring

Figure 8.4 shows a guarded method in class A calling class B's DoIt method. The DoIt method is guarded. If the DoIt method is called only from guarded methods of class A, then as an optimization, it is possible to make the DoIt method an unguarded method. It will still be executed by only one thread at a time, because it is only called by methods that are executed by one thread at a time.

This optimization is called *lock factoring*. Lock factoring is an unsafe optimization in the sense that if the program is modified so that concurrent calls can be made to the DoIt method, it will stop working correctly. If you decide this optimization is worth doing manually, you should put comments in design diagrams and code to warn and remind people that the optimization has been performed.

CONSEQUENCES

- ☺ If a class has methods that access variables or other resources in a way that is not thread-safe, you can make the class's methods thread-safe by making them guarded.

- • Making methods guarded that do not need to be can reduce performance. There are two reasons for this. One reason is the additional overhead of the SyncLock statement. The other reason is that if a method is guarded but does not need to be, then its callers may wait for a lock when there is no need to wait.

- ☹ Making methods guarded can introduce the opportunity for threads to become *deadlocked*. Deadlock occurs when two threads each have exclusive use of a resource, and each thread is waiting for the other to release its resource before continuing. Since each thread is waiting for a resource that the other thread already has exclusive access to, both threads will wait forever without gaining access to the resource they are waiting for. Consider the example in Figure 8.5.

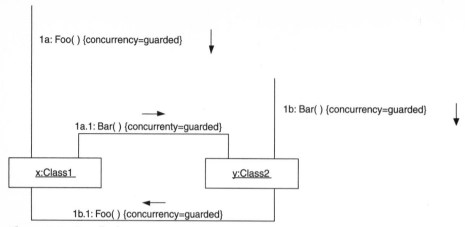

Figure 8.5   Deadlock

In Figure 8.5, thread 1a calls object x's Foo method, and thread 1b calls object y's Bar method at the same time. Thread 1a then calls object y's Bar method and waits for thread 1b to finish its call to that method. Thread 1b calls object x's Foo method and waits for thread 1a to finish its call to that method. At that point, the two threads are deadlocked. Each is waiting for the other to finish its call.

Deadlock can also involve more than two threads. Deadlock is sometimes called *deadly embrace*.

CODE EXAMPLE

The following is some of the code that implements the traffic sensor design discussed under the "Context" heading. A traffic sensor detects the passing of a vehicle over a place in a traffic lane. Each traffic sensor is associated with a TrafficSensor Controller object. When a traffic sensor detects a passing vehicle, it calls the TrafficSensorController object's VehiclePassed method. The Vehicle Passed method is responsible for maintaining a running total of the vehicles detected by the traffic sensor.

Here is a listing of the TrafficSensorController class:

```
Imports System

Namespace Traffic
    '
    ' Instances of this class maintain a running total of the
    ' number of vehicles that have passed the traffic sensors
    ' that notify them.
    '
    Public Class TrafficSensorController
        Private vehicleCount As Integer = 0
        Private lockObject As New Object
```

```
        Public Sub New()
        End Sub


        '
        ' This method is called when a traffic sensor detects
        ' a passing vehicle.  It increments the vehicle count
        ' by one.
        '
        Public Sub VehiclePassed()
            SyncLock lockObject
                vehicleCount += 1
            End SyncLock
        End Sub 'VehiclePassed

        Public Function GetAndClearCount() As Integer
            SyncLock lockObject
                Dim count As Integer = vehicleCount
                vehicleCount = 0
                Return count
            End SyncLock
        End Function 'GetAndClearCount
    End Class 'TrafficSensorController
End Namespace 'Traffic
```

Notice that both the `TrafficSensorController` class's `VehiclePassed` subroutine and its `GetAndClearCount` function are guarded.

The next class shown is the `TrafficTransmitter` class. Instances of the `TrafficTransmitter` class are responsible for transmitting the number of vehicles that have passed a place in the road each minute.

```
Imports System
Imports System.Messaging
Imports System.Threading

Namespace Traffic
    '
    ' Summary description for TrafficTransmitter.
    '
    Public Class TrafficTransmitter
        '
        ' The TrafficSensorController object that this
        ' object gets vehicle counts from.
        '
        Private controller As TrafficSensorController


        '
        ' A message queue that will provide reliable delivery
        ' of vehicle counts that this object transmits.
        '
        Private msgQue As MessageQueue
```

```
    '
    ' This object has its own thread so that it can
    ' initiate the transmission of vehicle counts
    ' independently of whatever else is going on.
    '
    Private myThread As Thread


    '
    ' Constructor
    '
    ' mq - A message queue object that will provice reliable
    ' delivery of vehicle counts to a central computer.
    Public Sub New( ByVal theController As TrafficSensorController, _
                    ByVal mq As MessageQueue)
        controller = theController
        msgQue = mq
        myThread = New Thread(AddressOf Me.Transmit)
        myThread.Start()
    End Sub 'New


    '
    ' Transmit a vehicle count every minute.
    '
    Private Sub Transmit()
        While True
            Thread.Sleep((60 * 1000))
            msgQue.Send(controller.GetAndClearCount())
        End While
    End Sub 'Transmit
End Class 'TrafficTransmitter
End Namespace 'Traffic
```

RELATED PATTERNS

Most other concurrency patterns use the Single Threaded Execution pattern.

Static Locking Order

This pattern was described previously in [Heaney99].

SYNOPSIS

If two objects need exclusive access to the same set of resources, they can become dead-locked with each holding a lock on one resource while waiting for the other to release its resource. Avoid such deadlocks by ensuring that all objects acquire locks on resources in the same order.

CONTEXT

Suppose that you work for a company that provides field service for computers. You have been asked to solve a problem that recently started happening.

Two of your company's applications occasionally hang. The problem is intermittent and only occurs in the evening. One of the applications is a program that field technicians use to enter information about what they did at a particular site, so that the appropriate parties can be billed and inventory levels adjusted.

The other program runs at a scheduled time every evening. It goes through the inventory transactions of the day and, when appropriate, sends messages to part vendors to register warranty information.

Most of the time, these programs work perfectly. Occasionally, a field technician working the evening shift will be entering information about a completed repair, and both the warranty registration program and the technician's session hang.

Upon investigation, you find that the problem is a deadlock between the two programs. The program that the technician uses gets a lock on records in the customer database when the technician indicates which customer(s) that last job was for. As the technician enters the parts that were used in the repair job, the program also locks records in the inventory database. The warranty registration program obtains lock on records in the inventory database and then tries to access the customer database to complete the warranty information for a part.

The problem is that occasionally the technician's program will have a customer record locked and want access to an inventory record. But the inventory program already has a lock on that inventory record and is trying to access the customer record that the other program already has locked. The two programs wait indefinitely to access the record that the other program has locked.

You solve the problem by modifying the warranty registration program so that it locks customer records before it locks the corresponding inventory record.

FORCES

☺ Multiple objects need to access a set of resources. The operations they perform on these resources require that some or all other objects be prevented from concurrently accessing the resources.

☺ Dynamically determining at run time whether granting an object access to a resource will result in a deadlock can be a very expensive operation.

☺ Some transaction management mechanisms automatically detect deadlocks among transactions that they manage. It will generally take them a while to detect the deadlock after it occurs. They way that most of these transaction managers handle a deadlock is to cause some or all of the transactions involved to fail. For the viewpoint of an application, such failures appear to be intermittent failures of the application.

If it is important that the transaction behave in a reliable and predictable way, then it is important for it to avoid such deadlocks.

☺ Objects access a set of resources that is either static or is a set of resources that always fill a static set of roles.

☹ If resources can fill multiple roles, then it may take a prohibitively long amount of time to determine in advance if a particular pattern of accessing resource can result in a deadlock.

SOLUTION

If objects lock multiple shared resources, ensure that the resources are always locked in the same relative order. For example, if there are four resources, A, B, C, and D, then you could require all objects to lock them in that order. So, one object may lock B, C, and D in that order. Another object may lock A and C in that order. However, no object may lock C and B in that order.

The same strategy applies to situations in which the specific resources that objects use vary, but the objects always fill the same roles. In this sort of situation, you apply the relative ordering to the roles rather than the resources. In the example under the "Context" heading, the specific database records that the programs use vary with the transaction; however, they always play the same roles.

CONSEQUENCES

☺ Use of the Static Locking Order pattern allows you to ensure that objects will be able to lock resources without deadlocking.

☹ Forcing all objects to lock resources in a predetermined order can sometimes increase the amount of time it takes some objects to perform an operation. For an example, consider the case of the warranty registration program discussed under the "Context" heading.

In its original implementation, it only needed to fetch an inventory record once. Forcing it to lock a customer record before locking an inventory record requires it to fetch the inventory record twice. The first time it fetches an inventory record, it may discover that there is a warranty to register and which customer is involved. It then locks the appropriate customer record. It must then fetch the inventory record a second time after locking it.

☹ If there are a large number of objects to be locked, the amount of time the amount of time that it takes to determine the proper locking order may be prohibitively large. In such cases, the Lock Object pattern may be a better solution.

IMPLEMENTATION

The usual way to get a lock on an object is to use a `SyncLock` statement. A `Sync Lock` statement uses the physical organization of code to determine what is locked and when. `SyncLock` statements are very convenient when there is a fixed set of objects to be locked in a fixed order.

Sometimes you want to apply the Static Locking Order pattern to a set of objects that is determined at run time. This sort of situation involves determining the number of objects to lock and the sequence in which to lock them at run time. Using `SyncLock` statements to do this is awkward at best. Fortunately, the .NET Framework gives us another way to lock objects that is more flexible.

The object-locking support provided by the .NET Framework is based on two static subroutines. Passing an object to the subroutine `System.Montor.Enter` causes the currently executing thread to get a lock on the object passed to `System.Montor. Enter`. The `Montor.Enter` subroutine does not return until it gets a lock on the object passed to it. The subroutine `System.Montor.Exit` releases the lock on the object passed to it.

The code generated for a `SyncLock` statement uses these two subroutines to obtain and release locks on an object. Consider this example:

```
SyncLock foo
    x += 2
    y += 5
End SyncLock
```

The preceding example is equivalent to this code:

```
Monitor.Enter(foo)
Try
    x += 2
    y += 5
Finally
    Monitor.Exit(foo)
End Try
```

The code example for this pattern uses these two subroutines.

KNOWN USES

The author has seen the Static Locking Order pattern used a number of proprietary applications.

CODE EXAMPLE

The code example for the Static Locking pattern is a utility class that allows you to lock multiple in-memory objects.

```vb
Imports System.Collections
Imports System.Threading

Namespace staticLockingOrder
    '
    ' Utility class for locking multiple objects in a way that
    ' avoids deadlock.
    '
    Public Class MultiMonitor

        '
        ' Lock all of the objects in the given collection.
        ' All of the objects in the collection must implement
        ' the ICollection interface.
        '
        ' objs - A collection of objects to be locked.  All
        ' objects in the collection must implement the
        ' IComparable interface.
        '
        ' This method locks all of the objects in the
        ' collection in a consistent.  It does not return
        ' until it has locked all of the objects in the
        ' collection.
        '
        ' This method guarantees that concurrent calls will
        ' not deadlock by locking the objects in the
        ' collection in their sorted order.
        '
        ' Exception InvalidCastException -
        '    If any of the objects in the collection do not
        '    implement the ICollection.
        Public Overloads Shared Sub Enter(ByVal objs As ICollection)
            Dim myArray(objs.Count) As IComparable
            objs.CopyTo(myArray, 0)
            Array.Sort(myArray)
            For i As Integer = 0 To myArray.Length - 1
                Monitor.Enter(myArray(i))
            Next i
        End Sub 'Enter


        '
        ' Lock all of the objects in the given collection.
        ' The locking order is determined using an
        ' IComparer object.
        '
```

```
' objs - A collection of objects to be locked.
' comparer -  An object to determine the locking order.
'
' This method locks all of the objects in the
' collection.  It does not return until it has
' locked all of the objects in the collection.
' This method guarantees that concurrent calls will
' not deadlock by locking the objects in the
' collection in their sorted order.
'
Public Overloads Shared Sub Enter(ByVal objs As ICollection, _
                                  ByVal comparer As IComparer)
    Dim myArray(objs.Count) As IComparable
    objs.CopyTo(myArray, 0)
    Array.Sort(myArray, comparer)
    For i As Integer = 0 To myArray.Length - 1
        Monitor.Enter(myArray(i))
    Next i
End Sub 'Enter


'
' Release the lock on all of the objects in the given
' collection.  The locking order is determined using
' an IComparer object.
'
' objs - A collection of objects whose locks are to be to be
' released.
'
Public Shared Sub MyExit(ByVal objs As ICollection)
    For Each obj As Object In objs
        Monitor.Exit(obj)
    Next obj
End Sub 'MyExit
End Class 'MultiMonitor
End Namespace 'staticLockingOrder
```

RELATED PATTERNS

Lock Object: The Lock Object pattern provides another way to gain single-threaded access to multiple objects without deadlocking. When there are a large number of objects involved, the Lock Object pattern may give significantly better performance.

The performance of the Static Locking Order pattern gets worse as the number of objects to be locked increases. The performance of the Lock Object pattern does not vary with the number of objects to be locked. However, the Lock Object pattern requires that objects to be locked and the classes that are supposed to respect the lock all be designed to cooperate.

Lock Object

SYNOPSIS

An operation is to be performed that requires single-threaded access to multiple objects. Save time and complexity by having an additional object that is locked instead of the multiple objects that participate directly in the operation.

CONTEXT

Suppose that you are writing a multiplayer game program. The game is played in real time. Each player is able to initiate operations that affect the state of multiple game objects. To ensure that each object's state change happens correctly, you use the Single Threaded Execution pattern.

For the game to work correctly, changes to some game objects must appear to happen at the same time. To happen at the same time without interference from the actions of another player, you want to ensure that the thread responsible for changing the state of the objects has exclusive access to the objects.

One way to arrange for threads to have exclusive access to the objects is to require threads to get a lock on each of the objects before they try to modify any of the objects' states. There are some difficulties with this type of solution:

- Simply having to get a lock on multiple objects requires a few extra CPU cycles, but that is the smallest of the problems.

- You need to ensure that when threads try to lock multiple objects, they do not get stuck in a deadlock. You don't want one thread to be waiting to get a lock on an object that another thread has a lock on and will not release until it can get a lock on an object that the first thread has a lock on.

  - It is possible to avoid deadlocks such as these by using the Static Locking Order pattern.

  - This sort of deadlock avoidance adds complexity and overhead.

Clearly, there are good reasons to look for an alternate solution to the problem of ensuring that a thread has exclusive access to multiple game objects. You want a solution that avoids the complexity and overhead of locking individual objects.

A way to simplify this problem is to insist that only one thread at a time will have access to any game objects. This restriction will sometimes force threads to wait that would not otherwise need to wait. However, you decide that the complexity and overhead that this saves you is more valuable.

To implement this simplified strategy, you create one additional object that will be used only as a lock object. The rule will be that no thread will do anything to affect the state of a game object unless it holds the lock on the lock object.

FORCES

☺ Operations are to be performed that require exclusive access to the objects they affect to ensure that they are correct.

☺ Having to lock an arbitrary set of objects in order to perform an operation adds complexity and overhead to the operation.

☺ It is acceptable if operations sometimes have to wait for other operations to complete before starting. Your performance requirements are soft enough that sometimes having to wait for another operation to complete even when it is not strictly necessary is acceptable.

SOLUTION

Arrange for threads to have exclusive access to a set of objects by having the threads acquire a lock on an object that exists only for this purpose. An object that exists only for the purpose of being the subject of locks is called a *lock object*. Collaborations involving a lock object follow the pattern shown in Figure 8.6.

In Figure 8.6, a Foo object's doIt method is called. The doIt method begins by getting a lock on the object lockObject. Once it has a lock on the lockObject object, it performs operations on other objects and then releases its lock on the lock object.

There are different ways that a lock object can be incorporated into the organization of some classes. Figure 8.7 shows a simple organization.

Figure 8.7 shows an abstract class. The class has a shared function called GetLock-Object. Subclasses of the abstract class call the GetLockObject function to get the lock object. This way of managing a lock object works well when you want all instances of one or more classes to share the same lock object.

Other ways of managing lock objects are discussed under the "Implementation" heading. Because there are a variety of reasonable ways to manage access lock objects, they are not really part of the pattern. This pattern is about using a lock object, not managing access to it.

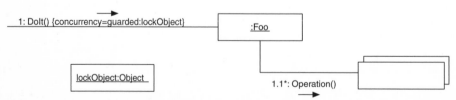

Figure 8.6 Lock Object Collaboration

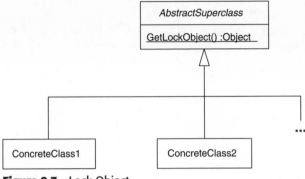

Figure 8.7   Lock Object

IMPLEMENTATION

There are a variety of ways to manage access to a lock object. The main considerations in choosing the way to manage a lock object is how diverse the objects are that will use the lock object and whether you need more than one lock object.

The example of lock object management in Figure 8.7 shows classes accessing a lock object through an inherited shared method. This organization works well when it is appropriate to lock all the instances of a class or classes to perform an operation.

When the set of objects to lock for an operation are not mostly instances of the same class, there are typically other groupings. In these cases, the way lock objects are managed is typically driven by the organization of the objects they are used to lock. For example, consider the case of objects organized into a tree, as shown in Figure 8.8.

Figure 8.8 shows objects organized in a tree. The objects are instances of different classes. However, all the objects have a method named GetLockObject that returns the lock object to use for operations on these objects. The way these objects implement the getLockObject method is that if they are not the root of the tree, their Get LockObject method calls the parent object's getLockObject method. If the object is the root of the tree, then it provides the actual lock object.

If an operation needs exclusive access to any objects in the tree, it arbitrarily picks one of the objects it needs exclusive access to and calls its GetLockObject method. The GetLockObject method of every object in the tree returns the same lock object. Once the operation has a lock on the lock object, it has exclusive access to all of the objects in the tree.

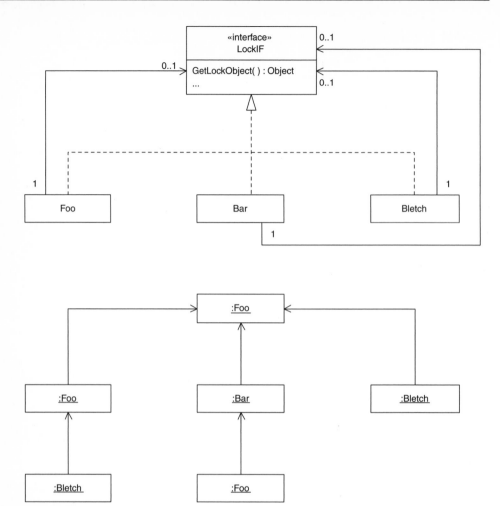

Figure 8.8 Objects in a Tree

CONSEQUENCES

☺ By using the Lock Object pattern, you can ensure that only one thread at a time is accessing a set of objects. You are able to accomplish this with very little complexity or overhead.

☹ An operation that uses the Lock Object pattern has exclusive access to all objects that may possibly be affected by the operation or any other operation. This means that if two operations could otherwise execute concurrently because they do not affect any of the same objects, they won't.

CODE EXAMPLE

The code example for this pattern involves some classes that follow the game object scenario described under the "Context" heading. Here is part of the abstract superclass for classes used to model game classes.

```
Namespace lockObject
    '
    ' Abstract class for objects that model object that are
    ' part of this game's state.
    '
    Public Class AbstractGameObject
        Private Shared myLockObject As New Object()
        '
        ' True if this object is glowing.
        '
        Private myGlowing As Boolean
        '
        ' Return the lock object to use for instances of all
        ' subclasses of this object.
        '
        Public Shared ReadOnly Property LockObject() As Object
            Get
                Return myLockObject
            End Get
        End Property
        '
        ' Determine whether this object is glowing.
        '
        Public Property Glowing() As Boolean
            Get
                Return myGlowing
            End Get
            Set(ByVal value As Boolean)
                myGlowing = Value
            End Set
        End Property
    End Class 'AbstractGameObject
End Namespace 'lockObject
```

Notice that the AbstractGameObject class has a LockObject property. The value of the LockObject property is an object to use as a lock object. The class also has a Boolean property to determine if an object is glowing. The next listing is for a subclass of the AbstractGameObject class that uses both of these.

```
Imports System.Collections

Namespace lockObject
    '
    ' This class is responsible for representing character in a
    ' game.
    '
    Public Class GameCharacter
        Inherits AbstractGameObject

        Private myWeapons As New ArrayList()

        Public Sub DropAllWeapons()
            SyncLock LockObject
                For Each thisWeapon As Weapon In myWeapons
                    thisWeapon.Glowing = True
                Next thisWeapon '...
            End SyncLock
        End Sub 'DropAllWeapons
    End Class 'GameCharacter
End Namespace 'lockObject
```

The GameCharacter class has a subroutine called DropAllWeapons that begins by getting a lock on the lock object that is the value of the LockObject property. It inherits the LockObject property from the AbstractGameObject class. The method then sets to true the Glowing property of the Weapon objects associated with the character. It continues doing other things while having exclusive access to all game objects.

RELATED PATTERNS

Single Threaded Execution: The Lock Object pattern is a refinement to the Single Threaded Execution pattern.

Static Locking Order: The Static Locking Order pattern provides another way to gain single-threaded access to multiple objects without deadlocking. The Static Locking Order does not require the level of cooperation between its participants that the Lock Object pattern requires.

Guarded Suspension

This pattern is based on material that appeared in [Lea97].

SYNOPSIS

If a condition exists that prevents a method from doing what it is supposed to do, suspend execution of the method until the condition no longer exists.

CONTEXT

Suppose that you have to create a class that implements a queue data structure. A queue is a first in, first out data structure. Objects are removed from a queue in the same order in which they are added. Figure 8.9 shows a Queue class.

The Queue class has two methods that are of particular interest:

- The push method adds objects to a queue.
- The pull method removes objects from the queue.

The .NET Framework does have a Queue class. However, the behavior of that class is not quite what you need. When you try to remove an object from an instance of System.Collections.Queue when it does not contain any objects, it throws an exception.

What you want to happen is that if a Queue object's pull method is called when the queue is empty, it does not return until there is an object in the queue for it to return. An object can be added to the queue while the pull method is waiting to return if another thread calls the push method. Both push and pull are guarded to allow multiple threads to safely make concurrent calls.

Simply making both methods guarded creates a problem when there is a call to a Queue object's pull method and the queue is empty. The pull method waits for a call to the push method to provide it with an object to return. However, because they are both guarded, calls to the push method cannot execute until the pull method returns, and the pull method will never return until a call to the push method returns.

A solution to the problem is to add a precondition to the pull method so that it does not execute while the queue is empty. Consider the collaboration diagram in Figure 8.10.

```
┌─────────────────────────────────────────────┐
│                   Queue                       │
├─────────────────────────────────────────────┤
│ Push(:Object) {concurrency=guarded}           │
│ Pull( ):Object {concurrency=guarded}          │
│ ...                                           │
└─────────────────────────────────────────────┘
```

Figure 8.9   Queue Class

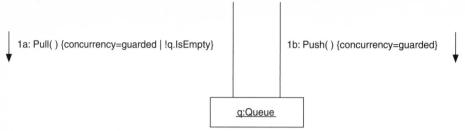

Figure 8.10   Queue Collaboration

The collaboration diagram in Figure 8.10 shows concurrent calls to a Queue object's Push subroutine and Pull function. If the pull function is called when the Queue object's IsEmpty property is true, then the thread waits until IsEmpty is false before executing the pull method. Because it does not actually execute the pull method while the queue is empty, there is no problem with a call to the push method being able to add objects to an empty queue.

FORCES

☺ A class's methods must be guarded to allow safe concurrent calls.

☺ An object may be in a state that makes it impossible for one of its guarded methods to execute to completion. In order for the object to leave that state, a call to one of the object's other guarded methods must execute. If a call to the first method is allowed to proceed while the object is in that state, it deadlocks and will never complete. Calls to the state-changing method that allows the first method to complete will have to wait until it does complete, which will never happen.

SOLUTION

Consider Figure 8.11. Figure 8.11 shows a class named Widget. It has two guarded methods named Foo and Bar. There is an exceptional state that Widget objects can enter. While a Widget object is in the exceptional state, its isOK method returns false; otherwise, it returns true. When a widget object is in the exceptional state, a call to its bar method may take it out of that state. There is no way to take it out of the exceptional state other than a call to bar. Taking a Widget object out of its exceptional state is a side effect of the bar method's main purpose, so it is not acceptable to call the bar method just to take a widget object out of its exceptional state.

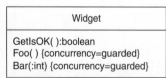

Figure 8.11   Unguarded Suspension Class

A call to a `Widget` object's `Foo` method cannot complete if the `Widget` object is in its exceptional state. If this happens, because the `Foo` and `Bar` methods are guarded, subsequent calls to the `Widget` object's `Foo` and `Bar` methods will not execute until the pending call to `Foo` returns. The call to `Foo` will not return until a call to `Bar` takes the `Widget` object out of its exceptional state.

The purpose of the Guarded Suspension pattern is to avoid the deadlock situation that can occur when a thread is about to execute an object's guarded method, and the state of the object prevents the method from completing. If a method call occurs when an object is in a state that prevents the method from executing to completion, the Guarded Suspension pattern suspends the thread until the object is in a state that allows the method to complete. This is illustrated in the collaboration diagram in Figure 8.12.

Notice that Figure 8.12 indicates a precondition that must be satisfied before a call to a `Widget` object's `Foo` method executes. If a thread tries to call a `Widget` object's `Foo` method when the value of the `Widget` object's `IsOK` property is false, the thread is forced to wait until the value of `IsOK` is true before it is able to execute the `Foo` method. While the thread is waiting for the value of `IsOK` to become true, other threads are free to call the `Bar` method.

IMPLEMENTATION

The Guarded Suspension pattern is implemented using the `System.Threading.Monitor` class's `Wait` and `Pulse` methods, like this:

```
Imports System.Threading

Public Class Widget
    Private myData As SomeDataClass

    Public Sub Foo()
        SyncLock (myData)
            While (Not myData.isOK())
                Monitor.Wait(myData)
            End While
            ...
            ' do something with myData
        End SyncLock
    End Sub 'Foo

    Public Sub Bar(ByVal x As Integer)
        SyncLock (myData)
            ' Do something to myData that makes isOK return true.
            ...
            Monitor.Pulse(myData)
        End SyncLock
    End Sub
End Class
```

```
Public Class SomeDataClass
    Public Function isOK() As Boolean
        Return True
    End Function
End Class
```

The way this works is that a method such as `Foo` must satisfy preconditions before it actually begins executing. The first thing such a method does is test its preconditions in a `while` loop. While the preconditions are false, it calls `Monitor.Wait`.

The `System.Threading.Monitor` class is responsible for managing object locks. If a thread requests ownership of an object's lock while another thread owns the object's lock, then the thread will have to wait until the other thread releases the object's lock before it can be granted ownership of the lock and proceed. If this sounds like the way the `SyncLock` statement works, there is a good reason. Consider this `SyncLock` statement:

```
SyncLock myData
    ...
End SyncLock
```

The `SyncLock` statement is equivalent to

```
System.Threading.Monitor.Enter(myData)
Try
    ...
Finally
    System.Threading.Monitor.Exit(myData)
End Try
```

When a thread passes an object to `Monitor.Wait`, it causes the thread to release the lock it holds on the object. `Monitor.Wait` then waits until it is notified that it may return by another thread passing the same object to `Monitor.Pulse` or `Monitor.PulseAll`. Then, as soon as the thread is able to recapture the lock, `Monitor.Wait` returns.

When `Monitor.Wait` returns, control returns to the top of the while loop, which tests the preconditions again. The reason for testing the preconditions in a loop is that between the time that the thread first tries to recapture the object lock and the time that it does capture it, another thread may have made the preconditions false.

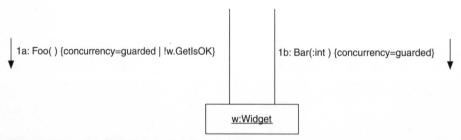

Figure 8.12 Guarded Suspension Collaboration

`Monitor.Wait` is notified that it should return when another method, such as `Bar`, calls `Monitor.Pulse`. Such methods call `Monitor.Pulse` after they have changed the state of the object in a way that may satisfy a method's preconditions. What `Monitor.Pulse` does is notify another thread waiting for `Monitor.Wait` to return that it should return.

If more than one thread is waiting, `Monitor.Pulse` chooses one to notify arbitrarily. Arbitrary selection works well in most situations. It does not work well for objects that have methods with different preconditions. Consider a situation in which multiple method calls are waiting to have their different preconditions satisfied. Arbitrary selection can result in a situation in which the preconditions of one method call are satisfied, but the thread that gets notified is waiting to execute a method with different preconditions that are not yet satisfied. In a situation like this, it is possible for a method call to never complete because the method is never notified when its preconditions are satisfied.

There is an alternative for classes where arbitrary selection is not a good way to decide which thread to notify. Their methods can call `Monitor.PulseAll`. Rather than choosing one thread to notify, `Monitor.PulseAll` notifies all waiting threads. This avoids the problem of not notifying the right thread. However, it may result in wasted machine cycles as a result of waking up threads waiting to execute method calls whose preconditions are not satisfied.

CONSEQUENCES

☺ Using the Guarded Suspension pattern allows a thread to cope with an object unable to perform an operation by waiting until the object is able to perform the operation.

• It is possible for multiple threads to be waiting to execute a call to the same method. The Guarded Suspension pattern specifically does not deal with selecting which of the waiting threads will be allowed to proceed when the object is in a state that will allow the method to be executed. Use the Scheduler pattern to accomplish this.

☹ Nested calls to guarded methods can make it difficult to use the Guarded Suspension pattern. Consider the collaboration diagram in Figure 8.13.

In Figure 8.13, access to the `Widget` object is through the guarded methods of a `Thing` object. This means that when thread `1a` calls the `Widget` object's `foo` method when the state of the `Widget` object causes its `isOK` method to return false, the thread will wait forever for the `Widget` object's `isOK` method to return true. The reason for this is that the methods of the `Thing` object are guarded without any preconditions. This gives us the same problem that the Guarded Suspension pattern was intended to solve.

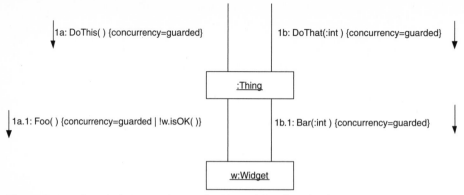

Figure 8.13   Guarded Suspension under Nested Synchronization

.NET API USAGE

All of the `System.Collections` classes provide a property called `SyncRoot`, which is an object that can be used to synchronize access to a particular instance.

CODE EXAMPLE

The following is code that implements the `Queue` class design discussed under the "Context" heading.

```
Imports System.Collections
Imports System.Threading

Namespace guardedSuspension
    '
    ' A queue class that handles a attempt to remove an object
    ' from an empty queue by waiting for another thread to put
    ' an object in the queue.
    '
    Public Class PatientQueue
        Private data As ArrayList

        '
        ' Construct a PatientQueue object.
        '
        Public Sub New()
            data = New ArrayList()
        End Sub 'New


        '
        ' Construct a PatientQueue object.
        '
        ' initialCapacity -
```

```
'    The initial capacity of the queue's internal data
'    structure.
'
Public Sub New(ByVal initialCapacity As Integer)
    data = New ArrayList(initialCapacity)
End Sub 'New


'
' Put an object on the end of the queue.
'
' obj - The object to put in the queue.
'
Public Sub Push(ByVal obj As Object)
    SyncLock data
        data.Add(obj)
        Monitor.Pulse(data)
    End SyncLock
End Sub 'Push


'
' Get and remove an object from the front of the
' queue.
' If the queue is empty this method waits until
' another thread puts an object in the queue and
' returns the object.
'
' returns - The object that was at the front of the queue.
'
Public Function Pull() As Object
    SyncLock data
        While data.Count = 0
            Monitor.Wait(data)
        End While
        Dim obj As Object = data(0)
        data.RemoveAt(0)
        Return obj
    End SyncLock
End Function 'Pull
End Class 'PatientQueue
End Namespace 'guardedSuspension
```

RELATED PATTERNS

Balking: The Balking pattern provides a different strategy for handling method calls to objects not in an appropriate state to execute the method call.

Balking

This pattern is based on material that appeared in [Lea97].

SYNOPSIS

If an object's method is called when the object is not in an appropriate state to execute the method, have the method return without doing anything.

CONTEXT

Suppose that you are writing a program to control an electronic toilet flusher. Such devices are intended for use in public bathrooms. They have a light sensor on the front of the flusher. When the light sensor detects an increased light level, it assumes that a person has left the toilet and triggers a flush. Electronic toilet flushers also have a button to manually trigger a flush. Figure 8.14 is a class diagram showing classes to model this behavior.

As shown in Figure 8.14, when a LightSensor object or a FlushButton object decides to flush, it requests the Flusher object to start a flush by calling its Flush subroutine. The Flush subroutine starts a flush and then returns once the flush is started. This arrangement raises some concurrency issues.

You must decide what will happen when the Flush subroutine is called while a flush is already in progress. You must also decide what happens when both the LightSensor object and the FlushButton object call the Flusher object's Flush subroutine at the same time.

These are the three most obvious choices for how to handle a call to the flush subroutine while there is a flush in progress:

- **Start a new flush immediately:** Starting a new flush while a flush is already in progress has the same effect as making the flush in progress last longer than a normal flush. The optimal length of a normal flush has been determined through experience. A longer flush will waste water, so this is not a good option.

- **Wait until the current flush finishes and immediately start another flush:** This option effectively doubles the length of a flush. It is a bigger waste of water than the first option.

- **Do nothing:** This option wastes no water, so it is the best choice.

When there are two concurrent calls to the flush subroutine, allowing one to execute and ignoring the other is also a good strategy.

Suppose that a call is made to an object's method when the object is not in a state to properly execute the method. If the method handles the situation by returning without performing its normal function, we say that the method balked. UML does not have a standard way of indicating a method call with balking behavior. This book represents a method call that exhibits balking behavior with an arrow that curves back on itself, as shown in Figure 8.15.

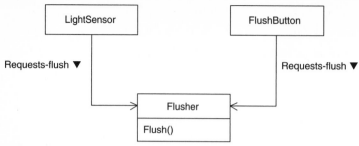

Figure 8.14   Flusher Classes

Figure 8.15 shows the balking behavior of the Flusher class's Flush subroutine.

FORCES

☺ An object may be in a state in which it is inappropriate to execute a method call.

☺ Postponing execution of a method call is not a good policy for the problem at hand. The method call must be executed immediately to produce the correct result.

☺ Calls made to an object's method when the object is not in an appropriate state to execute the method may be safely ignored.

SOLUTION

The collaboration diagram in Figure 8.16 shows objects collaborating in the Balking pattern.

In Figure 8.16, a Client object calls the DoIt method of a Service object. The bent-back arrow indicates that the call may balk. If the Service object's DoIt method is called when the Service object is in a state inappropriate for executing a call to its DoIt method, then the method returns without having performed its usual functions.

The DoIt method returns a result, indicated in the diagram as didIt. The result is either true or false, indicating whether the method performed its normal functions or balked.

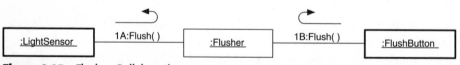

Figure 8.15   Flusher Collaboration

Figure 8.16   Balking Collaboration

IMPLEMENTATION

If a method can balk then, generally, the first thing it does is check the state of the object it belongs to, to determine if it should balk.

While an object's method is executing, after it has decided not to balk, you do not want the state of the object to become inappropriate for the method to execute. You can use the Single Threaded Execution pattern to prevent this inconsistency.

Instead of telling its callers that it balked by returning a value, it is also reasonable for a method to notify its callers that it balked by throwing an exception. If a method's callers do not need to be interested in whether it balked, the method does not need to return this information.

CONSEQUENCES

☺ Method calls are not executed if they are made when then method's object is in an inappropriate state.

• Calling a method that can balk means that the method may not perform its expected functions, but may do nothing instead.

CODE EXAMPLE

Following is code for the Flusher class discussed under the "Context" heading.

```
Namespace Balking
    '
    ' Summary description for Class1.
    '
    Public Class Flusher
        '
        ' This is true while a flush is in progress.
        '
        Private flushInProgress As Boolean


        '
        ' This method is called to start a flush.
        '
```

```
Public Sub Flush()
    SyncLock Me
        If flushInProgress Then
            Return
        End If
        flushInProgress = True
    End SyncLock
End Sub 'Flush
' code to start flush goes here.


' This method is called to notify this object that a
' flush has completed.

Public Sub flushCompleted()
    flushInProgress = False
End Sub 'flushCompleted
    End Class 'Flusher
End Namespace 'Balking
```

If the `Flush` method is called while a flush is in progress, the `Flush` method balks. Notice the use of the `SyncLock` statement in the `Flush` subroutine. It is there to ensure that if multiple calls to the `Flush` method occur at the same time, the result is predictable. Exactly one of the calls will proceed normally, and the others will balk. Without the lock statement, multiple calls could proceed normally at the same time.

Also, notice that the `FlushCompleted` method does not contain a `SyncLock` statement. This is because there is never a time when setting the `flushInProgress` variable to false causes a problem. Since the `flushCompleted` method does not modify any other state information, concurrent calls to the `flushCompleted` method are safe. However, there never should be concurrent calls to the `flushCompleted` method. The nature of the flusher mechanism makes it physically impossible for two flushes to complete at the same time.

RELATED PATTERNS

Guarded Suspension: The Guarded Suspension pattern provides an alternate way to handle method calls to objects that are not in an appropriate state to execute the method call.

Single Threaded Execution: The Balking pattern is often combined with the Single Threaded Execution pattern to coordinate changes to an object's state.

Scheduler

This pattern is based on material that appeared in [Lea97].

SYNOPSIS

Control the order in which threads are scheduled to execute single-threaded code using an object that explicitly sequences waiting threads. The Scheduler pattern provides a mechanism for implementing a scheduling policy. It is independent of any specific scheduling policy.

CONTEXT

Suppose that you are designing software to manage a building's physical security. The security system will support security checkpoints. At each checkpoint, a person must pass his or her identification badge through a scanner before passing through the checkpoint. When someone passes an identification badge through a checkpoint's scanner, the checkpoint either allows the person to pass through or rejects the badge. Whenever someone passes through a security checkpoint or a badge is rejected, an entry is printed on a hard-copy log in a central security office. Figure 8.17 shows the basic collaboration.

The interactions in Figure 8.17 diagram show SecurityCheckpoint objects creating JournalEntry objects and passing them to a Printer object's Print method. Simple though it is, there is a problem with this organization. The problem occurs when people go through three or more checkpoints at almost the same time. While the printer is printing the first of the log entries, the other print calls wait. After the first log entry is printed, there is no guarantee which log entry will be printed next. This means the log entries may not be printed in the same order that the security checkpoints sent them to the printer.

To ensure that journal entries are printed in the proper order, you could simply put each journal entry in a queue and then print the journal entries in the order that they arrived in the queue. Though this still leaves open the possibility of three or more journal entries arriving at the same time, the likelihood is greatly reduced. It may take as long as a second to print a journal entry. For the problem to occur, the other two journal entries must both arrive within that time period. Queuing a journal entry may take only about a microsecond. This reduces likelihood of journal entries printing out of sequence by a factor of 1,000,000.

You could make the queuing of journal entries to be printed the responsibility of the Printer class. However, the queuing of method calls to be executed sequentially is a capability that has a lot of potential reuse if it is implemented as a separate class. The interaction diagram in Figure 8.18 shows how a printer object could collaborate with another object to queue the execution of calls to its print method.

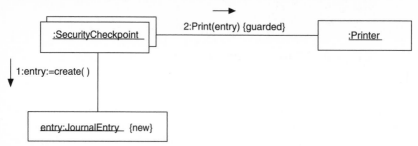

Figure 8.17 Security Journal Collaboration

In Figure 8.18, a `SecurityCheckpoint` object calls the `Printer` object's `Print` method. The `Print` method begins by calling the `Scheduler` object's `Enter` method. The `Enter` method does not return until the `Scheduler` object decides that it should. When the `Print` method is finished, it calls the `Scheduler` object's `Done` method. Between the time that the `Enter` method returns and the `Done` method is called, the `Scheduler` object assumes that the resource it is managing is busy. No call to the `Enter` method will return while the `Scheduler` object believes that the resource it is managing is busy. This ensures that only one thread at a time executes the portion of the `Print` method after its call to the `Scheduler` object's `Enter` method until it calls the `Scheduler` object's `done` method.

The actual policy the `Scheduler` object uses to decide when a call to the `Enter` method returns is encapsulated in the `Scheduler` object. This allows the policy to change without affecting other objects. In this example, the policy you want when more than one call to the `enter` method is waiting to return is as follows:

- If the `Scheduler` object is not waiting for a call to its `Done` method, then a call to its `Enter` method returns immediately. The `Scheduler` object then waits for a call to its `Done` method.

- While the `Scheduler` object is waiting for a call to its `Done` method, a call to its `Enter` method will wait to return until a call to the `Scheduler` object's `Done` method. When the `Scheduler` object's `Done` method is called, if any calls to its `Enter` method are waiting to return, then one of those `Enter` calls is chosen to return.

- If multiple calls to a `Scheduler` object's `Enter` method are waiting to return, then the `Scheduler` object must select the next `Enter` method call that will return. It selects the one passed a `JournalEntry` object with the earliest time-stamp. If more than one `JournalEntry` object has the same earliest time-stamp, then one of them is chosen arbitrarily.

In order for the `Scheduler` class to be able to compare the timestamps of `Journal Entry` objects and still be reusable, the `Scheduler` class must not refer directly to the `JournalEntry` class. However, it can refer to the `JournalEntry` class through an interface and still remain reusable. This is shown in Figure 8.19.

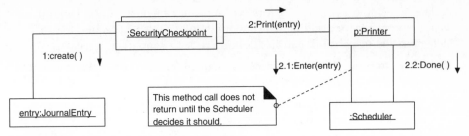

Figure 8.18 Security Journal with Scheduler

The Scheduler class does not know about the JournalEntry class. It just schedules processing for objects that implement the ScheduleOrdering interface. This interface declares the ScheduleBefore method that the IScheduler class calls to determine which of two IScheduleOrdering objects it should schedule first. Though the Scheduler class encapsulates a policy governing when processing will be allowed for a IScheduleOrdering object, it delegates the determination of the order they will be allowed to process in to the IScheduleOrdering object.

FORCES

☺ Multiple threads may need to access a resource at the same time, and only one thread at a time may access the resource.

☺ The program's requirements imply constraints on the order in which threads should access the resource.

SOLUTION

The Scheduler pattern uses an object to explicitly schedule concurrent requests by threads for nonconcurrent processing. The class diagram in Figure 8.20 shows the roles classes play in the Scheduler pattern.

Here are descriptions of the roles that the classes and interface play in the Scheduler pattern:

Request: Classes in this role must implement the interface in the ISchedule Ordering role. Request objects encapsulate a request for a Processor object to do something.

Processor: Instances of classes in this role perform a computation described by a Request object. They may be presented with more than one Request object to process at a time, but can process only one at a time. A Processor object delegates to a Scheduler object the responsibility for scheduling Request objects for processing, one at a time.

Scheduler: Instances of classes in this role schedule Request objects for processing by a Processor object. To promote reusability, a Scheduler class does not have any knowledge of the Request class. Instead, it accesses Request objects through the IScheduleOrdering interface that they implement.

A class in this role is responsible for deciding when the next request will run. It is not responsible for deciding which request will be the next request to run. It delegates that responsibility to an IScheduleOrdering interface.

IScheduleOrdering: Request objects implement the interface that is in this role. The interface in this role serves two purposes.

- By referring to an IScheduleOrdering interface, Processor classes avoid a dependency on a Request class.

- By calling methods defined by the IScheduleOrdering interface, Scheduler classes are able to delegate the decision of which Request object will be processed next. This increases the reusability of Scheduler classes. The class diagram in Figure 8.20 indicates one such method named ScheduleBefore.

The interaction between a Processor object and a Scheduler object occurs in two stages, as shown by the collaboration diagram in Figure 8.21.

The first interaction in Figure 8.21 is a call to a Processor object's DoIt subroutine. The first thing the DoIt method does is call the Enter subroutine of the Scheduler object associated with the Processor object. If there is no other thread currently executing the rest of the DoIt subroutine, then the Enter subroutine returns immediately. After the Enter subroutine returns, the Scheduler object knows that the resource it manages is busy. While its resource is busy, any calls to the Scheduler object's Enter subroutine will not return until the resource is not busy and the Scheduler object decides it is that call's turn to return.

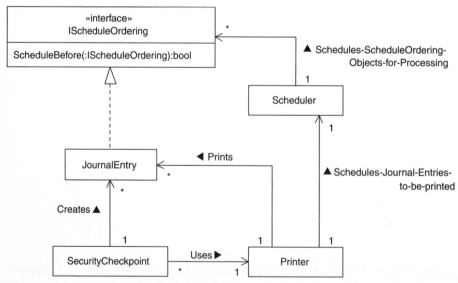

Figure 8.19 Journal Entry Scheduling Classes

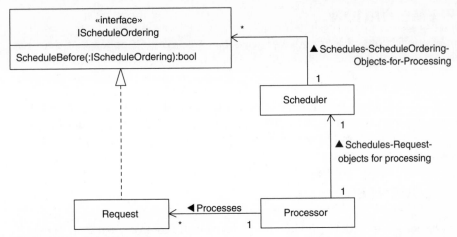

Figure 8.20 Scheduler Classes

A Scheduler object considers the resource it manages to be busy until the Scheduler object's Done subroutine is called. When one thread makes a valid call to a Scheduler object's Done subroutine, if any threads are waiting to return from the Scheduler object's Enter subroutine, then one of them returns.

If a call to a Scheduler object's Enter subroutine must wait before it returns and there are other Enter calls waiting to return, then the Scheduler object must decide which call will next return. It decides by consulting the Request objects that were passed into those calls. It does this indirectly by calling methods declared for the purpose by the ScheduleOrdering interface and implemented by the Request object.

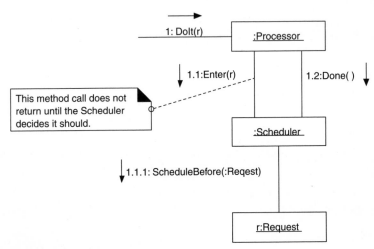

Figure 8.21 Scheduler Interaction

IMPLEMENTATION

In some applications, the `Scheduler` class has a scheduling policy that does not require it to consult `Request` objects to determine the order in which calls to its `Enter` subroutine will return. An example of such a policy is to allow calls to the `Enter` sub-routine to return in the order in which they were called. In such cases, there is no need to pass `Request` objects into the `Enter` subroutine or to have a `ScheduleOrdering` interface. Another example of such a policy is to not care about the order in which requests are scheduled, but to require at least five minutes between the end of one task and the beginning of another.

CONSEQUENCES

☺ The Scheduler pattern provides a way to explicitly control when threads may execute a piece of code.

☺ The scheduling policy is encapsulated in its own class and is reusable.

☹ Using the Scheduler pattern adds significant overhead beyond what is required to make a simple call to a thread-safe method.

CODE EXAMPLE

Following is some of the code that implements the print scheduling design discussed under the "Context" heading. The first listing is of the `Printer` class that manages the printing of security checkpoint journal entries.

```
Namespace Scheduler
    '
    ' Instances of this class manage the printing of
    ' JournalEntry objects.
    '
    Public Class Printer
        Private myScheduler As New Scheduler()

        '
        ' Print a journal entry.
        '
        ' j - The JournalEntry to print.
        '
        Public Sub Print(ByVal j As JournalEntry)
            myScheduler.Enter(j)
            Try
                ' ...
            Finally
                myScheduler.Done()
            End Try
        End Sub 'Print
    End Class 'Printer
End Namespace 'Scheduler
```

Each `Printer` object uses a `Scheduler` object to schedule concurrent calls to its `Print` subroutine so that they print sequentially in the order of their timestamps. It begins by calling the `Scheduler` object's `Enter` subroutine, passing it the `Journal Entry` object to be printed. The call does not return until the `Scheduler` object decides that it is the `JournalEntry` object's turn to print.

The `Print` subroutine ends by calling the `Scheduler` object's `Done` subroutine. A call to the `Done` subroutine tells the `Scheduler` object that the `JournalEntry` object has been printed and another `JournalEntry` object can have its turn to be printed.

The following is the source code for the `Scheduler` class.

```
Imports System.Collections
Imports System.Threading


Namespace Scheduler
    '
    ' Instances of this class manage the printing of
    ' JournalEntry objects.
    '
    Public Class Scheduler
        '
        ' The runningThread variable is Nothing when the
        ' managed resource is not busy.  It contains a
        ' reference to the thread that is using the resource
        ' when the resource is busy.
        '
        Private runningThread As Thread

        ' An invariant for this class is that a request and
        ' its corresponding thread are only in
        ' waitingRequests and waitingThreads
        ' while its call to enter is pending.
        Private waitingRequests As New ArrayList()
        Private waitingThreads As New ArrayList()


        ' This method is called before a thread starts using
        ' a managed resource.  This method does not return
        ' until the managed resource is not busy and this
        ' Scheduler object decides it is the method
        ' call's turn to return.
        '
        ' s - Determines the order in which pending calls return.
        '
        Public Sub Enter(ByVal s As IScheduleOrdering)
            Dim thisThread As Thread = Thread.CurrentThread

            ' For the case when the managed resource is not
            ' busy, lock on this object to ensure that two
            ' concurrent calls to enter do not both return
            ' immediately.
            SyncLock Me
```

```vb
            If runningThread Is Nothing Then
                runningThread = thisThread
                Return
            End If
            waitingThreads.Add(thisThread)
            waitingRequests.Add(s)
        End SyncLock
        SyncLock thisThread
            ' Wait until another thread's call to the Done
            ' method decides it is this thread's turn.
            While thisThread Is runningThread
                Monitor.Wait(thisThread)
            End While
        End SyncLock
        SyncLock Me
            Dim i As Integer = waitingThreads.IndexOf(thisThread)
            waitingThreads.RemoveAt(i)
            waitingRequests.RemoveAt(i)
        End SyncLock
    End Sub 'Enter

    Public Sub Done()
        SyncLock Me
            If runningThread Is Thread.CurrentThread Then
                Dim msg As String = "Wrong Thread"
                Throw New ApplicationException(msg)
            End If
            Dim waitCount As Integer = waitingThreads.Count
            If waitCount <= 0 Then
                runningThread = Nothing
            ElseIf waitCount = 1 Then
                runningThread = CType(waitingThreads(0), Thread)
            Else
                Dim [next] As Integer = waitCount - 1
                Dim nextRequest As IScheduleOrdering
                nextRequest = CType(waitingRequests([next]),
IScheduleOrdering)

                For i As Integer = waitCount - 2 To 0 Step -1
                    Dim r As IScheduleOrdering
                    r = CType(waitingRequests(i), IScheduleOrdering)
                    If r.ScheduleBefore(nextRequest) Then
                        [next] = i
                        nextRequest = CType(waitingRequests([next]),
IScheduleOrdering)
                    End If
                Next i
                runningThread = CType(waitingThreads([next]), Thread)
            End If
            SyncLock runningThread
                Monitor.PulseAll(runningThread)
```

```
            End SyncLock
        End SyncLock
    End Sub 'Done
End Class 'Scheduler
End Namespace 'Scheduler
```

The `Done` subroutine uses the `Monitor.PulseAll` subroutine to wake up a thread, rather than the `Monitor.Pulse` subroutine, because it has no guarantee that there will not be another thread waiting to regain ownership of the lock on the `runningThread` object. If it used the `Monitor.Pulse` subroutine, and there were additional threads waiting to regain ownership of the `runningThread` object's lock, then the `Monitor.Pulse` subroutine could fail to wake up the right thread.

The `Scheduler` class is independent of the specific type of resource it is scheduling access to. However, it does require that the class responsible for representing operations on the resource implement the `IScheduleOrdering` interface. When there are multiple operations waiting for access to a resource, the `Scheduler` class uses the `IScheduleOrdering` interface to determine the order in which it should schedule operations. Here is a listing of the `IScheduleOrdering` interface:

```
Namespace Scheduler
    '
    ' Objects used to specify the processing that the
    ' resource managed by a Scheduler object uses implement
    ' this interface.
    '
    Public Interface IScheduleOrdering
        Function ScheduleBefore(ByVal s As IScheduleOrdering) As Boolean
    End Interface 'IScheduleOrdering
End Namespace 'Scheduler
```

The final listing in this code example is a skeletal listing of the `JournalEntry` class that the `Printer` class is responsible for printing:

```
Namespace Scheduler
    '
    ' An instance of this class is created to detail the
    ' passing or rejection of someone from a security
    ' checkpoint.
    '
    <Serializable()> _
    Public Class JournalEntry
        Implements IScheduleOrdering
        '
        ' true if badge holder was passed through security
        ' checkpoint
        '
        Private passedFlag As Boolean

        Private myCheckpoint As SecurityCheckpoint
        Private myCreationTime As DateTime
```

```
'
' Constructor
'
' passed -
'   True if badge holder was passed through the
'   security checkpoint.
'
' theCheckpoint -
'   The security checkpoint a badge holder was passed
'   through or rejected from.
'

Public Sub New(ByVal passed As Boolean, ByVal theCheckpoint As
SecurityCheckpoint)
        passedFlag = passed
        myCheckpoint = theCheckpoint
        myCreationTime = DateTime.Now
End Sub 'New


'
' This JournalEntry's checkpoint.
'

Public ReadOnly Property Checkpoint() As SecurityCheckpoint
        Get
            Return myCheckpoint
        End Get
End Property


'
' True if badge holder passed throuth the checkpoint.
'

Public ReadOnly Property Passed() As Boolean
        Get
            Return passedFlag
        End Get
End Property


'
' The time that this JournalEntry was created.
'

Public ReadOnly Property CreationTime() As DateTime
        Get
            Return myCreationTime
        End Get
End Property

Public Function ScheduleBefore(ByVal s As IScheduleOrdering) As
Boolean _
    Implements IScheduleOrdering.ScheduleBefore
        If TypeOf s Is JournalEntry Then
            Dim that As JournalEntry = CType(s, JournalEntry)
            Return myCreationTime < that.CreationTime
```

```
            End If
            Return False
        End Function 'ScheduleBefore
      End Class 'JournalEntry
End Namespace 'Scheduler
```

RELATED PATTERNS

Read/Write Lock: Implementations of the Read/Write Lock pattern usually use the Scheduler pattern to ensure fairness in scheduling.

Read/Write Lock

This pattern is based on material that appeared in [Lea97].

SYNOPSIS

Allow concurrent read access to an object, but require exclusive access for write operations.

CONTEXT

Suppose that you are developing software for conducting online auctions. The way that these auctions work is that an item is put up for auction. People access the online auction to see the current bid for an item. People may then make a bid for an item that is greater than the current bid. At a predetermined time, the auction closes and the highest bidder at that time gets the item at the final bid price.

You expect that there will be many more requests to read the current bid for an item than to update it. You could use the Single Threaded Execution pattern to coordinate access to bids. Though this will ensure correct results, it can unnecessarily limit responsiveness. When multiple users want to read a current bid at the same time, Single Threaded Execution requires that only one user at a time be allowed to read the current bid. This forces users who just want to read the current bid to unnecessarily wait for other users who just want to read the current bid.

There is no reason to prevent multiple users from reading the current bid at the same time. Single-threaded execution is only required for updates to the current bid. Updates to the current bid must be processed one at a time to ensure that updates that would not increase the value of the current bid are ignored.

You can avoid unnecessary waiting to read data by allowing concurrent reads of data but only single-threaded access to data when it is being updated. Consider the collaboration diagram in Figure 8.22.

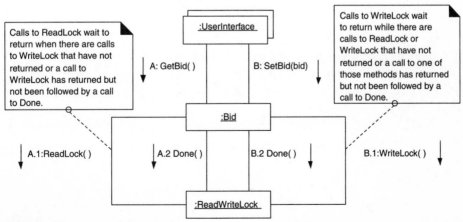

Figure 8.22   Bid Collaboration

Figure 8.22 shows multiple user interface objects calling a bid object's GetBid and SetBid methods. The GetBid method waits until there are no calls to SetBid waiting to complete before it returns the current bid. The SetBid method waits for any executing calls to GetBid or SetBid to complete before it updates the current bid. The ReadWriteLock object encapsulates the logic that coordinates the execution of Get Bid and SetBid to allow it to be reused.

All calls to a ReadWriteLock object's ReadLock method return immediately, unless there are any outstanding write locks. A write lock is considered to be outstanding from the time that a call to a ReadWriteLock object's WriteLock returns until it is released by a corresponding call to the ReadWriteLock object's Done subroutine. Calls to the ReadLock method wait until all outstanding write locks have been released.

Calls to a ReadWriteLock object's WriteLock method return immediately, unless one or more of the following are true:

- A previous call to WriteLock is waiting to execute.

- A previous call to WriteLock has finished executing, but there has been no corresponding call to the ReadWriteLock object's Done subroutine.

- There are any executing calls to the ReadWriteLock object's ReadLock method or there are outstanding read locks.

If a call to a ReadWriteLock object is made when any of the preceding conditions are true, it will not return until all of the conditions are false.

FORCES

☺ There is a need for read and write access to an object's state information.

☺ Any number of read operations may be performed on the object's state information concurrently. However, read operations are guaranteed to return the correct value only if there are no write operations executing at the same time as a read operation.

☺ Write operations on the object's state information must be performed one at a time, to ensure their correctness.

☺ There will be concurrently initiated read and write operations.

☺ Allowing concurrently initiated read operations to execute concurrently will improve responsiveness and throughput.

☺ The logic for coordinating read and write operations should be reusable.

SOLUTION

Organize a class so that concurrent calls to methods that fetch and store its instance information are coordinated by an instance of another class. The class diagram in Figure 8.23 shows the roles classes play in the Read/Write Lock pattern.

A class in the Data role has properties to get and set its instance information. On one hand, any number of threads may concurrently get a Data object's instance information, so long as no thread is setting its instance information at the same time. On the other hand, its set operations must occur one at a time, while there are no get operations being executed. Data objects must coordinate their set and get operations so that they obey these restrictions.

Data objects use an abstraction to coordinate get operations. The abstraction is a read lock. A Data object's properties do not get any information until they get a read lock. Associated with each Data object is a ReadWriteLock object. Before one of its properties gets anything, it calls the ReadWriteLock object's ReadLock method, which issues a read lock to the current thread. While the thread has a read lock, the property can be sure it is safe to get data from the object. This is so because while there are any outstanding read locks, the ReadWriteLock object will not issue any write locks. If there are any outstanding write locks when the ReadWriteLock object's ReadLock method is called, it does not return until all the outstanding write locks have been relinquished by calls to the ReadWriteLock object's Done method. Otherwise, calls to the ReadWriteLock object's ReadLock method return immediately.

When a Data object's property is finished getting data from the object, it calls the ReadWriteLock object's Done method. A call to that method causes the current thread to relinquish its read lock.

Similarly, Data objects use a write lock abstraction to coordinate set operations. A Data object's properties do not store any information until they get a write lock. Before one of a Data object's properties store any information, it calls the associated Read WriteLock object's WriteLock method, which issues a write lock to the current thread. While the thread has a write lock, the property can be sure that it is safe to store data in the object. This is because the ReadWriteLock object issues write locks only when there are no outstanding read locks and no outstanding write locks. If there are any outstanding locks when the ReadWriteLock object's WriteLock method is called, it does not return until all outstanding locks have been relinquished by calls to the ReadWriteLock object's Done method.

The preceding constraints that govern when read and write locks are issued do not address the order in which read and write locks are issued. The order in which read locks are issued does not matter, so long as read operations can be performed concurrently. Since write operations are performed one at a time, the order in which write locks are issued should be the order in which the write locks are requested.

The one remaining ambiguity occurs when there are calls to both of a ReadWrite Lock object's ReadLock and WriteLock methods waiting to return and there are no outstanding locks. If read operations are intended to return the most current information, then that situation should result in the WriteLock method returning first.

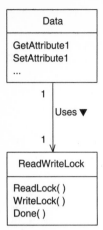

Figure 8.23   Read/Write Lock Classes

IMPLEMENTATION

Since read locks and write locks do not contain any information, there is no need to represent them as explicit objects. It is sufficient to just count them.

The scheduling policies described elsewhere in this description of the Read/Write Lock pattern give preference to granting read locks. If there is a call waiting to get a write lock because there are outstanding read locks, then any requests for additional read locks in this circumstance will be granted immediately. This is a good policy for many applications. However, there are some applications where it is more appropriate to have scheduling policies that give preference to granting write locks.

If the scheduling policy gives preference to write locks, it means that no read locks will be granted while there is a call waiting for a write lock to be granted. Other policies are possible. However, preference-based policies are the most common.

CONSEQUENCES

☺ The Read/Write Lock pattern coordinates concurrent calls to an object's get and set methods so that calls to the object's set methods do not interfere with each other or with calls to the object's get methods.

☺ If there are many concurrent calls to an object's get methods, using the Read/Write Lock pattern to coordinate the calls can result in better responsiveness and throughput than using the Single Threaded Execution pattern. This is because the Read/Write Lock pattern allows concurrent calls to the object's get methods to execute concurrently.

- If there are relatively few concurrent calls to an object's get methods, using the Read/Write Lock pattern will result in lower throughput than using the Single Threaded Execution pattern. This is because the Read/Write Lock pattern spends more time managing individual calls. When there are concurrent get calls for it to manage, this results in a net improvement.

☹ If the scheduling policy is to give preference to granting read locks, then it is possible that write locks will never be granted. If there is a steady enough stream of read lock requests for there to always be at least one outstanding read lock, then no write lock will ever be granted. This results in a situation called write starvation.

☹ Similarly, if the scheduling policy is to give preference to granting write locks, then it is possible that read locks will never be granted. If there is a steady enough stream of write lock requests for there to always be at least one call waiting to be granted a write lock, then no read lock will ever be granted. This results in a situation called read starvation.

One policy that avoids starvation problems is to reverse the read or write lock preference if the number of waiting requests exceeds a predetermined limit. Another way to avoid starvation is to determine preference randomly each time a scheduling choice is to be made. The drawback to policies like these is that they make the behavior of the ReadWriteLock class more difficult to analyze and debug.

.NET API USAGE

The .NET Framework's System.Threading.ReaderWriterLock class is designed to fill the ReadWriteLock role of the Read/Write Lock pattern. This class's scheduling policy gives preference to write locks. If a fixed preference for write locks is suitable for a particular purpose, then use the System.Threading.Reader WriterLock class.

If you need a different scheduling policy, consider using the class in the code example, which has a scheduling policy that gives preference to read locks. If a fixed policy of giving preference to read locks is not what is needed, you may be able to modify the class in the code example to have the needed scheduling policy.

CODE EXAMPLE

The code implements the design discussed under the "Context" heading. The first listing is the Bid class, which is rather straightforward.

```
Namespace ReadWriteLock
    '
    ' Instances of this class encapsulate the current bid for
    ' an auction.
    '
```

```
Public Class Bid
    Private myBid As Integer = 0
    Private lockManager As New ReadWriteLock()
    ...
    Public Property CurrentBid() As Integer
        Get
            lockManager.ReadLock()
            Dim thisBid As Integer = myBid
            lockManager.Done()
            Return thisBid
        End Get
        Set(ByVal value As Integer)
            lockManager.WriteLock()
            If value > myBid Then
                myBid = value
            End If
            lockManager.Done()
        End Set
    End Property
End Class 'Bid
End Namespace 'ReadWriteLock
```

As you can see, the Bid class uses a ReadWriteLock object to coordinate concurrent calls. Its methods begin by calling the appropriate lock method before getting or setting values. When finished, they call the ReadWriteLock object's Done method to release the lock.

The ReadWriteLock class is more complex. As you read through its listing, you will notice that there are two main things it focuses on:

■ It carefully tracks state information in a way that will be consistent for all threads.

■ It ensures that all preconditions are met before its lock methods return.

Any other class that is responsible for enforcing a scheduling policy will have these implementation concerns.

```
Imports System.Collections
Imports System.Threading

Namespace ReadWriteLock

    '
    ' Instances of this class manage read and write locks.
    '
    Public Class ReadWriteLock
```

A ReadWriteLock object uses the outstandingReadLocks variable to count the number of read locks it has issued to but not yet been released by the threads they were issued to.

A ReadWriteLock object uses the writeLockedThread variable to refer to the thread that currently has a write lock. If no thread currently has a write lock from the ReadWriteLock object, then the value of the writeLockedThread variable is Nothing. By having a variable that refers to the thread that has been issued the write lock, the ReadWriteLock object can tell if it awakened the thread to receive a write lock or if the thread was awakened for another reason.

```
Private waitingForReadLock As Integer = 0
Private outstandingReadLocks As Integer = 0


' The thread that has the write lock or Nothing.
'
Private writeLockedThread As Thread
```

A ReadWriteLock object uses these instance variables to keep track of threads that have requested or been issued a read or write lock. It uses the list referred to by the waitingForWriteLock variable to keep track of threads that are waiting to get a write lock. Using this list, it is able to ensure that write locks are issued in the same order in which they are requested.

```
'
' Threads waiting to get a write lock are tracked in
' this ArrayList to ensure that write locks are
' issued in the same order they are requested.
'
Private waitingForWriteLock As New ArrayList()
```

A ReadWriteLock object uses the waitingForReadLock variable to count the number of threads waiting to get a read lock. Simple counting is sufficient for this because all threads waiting for a read lock will be allowed to get them at the same time. There is no reason to keep track of the order in which threads requested read locks.

The ReadWriteLock class's ReadLock subroutine follows. It issues a read lock and returns immediately, unless there is an outstanding write lock. All it does to issue a read lock is to increment the outstandingReadLocks variable.

```
'
' Issue a read lock if there is no outstanding write
' lock or threads waiting to get a write lock.
'
Public Sub ReadLock()
    SyncLock Me
        If writeLockedThread IsNot Nothing Then
            waitingForReadLock += 1
            While writeLockedThread IsNot Nothing
                Monitor.Wait(Me)
            End While
            waitingForReadLock -= 1
        End If
```

```
            outstandingReadLocks += 1
        End SyncLock
    End Sub 'ReadLock
```

A listing of the `WriteLock` subroutine follows. Notice that it is longer than the `ReadLock` subroutine. This is because it manages threads and a data structure. It begins by checking for the case in which there are no outstanding locks. If there are no outstanding locks, it issues a write lock immediately. Otherwise, it adds the current thread to a list that the `Done` subroutine uses as a queue. The current thread waits until the `Done` subroutine issues it a write lock. The `WriteLock` subroutine then finishes by removing the current thread from the list of threads waiting for a write lock.

```
Public Sub WriteLock()
    Dim thisThread As Thread
    SyncLock Me
        If writeLockedThread Is Nothing And outstandingReadLocks _
= 0 Then
            writeLockedThread = Thread.CurrentThread
            Return
        End If
        thisThread = Thread.CurrentThread
        waitingForWriteLock.Add(thisThread)
    End SyncLock
    SyncLock thisThread
        While thisThread Is writeLockedThread
            Monitor.Wait(thisThread)
        End While
    End SyncLock
    SyncLock Me
        waitingForWriteLock.Remove(thisThread)
    End SyncLock
End Sub 'WriteLock
```

The final part of the `ReadWriteLock` class is the `Done` subroutine. Threads call a `ReadWriteLock` object's `Done` method to relinquish a lock that the `ReadWriteLock` object previously issued to them. The `Done` subroutine considers three cases:

1. **There are outstanding read locks, which implies that there is no outstanding write lock.**
   It relinquishes the read lock by decrementing the `outstandingReadLocks` variable. If there are no more outstanding read locks and threads are waiting to get a write lock, then it issues a write lock to the thread that has been waiting the longest to get a write lock. Finally, it wakes up the waiting thread.

2. **There is an outstanding write lock.**
   It causes the current thread to relinquish the write lock. If there are threads waiting to get a read lock, then it grants read locks to all of the threads that are waiting for a read lock. If there are no outstanding read locks and there are threads waiting to get the write lock, it transfers the write lock to the thread that has been waiting the longest by having the `writeLockedThread` variable refer to that thread instead of the current thread.

3. **There are no outstanding locks.**

   If there are no outstanding locks, then the done method has been called at an inappropriate time, so it throws an exception.

```
'
' Threads call this method to relinquish a lock that
' they previously got from this object.
'
' Exception ApplicationException -
'    if called when there are no outstanding locks or
'    there is a write lock issued to a different thread.
'
Public Sub Done()
    SyncLock Me
        If outstandingReadLocks > 0 Then
            outstandingReadLocks -= 1
            If outstandingReadLocks = 0 And waitingForWriteLock
.Count > 0 Then
                writeLockedThread = CType
(waitingForWriteLock(0), Thread)
                SyncLock writeLockedThread
                    Monitor.PulseAll(writeLockedThread)
                End SyncLock
            End If
        ElseIf Thread.CurrentThread Is writeLockedThread Then
            If outstandingReadLocks = 0 And waitingForWriteLock
.Count > 0 Then
                writeLockedThread = CType
(waitingForWriteLock(0), Thread)
                SyncLock writeLockedThread
                    Monitor.PulseAll(writeLockedThread)
                End SyncLock
            Else
                writeLockedThread = Nothing
                If waitingForReadLock > 0 Then
                    Monitor.PulseAll(Me)
                End If
            End If
        Else
            Dim msg As String = "Thread does not have lock"
            Throw New ApplicationException(msg)
        End If
    End SyncLock
End Sub 'Done
    End Class 'ReadWriteLock
End Namespace 'ReadWriteLock
```

One last detail to notice about the Done subroutine is that is uses the Monitor. PulseAll subroutine, rather than the Monitor.Pulse subroutine. When it wants to allow read locks to be issued, it calls Monitor.PulseAll to allow all the threads waiting to get a read lock to proceed. When it issues the write lock to a thread, it passes the thread to `Monitor.PulseAll`. Calling `Monitor.Pulse` would work in most cases. However, in the case that another thread is waiting to gain the synchronization lock of the thread to be issued the write lock, using `Monitor.Pulse` could cause the wrong thread to wake up. Using `Monitor.PulseAll` guarantees that the right thread will wake up.

RELATED PATTERNS

Single Threaded Execution: The Single Threaded Execution pattern is a good and simpler alternative to the Read/Write Lock pattern when most of the accesses to data are write accesses.

Scheduler: The Read/Write Lock pattern is a specialized form of the Scheduler pattern.

Producer-Consumer

SYNOPSIS

Coordinate the asynchronous production and consumption of information or objects.

CONTEXT

Suppose that you are designing a trouble ticket–dispatching system. Customers will enter trouble tickets through Web pages. Dispatchers will review the trouble tickets and forward them to the person or organization best suited to resolve the problem.

Any number of people may submit trouble tickets at given time. There will usually be multiple dispatchers on duty. If any dispatchers are not busy when a trouble ticket comes in, the system immediately gives the trouble ticket to one of them. Otherwise, it places the trouble ticket in a queue, where the trouble ticket waits its turn to be seen by a dispatcher and be dispatched. Figure 8.24 is a class diagram showing a design for classes that implement this behavior.

Figure 8.24 shows a `Client` class whose instances are responsible for getting trouble tickets filled out by users and placed in a `Queue` object. Trouble tickets stay in the `Queue` object until a `Dispatcher` object pulls them out of the `Queue` object.

The `Dispatcher` class is responsible for displaying trouble tickets to a dispatcher and then forwarding them to the destination selected by the dispatcher. When an instance of the `Dispatcher` class is not displaying a trouble ticket or forwarding it, it calls the `Queue` object's `Pull` method to get another trouble ticket. If there are no trouble tickets in the `Queue` object, the `Pull` method waits until it has a trouble ticket to return.

Figure 8.25 is a collaboration diagram that shows the interactions previously described.

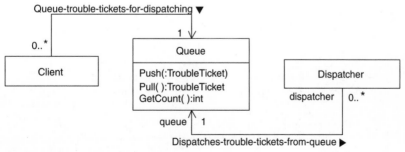

Figure 8.24   Trouble Ticket Classes

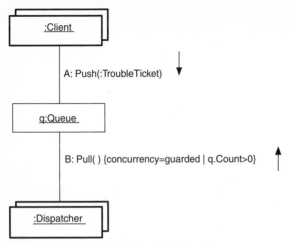

Figure 8.25   Trouble Ticket Collaboration

FORCES

☺ Objects are produced or received asynchronously of their use or consumption.

☺ When an object is received or produced, there may not be any object available to use or consume it.

SOLUTION

The class diagram in Figure 8.26 shows the roles in which classes participate in the Producer-Consumer pattern.

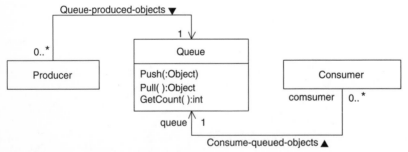

Figure 8.26   Producer-Consumer Classes

Here are descriptions of the roles that classes can play in the Producer-Consumer pattern.

Producer: Instances of classes in this role supply objects that are used by Con-sumer objects. Instances of `Producer` classes produce objects asynchronously of threads that consume them. This means that sometimes a `Producer` object will produce an object when all `Consumer` objects are busy processing other objects. Rather than wait for a `Consumer` object to become available, instances of `Producer` classes put objects they produce in a queue and then continue with whatever they do.

Queue: Instances of classes in this role act as a buffer for objects produced by instances of `Producer` classes. Instances of `Producer` classes place the objects that they produce in an instance of a `Queue` class. The objects remain there until a `Consumer` object pulls them out of the `Queue` object.

Consumer: Instances of `Consumer` classes use objects produced by `Producer` objects. They get the objects they use from a `Queue` object. If the `Queue` object is empty, a `Consumer` object that wants to get an object from it must wait until a `Producer` object puts an object in the `Queue` object.

The collaboration diagram in Figure 8.27 shows the interactions between objects that participate in the Producer-Consumer pattern.

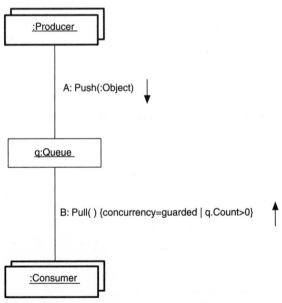

Figure 8.27 Producer-Consumer Collaboration

IMPLEMENTATION

Some implementations of the Producer-Consumer pattern limit the queue to a maximum size. In such implementations, a special case to consider is when the queue is at its maximum size and a producer thread wants to put an object in the queue. The usual way to handle this is for the queue to use the Guarded Suspension pattern to force the producer thread to wait until a consumer thread removes an object from the queue. When there is room for the object that the producer wants to put in the queue, the producer thread is allowed to finish and proceed with whatever else it does.

CONSEQUENCES

- ☺ `Producer` objects can deliver the objects they produce to a `Queue` object without having to wait for a `Consumer` object.

- • When there are objects in the `Queue` object, `Consumer` objects can pull an object out of the queue without waiting. However, when the queue is empty and a `Consumer` object calls the `Queue` object's `Pull` method, the `Pull` method does not return until a `Producer` object puts an object in the queue.

.NET API USAGE

The class `System.Messaging.MessageQueue` supports a variety of architectures for distributing messages, including the Producer-Consumer pattern.

CODE EXAMPLE

The following listings implement the design discussed under the "Context" heading: The first two listings are skeletal listings of the `Client` and `Dispatcher` classes.

```
Namespace producerConsumer
    Public Class Client
        Private myQueue As ProductQueue(Of TroubleTicket)

        Public Sub New(ByVal myQueue As ProductQueue(Of TroubleTicket))
            Me.myQueue = myQueue
        End Sub 'New

        Public Sub run()
            Dim tkt As TroubleTicket = Nothing
            myQueue.Enqueue(tkt)
        End Sub 'run
    End Class 'Client
End Namespace 'producerConsumer
```

```
Namespace producerConsumer
    Public Class Dispatcher
        Private myQueue As ProductQueue(Of TroubleTicket)
        Public Sub New(ByVal myQueue As ProductQueue(Of TroubleTicket))
            Me.myQueue = myQueue
        End Sub 'New
        Public Sub run()
            Dim tkt As TroubleTicket = myQueue.Dequeue()
        End Sub 'run
    End Class 'Dispatcher
End Namespace 'producerConsumer
```

The last listing is of the ProductQueue class.

```
Imports System.Collections
Imports System.Threading

Namespace producerConsumer
    '
    ' A Queue data structure to support a producer-consumer
    ' architecture.
    '
    Public Class ProductQueue(Of T)
        Private myQueue As New Queue(Of T)()
        '
        ' Put an object on the end of the queue.
        '
        ' tkt - The object to put at end of queue.
        '
        Public Sub Enqueue(ByVal tkt As T)
            SyncLock myQueue
                myQueue.Enqueue(tkt)
                Monitor.Pulse(Me)
            End SyncLock
        End Sub 'Enqueue


        '
        ' Get an TroubleTicket from the front of the queue.
        ' If queue is empty, waits until it is not empty.
        '
        Public Function Dequeue() As T
            SyncLock myQueue
                While myQueue.Count = 0
                    Monitor.Wait(myQueue)
                End While
                Return myQueue.Dequeue()
            End SyncLock
        End Function 'Dequeue
```

```
'
'  The number of trouble tickets in this queue.
'

Public ReadOnly Property Count() As Integer
    Get
        SyncLock myQueue
            Return myQueue.Count
        End SyncLock
    End Get
End Property
End Class 'Queue
End Namespace 'producerConsumer
```

RELATED PATTERNS

Guarded Suspension: The Producer-Consumer pattern uses the Guarded Suspension pattern to manage the situation of a `Consumer` object wanting to get an object from an empty queue.

Pipe: The Pipe pattern is a special case of the Producer-Consumer pattern that involves only one `Producer` object and only one `Consumer` object. The Pipe pattern usually refers to the `Producer` object as a data source and the `Consumer` object as a data sink.

Scheduler: The Producer-Consumer pattern can be viewed as a special form of the Scheduler pattern that has a scheduling policy with two notable features.

- The scheduling policy is based on the availability of a resource.
- The scheduler assigns the resource to a thread but does not need to regain control of the resource when the thread is done so it can reassign the resource to another thread.

Double Buffering

This pattern is also known as Exchange Buffering.

SYNOPSIS

You have an object that consumes data. Avoid delays in the consumption of data by asynchronously producing data with the goal of the data being ready for consumption before the consumer needs it.

CONTEXT

Suppose that you are maintaining software that loads a day's transactions from a point-of-sale system (POS) into a database that supports a data warehouse. Your task is to reduce the amount of time it takes to load POS transactions into the database.

You discover that the program is spending a lot of time reading the files that contain the transaction records. You notice that the program is using an instance of `System.IO.BufferedStream` to buffer reads. To reduce the number of read operations that it needs to perform, you try increasing the size of the buffer that the `BufferedStream` object is using.

The result of increasing the buffer size is that the program spends less time reading POS transaction records. However, the program is still waiting for transactions to be read from a file before adding them to the database. Since the database is stored on different physical disks than the transaction files, you know that it is possible for the reading of transactions and the updating of the database to happen concurrently. While some POS transactions are being added to the database, you would like the next transaction records to have already been read by the time that the preceding POS transactions have been added to the database. This way the program does not have to wait for more POS transactions to be read.

You consider solving the problem by using an asynchronous read function (`BeginRead`) to read the POS transactions. However, you are concerned that directly using asynchronous reads will require changes to the classes that call the read operations. If further tweaking or tuning of the read process is needed, additional changes to the classes that call the read operations may be needed. You search for a more structured solution that will better encapsulate the strategy you are using to minimize the time spent waiting for read operations to finish.

You decide to solve the problem of the program having to wait for POS transactions to be read by creating a class similar to `BufferedStream`. The new class will be called `DoubleBufferedStream`. This new class will use two buffers instead of one. The first time one of its read methods is called, it synchronously fills one of its buffers. From this point on, each buffer will fill one of two roles.

One role is called active buffer. The other role is called reserve buffer. The buffer that is synchronously filled during the first read call is initially the active buffer. The other buffer is initially the reserve buffer. As soon as the active buffer is full of its initial contents, two things happen:

- The read method reads bytes from the active buffer.
- At the same time, bytes are asynchronously read from the underlying input stream to fill the reserve buffer.

When the active buffer is empty and the asynchronous filling of the reserve buffer is finished, the two buffers switch roles. If the reading of bytes into the reserve buffer has not yet finished, the role switch is delayed until the reading is finished. After the role switch, the read method reads bytes from the active buffer and bytes are asynchronously read from the underlying input stream to fill the reserve buffer. Figure 8.28 shows these interactions.

FORCES

☺ An object consumes many pieces of data at once.

☺ Data is pulled by the consuming object from a data-producing object. The data-producing object has no control over when the data-consuming object will want more data.

☺ If data is not available when a consuming object wants it, the performance of the consuming object will suffer in some way.

☺ Over time, the average rate that data is consumed is not faster than the rate at which it can be produced.

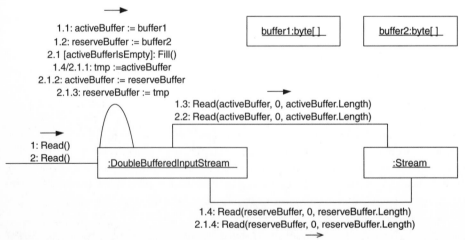

Figure 8.28 DoubleBufferedStream Collaboration

SOLUTION

You have an object that consumes data. Avoid delays in the consumption of data by asynchronously producing the data with the goal of the data being ready for consumption before the consumer needs it. You do this by putting data in a buffer before it is needed.

The behavior of some data-consuming objects is that they consume an entire buffer of data and then don't want another buffer for some indeterminate amount of time. If that amount of time is generally more than the amount of time that it takes to fill the buffer with data again, then you can reuse the same buffer. However, if the data-consuming objects do not use the entire buffer of data all at once or do not wait long enough between the times that they want data to refill a buffer, then you will need more than one buffer. The general case is that you will need more than one buffer.

Figure 8.29 shows the interactions between objects that participate in the Double Buffering pattern. The `DataProvider` object provides data to objects that call its `Get Data` method. The `buffer1` and `buffer2` objects are used by the `DataProvider` object to temporarily keep data in memory from when the data is fetched or created until the time it is returned by the `GetData` method. The `DataSource` object is responsible for fetching or creating data.

Here are descriptions of the interactions shown in Figure 8.29:

1 This is the first request to get data from wherever it comes from.

   1.1 The `buffer1` object becomes the active buffer.

   1.2 The `buffer2` object becomes the reserve buffer.

   1.3 The active buffer is synchronously filled.

   1.4 The reserve buffer is asynchronously filled. This call returns immediately without waiting until the reserve buffer is filled. A separate thread is responsible for filling the reserve buffer.

2 This is a request for more data. If there is sufficient data in the active buffer, the data is used to satisfy the request. Otherwise, more data is needed and the call continues to 2.1. After 2.1 is complete, there is more data available. It is used to satisfy the request for more data.

   2.1 This step happens only if the active buffer is empty. The purpose of this step is to ensure that the buffer being used as the active buffer is full, or as full as it is going to get.

      2.1.1 If the asynchronous filling of the reserve buffer is not finished, then this step waits until it is finished before proceeding. When this step does proceed, it is the first step in swapping the active buffer and the reserve buffer.

  2.1.2, 2.1.3 These steps complete the swapping of the active and reserve buffers. After step 2.1.3, the buffer that was the reserve buffer before 2.1.1 is the active buffer and the buffer that was the active buffer is the reserve buffer.

      2.1.4 The reserve buffer is asynchronously filled. This method returns immediately without waiting until the reserve buffer is filled. A separate thread is responsible for filling the reserve buffer.

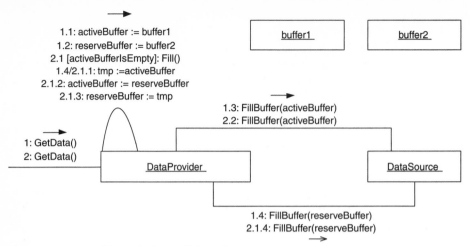

Figure 8.29   Double Buffering Collaboration

IMPLEMENTATION

Each request for data consumes some amount of data. The buffers should be large enough to hold enough data to satisfy one request.

Multiple Buffers

One of the assumptions underlying the Double Buffering pattern is that over time the average rate at which data is produced is at least as fast as it is consumed. Some applications may occasionally have multiple requests for data in rapid succession and then none for a while. In situations like this, data is sometimes consumed faster than a buffer can be filled. To avoid having to wait for data when requests for data come in bursts, use more buffers.

The additional buffers are used as reserve buffers. Having enough reserve buffers filled in advance of when their contents are needed means that bursts of requests for data will not have to wait for data.

Threads

The essence of double buffering is that one buffer may be filled while the contents of another buffer are being consumed. This implies that there are at least two threads involved. If you are using asynchronous read functions to fill the buffers, the thread that fills reserve buffers is managed by the .NET library.

The example under the "Code Example" heading reads data from a `Stream` object. It uses the `Stream` object's `BeginRead` function to ask a `Stream` object to fill a buffer using its own thread.

Because the thread that fills the buffers is managed by the .NET library, an implementation of the Double Buffering pattern does not need to deal with any threading issues if it uses only two buffers. If an implementation of the Double Buffering pattern is capable of using more than two buffers, then it will need a way to asynchronously initiate the filling of the next available reserve buffer after the previous reserve buffer is filled. To ensure the best performance, the filling of the next available reserve buffer should be initiated asynchronously of threads that request data from the Double Buffering implementation.

If turns out that because of the way .NET asynchronous reads are organized, we don't need to create a separate thread just to manage multiple reserve buffers. Instead, we can use the thread that performs the asynchronous read. We can ask that when an asynchronous read finishes, it calls a method we provide that is responsible for initiating an asynchronous read into the next reserve buffer.

Exception Handling

Having recognized that we will need to have a thread to asynchronously manage multiple reserve buffers, we discover the next challenge in implementing the Double Buffering pattern. The logic for managing reserve buffers may throw an exception, either as a result of a problem in a read operation or as a result of something that happens within the buffer management logic. Exceptions thrown from these operations require some special handling. There are two difficulties associated with handling these exceptions.

The first problem is that these exceptions are thrown in a different thread than the thread that is requesting data from the implementation of the Double Buffering pattern. It is usually more inconvenient and less useful to handle exceptions in this thread than to handle the exceptions in the data-requesting thread. To make this happen, you will need to catch exceptions in the data-reading thread and re-throw them in the data-requesting thread. However, simply re-throwing the exceptions is not usually good enough. There is a timing issue.

When an exception is thrown in the data-reading thread, it will usually be at a point in the data after what has already been returned by requests for data. If you immediately re-throw the exception in the data-requesting thread, the data-requesting thread might not get to see the good data between what it has already seen and the place where the exception was thrown. It would be better not to re-throw the exception in the data-requesting thread until the data requesting thread sees all the data up to the point that the exception occurred.

The example under the "Code Example" heading includes code that handles exceptions in this way.

CONSEQUENCES

☺ Using the Double Buffering pattern avoids situations where an application must wait for more data to be fetched or created before it can continue processing data.

☺ Use of the Double Buffering pattern keeps classes that use data from having any dependencies on the strategy being used to avoid waiting for more data to be read.

• The Double Buffering pattern increases the amount of memory that a program uses so that it can run faster.

☹ The Double Buffering pattern is an optimization that adds complexity to a program.

.NET API USAGE

The .NET Framework utilizes the double buffering technique in order to display images during an image move, without visible stuttering. Setting the `Control Styles.DoubleBuffer` to true prevents the flicker sometimes observed during the redrawing of a control.

CODE EXAMPLE

The code example for this pattern is a subclass of `System.IO.Stream`. It is similar to the `System.IO.BufferedStream` class, except that instead of using single buffering to just reduce the number of physical read operations needed to read a file, it uses double buffering to also avoid having to wait for physical reads.

```
Imports System.IO
Imports System.Threading

Namespace doubleBuffering
    '
    ' Perform true double buffering, using two or more buffers
    ' for reading and relying on a wrapped Stream object
    ' to implement truely asynchronous reads.
    ' This class does not buffer writes.
    '
    Public Class DoubleBufferedStream
        Inherits StreamWrapper
        Private Const DEFAULT_BUFFER_COUNT As Integer = 2
        Private Const DEFAULT_BUFFER_SIZE As Integer = 65536


        '
        ' An array of input buffers.
        '
        Private inBuffers()() As Byte


        '
        ' An array to track asynchronous read operations
        ' associated this the corresponding buffer in
        ' inBuffers.
        '
        Private reads() As IAsyncResult
```

An instance of this class performs read operations by asking its underlying Stream object to asynchronously read data and fill a buffer. It asks the underlying Stream object to asynchronously read data by calling the Stream object's BeginRead method. The BeginRead method returns an IAsynchResult object, which is put in an array element that corresponds to the buffer that the Stream object was asked to fill.

Before a buffer can become the active buffer, we must be sure that the previously requested read operation has finished filling the buffer. This is determined by checking the IsCompleted property of the IAsynchResult object that corresponds to the buffer in the reads array.

```
'
' Index of the active buffer in inBuffers.
'

Private activeInBuffer As Integer = 0


'
' The number of bytes in each input buffer.
'

Private inByteCounts() As Integer
```

When buffers are filled, this class tries to fill them completely. However, that is not always possible. The actual number of bytes of data that a buffer contains is in the element of the counts array that corresponds to the buffer.

```
'
' The index of the next character to be read from the
' active input buffer.
' It will always be the case that
'
'    0 <= pos <= inBytecounts[activeInBuffer]
'
' If inPos==inByteCounts[activeInBuffer] then
' the active input buffer is empty.
'

Private inPos As Integer


'
' If this is true then the contents of the
' underlying input stream have been exhausted.
'

Private exhausted As Boolean


'
' This is true after the entire underlying input
' stream has been read into buffers.
'

Private inEof As Boolean
```

```
    '
    ' True if this stream is closed.
    '
    Private closed As Boolean


    '
    ' If an asynchronous read throws an exception, this
    ' variable is set to the thrown exception so it can
    ' be re-thrown in a thread that makes a synchronous
    ' request.
    '
    Private readException As Exception


    '
    ' This object is used to coordinate asynchronous
    ' reads with synchronous read operations.
    '
    Private readLockObject As New Object()


    '
    ' The current position within the file.
    '
    Private myPosition As Long


    '
    ' Construct a DoubleBufferedStream with two
    ' buffers and a default buffer size.
    '
    ' underlyingStream -
    '   The underlying stream for which this object will
    '   buffer bytes.
    '
    Public Sub New(ByVal underlyingStream As Stream)
        MyClass.New(underlyingStream, DEFAULT_BUFFER_COUNT)
    End Sub 'New


    '
    ' Construct a DoubleBufferedStream with two
    ' buffers and a default buffer size.
    '
    ' underlyingStream -
    '   The underlying stream for which this object will
    '   buffer bytes.
    '
    ' bufferCount -
    '   The number of buffers that this object should use.
    '   Values less that two are ignored.
    '
    Public Sub New(ByVal underlyingStream As Stream, ByVal
bufferCount As Integer)
        MyClass.New(underlyingStream, bufferCount,
```

```
DEFAULT_BUFFER_SIZE)
        End Sub 'New


    '
    ' Construct a DoubleBufferedStream with two
    ' buffers and a default buffer size.
    '
    ' underlyingStream -
    '    The underlying stream for which this object will
    '    buffer bytes.
    '
    ' bufferCount -
    '    The number of buffers that this object should use.
    '    Values less that two are ignored.
    '
    ' bufferSize -
    '    The size of the buffers to use.  The value must be
    '    greater than 1.
    '
    Public Sub New(ByVal underlyingStream As Stream, _
      ByVal bufferCount As Integer, ByVal bufferSize As Integer)
        MyBase.New(underlyingStream)
        If bufferSize < 1 Then
            Throw New ArgumentException("bufferSize < 1")
        End If
        If bufferCount < 2 Then
            bufferCount = 2
        End If
        'CanRead is inherited from Stream
        If CanRead Then
            Dim inBuffers(bufferCount)() As Byte
            For i As Integer = 0 To bufferCount - 1
                Dim tmp(bufferSize) As Byte
                inBuffers(i) = tmp
            Next i
            inByteCounts = New Integer(bufferCount) {}
            reads = New IAsyncResult(bufferCount) {}

            ' Do first read-ahead
            inEof = Not advanceBuffer()
        End If
    End Sub 'New


    '
    ' Throw an exception if this Stream has been closed.
    '
    Private Sub CheckClosed()
        If closed Then
            Throw New IOException("Stream closed")
        End If
    End Sub 'CheckClosed
```

```vb
    Private Sub CheckReadSupported()
        If Not CanRead Then
            Dim msg As String = "Stream cannot read"
            Throw New NotSupportedException(msg)
        End If
    End Sub 'CheckReadSupported


    ' Gets or sets the position within this stream.
    '
    Public Overrides Property Position() As Long
        Get
            Return myPosition
        End Get
        Set(ByVal Value As Long)
            Seek(Value, SeekOrigin.Begin)
        End Set
    End Property


    ' If this object is able to read, then it may not seek.
    '
    Public Overrides ReadOnly Property CanSeek() As Boolean
        Get
            Return Not CanRead
        End Get
    End Property


    ' Reads a byte from the stream and advances the
    ' position within the stream by one byte, or returns
    ' -1 if at the end of the stream.
    '
    ' returns -
    '    The unsigned byte cast to an Int32, or -1 if at the
    '    end of the stream.
    '
    ' Exceptions:
    ' IOException -
    '    An I/O error occured, such as the file being closed.
    ' NotSupportedException -
    '    The stream does not support reading, or the stream
    '    is already closed.
    '
    Public Overrides Function ReadByte() As Integer
        CheckClosed()
        CheckReadSupported()

        If inEof Then
            Return -1
        End If
```

```
            If inPos >= inByteCounts(activeInBuffer) Then
                inEof = Not advanceBuffer()
            End If
            If exhausted Then
                Return -1
            End If

            Dim c As Integer = inBuffers(activeInBuffer)(inPos)
            inPos += 1
            myPosition += 1

            If inPos >= inByteCounts(activeInBuffer) Then
                If Not advanceBuffer() Then
                    Return -1
                End If
            End If
            Return c
        End Function 'ReadByte

        '
        ' Read a sequence of bytes from this stream and
        ' advance the position within the stream by the
        ' number of bytes read.
        '
        ' buffer -
        '   An array of bytes. When this method returns, the
        '   buffer contains the specified byte array
        '   with the values between offset and
        '   (offset + count) replaced by the
        '   bytes read from this stream.
        '
        ' offset -
        '   The zero-based byte offset in buffer at
        '   which to begin storing the data read from this
        '   stream.
        '
        ' count -
        '   The maximum number of bytes to be read from this
        '   stream.
        '
        ' returns -
        '   The total number of bytes read into the buffer.
        '   This may be less than the number of bytes requested
        '   if that many bytes are not currently available, or
        '   zero (0) if the end of the stream has been reached.
        '
        ' Exception:
        ' ArgumentException -
        '   The sum of offset and count is larger
        '   than the buffer length.
```

```vbnet
' ArgumentNullException -
'   buffer is Nothing.
' ArgumentOutOfRangeException -
'   offset or count is negative.
' IOException -
'   An I/O error occurs.
' NotSupportedException -
'   The stream does not support reading.
' ObjectDisposedException -
'   Methods were called after the stream was closed.
'
Public Overrides Function Read(ByVal buffer() As Byte, _
  ByVal offset As Integer, ByVal count As Integer) As Integer
    CheckClosed()
    CheckReadSupported()

    ' Sanity checks
    If offset < 0 Then
        Dim msg As String = offset.ToString()
        Throw New ArgumentOutOfRangeException("offset", msg)
    End If
    If count < 0 Then
        Dim msg As String = count.ToString()
        Throw New ArgumentOutOfRangeException("count", msg)
    End If
    If buffer Is Nothing Then
        Throw New ArgumentNullException("buffer")
    End If
    If offset + count > buffer.Length Or offset + count < 0 Then
        Throw New ArgumentException()
    End If
    If count = 0 Then
        Return 0
    End If

    Dim howMany As Integer = 0
    Do
        Dim remaining As Integer
        remaining = inByteCounts(activeInBuffer) - inPos
        Dim thisBuffer As Byte() = inBuffers(activeInBuffer)
        If count <= remaining Then
            Array.Copy(thisBuffer, inPos, buffer, offset, count)
            howMany += count
            inPos += count
            count = 0
        Else
            Array.Copy(thisBuffer, inPos, buffer, offset, remaining)
            howMany += remaining
            inPos += remaining
            count -= remaining
            offset += remaining
```

```
            End If
            If inPos >= inByteCounts(activeInBuffer) Then
                If Not advanceBuffer() Then
                    Exit Do
                End If
            End If
        Loop While Not inEof And count > 0

        myPosition += howMany
        Return howMany
End Function 'Read
```

Because this class fills buffers asynchronously of calls to its `Read` and `ReadByte` methods, implementing asynchronous read requests is a problem. The problem is that it is not entirely clear how an asynchronous read can interact with asynchronous buffer filling in a predictable way. To avoid surprises from this type of interaction, this class implements asynchronous read requests synchronously.

```
'
' Begin an asynchronous read operation.
'
' buffer -
'    The buffer to read the data into.
'
' offset -
'    The byte offset in buffer at which to begin
'    writing data read from the stream.
'
' count -
'    The maximum number of bytes to read.
'
' callback -
'    An optional asynchronous callback, to be called
'    when the read is complete.
'
' state -
'    A user-provided object that distinguishes this particular
'    asynchronous read request from other requests.
'
' returns -
'    An IAsyncResult that represents the asynchronous
'    read, which could still be pending.
'
' IOException -
'    An I/O error occurred.
'
' ArgumentException -
'    One or more arguments is invalid.
'
' NotSupportedException -
'    The stream does not support reading.
'
```

```vbnet
' ObjectDisposedException -
'    Methods were called after the stream was closed.
'
Public Overrides Function BeginRead(ByVal buffer() As Byte, _
    ByVal offset As Integer, ByVal count As Integer, _
    ByVal callback As AsyncCallback, ByVal state As Object) As
IAsyncResult
        Dim readCount As Integer = Read(buffer, offset, count)
        Dim theResult As IAsyncResult
        theResult = New Result(state, readCount)
        callback(theResult)
        Return theResult
End Function 'BeginRead


'
' This class is used by the BeginRead method
' to reflect its non-asynchronous implementation.
' Instances of this class are used to encapsulate the
' result of an asynchronous read into a reserve buffer.
'
Private Class Result
    Implements IAsyncResult
    Private state As Object
    Private myCount As Integer

    '
    ' Constructor
    '
    ' state -
    '    The state object to be encapsulated by this
    '    object.
    '
    ' theCount -
    '    The result that should by returned by
    '    EndRead.
    '
    Public Sub New(ByVal state As Object, ByVal theCount As
Integer)
        Me.state = state
        myCount = theCount
    End Sub 'New


    '
    ' Gets a user-defined object that qualifies or
    ' contains information about an asynchronous
    ' operation.
    '
    Public ReadOnly Property AsyncState() As Object _
        Implements IAsyncResult.AsyncState
        Get
```

```vbnet
            Return state
        End Get
    End Property


    '
    ' Gets a WaitHandle that is used to wait for an
    ' asynchronous operation to complete.  The
    ' returned WaitHandle will never make a
    ' caller wait, since the caller will never see
    ' this object until the synchronously implemented
    ' operation has completed.
    '
    Public ReadOnly Property AsyncWaitHandle() As WaitHandle _
        Implements IAsyncResult.AsyncWaitHandle
        Get
            Return New ManualResetEvent(True)
        End Get
    End Property


    '
    ' Gets an indication of whether the asynchronous
    ' operation completed synchronously.  This
    ' implementation is always true.
    '
    Public ReadOnly Property CompletedSynchronously() As Boolean _
        Implements IAsyncResult.CompletedSynchronously
        Get
            Return True
        End Get
    End Property


    '
    ' Gets an indication whether the asynchronous
    ' operation has completed.  Because this is for
    ' a synchronous implementation, instances of this
    ' class will never be seen until the operation
    ' has completed.
    '
    Public ReadOnly Property IsCompleted() As Boolean _
        Implements IAsyncResult.IsCompleted
        Get
            Return True
        End Get
    End Property

    Public ReadOnly Property Count() As Integer
        Get
            Return myCount
        End Get
    End Property
End Class 'Result
```

```
        ' Wait for the pending asynchronous read to complete.
        '
        ' asyncResult -
        '   The reference to the pending asynchronous request
        '   to finish.
        '
        ' returns -
        '   The number of bytes read from the stream, between
        '   zero (0) and the number of bytes you requested.
        '   Streams only return zero (0) at the end of the
        '   stream, otherwise, they should block until at least
        '   one byte is available.
        '
        '
        ' ArgumentNullException -
        '   asyncResult is Nothing.
        '
        ' ArgumentException -
        '   asyncResult did not originate from a
        '   BeginWrite method on this stream.
        '
        Public Overrides Function EndRead(ByVal asyncResult As
IAsyncResult) As Integer
            If Not TypeOf asyncResult Is Result Then
                Throw New ArgumentException("asyncResult")
            End If
            Return CType(asyncResult, Result).Count
        End Function 'EndRead


        '
        ' This method makes the current active buffer an
        ' empty reserve buffer and the next reserve buffer
        ' the new active buffer.  If the next reserve buffer
        ' has not yet been filled and there is reason to
        ' believe that it will be filled then this method
        ' waits until then.
        '
        ' returns -
        '   true if the this call was successful in advancing
        '   to another filled buffer.
        '
        ' IOException - If there is a problem.
        '
        Private Function advanceBuffer() As Boolean
            Dim nextActiveBuffer As Integer
            nextActiveBuffer = (activeInBuffer + 1) Mod
inByteCounts.Length
            SyncLock readLockObject
                If inByteCounts(nextActiveBuffer) = 0 Then
                    If inEof Then
                        exhausted = True
```

```
                    Return False
                End If


            ' If there is not an asynchronous read
            ' operation in progress for the next buffer
            ' make sure that there is.
            EnsureReadInProgress(nextActiveBuffer)

            While Not inEof And inByteCounts(nextActiveBuffer) = 0
                Monitor.Wait(readLockObject)
            End While
            RethrowReadException()
            If inEof Then
                Return False
            End If
        End If
    End SyncLock


    ' At this point we know that the next buffer has data
    ' in it, so we can make that the active buffer.
    inByteCounts(activeInBuffer) = 0
    activeInBuffer = nextActiveBuffer
    inPos = 0

    Return True
End Function 'advanceBuffer


'
' If there is not an asynchronous read
' operation in progress for the next buffer
' make sure that there is.
'
' index -
'    The index of the buffer to ensure there is an
'    active read operation for.
'
Private Sub EnsureReadInProgress(ByVal index As Integer)
    If reads(index) Is Nothing Or Not reads(index).IsCompleted
Then
        Dim callback As AsyncCallback
        callback = AddressOf Me.FinishRead
        Dim thisBuffer As Byte() = inBuffers(index)
        reads(index) = MyBase.BeginRead(thisBuffer, 0, thisBuffer
.Length, _
                                        callback, index)
    End If
End Sub 'EnsureReadInProgress


'
' This method is called when an asynchronous read finishes.
```

```
        '
        Private Sub FinishRead(ByVal result As IAsyncResult)
            SyncLock readLockObject
                Dim index As Integer = CInt(result.AsyncState)
                Try
                    inByteCounts(index) = MyBase.EndRead(result)
                Catch e As Exception
                    readException = e
                    exhausted = True
                End Try
                If inByteCounts(index) = 0 Then
                    inEof = True
                End If
                Dim nextIndex As Integer = (index + 1) Mod
inByteCounts.Length
                If nextIndex <> activeInBuffer Then
                    EnsureReadInProgress(nextIndex)
                End If
                Monitor.Pulse(readLockObject)
            End SyncLock
        End Sub 'FinishRead


        '
        ' Re-throw any exception thrown while reading ahead
        ' in the current thread.
        '
        Private Sub RethrowReadException()
            SyncLock Me
                If readException IsNot Nothing Then
                    Dim excp As Exception = readException
                    readException = Nothing
                    Throw excp
                End If
            End SyncLock
        End Sub 'RethrowReadException


        '
        ' Set the current position in this stream.
        '
        ' offset -
        '   A byte offset relative to origin. If
        '   offset is negative, the new position will
        '   precede the position specified by origin by
        '   the number of bytes specified by offset.
        '   If offset is zero, the new position will
        '   be the position specified by origin. If
        '   offset is positive, the new position will
        '   follow the position specified by origin by
        '   the number of bytes specified by offset.
        '   Note: This implementation does not support seek.
```

```
' origin -
'    A value of type SeekOrigin indicating the
'    reference point used to obtain the new position.
'
' returns -
'    The new current position in this stream.
'
' NotSupportedException -
'    The stream does not support reading.
'

Public Overrides Function Seek(ByVal offset As Long, _
                              ByVal origin As SeekOrigin) As Long
    If CanRead Then
        Throw New NotSupportedException()
    End If
    Return MyBase.Seek(offset, origin)
End Function 'Seek


    '
    ' Closes the current stream and releases any
    ' resources (such as sockets and file handles)
    ' associated with the current stream.
    '
    Public Overrides Sub Close()
        MyBase.Close()
        closed = True
    End Sub 'Close
End Class 'DoubleBufferedStream
End Namespace 'doubleBuffering
```

The base class of the DoubleBufferedStream class is StreamWrapper. The StreamWrapper class is a subclass of the Stream class that overrides all its methods and properties with implementation that delegate to an object passed to the Stream Wrapper object's constructor.

```
Public Class StreamWrapper
    Inherits Stream
    ' Reference to wrapped object
    Private myWrappedObject As System.IO.Stream

    '
    ' Construct a StreamWrapper.
    '
    ' myStream -
    ' The Stream object to be wrapped by this
    ' object.
    '
    Public Sub New(ByVal myStream As System.IO.Stream)
        myWrappedObject = myStream
    End Sub 'New
```

```
        '
        ' The wrapped Stream object to delegate
        ' operations to.
        '

        Protected ReadOnly Property WrappedObject() As Stream
            Get
                Return myWrappedObject
            End Get
        End Property


        '
        ' True if this stream supports reading.
        '

        Public Overrides ReadOnly Property CanRead() As Boolean
            Get
                Return myWrappedObject.CanRead
            End Get
        End Property
...
        '
        ' Closes the current stream and releases any
        ' resources (such as sockets and file handles)
        ' associated with the current stream.
        '

        Public Overrides Sub Close()
            myWrappedObject.Close()
        End Sub 'Close
        ...
    End Class 'StreamWrapper
```

RELATED PATTERNS

Producer-Consumer: The Double Buffering pattern is a specialized form of the Producer-Consumer pattern.

Guarded Suspension: The Guarded Suspension pattern is used in the implementation of the Double Buffering pattern to coordinate the actions of data-requesting threads with the read-ahead thread.

Asynchronous Processing

SYNOPSIS

An object receives requests to do something. Do not process the requests synchronously. Instead, queue them and process them asynchronously.

CONTEXT

Because objects are requested to process things in very diverse circumstances, the description of this pattern includes two different scenarios to make clear the breadth of the problem this pattern solves: a server-based scenario and a client-based scenario. First we consider the server-based scenario.

Suppose that you are designing a server to generate form letters on behalf of applications. The way it is supposed to work is that applications will pass an object to the server that contains the information needed to generate a form letter. If the server determines that the object contains valid data, it returns an ID number to the application. The ID number can be used later by the application to uniquely refer to the generated form letter and send it on.

The simplest way for this server software to work would be to generate a form letter synchronously. This would mean that the server would have a thread that receives a request, generates the form letter, returns the letter's ID to the requesting application and then waits for the next request. Figure 8.30 shows these interactions. However, there are some problems with this design that lead you to decide to look for an alternative.

The first problem is a performance problem. The simplest way for clients to work with a form letter server is to pass the data for a form letter to the server and then wait for the server to return the letter's ID. The longer an application finds itself waiting for the server to return a letter's ID, the more likely there is something more useful it could be doing than waiting. If the server processes requests synchronously, then there is no telling how long a client might find itself waiting for the server.

Applications can be designed to work around this problem by firing off a thread whose only purpose is to wait for the form letter ID. Designing applications to work this way avoids the problem of them having to wait for the server. This is done at the expense of the additional complexity of coordinating the additional thread on each application.

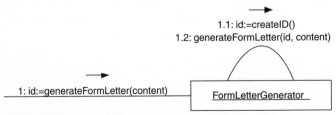

Figure 8.30 Synchronous Form Letter Generation

There is another problem with the synchronous design that is more serious. The problem manifests itself when the server is subject to a burst of requests arriving at about the same time. To service each request synchronously, the server needs to needs to have at least as many active threads as there are pending requests.

If the server does not limit the number of threads it allows to run concurrently, then a sufficiently big burst of requests will overload the server. When the number of threads exceeds some number, performance quickly goes down. A sufficiently large number of threads (perhaps just a few hundred) will cause the server to run out of memory.

If the server does limit the number of threads it allows to run concurrently, then a problem can occur when the server is using its maximum number of threads. Since the server needs a thread for every request it processes, it must refuse to process requests until some pending requests complete and the threads running them become available to process other requests.

The alternative to processing requests synchronously is to process them asynchronously. Figure 8.31 shows how this interaction works. Here are descriptions of the interactions that appear in Figure 8.31:

1   A client asks the server to generate a form letter based on data in a given object. This call returns after the form letter has been assigned an ID number but usually before the form letter is generated.

1.1   The server assigns an ID to the form letter prior to its generation.

1.2   The server initiates the asynchronous generation of the form letter.

1.2.1   The form letter is generated.

1.2.2   The form letter is put in a database, where it can be the subject of further operations.

Making the generation of form letters asynchronous solves the problems that we had with synchronous processing. Clients do not have to wait any longer than it takes to assign an ID to the form letter. The server can limit the number of threads that it devotes to generating form letters to as few a one. If there isn't a thread immediately available to process a request, it can queue the request using the Producer-Consumer pattern. Putting the asynchronous processing in the server does complicate the server slightly. However, the server is the only place that has this complication. All of its clients are relieved of this complexity.

Now let us consider a client-based scenario.

Suppose that you are designing the implementation of a GUI. The GUI is supposed to look like the picture shown in Figure 8.32.

When the menu item labeled "Do It" is clicked, a lengthy operation takes place that lasts many seconds. If the operation is not run asynchronously of the GUI event that triggered it, the GUI and the operation will not behave properly. The problem stems from the fact that delivery of GUI events is single threaded. If a command is run synchronously in response to the GUI event then no other GUI events will be processed until the command completes. While this is happening, the user interface appears to be frozen and unresponsive.

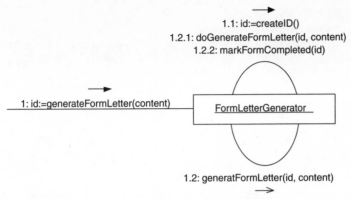

Figure 8.31 Asynchronous Form Letter Generation

The usual way to run a lengthy command while allowing the user interface to continue responding to events normally is to process the command asynchronously of the thread that delivers GUI events. Respond to the event by running the command in a different thread.

FORCES

☺ An object is expected to respond to requests to process things.

☺ An object's clients may not need to wait for its response to a request.

☺ Requests arrive asynchronously of each other.

☺ It is possible for an object to receive a request while it is still in the process of responding to previous requests.

☺ There may be no practical limit on how many requests arrive at about the same time.

☺ An object is required to respond to a request within a specified amount of time from when it received the request.

SOLUTION

Design objects to processes requests asynchronously of when it receives them. The general organization of this is shown in Figure 8.33.

Conceptually, this is one of the simplest patterns in this book. However, like many conceptually simple ideas, there are many implementation-specific details to be filled in.

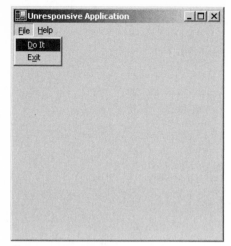

Figure 8.32 Simple GUI

IMPLEMENTATION

There are two main issues in designing an implementation of this pattern. The first issue is how the requests will be managed and how the threads that will process them will be allocated. The second issue arises if the other objects need to know that the request has been processed or what the outcome of its processing was.

Request Management and Thread Allocation

There are many ways to manage requests and the allocation of threads to process them. What is meant here by managing requests is determining when a request *may not be* processed. The possibilities include the following:

- Allow a request to be scheduled for processing immediately.
- Postpone processing a request for a specific period of time.
- Postpone processing a request until a condition is satisfied.
- Reject a request so that it will never be processed.

What is meant here by allocating a thread to process a request is to determine when a request *may be* processed. This involves allocating a thread to process the request and may also involve setting the thread's priority.

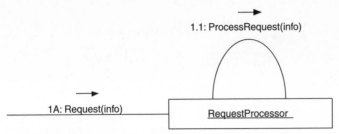

Figure 8.33   Asynchronous Processing

The simplest way of matching requests with threads is to start a new thread every time a request is to be processed. This has the virtue of simplicity. The drawbacks are that it provides minimal control over request management and thread allocation. This organization allows a request to be rejected but provides no way to postpone its processing. There is no real thread allocation policy or limit on the number of threads. This is a problem if it is possible for multiple events notifications to arrive at about the same time. If too many events are being processed at the same time, then the sheer number of threads may cause the request processing to slow down or break due to a lack of resources.

A simple thread allocation policy is to have a fixed number of threads available to process events and arbitrarily assign events to threads as each becomes available. This is essentially an application of the Producer-Consumer pattern. The thread responsible for receiving and queuing requests is the producer. The threads that process the requests are consumers.

A more sophisticated thread allocation policy can be implemented using the Thread Pool pattern (described in [Grand01]). Passing requests to a thread pool allows more sophisticated thread allocation policies. The number of threads in use may be allowed to vary, based on the demand. The priority of threads may also be varied, based on the nature of the request.

Request management may be accomplished by using the Scheduler pattern. The nature of a scheduler object is that it prevents threads from running until a condition is met. Using a scheduler object can allow you to postpone the processing of a request using almost any criteria.

Figure 8.34 shows the interactions between a schedule object and a thread pool. If you use a simple queue instead of a thread pool, the interactions are similar.

1A   A request is delivered to the object labeled `RequestProcessor`.

　1A.1 The `RequestProcessor` object passes the request information to the `scheduler` object.

1B   When the `scheduler` object decides that it is time to process a request, it passes the request information to the `threadPool` object.

1C   The `threadPool` object allocates a thread to process the request and the `RequestProcessor` provides the logic and state information.

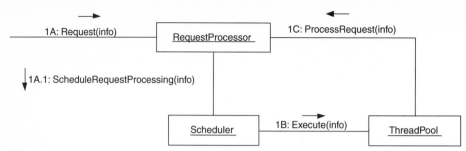

Figure 8.34 Request Processing with Scheduler and Thread Pool

The `scheduler` object shown in Figure 8.36 is an active object that has its own thread. It is able to recognize when a request is ready to be processed and pass it to the thread pool independently of what any other thread is doing.

If there is a need to conserve threads, you can implement the `scheduler` object as a passive object that does not have its own thread. The way this works is that every time a request is passed to a `scheduler` object, the `scheduler` object checks if it has any requests ready to be passed to the thread pool. Optionally, when one of the thread pool's threads finishes processing a request, it may call a method of the `scheduler` object that checks for requests ready to process.

Outcome Management

In some cases, after the processing of a request is completed, another object is supposed to discover the fact that the request processing is completed. Most commonly, the object that is supposed to be aware of the completed request processing is the object that originated the request. Here are two common ways that other objects learn that the processing of a request has completed:

- The object responsible for the completed request processing may send an event to objects that have been registered to receive such events.

- The outcome of the request processing may be stored in a place that interested objects will poll for the purpose of discovering requests and their outcomes.

If the object that originated a request is supposed to become aware of the outcome of request processing, it may use the Future pattern to coordinate the outcome of the request processing with any other activities it is involved in.

CONSEQUENCES

☺ An object that is the source of a request does not have to wait for the request to be processed before it can do other things, such as send out more events.

☺ A request can be queued for processing without having a thread allocated to it. This is a big savings on resources, because each thread consumes a significant amount of memory even if it is doing nothing.

☺ The Asynchronous Processing pattern makes it possible to have explicit policies to determine when or if a request will be processed.

☹ The Asynchronous Processing pattern makes it difficult to guarantee that a request will be processed within a fixed amount of time.

.NET API USAGE

`System.Windows.Forms` based user interfaces use the Asynchronous Processing pattern. They manage keyboard and mouse events using the Producer-Consumer pattern and schedule them sequentially using a single thread.

The way this works is that when the user does something with the mouse or keyboard, an event is generated. Events can be then be handled by an associated `EventHandler`.

CODE EXAMPLE

The code example for this pattern is an example of a client program that processes some user interface events asynchronously. It is a subclass of the `Form` class that looks like the picture in Figure 8.32. On its `File` pull-down menu is a menu item labeled "Do It". There is also a progress bar at the bottom of the frame.

When a user clicks the "Do It" menu option, the progress bar goes from 0 to 100 percent over the course of about 4 seconds. While the progress bar is being incremented, the "Do It" menu item does not appear on the `File` pull-down menu. In its place, there appears a menu item labeled "Stop Doing It". If the user clicks on the "Stop Doing It" menu item, then the progress bar stops changing.

Whether the progress bar stops changing because it is at 100 percent or because the user clicks the "Stop Doing It" menu item, when the progress bar stops changing, the "Stop Doing It" menu item is replaced by the "Do It" menu item.

```
Imports System.Threading

Public Class Form1
    Private Sub MenuItem3_Click(ByVal sender As System.Object, _
    ByVal e As System.EventArgs) Handles MenuItem3.Click
        simStop()

        Me.ProgressBar1.Visible = True
        Me.Button1.Visible = True
        Me.ProgressBar1.Invalidate()
        Me.Button1.Invalidate()

        Dim file As New FileSimProc(ProgressBar1, New
FileSimDone(AddressOf simDone))
        sim = New Thread(New ThreadStart(AddressOf file.RunSim))
        sim.IsBackground = True
        sim.Start()
    End Sub
```

```
        Private sim As Thread

        Private Sub simStop()
            If Not (sim Is Nothing) Then
                sim.Interrupt()
            End If
            sim = Nothing
            ProgressBar1.Visible = False
            Button1.Visible = False
        End Sub 'simStop


        Private Sub simDone()
            ProgressBar1.Visible = False
            Button1.Visible = False
        End Sub 'simDone


        Private Sub Button1_Click(ByVal sender As System.Object, _
         ByVal e As System.EventArgs) Handles Button1.Click
            simStop()
        End Sub
    End Class


    Public Delegate Sub FileSimDone()

    Public Class FileSimProc
        Private bar As ProgressBar
        Private done As FileSimDone

        Private Sub New()
        End Sub

        Public Sub New(ByVal p As ProgressBar, ByVal d As FileSimDone)
            bar = p
            done = d
            bar.Value = 0
        End Sub

        Public Sub RunSim()
            Try
                Dim m As New MethodInvoker(AddressOf Me.Update)
                While bar.Value < bar.Maximum
                    bar.BeginInvoke(m) ' call our update on the controls thread
                    Thread.Sleep(1000)
                End While
                bar.BeginInvoke(done)
            Catch e As ThreadInterruptedException ' occurs on interrupt
                ' ignore and exit
            End Try
        End Sub 'RunSim
```

```
      Private Sub Update()
          If bar.Value < bar.Maximum Then
              bar.PerformStep()
          End If
      End Sub 'Update
  End Class
```

RELATED PATTERNS

Thread Pool: The Thread Pool pattern (described in [Grand01]) may be used in implementing the Asynchronous Processing pattern.

Producer-Consumer: The Producer-Consumer pattern may be used in implementing the Asynchronous Processing pattern.

Scheduler: The Scheduler pattern may be used in implementing the Asynchronous Processing pattern.

Façade: An implementation of a request processing class may use classes that are artifacts of using the Thread Pool, Producer-Consumer or Scheduler patterns. Request processing classes generally act as a façade to hide these details from their client classes.

Future: The object that originates a request may need to be aware of the outcome of the request being asynchronously processed by another object. The originating object may use the Future pattern to coordinate the outcome of processing with any other activities the originating object is involved in.

Active Object: The Active Object pattern described in [SSRB00] describes a way of combining the Future pattern with the Asynchronous Processing pattern.

Future

This pattern is also known as Promise.

SYNOPSIS

Use an object to encapsulate the result of a computation in a way that hides from its clients whether the computation is synchronous or asynchronous. The object will have a method to get the result of the computation. The method waits for the result if the computation is asynchronous and in progress or performs the computation if it is synchronous and not yet performed.

CONTEXT

Suppose that you are designing a reusable class that will allow a program to get current weather data for a given location. A common type of application for this weather class is expected to be a display that includes weather information along with many other pieces of information. For example, the weather class might be used to generate the HTML for a Web page that displays weather information to the side of some news.

The amount of time it will take to get weather information will vary greatly. It could be a fraction of a second or it could be many minutes. You want to design the weather class in a way that minimizes the impact on its clients.

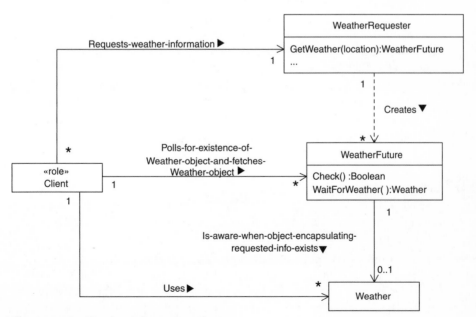

Figure 8.35   Weather Information Classes

You consider having instances of the weather class send an event to interested objects when it receives requested weather information. You decide against this. You are concerned that requiring the weather class's clients to receive an asynchronous call that delivers an event notification forces too much complexity on them. A method to receive such a notification must arrange for the client to take notice of the new weather information in a thread-safe way.

Finally, you decide on the organization shown in Figure 8.35. Here are descriptions of the classes shown in Figure 8.35:

Weather: Instances of this class *encapsulate* information about the current weather conditions at a particular location.

Client: Instances of a class in this role use the information in `Weather` objects.

WeatherRequester: When a `Client` object wants to get a `Weather` object that contains the current information for a given location, it asks a `Weather Requester` object to request the information on its behalf. The `Client` object does this by calling the `WeatherRequester` object's `GetWeather` method. The `GetWeather` method does not wait for the weather information to be fetched. It returns immediately. The value it returns is a `WeatherFuture` object. The requested weather information is fetched asynchronously.

WeatherFuture: This class is responsible for allowing other threads to coordinate their actions with a thread that is fetching weather information. When a `WeatherRequester` object's `GetWeather` method is called, it initiates the asynchronous fetching of requested weather information. It immediately returns a `WeatherFuture` object associated with the request.

A `WeatherFuture` object has a method named `Check` that returns false if it is called before the requested information has been fetched and a `Weather` object containing the information has been created. After the `Weather` object has been created, calls to the `Check` method return true.

A `WeatherFuture` object has another method named `WaitForWeather`. If this method is called before the `Weather` object has been created, it waits until the `Weather` object has been created. Once the `Weather` object has been created, calls to the `waitForWeather` method immediately return the `Weather` object.

FORCES

☺ A computation takes place asynchronously of other threads that use the result of the computation.

☺ An asynchronous computation can notify objects that use its result that the result is available by using the Observer pattern or passing the object an event. For this to work properly, it may be necessary to have single-threaded access to some methods or sections of code. In some situations, this may add an unacceptable level of overhead or complexity to a class.

☺ You want to encapsulate a computation so that its clients do not need to know if it is synchronous or asynchronous.

SOLUTION

Instead of designing a method to directly return the result of a computation, have it return an object that encapsulates the result of the computation. The object that encapsulates the result will have a method that can be called to get the result of the computation. Callers of this method do not know whether the computation is performed synchronously or asynchronously of their thread.

Figure 8.36 shows the roles that classes play in this solution. Here are descriptions of the roles that classes play in the Future pattern.

Result: Instances of a class in this role encapsulate the result of a computation.

Client: Instances of classes in this role use Result objects. Client objects initiate the process of getting a Result object by passing the appropriate parameters to a Requester object's DoIt method.

Requester: A class in this role has a method that can be called to initiate the computation of a Result object. In Figure 8.36, this method is indicated with the name DoIt. The DoIt method returns a Future object that encapsulates that computation.

Future: Each instance of a class in this role encapsulates the computation of a Result object. The computation may be synchronous or asynchronous. If the computation is asynchronous, then it is computed in its own thread. An asynchronous computation may already be underway when the Future object that encapsulates it is created.

Future objects have a method that Client objects call to get the result of a computation. In Figure 8.36, this method is indicated with the name get Result. The way that this method works depends on whether the computation is synchronous or asynchronous.

If the computation is asynchronous and the method is called before the computation has completed, then the method waits until the computation is complete and then returns the result. If the method is called after the computation has completed, then the method immediately returns the result.

If the computation is synchronous, the first time the method is called the computation is synchronously performed and its result is returned. Subsequent calls to the method just return the result. Alternatively, the computation may be performed when the Future object is created.

Figure 8.37 is a collaboration diagram that shows the interactions between objects in the Future pattern. Here are descriptions of the interactions shown in Figure 8.37:

1. A Client object calls a Requester object's doIt method. This initiates a computation that is encapsulated by the Future object that the DoIt method returns.

2. After spending some time doing other things, the Client object calls the Future object's GetResult method. The GetResult method returns the result of the computation.

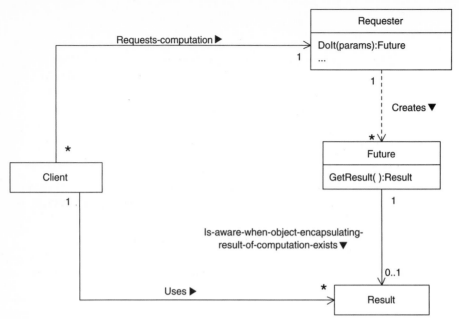

Figure 8.36 Future Pattern

IMPLEMENTATION

The Future pattern has a few interesting implementation issues.

Polling

A common usage pattern for the Future pattern is for the Client object to call a Requester object's DoIt method to start a computation before it needs the result. It then does some other things. When it finally needs the result of the computation, it calls the Future object's GetResult method. If the computation is asynchronous, initiating the computation as soon as possible and then getting its result as late as possible maximizes the advantages of the asynchronous processing.

In some situations this usage is not appropriate. One such situation is when the client has an ongoing task it performs continuously. Consider the example of a program that serves a Web page containing news articles and weather information. Suppose that this program uses the weather-related classes discussed under the "Context" heading. After it has requested weather information, there is no one point in what this program does that you can regard as the latest possible time to get the weather information. The program is continuously updating the information it uses for the content of the Web page it serves. You don't want any request for the program to provide Web content to be delayed by having to wait for an update to weather information.

One way to resolve this problem would be to have a separate thread for each request for weather information. Using a thread for this purpose does not add much value and seems like a waste of resources.

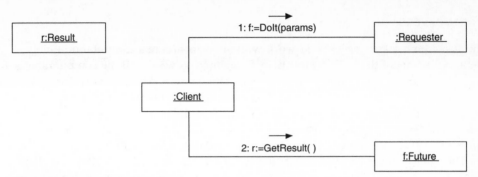

Figure 8.37 Future Interactions

A better solution is to add another method to the Future class. For the purposes of this discussion, we will call the method isCompleted. The purpose of this isCompleted method is to check whether a Client object will wait idly if it calls the Future object's GetResult method. An isCompleted method may be helpful if the encapsulated computation is asynchronous. The isCompleted method will return false if it is called before the computation has completed or true if it is called after the computation has completed. If the computation is synchronous, then the isCompleted method always returns true.

Having an isCompleted method allows Client objects to poll Future objects. Each request for content can poll a Future object by calling its isCompleted method. If the isCompleted method returns true, the program updates the weather information it uses for the Web page's content. If the check method returns false, then the program continues using information it already has.

Proxy

The Future pattern is sometimes used with the Proxy pattern. This is generally done by having the class in the Future role implement an interface that allows it to be used as a proxy to the class performing the computation. When used this way, the object that initiates the computation and creation of the Future object and the object that gets the result from the Future object are usually not the same object.

An object will initiate the creation of the Future object. It will pass the Future object to other objects that will access the object through an interface without any knowledge of the Future object's class or its participation in the Future pattern. When the Future and Proxy patterns are combined in this way and the computation is synchronous, the result is the Virtual Proxy pattern.

Launching a Synchronous Computation

If a Future object encapsulates a synchronous computation, it must be able to launch the computation the first time that its GetResult method is called. To launch the computation, the Future object must be able to provide the computation with its parameters. For this reason, if a Future class encapsulates a synchronous computation, the class's constructor will take the necessary parameters to provide the parameter values to the computation.

Rendezvous

Implementing a `Future` class to work with an asynchronous computation involves getting the thread that calls its `getResult` method to wait until the computation is finished. There is a name for the technique of getting multiple threads to wait until one or more of them reach a certain point. The name of this technique is *rendezvous*.

A general-purpose way to implement rendezvous involves using `Monitor.Wait` and `Monitor.NotifyAll`. The code listing of the `AsynchronousFuture` class under the "Code Example" heading shows an example of this technique.

The .NET Framework provides the `System.Threading.WaitHandle` class, which is a more specialized mechanism for waiting until a computation has completed. This is discussed in more detail under the ".NET API Usage" heading.

Exceptions

If the computation associated with a `Future` object throws an exception, you want the exception to be thrown out of the `Future` object's `getResult` method. If the computation is performed synchronously, then any exceptions it throws will, as a natural consequence, be thrown out of the `Future` object's `getResult` method.

If the computation is asynchronous and it throws an exception, the natural course of events is for it to throw the exception in the currently running thread. In order for the exception to be thrown out of the `Future` object's `getResult` method, you will need to catch the exception and set one of the `Future` object's instance variables to refer to it. You can then code the `getResult` method so that if the instance variable is not null, the `getResult` method throws the exception that it refers to.

CONSEQUENCES

☺ The classes that use a computation are relieved of any responsibility for concurrency.

☺ If the computation is asynchronous, all of the complexity related to synchronization is in the `Future` class.

.NET API USAGE

The .NET API includes support for a variation on the Future pattern that involves the uses of the `System.IAsyncResult` interface. A method that starts an asynchronous computation returns a `IAsyncResult` object. The `IAsyncResult` object is used to determine when the computation has completed, by polling or waiting. However, the result of the computation is not available through that `IAsyncResult` object. To get the result of the computation, it is necessary to call a method of the object that created the `IAsyncResult` object.

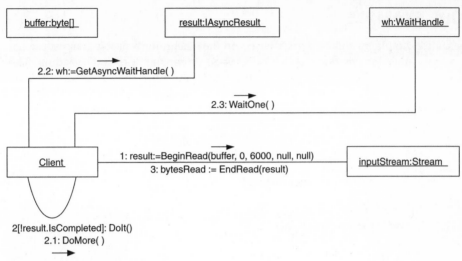

Figure 8.38 Asynchronous Read

Figure 8.38 shows how this is used with the System.IO.Stream class to request an asynchronous read and then determine what then find out when the read has finished and how many bytes were read. Here are descriptions of the interactions shown in Figure 8.38:

1 Ask the inputStream object to start an asynchronous read operation to put 6,000 bytes of data into the buffer. The method call returns the object labeled result that can be used to determine when the read operation is done.

2 Ask the result object if the read operation is done. If it is not done, then call the DoIt method to do something useful while we are waiting for the read operation to finish.

2.1 This method call does something useful.

2.2 Get the WaitHandle object from the result object.

2.3 Call the WaitHandle object's waitOne method to wait until the read operation is finished.

3 Get the results of the read operation by calling inputStream.EndRead, which will either return the actual number of bytes read or rethrow any exceptions that were thrown from the read operation.

The simplest use of the Future pattern is for a client object to start a single asynchronous operation and then get the results of the operation. This variation that uses the IAsyncResult interface makes this simplest case a bit more complicated for client classes. However, it simplifies more complicated cases.

Using IAsyncResult objects makes some situations that involve multiple concurrent operations simpler. For example, it simplifies the situation when there are multiple concurrent operations and another operation to happen after all of the concurrent operations have completed.

CODE EXAMPLE

The code example for this pattern is based on the design for reusable classes to fetch current weather information that was discussed under the "Context" heading. The first class presented is the WeatherRequester class that fills the Requester role.

```
Namespace Future
    '
    ' This class is used to request current weather
    ' information for a location at the given coordinates.
    '
    Public Class WeatherRequester
        '
        ' The object that does the real work of fetching
        ' weather information.
        '
        Private fetcher As IWeatherFetch


        '
        ' Constructor
        '
        ' fetcher -
        '     The object that will be used to fetch weather
        '     information.
        '
        Public Sub New(ByVal fetcher As IWeatherFetch)
            Me.fetcher = fetcher
        End Sub 'New


        '
        ' Initiate the process of getting current weather
        ' data for the given geographical coordinates.
        '
        ' location -
        '     The location for which weather information is to
        '     be fetched.
        '
        ' returns -
        '     A future object that can later be used to access
        '     the requested weather information.
        '
        Public Function GetWeather(ByVal location As Coordinate) As
    WeatherFuture
            SyncLock Me
                Return New WeatherFuture(fetcher, location)
            End SyncLock
        End Function 'GetWeather
    End Class 'WeatherRequester
End Namespace 'Future
```

The constructor for the `WeatherRequester` class is passed the object that will do the real work of fetching current weather information for a given location. Its `GetWeather` method is passed a location and creates a `WeatherFuture` object by passing the weather fetching object and the location to the `WeatherFuture` class's constructor. The `WeatherFuture` class fills the `Future` role.

```vb
Imports System.Threading

Namespace Future
    '
    ' Instances of this class encapsulate the asynchronous
    ' fetching of current weather information.
    '
    Public Class WeatherFuture
        '
        ' When a coordinate is passed to the constructor, it
        ' puts the coodinate for the request in this
        ' instance variable so that it is visible to the new
        ' thread that it starts.
        '
        Private location As Coordinate
        '
        ' The object to use to fetch current weather
        ' information.
        '
        Private fetcher As IWeatherFetch
        '
        ' An object to provide support logic.
        '
        Private futureSupport As AsynchronousFuture
        '
        ' Construct a WeatherFuture object that encapsulates
        ' the fetching of weather information for the given
        ' coordinate using the given WeatherFetchIF object.
        '
        ' fetcher -
        '    The object that will fetch the weather data.
        '
        ' location -
        '    The location for which weather information is to
        '    be fetched.
        '
        Public Sub New(ByVal fetcher As IWeatherFetch, ByVal location As Coordinate)
            Me.fetcher = fetcher
            Me.location = location
            futureSupport = New AsynchronousFuture()
            Dim asyncThread As Thread
            asyncThread = New Thread(New ThreadStart(AddressOf Run))
            asyncThread.Start()
        End Sub 'New
```

```vb
    '
    ' Return true if the requested weather info has been
    ' fetched.
    '
    Public ReadOnly Property IsResultAvailable() As Boolean
        Get
            Return futureSupport.IsResultAvailable
        End Get
    End Property


    '
    ' Return the result object for this future.  If it
    ' has not yet been set, wait until it is set.
    '
    ' returns - the result object for this future.
    '
    Public Function WaitForWeather() As IWeather
        Return CType(futureSupport.Result, IWeather)
    End Function 'WaitForWeather


    '
    ' This private class provides the top-level logic for
    ' asynchronously fetching current weather
    ' information.
    '
    Public Sub Run()
        Try
            Dim info As IWeather = fetcher.fetchWeather(location)
            futureSupport.SetResult(info)
        Catch e As Exception
            futureSupport.SetException(e)
        End Try
    End Sub 'Run
End Class 'WeatherFuture
End Namespace 'Future
```

When the weather information has been fetched, it is encapsulated in an instance of a class that implements an interface named `WeatherIF`. The core logic for managing the asynchronous computation is delegated to a reusable class named `Asynchronous Future`.

```vb
Imports System.Threading

Namespace Future
    '
    ' This class provides reusable logic for implementing
    ' Future classes that encapsulate an asynchronous
    ' computation.
    '
```

```
Public Class AsynchronousFuture
    Private myResult As Object
    Private resultIsAvailable As Boolean
    Private problem As Exception

    '
    ' True if the result has been set.
    '
    Public ReadOnly Property IsResultAvailable() As Boolean
        Get
            Return resultIsAvailable
        End Get
    End Property

    '
    ' The result object for this future.  If it has not
    ' yet been set, wait until it is set.
    '
    Public ReadOnly Property Result() As [Object]
        Get
            SyncLock Me
                While Not resultIsAvailable
                    Monitor.Wait(Me)
                End While
                If problem IsNot Nothing Then
                    Throw problem
                End If
                Return myResult
            End SyncLock
        End Get
    End Property

    '
    ' Call this method to set the result of a
    ' computation.  This method should only be called
    ' once.
    '
    ' theResult - The object that is the result of the computation.
    '
    Public Sub SetResult(ByVal theResult As [Object])
        SyncLock Me
            If resultIsAvailable Then
                Dim msg As String = "Result is already set"
                Throw New ThreadStateException(msg)
            End If ' if
            myResult = theResult
            resultIsAvailable = True
            Monitor.PulseAll(Me)
        End SyncLock
    End Sub 'SetResult
```

```
        '
        ' If the asynchronous computation associated with
        ' this object throws an exception, pass the exception
        ' to this method and the exception will be rethrown
        ' by the getResult method.
        '
        ' e - The object that was thrown
        Public Sub SetException(ByVal e As Exception)
            SyncLock Me
                problem = e
                resultIsAvailable = True
                Monitor.PulseAll(Me)
            End SyncLock
        End Sub 'SetException
    End Class 'AsynchronousFuture
End Namespace 'Future
```

RELATED PATTERNS

Asynchronous Processing: The Asynchronous Processing pattern provides guidance on when to make a computation asynchronous. It is often used with the Future pattern.

Observer: Using the Observer pattern is an alternative to polling a `Future` object to determine if its associated asynchronous computation has completed.

Proxy: The Future pattern can be combined with the Proxy pattern so that the `Future` object is also a proxy for the object that performs that underlying computation.

Virtual Proxy: If the Future pattern is combined with the Proxy pattern and the computation is synchronous, then what you have is equivalent to the Virtual Proxy pattern.

Active Object: The Active Object pattern described in [SSRB00] describes a way of combining the Future pattern with the Asynchronous Processing pattern.

Bibliography

[Appleton97] Brad Appleton. "Patterns and Software: Essential Concepts and Terminology". www.enteract.com/~bradapp/docs/patterns-intro.html.

[ASU86] Alfred V. Aho, Ravi Seti, Jeffery D. Ullman. *Compilers, Principles, Techniques and Tools*. Addison-Wesley, Reading, MA, 1986.

[Bentley] Jon Louis Bentley. *Programming Pearls*. ACM, New York, NY, 1986.

[BMMM98] William J. Brown, Raphael C Malveau, Hays W. "Skip" McCormick III, and Thomas J. Mowbray. *AntiPatterns*. Wiley Publishing, Inc., New York, NY, 1998.

[BMRSS96] Frank Buschmann, Regine Meunier, Hans Rohnert, Peter Sommerlad, and Michael Stal. *Pattern-Oriented Software Architecture, Volume 1: A System of Patterns*. John Wiley & Sons, Inc., West Sussex, England, 1996.

[GoF95] Erich Gamma, Richard Helm, Ralph Johnson, and John Vlissides. *Design Patterns: Elements of Reusable Object-Oriented Software*. Addison-Wesley, Reading, MA, 1995.

[Grand98] Mark Grand. *Patterns in Java*, Volume 2. Wiley Publishing, Inc., New York, NY, 1998.

[Grand01] Mark Grand. *Java Enterprise Design Patterns*. Wiley Publishing, Inc., New York, NY, 2001.

[Grand02] Mark Grand. *Patterns in Java*, Volume 1, Second Edition. Wiley Publishing, Inc., New York, NY, 2002.

[Heany99] Matthew Heaney. "Static Locking Order", http://listserv.acm.org/scripts/wa.exe?A2=ind9904&L=patterns&F=&S=&P=877, April 9, 1999.

[Kaplan94] Randy M. Kaplan. *Constructing Language Processors for Little Languages*. Wiley Publishing, Inc., New York, NY, 1994.

[Larman01] Craig Larman. *Applying UML and Patterns*, Second Edition. Prentice Hall PTR, Upper Saddle River, NJ, 2001.

[Lea97] Doug Lea. *Concurrent Programming in Java*. Addison-Wesley, Reading, MA, 1997.

[LL01] Timothy C. Lethbridge and Robert Laganière. "Object-Oriented Software Engineering: Practical Software Development using UML and Java." McGraw Hill, Summer 2001.

[LLLMP02] Brian A. LaMacchia, Sebastian Lange, Matthew Lyons, Rudi Martin, and Kevin T. Price. *.NET Framework Security*. Addison-Wesley, Reading, MA, 2002.

[Rhiel00] Dirk Rhiel. "Fundamental Class Patterns in Java." Unpublished manuscript (in 2000). www.riehle.org/papers/2000/plot-2000-class-patterns.html.

[Ritchie84] D. Ritchie, "A Stream Input-Output System," *AT&T Bell Labs Technical Journal*, Volume 63, pp. 311–324, Oct 1984.

[SSRB00] Douglas Schmidt, Micheal Stal, Hans Rohnert, and Frank Buschmann. *Pattern Oriented Software Architecture*, Volume 2. John Wiley & Sons, West Sussex, England, 2000.

[Woolf97] Bobby Woolf. "The Null Object Pattern". www.ksccary.com/nullobj.htm.

Index

- (private) visibility indicator, meaning, 2
(protected) visibility indicator,
    meaning, 2
+ (public) visibility indicator, meaning, 2

A

ABCJournalRecordFactory class, Factory
    Method pattern, 104
Abstract Base Class pattern
  abstract base classes, 61
  class roles, 63–64
  code example, 64–67
  concrete classes, 64
  dependencies, 64
  IEnumerator interface, 61
  implementation, 64
  Interface and Abstract Class
      pattern and, 67
  .NET Framework and, 64
  Template Method pattern and, 67
abstract base classes, behavior, 61
Abstract Class pattern, Interface and
    Abstract Class pattern, 72
abstract classes
  extension, 99
  Template Method pattern, 407
abstract factory class
  abstract class instances and, 109
  instantiation and, 132

Abstract Factory pattern
  Bridge pattern and, 223
  class roles, 111
  Client role, 112
  code example, 114–119
  ConcreteFactory1 role, 112
  ConcreteFactory2 role, 112
  Factory Method pattern and, 107, 119
  IFactory interface, 112
  implementation, 113
  instances of classes, 110
  IWidgetA interface, 112
  IWidgetB interface, 112
  Kit, 109
  object creation and, 94
  Product1WidgetA role, 112
  Product2WidgetA role, 112
  Prototype pattern and, 139
  Singleton pattern and, 119
  Toolkit, 109
Abstract Superclass, 61
AbstractBaseclass, 63–64
AbstractBuilder class, Builder pattern, 125
AbstractCommandHandler class, Chain of
    Responsibility pattern, 297
AbstractComposite class, Composite pat-
    tern, 177
AbstractDoorControllerWrapper class,
    Decorator pattern, 266–267

AbstractElement class, Visitor pattern, 419
AbstractFlyweight class, 238
Abstraction class, Bridge pattern, 216
AbstractionImpl interface, Bridge pattern, 217
abstractions
  Bridge pattern, 213
  hierarchies, combining, 216
  implementations, creating, 216
  logic reuse, 216
AbstractLoadableClass class
  Dynamic Linkage pattern, 248
  subclasses, 249
AbstractPullFilter class, Filter pattern, 167
AbstractPushFilter class, Filter pattern, 169
AbstractTemplate class, Template Method pattern, 409
AbstractVisitor class, Visitor pattern, 419
AbstractWrapper class, Decorator pattern, 268
accessor methods, attributes, 35
Action class, Hashed Adapter Objects pattern and, 431
ActionKey class, Hashed Adapter Objects pattern and, 431
active buffer, 500
Active Object pattern
  Asynchronous Processing pattern and, 527
  Future pattern and, 540
Adaptee classes, Adapter pattern, 197
Adapter classes, Adapter pattern, 197
adapter classes, interfaces, 195
adapter objects, Hashed Adapter Objects pattern, 427
Adapter pattern
  Adaptee classes, 197
  Adapter classes, 197
  adapter classes, 195
  Client class, 197
  code example, 199–206
  Façade pattern, 204, 231
  Hashed Adapter Objects pattern and, 435
  implementation, 198–199
  Interface pattern, 59
  ITarget interface, 197

Iterator pattern, 204, 211
  Observer pattern and, 382
  overview, 193
  Proxy pattern, 204
  Read-Only interface pattern, 192
  Strategy pattern, 204, 400
aggregations
  class relationships, 8
  composite, 9
algorithms, encapsulation (Strategy pattern), 395–400
application-independent objects, 97–98
application-specific classes, creation, 96
arbitrary objects, Hashed Adapter Objects pattern, 427
ArrayCopier class, 195
arrowheads, asynchronous calls, 20–21
ASP.NET, Interface and Abstract Class pattern and, 70–71
assemblies, packages and, 11
associations
  association names, 7
  classes, 7
  dependencies, 10
  multiplicity indicators, 8
  navigation arrows, 7
  role names, 7
assumptions, requirements and, 29
asynchronous calls, arrowheads, 20–21
asynchronous interactions, collaborative diagram, 19
Asynchronous Processing pattern
  Active Object pattern and, 527
  code example, 525–527
  Façade pattern and, 527
  Future pattern and, 527, 540
  implementation, 522–524
  introduction, 438
  .NET, 525
  overview, 519
  Producer-Consumer pattern and, 527
  request management, 522–524
  Scheduler pattern and, 527
  thread allocation, 522–524
  Thread Pool pattern and, 527

B

Backus-Naur Form (BNF), tokens, 320
Balking pattern
  code example, 469–470
  Guarded Suspension pattern and, 465,
    470
  implementation, 469
  introduction, 438
  Mediator pattern and, 354
  Single Threaded Execution pattern and,
    470
  state and, 467–470
batching notifications, Observer pattern,
  378
behavioral patterns
  categories, 293
  Chain of Responsibility pattern, 295–304
  Command pattern, 305–315
  Hashed Adapter Objects pattern, 427–435
  Little Language pattern, 317–342
  Mediator pattern, 343–354
  Null Object, 401–405
  Observer pattern, 373–382
  Snapshot pattern, 355–372
  State pattern, 383–394
  Strategy pattern, 395–400
  Template Method, 407–413
  Visitor, 415–425
behaviors
  delegation and, 51
  IEnumerator interface, 61
  operations, 1
  Strategy pattern and, 396
Bentley, Jon, 317
BNF (Backus-Naur Form), tokens, 320
Both Dirty state, 385
Bridge pattern
  Abstract Factory pattern and, 223
  Abstraction class, 216
  abstraction hierarchies, 213
  AbstractionImpl interface, 217
  code example, 218–223
  Decorator pattern and, 223
  Factory Method object, 219
  hierarchy extension, 218
  implementation, 218

  Layered Architecture pattern and, 223
  .NET Framework, 218
  overview, 193
  SpecializedAbstraction class, 216
  SpecializedAbstractionImpl interface,
    217
buffers
  active, 500
  Double Buffering pattern and, 502–503
  reserve, 500
Builder pattern
  AbstractBuilder class, 125
  client classes, 125
  code example, 128–129
  Composite pattern and, 129
  Concrete Builder class, 125
  consequences, 127
  Director object, 125
  external data representation, 124
  Factory Method pattern and, 129
  implementation, 126–127
  Interface pattern and, 129
  IProduct interface, 124
  .NET Framework, 128
  Null Object pattern and, 129
  object creation and, 94
  overview, 121
  Product class, 124
  Strategy pattern and, 129
  Template Method pattern and, 129
  Visitor pattern and, 129

C

cache, object limits, 280
Cache class, Cache Management pattern,
  275
Cache Management pattern
  ArrayList, 278
  Cache class, 275
  CacheManager class, 275
  Client classes, 275
  code example, 282–292
  Ephemeral Cache Item pattern and, 292
  Façade pattern and, 292
  Flyweight pattern and, 244

Cache Management pattern *(continued)*
  GetHashCode( ) method, 281
  Hashtable, 279
  hit rate, 277
  implementation, 275–281
  object access, 273
  Object Pool pattern and, 161
  Object Replication pattern and, 292
  ObjectCreator class, 275
  ObjectKey class, 275
  Optimistic Concurrency pattern and, 292
  overview, 193
  performance tuning and, 277–281
  prefetching objects, 277
  ProductCacheManager class and, 274
  ProductInfoFetcher object, 274
  read consistency, 282
  Singleton pattern and, 147
  Template Method pattern and, 292
  Virtual Proxy pattern and, 292
  write consistency, 282
CacheManager class
  Cache Management pattern, 275
  hit rate and, 280
  ObjectCreator class and, 275
Caretaker class, Snapshot pattern, 360
CAS (code access security), Dynamic Linkage Pattern and, 249
case studies
  business case in deployment, 28–29
  essential use cases, 30–32
  object-oriented analysis, 32–34
  object-oriented design, 34–43
  requirements for deployment, 29–30
Chain of Responsibility pattern
  AbstractCommandHandler class, 297
  behavior and, 293
  code example, 299–304
  Command pattern and, 304
  commands, 295
  CommandSender class, 297
  Composite pattern and, 185, 304
  ICommandHandler interface, 297
  implementation, 297–298
  .NET API, 299
  object coupling, 299
  Template Method pattern and, 304

class diagrams
  classes and, 6
  definition, 2
  interfaces and, 6
  objects, 12
classes
  ABCJournalRecordFactory, 104
  Abstract Base Class pattern, 63–64
  abstract factory class, 109
  AbstractBaseclass, 63–64
  AbstractPushFilter, 169
  adapter classes, 195
  aggregations, 8
  application-specific, 96
  ArrayCopier, 195
  associations, 7
  attributes, 1
  class diagrams and, 6
  Client, 56
  Client, Object Pool pattern, 153
  compartments, 4
  compatibility, Dynamic Linkage pattern and, 248
  concrete, Abstract Base Class pattern, 64
  ConcretePushFilter, 169
  constructors, interfaces and, 56
  CSharpCodeProvider, 128
  data-driven, Factory Method pattern, 100–101
  data filter classes, 166
  delegation and, 47
  DoubleLinkedList, 71–72
  ellipsis (...), 3
  Façade pattern, 225
  factory method, 132
  Game Snapshot, 356
  hiding, 69
  inheritance, 47
  LazyCloneDictionary, 86–87
  loading, deferred, 259–260
  loading arbitratry, 245–253
  Mediator pattern, 345
  nested, 11
  proxy objects, 81
  RecordFactoryFactory, 104
  rectangles, 2
  relationships, 7

SaleLineItem, 104
simplified, 4
Singleton pattern, 142
StartOfSale, 104
State pattern, 386–388
two-compartment classes, 4
UserInterface, 356
VBCodeProvider, 128
word combination language, 327
wrapper classes, 121
WrapperGenerator, 123–124
XYZJournalRecordFactory, 104
Client class
  Abstract Factory pattern, 112
  Adapter pattern, 197
  Builder pattern, 125
  Cache Management pattern, 275
  concrete widget classes and, 113
  Future pattern, 531
  Hashed Adapter Objects pattern and, 431
  IFactory interface and, 113
  IIndirection interface, 56
  Little Language pattern, 328
  Object Pool pattern, 153
  problem domain and, 50
  Prototype pattern, 132
  Strategy pattern, 396
  Virtual Proxy pattern, 257–258
  Visitor pattern and, 418
client objects, complex object creation,
    Builder pattern, 121–129
Clone function
  deep copies, 84, 133
  shallow copies, 84, 133
code example
  Abstract Base Class pattern, 64–67
  Abstract Factory pattern, 114–119
  Adapter pattern, 199–206
  Asynchronous Processing pattern,
    525–527
  Balking pattern, 469–470
  Bridge pattern, 218–223
  Builder pattern, 128–129
  Cache Management pattern, 282–292
  Chain of Responsibility pattern, 299–304
  Command pattern, 310–315
  Composite pattern, 180–185

Decorator pattern, 270–271
delegation example, 52–54
Double Buffering pattern, 504–518
Dynamic Linkage pattern, 250–253
Façade pattern, 228–231
Factory Method pattern, 102–107
Filter pattern, 170–174
Flyweight pattern, 239–244
Future pattern, 536–540
Guarded Suspension pattern, 464–465
Hashed Adapter Objects pattern, 433–435
Immutable pattern, 78–79
Interface and Abstract Class pattern,
    71–72
Interface pattern example, 58–59
Iterator pattern, 209–211
Little Language pattern, 331
Lock Object pattern, 457–458
Mediator pattern, 349–354
Null Object pattern, 404–405
Object Pool pattern, 156–161
Observer pattern, 379–381
Producer-Consumer pattern, 496–498
Prototype pattern, 135–139
Proxy pattern, 83–91
Read-Only interface pattern, 190–192
Read/Write Lock pattern, 487–492
Scheduler pattern, 476–481
Single Threaded Execution pattern,
    444–446
Singleton pattern, 146–147
Snapshot pattern, 370–371
State pattern, 389–394
Static Locking Order pattern, 450–451
Strategy pattern, 398–399
Template Method pattern, 410–413
Virtual Proxy pattern, 261–263
Visitor pattern, 422–425
coding, deployment and, 27
collaboration diagram
  example, 14
  interactions, 14
  links, 14
collaborations, 14
Colleague classes, Mediator pattern, 349
Collection class, Iterator pattern and, 207

Collection interface, Iterator pattern and, 207

collections
  access, Iterator pattern, 206
  object modification during iteration, 208
  remote, access, 206

Command pattern
  behavior and, 293
  Chain of Responsibility pattern and, 304
  code example, 310–315
  CommandManager class, 306
  commands, encapsulating, 305
  ConcreteCommand class, 306
  do function, 305
  Factory Method pattern and, 315
  ICommand interface, 306
  implementation, 307–309
  interface dependencies, 308–309
  Invoker class, 306
  Little Language pattern and, 315
  Marker Interface pattern and, 315
  .NET, 310
  Snapshot pattern and, 315, 372
  Template Method pattern and, 315
  undo function, 305

CommandManager class
  Command pattern, 306
  objects, undo/redo, 307–308

CommandSender class, Chain of Responsibility pattern, 297

comments, Delegation pattern, 52

compartments, classes, 2, 4

compatibility of classes, Dynamic Linkage pattern and, 248

composite aggregations, classes, 9

Composite pattern
  AbstractComposite class, 177
  Builder pattern and, 129
  Chain of Responsibility pattern and, 185, 304
  code example, 180–185
  Element1 class, 177
  Filter pattern and, 174
  Flyweight pattern and, 244
  Frame objects, 175
  hierarchy and, 177
  IElement interface, 177

implementation, 179
  introduction, 163
  Little Language pattern and, 342
  .NET Framework, 180
  Page objects, 175
  Prototype pattern and, 139
  recursion, 175
  Recursive Composition pattern, 175
  Visitor pattern and, 185, 425

Concrete Builder class, Builder pattern, 125

concrete classes
  Abstract Base Class pattern, 64
  interface implementation, 109
  widget classes, client classes and, 113

ConcreteCommand class, Command pattern, 306

ConcreteLoadableClass class, Dynamic Linkage pattern and, 248

ConcretePullFilter class, Filter pattern, 168

ConcretePushFilter class, Filter pattern, 169

ConcreteService class, Decorator pattern, 268

ConcreteTemplate class, Template Method pattern, 409

concurrency patterns
  Asynchronous Processing, 519–527
  Balking pattern, 467–470
  Double Buffering pattern, 499–518
  Future pattern, 529–540
  Guarded Suspension pattern, 459–465
  Lock Object pattern, 453–458
  Producer-Consumer pattern, 493–498
  Read/Write Lock pattern, 483–492
  Scheduler pattern, 471–481
  sequence of operations and, 437
  shared resources and, 437
  Single Threaded Execution, 439–446
  Static Locking Order, 447–451

connections
  dynamic, 165–174
  IDbConnection interface and, 149–150

constructors
  Immutable pattern and, 77
  interfaces, 56, 57–58
  .NET Framework, 57–58

singleton classes, 143
   wrapper classes, 121
Consumer class, Producer-Consumer pat-
   tern, 495
Context class, State pattern, 387
Controller pattern, Mediator pattern and,
   354
copy, serialization and, 144
creational patterns
   Abstract Factory pattern, 94, 109–119
   Builder pattern, 94, 121–129
   Factory Method pattern, 94, 95–108
   object creation and, 93
   Object Pool pattern, 94
   Prototype pattern, 94, 131–139
   Singleton pattern, 94, 141–147
CreationRequester role class, Factory
   Method pattern, 98
CSharpCodeProvider class, Builder pat-
   tern, 128

D
data analyses
   data filter classes, 166
   implementation, 166
data-driven classes, Factory Method pattern and, 100–101
data filter classes
   analysis, 166
   transformations, 166
data structure
   Hashed Adapter Objects pattern, 433
   object pool, 155
data transformations. *See* transformations
deadlocked threads
   Single Threaded Execution pattern and,
      443
   Static Locking Order pattern, 447–449
deadly embrace, threads (Single Threaded
   Execution pattern), 444–446
decorator classes, implementation,
   121–122
Decorator pattern
   AbstractWrapper class, 268
   Bridge pattern and, 223
   code example, 270–271
   ConcreteService class, 268

delegation, 54
   Delegation pattern and, 272
   Filter pattern and, 174, 272
   IAbstractService interface, 268
   implementation, 269
   inheritance, 269
   object functionality, 265
   overview, 193
   Prototype pattern and, 139
   Proxy pattern and, 91
   Strategy pattern and, 272
   Template Method pattern and, 272
   wrapper classes, 121
   Wrapper pattern, 265
deep copies, objects
   Clone function, 84
   Prototype pattern, 133
deferred class loading, Virtual Proxy pattern, 259–260
delegation of object creation, Object Pool
   pattern, 155
Delegation pattern
   behaviors and, 51
   behaviors and, run time, 52
   classes and, 47
   code example, 52–54
   comments, 52
   Decorator pattern and, 54, 272
   disadvantages, 52
   implementation, 51
   indirect, 52
   indirect delegations, 52
   inheritance and, 47–54
   Interface pattern and, 59
   .NET and, 52
   Observer pattern and, 382
   Proxy pattern and, 54
   roles, 48
Delegator class, Null Object pattern, 403
dependencies
   Abstract Base Class pattern, 64
   dialog boxes, Mediator pattern, 344–345
   dynamically registering, 373
   Façade pattern, 38, 226
   interfaces, Command pattern, 308–309
   logic, Mediator pattern, 349
   minimizing, 38

dependencies *(continued)*
  Observer pattern, 373
  requirements and, 29
  state-related, Mediator pattern classes,
      345–346
dependent objects, classes, 56
deployment
  activities leading up to, 26
  coding and, 27
  essential use cases, 27
  high-level system architecture, 27
  object-oriented analysis and, 27
  object-oriented design, 27
  planning, 26
  prototype creation, 27
  requirements, 26–27
  testing and, 27
Deserializer class, Snapshot pattern, 358
dialog boxes, Mediator Pattern and,
    343–345
Director object, Builder pattern, 125
DirectShow API, filters, 170
do function, Command pattern, 305
DocChar class, Flyweight pattern, 234
documentation, IEnumerator interface, 61
DocumentContainer class, Flyweight pat-
    tern, 234
DocumentManager object, Factory Method
    pattern and, 95–97
DocumentVisitor class, Visitor pattern, 417
Double Buffering pattern
  code example, 504–518
  DoubleBufferedStream class, 499
  exception handling, 503
  Guarded Suspension pattern and, 518
  implementation, 502–503
  introduction, 438
  multiple buffers, 502
  .NET, 504
  Producer-Consumer pattern and, 518
  threads, 502–503
DoubleLinkedList class, 71–72
doubly linked lists, inserting/deleting
    objects, 73
dynamic connections, Filter pattern, 165
dynamic linkage, instantiation and, 132

Dynamic Linkage pattern
  AbstractLoadableClass class and, 248
  arbitrary classes, loading, 245
  ConcreteLoadableClass class, 248
  Environment class, 247
  IEnvironment interface, 247
  implementation, 248–249
  loading time, 250
  .NET Framework and, 250
  overview, 193
  Protection Proxy pattern and, 253
  security and, 249
  Virtual Proxy pattern and, 253
dynamic registration of dependencies, 373

E
ellipsis (...), classes and, 3
encapsulation, algorithms (Strategy pat-
    tern), 395–400
Environment class, Dynamic Linkage pat-
    tern and, 247
Ephemeral Cache Item pattern, Cache
    Management pattern and, 292
essential use cases
  case study, 30–32
  deployment and, 27
events
  recursive, Mediator pattern, 348
  state and, 22
exception handling, Double Buffering pat-
    tern and, 503
execution order of threads, Schedule pat-
    tern and, 471–481
execution suspension, Guarded Suspen-
    sion pattern, 459–465
Expect subroutine, Parser class, 337
external data representation, Builder pat-
    tern and, 124

F
Façade pattern
  Adapter pattern and, 204, 231
  Asynchronous Processing pattern and,
      527
  Cache Management pattern and, 292
  code example, 228–231

dependencies and, 38, 226
implementation, 227–228
Interface pattern and, 231
.NET Framework, 228
object access, 225
Object Pool pattern and, 161
overview, 193
Prototype pattern and, 139
Proxy pattern and, 91
Virtual Proxy pattern and, 263
wrapper classes, 121
Factory class
  Factory Method pattern, 99
  journal-file-related, 103
factory method classes, instantiation and,
  132
Factory Method object, Bridge pattern, 219
Factory Method pattern
  ABCJournalRecordFactory class, 104
  abstract class extension, 99
  Abstract Factory pattern and, 107, 119
  Builder pattern and, 129
  class determination, data-driven, 100–101
  Command pattern and, 315
  consequences, 101
  CreationRequester class, 98
  Factory class, 99
  Flyweight pattern and, 244
  Hashed Adapter Objects pattern and, 107
  IFactory interface, 98–99
  IJournalRecord interface, 104
  IJournalRecordFactory interface, 104
  implementation, 99
  IProduct interface, 98
  Iterator pattern and, 211
  .NET Framework, 101–102
  object creation and, 94
  Object Pool pattern and, 161
  overview, 95
  Prototype pattern and, 108, 139
  RecordFactoryFactory class, 104
  StartOfSale class, 104
  Strategy pattern and, 108
  Template Method pattern and, 108
  XYZJournalRecordFactory class, 104
File Dirty state, 385
FileStream class, Snapshot pattern, 358

Filter pattern
  AbstractPullFilter class, 167
  AbstractPushFilter class, 169
  code example, 170–174
  Composite pattern and, 174
  ConcretePullFilter class, 168
  ConcretePushFilter class, 169
  connecting objects dynamically, 165–174
  data analyses, 166
  data transformations, 166
  Decorator pattern and, 174, 272
  implementation, 169
  introduction, 163
  ISink interface, 169
  ISource interface, 167
  .NET Framework, 170
  Pipe pattern and, 174
  pull filters, 166
  Sink class, 168, 169
  Source class, 167
  state and, 170
Flyweight pattern
  AbstractFlyweight class, 238
  Cache Management pattern and, 244
  code example, 239–244
  Composite pattern and, 244
  DocChar class, 234
  DocumentContainer class, 234
  Factory Method pattern and, 244
  FlyweightFactory class, 238
  IDocumentElement interface, 234
  Immutable pattern and, 244
  implementation, 238
  instances, multiple, 233
  .NET Framework and, 239
  objects, shared, 239
  overview, 193
  SharedConcreteFlyweight class, 238
  State pattern and, 394
  Strategy pattern and, 400
  UnsharedConcreteFlyweight class, 238
FlyweightFactory class, 238
For Each statement (.NET), Iterator pattern
  and, 206
formal parameters, 3
Frame objects, Composite pattern, 175

function calls, Single Threaded Execution
   pattern, 439
functions
   Clone, 84
   interfaces and, 196
   Iterator pattern, 208
   multiple parameters, 3
   subroutines and, 1
   threads, multiple, 18
   visibility indicators, 2
Future class, Future pattern, 531
Future pattern
   Active Object pattern and, 540
   Asynchronous Processing pattern and,
      527, 540
   Client class, 531
   code example, 536–540
   encapsulation, 529
   exceptions, 534
   Future class, 531
   implementation, 532–534
   introduction, 438
   .NET, 534–535
   Observer pattern and, 540
   Promise pattern, 529
   Proxy pattern and, 533, 540
   rendezvous, 534
   Requester class, 531
   Result class, 531
   synchronous computation launch, 533
   Virtual Proxy pattern and, 540

G

Game Snapshot classes, 356
GameModel class, Snapshot pattern, 357
generics, Iterator pattern, 207
GetClassname method, singleton classes,
   143
GetHashCode( ) function
   Cache Management pattern, 281
   Hashed Adapter Objects pattern, 432
GetInstance method
   concurrent calls, 144–145
   singleton classes, 143
grammar, language
   definition, 317
   tokens, 320

Guarded Suspension pattern
   Balking pattern, 465
   Balking pattern and, 470
   code example, 464–465
   Double Buffering pattern and, 518
   execution suspension, 459–465
   implementation, 461–463
   introduction, 438
   .NET, 464
   Producer-Consumer pattern and, 498

H

hash tables, data structure, 432–433
Hashed Adapter Objects pattern
   Action class, 431
   ActionKey class, 431
   adapter objects, 427
   Adapter pattern and, 435
   arbtrary objects, 427
   behaviors and, 293
   Client class, 431
   code example, 433–435
   data structures, alternate, 433
   Factory Method pattern and, 107
   GetHashCode( ) function, 432
   hash table data structure, 432–433
   IAction interface, 431
   implementation, 432–433
   Lookup Table pattern and, 435
   Polymorphism pattern and, 435
   Single Threaded Execution pattern and,
      435
   Strategy pattern and, 435
Hashtable, Cache Management pattern,
   279
hierarchy
   Composite pattern and, 177
   extending, Bridge pattern, 218
high-level system architecture, deployment, 27
hit rate, cache manager and, 277

I

IAbstractService interface, Decorator pattern, 268
IAction interface, Hashed Adapter Objects
   pattern and, 431

IBuilder interface, Builder pattern, 125

ICloneable interface, 84, 131

ICommand interface, Command pattern, 306

ICommandHandler interface, Chain of Responsibility pattern, 297

ICopyFilter interface, 195

IDbConnection interface, data source connections, 149–150

IDescription interface
   browser object, 55
   code example, 58–59

IDictionary object, cloning, 85

IDocumentElement interface, Flyweight pattern, 234

IElement interface, Composite pattern, 177

IEnumerable interface, Iterator pattern and, 207

IEnumerator interface
   behavior implementation, 61
   documentation, 61
   Iterator pattern and, 207

IEnvironment interface, Dynamic Linkage pattern and, 247

IFactory interface
   Abstract Factory pattern, 112
   client classes and, 113
   Factory Method pattern, 98–99

IFormatter interface, Snapshot pattern, 361

IInderection interface, Client class, 56

IJournalRecord interface, Factory Method pattern, 104

IJournalRecordFactory interface, Factory Method pattern, 104

IMemento interface, Snapshot pattern, 360

IMilestoneMemento interface, Snapshot pattern, 357

Immutable pattern
   code example, 78–79
   constructors and, 77
   Flyweight pattern and, 244
   implementation, 77
   instance variables, 77
   .NET and, 78
   Read-Only interface pattern and, 79
   robustness and, 75

shared references and, 75

Single Threaded Execution pattern and, 79

state information, 75, 76

String class and, 78

threads, 76

value objects and, 75, 76

impelementation, Read/Write Lock pattern, 486

implementation
   Abstract Base Class pattern, 64
   Abstract Factory pattern, 113
   Adapter pattern, 198–199
   Asynchronous Processing pattern, 522–524
   Balking pattern, 469
   Bridge pattern, 218
   Builder pattern, 126–127
   Cache Management pattern, 275–281
   Chain of Responsibility pattern, 297–298
   Command pattern, 307–309
   Composite pattern, 179
   decorator classes, 121–122
   Decorator pattern, 269
   delegation, 51
   Double Buffering pattern, 502–503
   Dynamic Linkage pattern, 248–249
   Façade pattern, 227–228
   Filter pattern, 169
   Flyweight pattern, 238
   Future pattern, 532–534
   Guarded Suspension pattern, 461–463
   Hashed Adapter Object pattern, 432–433
   Immutable pattern, 77
   Iterator pattern, 207–209
   Little Language pattern, 329–330
   Lock Object pattern, 455–456
   Mediator pattern, 347–348
   Null Object pattern, 403
   Object Pool pattern, 154–156
   Observer pattern, 376–378
   parser, recursive descent, 334
   Producer-Consumer pattern, 496
   Prototype pattern, 133–134
   Proxy pattern, 83
   Read-Only interface pattern, 190–192

implementation (*continued*)
Scheduler pattern, 476
Single Threaded Execution pattern, 442–443
Singleton pattern, 143–145
Snapshot pattern, 363–370
State pattern, 388–389
Static Locking Order pattern, 449
Strategy pattern, 397
Template Method pattern, 410
Virtual Proxy pattern and, 259–260
Visitor pattern, 421
indirect delegations, intermediate classes and, 52
inheritance
classes and, 47
Decorator pattern, 269
delegation, 47–54
inappropriate use, 51
roles, 48
INonterminal interface, Little Language pattern, 328
instance variables, Immutable pattern and, 77
instances
Abstract Factory pattern and, 110
Immutable pattern and, 76
interfaces and, 55
loaded classes, 247
maximum number, Object Pool pattern, 155
modification, 189
multiple, singleton classes, 143
Object Pool pattern, 151
object reuse, 151
singleton classes, 145
Strategy pattern, 396
instantiation
abstract factory classes, 132
dynamic linkage and, 132
factory method classes and, 132
singleton classes, 143
Singleton pattern and, 141–147
Virtual Proxy pattern, 255–263
interactions
asynchronous, 19
collaborations, 14

collaborative diagrams, 14
multilevel sequence numbers, 15
preconditions, 20
repeated, 16
sequence numbers, 14
sequence numbers, multilevel, 15
Interface and Abstract Class pattern
Abstract Base Class pattern and, 67
Abstract Class pattern and, 72
ASP.NET and, 70–71
code example, 71–72
Interface pattern and, 72
overview, 69
Interface pattern
Adapter pattern, 59
Builder pattern and, 129
code example, 58–59
constructors, 57–58
delegates, 57
Delegation pattern and, 59
dependent objects, 56
Façade pattern and, 231
IDescription, 55
IDescription interface, 55
IInderection interface, 56
implementation, 56–58
instances and, 55
Interface and Abstract Class pattern, 72
.NET delegates, 57
Read-Only interface pattern, 192
Reference Interface, 55
Strategy pattern, 59
interfaces
class diagrams and, 6
compartments, 5
constructors, 56, 57–58
dependencies, Command pattern, 308–309
function calls, 196
IAbstractService, 268
IAction, 431
IBuilder interface, 125
ICloneable interface, 84
ICommandHandler, 297
ICopyFilter, 195
IDbConnection, 149–150
IDocumentElement, 234

IEnvironment, 247
IFactory interface, 98–99
IFormatter, 361
IJournalRecord, 104
IJournalRecordFactory, 104
IMilestoneMemento, 357
implementation, concrete classes and, 109
INonterminal, 328
IObservable, 375
IObserver, 375
IOperation, 403
IReadOnly interface, 190
IScheduleOrdering, 474
ISerializable, 365
IService, 259
ISink, 169
IStrategy, 396
ITarget interface, 197
Mediator pattern, 345
stereotype, 5
subroutine calls, 196
internal ToC table, Visitor pattern, 415
Invoker class, Command pattern, 306
IObservable interface, 376–377
IObserver interface, Observer pattern, 375
IOperation interface, Null Object pattern, 403
IProduct interface, Builder pattern, 124
IPrototype interface, Prototype pattern and, 132
Iprotype interface, Prototype pattern and, 133
IReadOnly interface, Read-Only interface pattern, 190
is-a-part-of relationships, 36
is-a relationships, 35
IScheduleOrdering interface, 474
ISerializable interface, 365
IService interface, Virtual Proxy pattern, 259
ISink interface, Filter pattern, 169
IStrategy interface, Strategy pattern, 396
ITarget interface, Adapter pattern, 197
Iterator class, Iterator pattern and, 207

Iterator pattern
    Adapter pattern, 204, 211
    code example, 209–211
    collection access, 206
    Collection class, 207
    Factory Method pattern, 211
    functions, 208
    generics, 207
    ICollection interface, 207
    IEnumerable interface, 207
    IEnumerator interface, 207
    implementation, 207–209
    Iterator class, 207
    multiple orderings, 208
    .NET Framework, 209
    null iterator, 208
    Null Object pattern, 211
    overview, 193
    sequential access, 205
    Visitor pattern and, 425
IWidgetA interface, Abstract Factory pattern, 112
IWidgetB interface, Abstract Factory pattern, 112

L

languages, 317. *See also* Little Language pattern
    combinations of words, 318
    lexical rules for word combination language, 326
    parse tree, 323
    precedence rule, 319
    regular expression, 325
    semantics, 317
    syntax, 317
    tokens, grammar, 320
    white space, 324
Layered Architecture pattern
    Bridge pattern and, 223
    Object Pool pattern and, 161
lazy instantiation, Virtual Proxy pattern and, 255
LazyCloneDictionary class, 86–87
lexical rules for word combination language, 326

LexicalAnalyzer, Little Language pattern, 328
links, collaborative diagrams, 14
Little Language pattern
  behavior and, 293
  Client class, 328
  code example, 331
  combinations of words, 318
  Command pattern and, 315
  Composite pattern and, 342
  implementation, 329–330
  INonterminal interface, 328
  Interpreter pattern and, 317
  lexical rules for word combination language, 326
  LexicalAnalyzer, 328
  little languages (Jon Bentley), 317
  .NET, 331
  Parser class, 328
  reserved words, 318
  TerminalToken class, 329
  tokens, grammar, 320
  Visitor pattern and, 342, 425
  word combination language classes, 327
  WordCombination class, 339
Lock Object pattern
  code example, 457–458
  implementation, 455–456
  introduction, 438
  Object Pool pattern and, 161
  Single Threaded Execution pattern and, 458
  Static Locking Order pattern and, 451, 458
  threads, object locks and, 454
lock objects, threads, 454
logic, Visitor pattern, 415–425
Lookup Table pattern, Hashed Adapter Objects pattern and, 435
Low Coupling/High Cohesion pattern, Mediator pattern and, 354

M
Marker Interface pattern, Command pattern and, 315
Mediator pattern
  Balking pattern and, 354
  classes, 345
  code example, 349–354
  Colleague classes, 349
  Controller pattern and, 354
  dialog boxes, dependencies, 344–345
  dialog boxes and, 343–344
  implementation, 347–348
  interfaces and, 345
  Low Coupling/High Cohesion pattern and, 354
  Mediator object, 346–347
  Observer pattern and, 354, 382
  recursive events, 348
  state and, 343
  State pattern and, 394
  White Box Testing pattern and, 354
MemberwiseClone function, 84
Memento class, Snapshot pattern, 360
Memento objects
  serialization comparison, 362
  Snapshot pattern, 359–360
  state, 362
Memento pattern, Snapshot pattern, 355
MilestoneMemento class, Snapshot pattern, 357
MilestoneMementoManager class, Snapshot pattern, 357
Multicaster class, Observer pattern and, 376, 377
multilevel sequence numbers, 15
  interactions, 15
multiobjects, 15
multiplicity indicators, associations, 8
Mutable class, Read-Only interface pattern, 190
MutatorClient class, Read-Only interface pattern, 190

N
names, association names, 7
namespaces, packages and, 11
navigation arrows, associations, 7
nested classes, 11
.NET
  Abstract Base Class pattern and, 64
  Asynchronous Processing pattern, 525
  Bridge pattern, 218
  Builder pattern, 128
  Chain of Responsibility pattern, 299

Command pattern, 310
Composite pattern, 180
constructors, 57–58
delegate, stereotype, 5
delegation and, 52
Double Buffering pattern and, 504
Dynamic Linkage pattern, 250
Façade pattern, 228
Factory Method pattern and, 101–102
Filter pattern, 170
Flyweight pattern, 239
Future pattern, 534–535
Guarded Suspension pattern, 464
Immutable pattern and, 78
Iterator pattern, 209
Little Language pattern, 331
Observer pattern, 379
Producer-Consumer pattern, 496
Prototype pattern, 135
Read/Write Lock pattern, 487
Singleton pattern, 145
Strategy pattern, 397
.NET delegates, Interface pattern, 57
non-terminal tokens, language, 320
Not Dirty state, 384
notifications, batching, Observer pattern,
    378
null iterator, Iterator pattern, 208
Null Object pattern
    Builder pattern and, 129
    code example, 404–405
    Delegation class, 403
    implementation, 403
    IOperation interface, 403
    Iterator pattern and, 211
    NullOperation class, 403
    object absence, 401
    RealOperation class, 403
    Singleton pattern and, 405
    Strategy pattern and, 400, 405
NullOperation class, Null Object pattern,
    403

O

object diagrams, example, 13
object-oriented analysis
    case study, 32–34
    deployment and, 27

object-oriented design
    case study, 34–43
    deployment, 27
object pool
    hiding, 154–155
    size limit, 155–156
    stateful objects, 156
    structure, 155
Object Pool pattern
    Cache Management pattern and, 161
    Client class, 153
    code example, 156–161
    Façade pattern and, 161
    Factory Method pattern and, 161
    implementation, 154–156
    instances, 151
    instances, maximum number, 155
    Layered Architecture pattern and, 161
    Lock Object pattern and, 161
    object creation, 94, 156
    object reuse, 149–161
    Reusable object, 153
    ReusablePool object, 154
    Singleton pattern and, 147, 161
    Thread Pool pattern and, 161
    Virtual Proxy pattern and, 263
Object Replication pattern, Cache Manage-
    ment pattern and, 292
Object Request Broker pattern, Proxy pat-
    tern and, 91
object reuse
    instances, 151
    Object Pool pattern, 149–161
ObjectCreator class, Cache Management
    pattern, 275
ObjectKey class, Cache Management pat-
    tern, 275
objects
    cache limits, 280
    class diagrams, 12
    commands, Chain of Responsibility pat-
        tern, 295
    commands, Command pattern, 305
    creation, delegating, 155
    creation, Object Pool pattern and, 156
    creational patterns and, 93
    custom, Prototype pattern and, 131
    deep copies, 84

objects *(continued)*
  deep copies, Prototype pattern and, 133
  deleting, doubly linked lists and, 73
  dependent, 56
  flyweight, shared, 239
  inserting, double linked lists and, 73
  modifying, iteration and, 208
  modifying, Read-Only interface pattern, 187–192
  multiobjects, 15
  prototypes, 131, 132–139 (*See also* Prototype pattern)
  proxy objects (*See* proxy objects)
  read-only status, 189
  read/write access, 483–492
  Reusable, Object Pool pattern, 153
  serialization, 144
  ServiceProxy, 82–83
  shallow copies, 84
  shallow copies, Prototype pattern and, 133
  shared references, Immutable pattern and, 75
  shared service objects, Virtual Proxy pattern, 259
  temporary, 15
ObjectStructure class, Visitor pattern and, 418
Observer pattern
  Adapter pattern and, 382
  batching notifications, 378
  behavior and, 293
  code example, 379–381
  Delegation pattern and, 382
  dependencies, 373
  Future pattern and, 540
  implementation, 376–378
  IObservable interface and, 375
  IObserver interface and, 375
  Mediator pattern and, 354, 382
  Multicaster class and, 376, 377
  .NET, 379
  Observable class, 375, 376–377
  Observer class, 375
  Publish-Subscribe pattern and, 382
  veto changes, 378

operations
  behaviors, 1
  meaning, 1
  sequence, concurrency patterns and, 437
Optimistic Concurrency pattern, Cache Management pattern and, 292
Originator class, Snapshot pattern, 360

P
packages
  assemblies, 11
  namespaces, 11
  visibility indicators, 11
Page objects, Composite pattern, 175
Param Dirty state, 385
parameters
  formal, 3
  multiple, functions, 3
  multiple, subroutines, 3
parse tree
  introduction, 323
  token sequences, 323
parser, recursive descent, 334
Parser class
  Expect subroutine, 337
  Little Language pattern, 328
partitioning patterns
  Composite pattern, 163, 175–185
  Filter pattern, 163, 165–174
  Read-Only interface pattern, 187–192
  Read-Only pattern, 163
performance tuning, Cache Management pattern and, 277–281
persistence, serialization and, 144
Pipe pattern
  Filter pattern and, 174
  Producer-Consumer pattern and, 498
planning, deployment and, 26
polling, Future pattern, 532–533
Polymorphism pattern
  Hashed Adapter Objects pattern and, 435
  State pattern and, 394
precedence rule, language, 319
preconditions, interactions, 20
prefetching objects, Cache Management pattern and, 277

private (-) visibility indicator, meaning, 2
problem domain, client classes, 50
Processor class, Scheduler pattern, 473
Producer class, Producer-Consumer pattern, 495
Producer-Consumer pattern
  Asynchronous Processing pattern and, 527
  code example, 496–498
  Consumer class, 495
  Double Buffering pattern and, 518
  Guarded Suspension pattern and, 498
  implementation, 496
  introduction, 438
  .NET, 496
  Pipe pattern and, 498
  Producer class, 495
  Queue class, 495
  Scheduler pattern and, 498
Product class, Builder pattern, 124
ProductCacheManager class, Cache Management pattern, 274
ProductInfoFetcher object, Cache Management pattern, 274
protected (#) visibility indicator, meaning, 2
Protection Proxy pattern
  Dynamic Linkage pattern and, 253
  Proxy pattern and, 91
Prototype Builder class, roles, 133
prototype, deployment and, 27
Prototype pattern
  Abstract Factory pattern and, 139
  code, 135–139
  Composite pattern and, 139
  consequences, 134–135
  custom objects, 131
  Decorator pattern and, 139
  deep copying, 133
  Façade pattern and, 139
  Factory Method pattern and, 108, 139
  ICloneable interface, 131
  implementation, 133–134
  IProrotype interface and, 132
  Iprotype, 133
  .NET Framework and, 135

object creation and, 94
overview, 131
shallow copying, 133
symbol objects, 131
SymbolBuilder objects, 132
PrototypeBuilder objects, Prototype pattern implementation, 133–134
proxy objects
  classes, 81
  description, 81
  function calls, 81–82
  Proxy pattern and, 81
  uses, 81–82
Proxy pattern
  Adapter pattern, 204
  code example, 83–91
  Decorator pattern and, 91
  delegation, 54
  Façade pattern and, 91
  Future pattern and, 532–533, 540
  implementation, 83
  Object Request Broker pattern and, 91
  organization, 82–83
  Protection Proxy pattern and, 91
  proxy objects and, 81
  Virtual Proxy pattern and, 91, 263
  wrapper classes, 121
public (+) visibility indicator, meaning, 2
Publish-Subscribe pattern, Observer pattern and, 382
pull filters
  AbstractPullFilter class, 167
  introduction, 166
pull method, Queue class, 459
push method, Queue class, 459

Q

Queue class
  Producer-Consumer pattern, 495
  pull method, 459
  push method, 459

R

read consistency, cache management and, 282
read-only access, IEnumerator interface, 61

Read-Only Interface pattern
  Adapter pattern and, 192
  code example, 190–192
  Immutable pattern and, 79
  implementation, 190–192
  Interface pattern and, 192
  IReadOnly interface, 190
  Mutable class, 190
  MutatorClient class, 190
  object modification, 187–192
  ReadOnly Client class, 190
  Snapshot pattern and, 372
Read-Only pattern, 163
Read/Write Lock pattern
  code example, 487–492
  concurrent read access, 483–492
  impelementation, 486
  introduction, 438
  .NET, 487
  Scheduler pattern and, 481, 492
  Single Threaded Execution pattern and,
    492
ReadOnlyClient class, Read-Only interface
  pattern, 190
RealOperation class, Null Object pattern,
  403
RecordFactoryFactory class, Factory
  Method pattern, 104
rectangles, classes, 2
recursion
  Composite pattern, 175
  Mediator pattern, 348
  tail recursion, 335
Recursive Composition pattern, 175
recursive descent parsers, 334
redo commands, 307–308
Reference Interface, indirection, 55
references, shared (Immutable pattern), 75
regular expression languages, 325
relationships
  is-a, 35
  is-a-part-of, 36
remote procedure calls, serialization and,
  144
renderer filter, DirectShow API filters, 170
rendezvou, Future pattern, 534
ReorgVisitor class, Visitor pattern, 417

Request class, Scheduler pattern, 473
request management, Asynchronous Processing pattern, 522–524
Requester class, Future pattern, 531
requirements
  assumptions, 29
  case study, 29–30
  dependencies, 29
  deployment and, 26–27
  risks, 29
reserve buffer, 500
reserved words, Little Language pattern,
  318
Result class, Future pattern, 531
Reusable object, Object Pool pattern, 153
ReusablePool object, Object Pool pattern,
  154
reusing objects, Object Pool pattern,
  149–161
risks, requirements and, 29
role names, associations, 7
roles
  delegation, 48
  inheritance, 48

S

Scheduler class, Scheduler pattern, 473
Scheduler pattern
  Asynchronous Processing pattern and,
    527
  code example, 476–481
  implementation, 476
  IScheduleOrdering interface, 474
  Processor class, 473
  Producer-Consumer pattern and, 498
  Read/Write Lock pattern and, 481, 492
  Request class, 473
  Scheduler class, 473
  thread execution, 471–481
security
  Dynamic Linkage pattern, 249
  object modification, 187–192
semantics, language, 317
sequence numbers, interactions
  introduction, 14
  multilevel, 15

sequence of operations, concurrency patterns and, 437

sequential access
  IEnumerator interface, 61
  Iterator pattern, 205

serialization
  Memento object comparison, 362
  objects, 144
  persistence and, 144
  remote procedure calls and, 144
  SOAP and, 144
  XML (Extensible Markup Language) and, 144

Serialize method, Snapshot pattern and, 363–365

Serializer class, Snapshot pattern, 358

Service class, Virtual Proxy pattern, 257

ServiceProxy class, Virtual Proxy pattern, 258–259

ServiceProxy objects, 82–83

shallow copies, objects
  Clone function, 84
  Prototype pattern, 133

shared references, Immutable pattern and, 75

shared resources, concurrency patterns and, 437

SharedConcreteFlyweight class, 238

Single Threaded Execution pattern
  Balking pattern and, 470
  code example, 444–446
  deadlocked threads, 443
  function calls, concurrent, 439
  Hashed Adapter Objects pattern and, 435
  Immutable pattern and, 79
  implementation, 442–443
  Lock Object pattern and, 458
  Read/Write Lock pattern and, 492
  shared resources and, 437
  TrafficSensor class, 440
  TrafficSensorController class, 440
  TrafficTransmitter class, 440

singleton classes
  access, 143
  constructors, 143
  instances, 145
  instantiation, 143

object copies, 143
subclassing, 145
variables, 143

Singleton pattern
  Abstract Factory pattern and, 119
  Cache Management pattern and, 147
  classes, 142
  code example, 146–147
  implementation, 143–145
  instantiation and, 141–147
  .NET API, 145
  Null Object pattern and, 405
  object creation and, 94
  Object Pool pattern and, 147, 161
  State pattern and, 394

Sink class, Filter pattern, 168, 169

Snapshot pattern
  Caretaker class, 360
  code example, 370–371
  Command pattern and, 315, 372
  Deserializer class, 358
  FileStream class, 358
  Game Snapshot classes, 356
  GameModel class, 357
  IFormatter interface, 361
  IMemento interface, 360
  IMilestoneMemento interface, 357
  implementation, 363–370
  Memento class, 360
  Memento objects and, 359–360
  Memento pattern and, 355
  MilestoneMemento class, 357
  MilestoneMementoManager class, 357
  Originator class, 360
  Read-Only Interface pattern and, 372
  Serializer class, 358
  Stream class, 361
  Target object, 361
  TextFileReader class, 369
  UserInterface class, 356

SOAP (Simple Object Access Protocol), serialization and, 144

software, deployment, activities leading up to, 26

software lifecycle, 25–26

Source class, Filter pattern, 167

source filter, DirectShow API filters, 170

SpecializedAbstraction class, Bridge pattern, 216
SpecializedAbstractionImpl interface, Bridge pattern, 217
StartOfSale class, Factory Method pattern, 104
state
  Balking pattern, 467–470
  Both Dirty state, 385
  dependencies, Mediator pattern, 345–346
  encapsulation, State pattern, 383–394
  events, 22
  File Dirty state, 385
  filter objects, 170
  Immutable pattern and, 75
  Mediator pattern, 343–354
  Memento objects, 362
  Not Dirty state, 384
  notification batching, Observer pattern, 378
  object pool, 156
  Param Dirty state, 385
  serialization and, 362
  Snapshot pattern, 355–372
  transitions, 23
State class, State pattern, 387
state machines
  implementation, 42
  statechart diagrams, 22
State pattern
  Both Dirty state, 385
  classes, 386–388
  code example, 389–394
  Context class, 387
  File Dirty state, 385
  Flyweight pattern and, 394
  implementation, 388–389
  Mediator pattern and, 394
  Not Dirty state, 384
  Param Dirty state, 385
  Polymorphism pattern and, 394
  Singleton pattern and, 394
  State class, 387
  state encapsulation, 383–394
statechart diagrams
  state machines and, 22
  transition lines, 23

stateful objects, 383
Static Locking Order pattern
  code example, 450–451
  deadlocks, 447–449
  implementation, 449
  introduction, 438
  Lock Object pattern and, 451, 458
static relationships, inheritance and, 50
stereotypes
  definition, 3
  interfaces, 5
  .NET delegate, 5
Strategy pattern
  Adapter pattern, 204, 400
  algorithm encapsulation, 395
  Builder pattern and, 129
  Client class, 396
  code example, 398–399
  Decorator pattern and, 272
  Factory Method pattern and, 108
  Flyweight pattern and, 400
  Hashed Adapter Objects pattern and, 435
  implementation, 397
  Interface pattern and, 59
  IStrategy interface, 396
  .NET API usage, 397
  Null Object pattern and, 400, 405
  Template Method pattern and, 400, 413
Stream class, Snapshot pattern, 361
String class, Immutable pattern and, 78
structural patterns
  Adapter pattern, 195–206
  Bridge pattern, 213–223
  Cache Management, 273–292
  Decorator pattern, 265–272
  Dynamic Linkage pattern, 245–253
  Façade pattern, 225–228
  Flyweight pattern, 233–244
  Iterator pattern, 205–211
  Virtual Proxy pattern, 255–263
subclassing, singleton classes, 145
subroutines
  functions and, 1
  interfaces and, 196
  multiple parameters, 3
  threads, multiple, 18
  visibility indicators, 2

suspended execution, Guarded Suspension pattern, 459–465
Symbol objects, SymbolBuilder objects, 132
symbol objects, Prototype pattern and, 131
SymbolBuilder objects, 132
synchronous design, 519
syntax, language
  combinations of words, 318
  definition, 317
  grammar, 317
system architecture, deployment and, 27

T

tail recursion, 335
Target object, Snapshot pattern, 361
Template Method pattern
  Abstract Base Class pattern and, 67
  abstract classes, 407
  AbstractTemplate class and, 409
  behavior and, 294
  Builder pattern and, 129
  Cache Management pattern and, 292
  Chain of Responsibility pattern and, 304
  code example, 410–413
  Command pattern and, 315
  ConcreteTemplate class and, 409
  Decorator pattern and, 272
  Factory Method pattern and, 108
  implementation, 410
  Strategy pattern and, 400, 413
temporary objects, collaboration, 15
terminal tokens, language, 320
TerminalToken class, Little Language pattern, 329
testing, deployment and, 27
TextFileReader class, Snapshot pattern, 369
Thread Pool pattern
  Asynchronous Processing pattern and, 527
  Object Pool pattern and, 161
threads
  Asynchronous Processing pattern, 522–524
  deadlocked, Single Threaded Execution pattern, 443
  deadlocked, Static Locking Order pattern, 447–449
deadly embrace, Single Threaded Execution pattern, 444–446
Double Buffering pattern and, 502–503
execution order, Schedule pattern and, 471–481
functions, 18
Immutable pattern and, 76
lock objects and, 454
multiple, 18
subroutines, 18
TOCVisitor class, Visitor pattern, 417
tokens, grammar, 320, 323
transform filter, DirectShow API filters, 170
transformations
  data filter classes, 166
  implementation, 166
transition lines, state charts, 23
transitions, state, State pattern, 388
two-compartment classes, example, 4

U

UML (Unified Modeling Language), 1
undo function, 305, 307–308
UnsharedConcreteFlyweight class, 238
user interface, windowing systems, 109
UserInterface class, Snapshot pattern, 356

V

value objects
  Immutable pattern and, 75, 76
  purpose, 75
variables
  singleton classes, 143
  visibility indicators, 2
VBCodeProvider class, Builder pattern, 128
VB.NET. *See also* .NET
  assumptions about, 1
  interfaces and, 57
veto changes, Observer pattern, 378
Virtual Proxy pattern
  Cache Management pattern and, 292
  Client class, 257–258
  code example, 261–263
  deferred class loading, 259–260

Virtual Proxy pattern *(continued)*
  Dynamic Linkage pattern and, 253
  Façade pattern, 263
  Future pattern and, 540
  implementation, 259–260
  instantiation and, 255–263
  IService interface, 259
  Object Pool pattern, 263
  overview, 193
  Proxy pattern, 91, 263
  Service class, 257
  ServiceProxy class, 258–259
  shared service objects, 259
visibility indicators
  meanings, 2
  packages, 11
Visitor pattern
  AbstractElement class and, 419
  AbstractVisitor class and, 419
  Builder pattern and, 129
  Client class and, 418
  code example, 422–425
  Composite pattern and, 185, 425
  DocumentVisitor class, 417
  implementation, 421
  Iterator pattern and, 425
  Little Language pattern and, 342, 425
  logic and, 415
  ObjectStructure class and, 418
  ReorgVisitor class, 417
  TOCVisitor class, 417
  WordProcessor class, 416

W

White Box Testing pattern, Mediator pattern and, 354
white space, 324
word combination language classes, 327
word combination language lexical rules, 326
WordCombination class, Little Language pattern, 339
WordProcessor class, Visitor pattern, 416
words. *See* languages; Little Language pattern
wrapper classes
  constructors, 121
  Decorator pattern, 121
  definition, 121
  Façade pattern and, 121
  Proxy pattern and, 121
  source creation, 123
wrapper objects, inheritance and, 269
Wrapper pattern. *See* Decorator pattern
WrapperGenerator class, 123–124
write consistency, cache management and, 282

X–Y–Z

XML (Extensible Markup Language), serialization and, 144
XYZJournalRecordFactory class, Factory Method pattern, 104